W9-BCI-252

THE ORIENTAL RELIGIONS AND AMERICAN THOUGHT

Contributions in American Studies
Series Editor: Robert H. Walker

In the Trough of the Sea: Selected American Sea-Deliverance Narratives, 1610-1766
Donald P. Wharton, editor

Aaron Burr and the American Literary Imagination
Charles J. Nolan, Jr.

The Popular Mood of Pre-Civil War America
Lewis O. Saum

The Essays of Mark Van Doren
William Claire, editor

Touching Base: Professional Baseball and American Culture in the Progressive Era
Steven A. Riess

Late Harvest: Essays and Addresses in American Literature and Culture
Robert E. Spiller

Steppin' Out: New York Nightlife and the Transformation of American Culture, 1890-1930
Lewis A. Erenberg

For Better or Worse: The American Influence in the World
Allen F. Davis, editor

The Silver Bullet: The Martini in American Civilization
Lowell Edmunds

Boosters and Businessmen: Popular Economic Thought and Urban Growth in the Antebellum Middle West
Carl Abbott

Democratic Dictatorship: The Emergent Constitution of Control
Arthur S. Miller

THE ORIENTAL RELIGIONS AND AMERICAN THOUGHT

Nineteenth-Century Explorations

Carl T. Jackson

GP CONTRIBUTIONS IN AMERICAN STUDIES, NUMBER 55
GREENWOOD PRESS
WESTPORT, CONNECTICUT • LONDON, ENGLAND

Library of Congress Cataloging in Publication Data

Jackson, Carl T 1934-
The oriental religions and American thought.

(Contributions in American studies ; no. 55
ISSN 0084-9227)
Bibliography: p.
Includes index.
1. Asia—Religion—Influence. 2. United States—Civilization—Oriental influences. 3. Religious thought—United States. I. Title.
BL1032.J3 291 80-25478
ISBN 0-313-22491-9 (lib. bdg.)

Library of Congress Catalog Card Number: 80-25478
ISBN: 0-313-22491-9
ISSN: 0084-9227

First published in 1981

Greenwood Press
A division of Congressional Information Service, Inc.
88 Post Road West
Westport, Connecticut 06881

Printed in the United States of America

10 9 8 7 6 5 4 3 2 1

To my Mother and the memory
of my Father

Contents

Preface

The growing American recognition of the importance and profundity of Asian religions represents one of the major intellectual events of our time. For many years American scholars indicated little interest in this crucial development. This began to change in the 1930s with Frederic Carpenter's and Arthur Christy's pioneering studies of Oriental influence on Transcendentalism. Interest had increased in the 1960s and 1970s, although the field remains largely unexplored. The pervasive evidence of Oriental religious influence since World War II has made it impossible to ignore the Asian religions any longer. Critics still dismiss interest in Oriental thought as a passing fad, caricaturing and minimizing the East's influence by associating it with the more bizarre forms that Eastern cults have taken in the West. The argument of this book is that American interest in Oriental religion is definitely *not* a passing fad. Americans began to discover Asian religion as early as the 1700s, and during the nineteenth century this interest exploded.

This study represents an attempt to establish the beginnings and to map the rise of America's discovery of the Asian religions—of Hinduism and Buddhism principally, but occasionally also of Confucianism, Shintoism, and Taoism. Beginning with the earliest perceptions of Asia in the eighteenth century, it follows America's rising consciousness of Eastern religions to the 1893 World's Parliament of Religions. Previous scholars have sketched parts of the story, often based as much on speculation as on careful research; this is the first systematic examination based on wide-ranging research in the sources. The coverage is wide, including most significant people and movements; I have taken pains to suggest the richness of the nineteenth-century reaction by heavy documentation and an emphasis on widely divergent movements. Readers will be quick to recognize that I write as a student of American intellectual history, not as an Oriental scholar. My focus is not so much the Asian religions as the influence of Asian religion in America.

I hope that I may be forgiven for introducing a personal note, which will help explain how this study came to be. I first became aware of the Asian religions as a graduate student during the late 1950s, the era of the so-called Silent Generation and the Beats. Like countless others, I was attracted to Zen Buddhism by D. T. Suzuki and Alan Watts; this led to general reading in the other Asian philosophies. Raised in a small southwestern town and educated at the state university, I do not recall the slightest awareness of these alien conceptions before graduate school. Several years' residence in southern California did much to change that. I chose a doctoral dissertation on one of the most important Hindu movements to take up work in the United States—the Ramakrishna movement. The introductory chapter of the dissertation became the outline for the present work.

The limitations of this study are depressingly numerous. The ability to read Asian sources as well as a deeper acquaintance with Asian history would have helped immensely. Oriental scholars will surely find much to criticize; my only rejoinder is that perhaps my failures will stimulate Asian experts to focus more attention on the influence of Asian thought in America. I have restricted my analysis to literary materials; obviously, much would be gained from examining Asian influences in art, architecture, music, and, in the twentieth century, film. At the outset, my ambition was to survey all significant intellectual figures and developments, but as the manuscript fattened, more and more cuts had to be made. One can immediately think of important people who have been omitted, including poets Walt Whitman and John Greenleaf Whittier, philosophers William Torrey Harris and Josiah Royce, world travelers Richard Henry Dana and William H. Seward, diplomats Townshend Harris and Caleb Cushing, and missionary scholars S. Wells Williams and William Elliott Griffis, all of whom had significant things to say about Eastern religions. My only defense is that space requirements forced selection and that these did not fit or failed to survive the cutting process. Another scholar would undoubtedly have written a different book.

Several end-of-the-century people and movements that might have been included have been reserved for a twentieth-century sequel: these include the comparative religions movement, Paul Carus (a crucial prophet of the meeting of East and West), the New Thought movement, and important

Vedanta and Buddhist movements inaugurated in America by Swami Vivekananda and Anagarika Dharmapala. The field is wide open: every chapter in the present study might have been expanded into a separate book.

A word should also be said about my heavy emphasis on discovery and exploration—motifs that extend throughout the study. I argue that Americans first discovered and explored Oriental religions in the nineteenth century, not the twentieth century as many seem to believe. This, of course, is not a new thesis; previous scholars have recognized the nineteenth-century roots of America's discovery. My emphasis grows out of the feeling that the powerful nineteenth-century interest has not been sufficiently appreciated, as well as a recognition that, in fact, discovery and exploration best describe America's first encounters with Eastern conceptions. In the American colonies in the 1600s the Oriental religions formed as much of an unknown territory as the entire New World in 1492. The region to be explored was a world of ideas rather than a physical body of land; however, the processes at work are strikingly similar. Historian William Goetzmann's observation, "The nineteenth century, for Americans as well as for Europeans, was an age of Exploration,"[1] applies to the unknown expanses of Oriental religion as much as to unexplored islands and continents. In Asian religion as much as global geography, the nineteenth century was, indeed, an age of exploration.

Several procedural restrictions should be noticed. I have arbitrarily limited the term "Oriental religion" to the religions of the eastern half of the Asian continent, mainly to India, China, and Japan. Islam, Zoroastrianism, and Sufiism, religions of western Asia, might of course also be treated as "Oriental" religions. (Some scholars have even viewed Christianity as fundamentally "Oriental" in spirit.) The reasons for the restriction should be obvious. Secondly, I have arbitrarily focused upon those Americans who revealed a sympathetic view of the Asian religions. (The exception is the Christian missionary, treated in chapter 5.) Probably most nineteenth-century Americans were either unaware of or hostile toward the Oriental religions. However, from the beginning, there has always been a counterview that looked to the East for wisdom. I have chosen to spotlight the sympathizers, but I would be the first to concede that one should not forget the widespread negative view.

The spelling of Asian terms has presented a constant problem throughout the manuscript. The only satisfactory procedure in a work of this kind was to eliminate the complex diacritical markings and to employ standard dictionary spellings taken from the *Random House Dictionary of the English Language* and other sources.

My thanks go out to the following people who in differing ways contributed to the conception and realization of this study: Joseph Botond-

Blazek and Joseph Brent, friends, who helped awaken my first interest in Oriental thought; Donald Meyer and George Mowry, mentors, who taught me to see history in a new way; and Roger Mueller, a coworker, who read and suggested improvements in the manuscript. Library staffs at the following institutions greatly aided me with the research: the University of Texas at El Paso (UTEP), University of California at Los Angeles, Library of Congress, Harvard University, University of Texas, Oregon State University, University of Wisconsin, and Yale University. I should especially thank Jeanne Reynolds, for a number of years, director of the UTEP inter-library loan service, upon which geographical isolation forced an unusually heavy reliance. I would also like to acknowledge and thank the Research Committee of the University of Texas at El Paso for a series of grants that underwrote much of my research and the National Endowment for the Humanities, which provided a summer stipend to support part of the writing. Liberal Arts Dean Diana Natalicio and Anne Kugielsky of Greenwood Press were both very helpful in the manuscript's final stages. Though traditionally reserved for last, my first debt by far is to my family—Margaret, Forrest, Laura, and Jonathan—who have patiently endured the long preparation of this manuscript.

Notes

1. William H. Goetzmann, *Exploration and Empire: The Explorer and the Scientist in the Winning of the American West* (New York: Alfred Knopf, 1966), p. ix.

THE ORIENTAL RELIGIONS AND AMERICAN THOUGHT

1
First American Contacts with the Orient: The Eighteenth Century

Serious American interest in Oriental religions arose late, several centuries after Europeans had begun to show such interest. The reasons for this should be fairly obvious. Life was difficult in the New World: the sheer effort required to subjugate the new environment and to establish an ordered life in the midst of a wilderness left early settlers with little leisure for such curiosities. Physically, the East was extremely remote, thousands of miles away over the largely unknown expanse of the Pacific Ocean. And, finally, most of the first Americans were inflexibly Christian in outlook, and inhospitable to alien religious ideas. Until there was more leisure, less rigidity of belief, and more physical contact—conditions that did not exist until the nineteenth century—Asian thought would remain largely unknown. And yet preliminary contacts were made that paved the way for the later nineteenth-century intellectual discoveries.

One of the earliest Americans to express interest in Asia was, inevitably, Cotton Mather, that indefatigable Puritan divine and amateur scholar, who looked upon both this world and the world beyond as his territory. As Professor Mukhtar Isani has emphasized, Mather's Oriental interests were fairly significant. He "read fairly widely about the Orient," kept informed about news from the East, particularly the Turkish empire, and "maintained an active interest in missionary efforts in the Orient."[1] His father's library provided access to Purchas's *Hakluyt Posthumus or Purchas his Pilgrimes* (he later acquired his own set) and Robert Knox's *Historical Relation of the Island Ceylon*; he also had contacts with several individuals who had lived in India, including Elihu Yale, the American-born governor of Madras.[2]

The most remarkable testimony to Mather's interest in Asia, however, is to be found in a fascinating correspondence he carried on over several years with August Hermann Francke, leader of the German Pietist movement and professor of divinity and Oriental languages at the University of Halle.[3] It is easy to understand Mather's attraction to Francke: Pietism revealed close affinities with Puritanism, while Francke's support of an orphanage in Halle and of missionary work in India exemplified Mather's conception of "Doing Good."[4] Francke drew Mather's attention to pioneer missionary work being conducted by Danes in southern India and arranged for him to correspond with one of the missionaries, Bartholomew Ziegenbalgh. Mather followed the Danish mission's progress in the "East Indies" for several years, keeping Ziegenbalgh and Francke informed of the religious situation in the "West Indies." His diary entries during the period indicate both his fascination and his itch to become involved.[5] He sent advice, books, and "small presents of Gold" and in return received several religious tracts and a New Testament printed in Tamil, perhaps the first Asian publications to reach America.

Here was a beginning, but only a beginning. There is no evidence that Mather knew anything or cared to know anything about the Oriental religions or that he looked upon Asia in a positive way.[6] On the contrary, the real impact of the Asian correspondence seems to have been the inspiration it contributed for a more strenuous missionary effort at home. In 1721 he expanded and published two of the Indian letters as *India Christiana*, including an outline of the methods best suited to convert the Hindu people to Christianity. Nothing came of these events; when the first American missionaries sailed for India a hundred years later, they proceeded in apparent ignorance of Mather's earlier contacts. The episode does have symbolic significance, however, indicating that despite a wilderness condition and immense distances, contacts with Asia were made from an early date.

For many Americans the "Oriental tale," a literary genre that had arisen as far back as the Middle Ages, provided the first blurred image of Asia.[7] One has to wonder whether it did more to retard than to encourage American awareness of Oriental thought. There were several types of tales—the moral tale, satiric tale, philosophic tale, and imaginative or romantic tale—but all sought to evoke an "Oriental" mood. The tale was usually played out in an exotic Eastern setting, with picturesque dress, bizarre customs, and strange Oriental or pseudo-Oriental words sprinkled about to heighten the illusion. Though a few of the tales were authentically Eastern, most were Western tales decked out in Oriental dress.[8] The most famous, of course, were the *Arabian Nights*, a genuine Eastern collection first published in

America in 1794, which went through numerous editions by the time of the Civil War.

The Oriental tale enjoyed a sensational vogue in England in the first half of the eighteenth century. Looking on the Oriental vogue with disapproval, the English satirist James Cawthorne would lament, "Of late, 'tis true, quite sick of Rome and Greece,/ We fetch our models from the wise Chinese,/ European artists are too cool and chaste,/ For Mand'rin only is the man of taste!"[9] Addison, Defoe, Samuel Johnson, and Goldsmith all tried their hands at writing such tales. Addison's efforts are especially noteworthy, since most of his tales were published in the *Spectator,* which was widely read in the American colonies. The three most enduring Oriental tales produced in England were Samuel Johnson's *Rasselas* (1759), Goldsmith's *The Citizen of the World* (1762), subtitled "Letters from a Chinese Philosopher Residing in London to his Friends in the East," and William Beckford's *History of the Caliph Vathek* (1786).

The genre was just catching on in America as it passed out of style in England, and it enjoyed its greatest vogue here at the end of the century. Many of the tales printed in America were culled from English sources, although after 1780 American authors began to compose their own. Most were published in magazines such as the *Royal American Magazine* (1774-1775), *Boston Magazine* (1783-1786), *Gentleman and Lady's Town and Country Magazine* (1784), and *American Magazine* (1787-1788). By the count of one investigator, American magazines carried "well over a hundred" Oriental stories in the last fifteen years of the century alone; "nearly two-thirds" were authored by American writers.[10] *New York Magazine* (1790-1797) published thirty and Boston's *Massachusetts Magazine* (1789-1796) thirty-eight tales.

If most of the tales published in America were set in the Middle East, there were also a sprinkling centered in the farther East. Probably the earliest written by an American was Henry Sherburne's *The Oriental Philanthropist,* published in 1800. The story concerns Prince Nytan, the heir-apparent to the Chinese throne, who is imprisoned by an evil minister. Escaping with the help of a fairy, Nytan is magically transported to an island in the East Indies and subsequently travels across Asia, Africa, and Europe preaching the ideals of virtuous living and good government.[11]

One of the rare American tales that refers to Oriental religion is Samuel Lorenzo Knapp's *Letters of Shahcoolen, a Hindu Philosopher Residing in Philadelphia to his Friend El Hassan an Inhabitant of Delhi,* published in Boston in 1802. The Hindu philosopher speaks of the "veda" and "Brumma" (Brahma) and devotes two of his fourteen letters to a sympathetic discussion of Jayadeva's *Gitagovinda.* Knapp was an undergraduate at Dartmouth when he prepared the sketches. Though his tale reveals only a superficial knowledge of Oriental philosophy, he at least had some knowledge of Indian literature. The letters had been printed earlier in the New York *Commercial Advertiser.*[12] Another series published in 1813-1814 in *Polyanthos* magazine also suggest some acquaintance with the Orient. Presented as the authentic letters of people who had been to India, the pieces include descriptions of Indian customs and beliefs. Introducing the series, the author declares, "Different as the inhabitants of different nations are from each other in their customs, laws, and religion, there are a few principles and feelings common to them all. . . ."[13] One other work may be cited, George Fowler's *The Wandering Philanthropist; or, Lettres from a Chinese Written during his Residence in the United States,* published in 1810. At best, the Oriental tale may have stimulated an interest in Asia; it did little, however, to clarify Oriental religion.

Trade offered another early contact with Asia and, for a few heady years following the Revolution, it almost seemed that it would become the dominant factor in the new American republic's economic survival. Forced by the break with England to look for new markets, American ships scoured the high seas. One of these, the *Empress of China,* reached Canton in mid-1784, inaugurating the trade with China. Backed by Robert Morris, the leading financier of the American Revolution, it had sailed with a load of furs, raw cotton, lead, and ginseng, a root gathered in the New England woods and cherished by the Chinese as a restorer of lost virility. The ship had returned to New York in 1785 with a cargo of teas and miscellaneous China goods. Impressed by the 25 percent profit realized on the venture and the incredible potential of the market, merchants and shippers in Boston, Salem, Providence, and Philadelphia rushed to join the trade.[14] Within a year of the return of the *Empress,* five other ships had sailed for Canton, including the celebrated *Grand Turk,* which inaugurated Salem's trade with the Orient.

Meanwhile, a similar trade was springing up with India, triggered by the arrival of the *United States* off the coast of Pondicherry in 1784. Elias Hasket Derby, who began in the China trade and redirected his ships to India after 1790, played the leading role. After Derby's death in 1799, domination of the trade passed to the Crowninshields—John, Jacob, and Benjamin—who were, like the Derbys, prominent citizens of Salem.[15] In spite of difficulties caused by the Napoleonic Wars and the almost fatal setback of the Jefferson Embargo, the Chinese and Indian trade grew rapidly until the War of 1812. The number of American ships reaching Canton increased from four in 1789 to thirty-four in the 1804-1805 season, forty-two in 1805-1806, and thirty-seven in 1809-1810.[16] Interrupted by the War of 1812, the commerce revived briefly only to decline again in the late 1820s. While the Chinese trade was reaching its greatest heights during the 1830s and early 1840s, the Indian trade languished, then revived somewhat in the 1850s.[17]

Van Wyck Brooks captures the cosmopolitan effects of America's expanding foreign trade in *The Flowering of New England*:

> In all these bustling ports, or ports that had recently bustled, where the forests of masts rose at the wharves and Portuguese sailors sauntered through the streets, the wide world was omnipresent. Everyone talked about voyages "up the Straits," or to Hong Kong and Calcutta, towns that seemed closer to Salem or Portsmouth than Hartford or New York had ever seemed. The lofty chambers of the great dwellings, hung with French or English tapestry, adorned with arches and columns and carved Italian mantel-pieces, were papered with bold designs, brilliantly coloured birds and tropical flowers and scenes from the Medeterranean lands. The massive bedsteads in the upper rooms were draped with curious curtains of India linen, covered with quaint pagodas and figures in turbans. Canton shawls and Smyrna silks were as common as linsey-woolsey. There were parrots and pet monkeys in half the houses. The children played with cocoanuts and coral and spent their pennies for tamarinds and ginger, or spent their Russian kopeks and their British coppers, which circulated as freely as American coins. The men wore Chinese gowns at the Salem assemblies. . . .[18]

In such port cities as Boston, Salem, and Providence one could hardly avoid some contact with the Orient: while browsing in the shops where one might purchase Bohea and Souchong teas, nankeens, India muslins, Chinaware, Bengal ginghams, lacquer boxes, camphor wood sea chests; while reading the newspaper where notices of new arrivals of vessels from Canton and Calcutta regularly appeared; or perhaps while sauntering along the wharves where one might encounter Chinese and Indian servant boys brought home by the sea captains. Lacquered desks, Chinese porcelain, wallpaper, and fans blossomed in many larger New England homes to add a touch of Oriental elegance.[19] And in 1796 Captain Jacob Crowninshield returned triumphantly bearing a Bengal elephant named "old Bet." The first ever seen in America, the giant animal was exhibited in Philadelphia, New York, Boston, Salem, and Beverly and was eventually sold for the princely sum of $10,000.[20]

While the China-India trade was colorful, one must not exaggerate its significance. The exotic products, distant lands, and strange peoples associated with the trade early created an aura of mystery and romance that has surrounded it ever since.[21] In fact, trade with the Orient never made up more than a fraction of America's total foreign commerce. Before 1840 the trade with China never exceeded 6 percent of America's total foreign trade in any year, and after 1840 it was always less than 2 percent.[22] The percentages for the Indian trade until 1820 are comparable and are much smaller thereafter. It is also clear that the postrevolutionary vogue of Oriental goods was largely a passing fad that testified more to the sheer availability and novelty of Eastern products than a deeper appreciation of their aesthetic merits. Few of the people who adorned their homes with Oriental things were aware of the civilization and people who had produced them. One may agree with Ping Kuo, who was not disposed to underestimate the cultural impact of the trade, that the American attraction was "in the main, hardly more than an interest in the exotic, a fantastic striving to escape the drabness and dry routine of their daily round of existence."[23] In retrospect, the trade was significant only as a sign of things to come, not as the opening of a new era in close economic and cultural exchange.

William Bentley, minister of the Second Congregational Church in Salem, was one of the few who seemed to sense the wider possibilities opened by the Asian trade. An unorthodox thinker, he became one of the country's earliest converts to Unitarianism after reading one of Joseph Priestley's antitrinitarian tracts. Scholarly by temperament, he spent his spare time studying languages. He is said to have read more than twenty—including Arabic and Persian—which would give him good claim to be remembered as the first American to comprehend an Asian language. He also wrote thirty-three hundred sermons and fifty-six volumes of manuscripts. Recognizing these accomplishments, Jefferson sought to recruit him as the first president of the University of Virginia. Apparently, he could also be difficult. Asked to offer an abbreviated prayer at the July Fourth celebration in 1810, the assembled musicians needing to proceed to another engagement, he was so outraged that he prayed on for nearly an hour. By the time he reached "Amen," the band had departed.[24]

Bentley's most important contribution for our purposes was his leadership role in the East India Marine Society, which built up one of the first American collections of Oriental artifacts and art pieces. Founded in 1799, the society and its museum were direct outgrowths of Salem's trade with Asia; the requirement for membership was that the individual had sailed in Asian waters. Bentley largely drafted the society's original articles of association including the provision directing sea captains to collect books and to take notes on the customs of the peoples they contacted. He personally directed the collections for many years, furnishing departing captains with information concerning localities where valuable specimens might be found.[25] The yearly meetings of the society became one of Salem's most memorable events. The high point was a colorful procession of the society's membership in Oriental garb through the town streets. Describing the 1804 procession, Bentley noted that "each of the brethren" carried "some Indian curiosity," while a "palanquin was borne by the negroes dressed nearly in the Indian manner." Another member had marched in "Chinese habits & mask."[26]

Bentley also kept a voluminous diary, which provides invaluable glimpses of the Asian trade. Skimming ghrough the diary entries, which extend over thirty-five years, one finds the observant minister constantly recording the "curiosities" that Salem's ships were disgorging: a two-foot mandarin statue, a specimen of Chinese writing, a Chinese pipe, Japanese tea tables, lacquer cabinets, and Japanese paintings ("totally destitute of perspective"). And in 1790 he recorded the unique experience of "seeing for the first time a native of the Indies from Madras." Looking him over intently, he noted his "very dark" complexion, "soft" countenance, and "well proportioned" body.[27] (This was not the first occasion for an American to view an Asian in the flesh: in 1785 the *Pallas* had returned with several Chinese who spent the winter as wards of the city of Philadelphia.[28]) He notes another kind of East-West traffic in later years as the first English and American missionaries were dispatched for Asia. He was unimpressed, dismissing the missionaries as "mere fanatics without common talents" and "these infatuated, now perhaps roguish men." The missionary movement would steadily gather momentum and become one of the crucial influences in America's encounter with the Orient. Bentley's doubts hinged on the inferior qualifications of the men chosen to inform the "heathen" and a belief that missionaries would do better to address problems nearer home. Sought out by a young man who was preparing for missionary work in the East Indies, he would bristle: "Totally uninformed he is enquiring means to learn Oriental languages. I found the youth totally unprepared & not apparently of a taste & capacity for his appointment."[29]

Though American travel to the Orient has been mainly restricted to the nineteenth and twentieth centuries, a small number of adventurous spirits reached Asia in the eighteenth and, in rare cases, the seventeenth centuries. One early example is Christopher Newport, identified as a participant in the founding of Jamestown colony, who made three voyages for the East India Company (1613-1616) and died in Java in 1617.[30] A more notable seventeenth-century example is Elihu Yale, the "American Nabob," who would spend twenty-seven years in India. Born in Boston in 1649, young Elihu spent only his first three years in America, before his family returned to England. Employed by the East India Company, he eventually became governor of Madras. When he retired to England in 1699, he hauled away a magnificent collection of Oriental *objets d'art*, including many paintings, jewels, and Indian and Japanese cabinets. Yale became a benefactor of the college that still bears his name, but apparently none of his Oriental treasures reached America.[31] The traffic increased during the eighteenth century. David Ochterlony, a graduate of New Hampshire's Dummer Academy, joined the British army in India, rose to the rank of major general, and was knighted in 1815. William Duane, who went to India in 1787, was less fortunate. For several years the publisher of a newspaper in Calcutta, he fell out with the English authorities and was arrested and deported back to America.[32]

The seamen and traders who sailed in the China and India trade made up the largest contingent of early travelers. Some made the incredible voyage three and four times, although the high death toll normal in the early years made this a mounting gamble.[33] No early Americans were in a better position to see past the dark wall of ignorance and fantastic images that dominated the first perception of Asia. Unfortunately, most seamen and traders were simple men who had neither the literary skill nor the curiosity to bother to report what they saw. There were exceptions, however; one is Major Samuel Shaw, who participated in the very first American voyage to Asia.

Though lacking advanced schooling, Shaw was not exactly an unlettered seaman.[34] The son of a prosperous merchant, he had attended Boston's common schools and the famous Boston Latin School and served as an officer during the Revolutionary War (Trenton, Princeton, Brandywine, the hard winter at Valley Forge). Following the Revolution, he signed on as supercargo on the historic *Empress of China* voyage and upon his return was named America's first consul to China. Besides the 1784-1785 voyage, he made three other journeys to China: in 1786-1789, 1790-1792, and 1793-1794. During the second trip he spent more than a year in south China and made a brief excursion to India. He died enroute to the United States in 1794 from a liver ailment contracted in Bombay. Happily, his *Journals* survived and were published in 1847.

Except for brief interludes, Chinese authorities have resisted contacts with the West for centuries. Thus, when Shaw first reached China, the government was still restricting foreigners to a very narrow zone in south China, including the port city of Canton and nearby Macao, where foreign traders were expected to reside. Shaw's impressions are therefore based on a very constricted view of Chinese life, although he apparently gathered further scraps of information from older European traders as well as from the limited literary sources available to him. To his credit, he was quite conscious of the possible distortions imposed by such a restriction. For a comparable handicap, one might suggest the attempt to capture contemporary Mexico based on a brief visit to one of the border cities—Juarez or Tijuana—not exactly the optimum situation for real understanding.

Most of the *Journals* are devoted to a detailed description of the Chinese management of foreign commerce—a matter that Shaw considered of utmost importance to the future of the United States. But spliced through the account are charming glimpses of Chinese society and religious life. One discovers a mixture of appreciation and censure. He visited the homes of several of the great hong merchants whom the Chinese government permitted to transact business with foreigners. Remarking that the "knavery of the Chinese, particularly of the trading class," had become "proverbial," he insisted that he had found the merchants "as respectable a set of men as are commonly found in other parts of the world. . . . They are intelligent, exact accountants, punctual to their engagements, and, though not the worse for being well looked after, value themselves much upon maintaining a fair character."[35] Other American shippers testified in favor of the high character of the hong merchants and, in a number of cases, established lasting friendships.[36]

If Shaw found himself reassured by the character of the people, the same was not true of Chinese government; on the contrary, he questioned whether there was a "more oppressive" government to "be found in any civilized nation upon earth."[37] Officials at all levels were being "squeezed," with the whole system based on payoffs and favoritism. He was also disappointed by Chinese art, noting the general agreement that though able to "imitate most of the fine arts," the Chinese did "not possess any large portion of original genius" of their own.[38] Unfortunately, this astonishing view would dominate the West until the twentieth century.

Though brief, Shaw's statements concerning Chinese religion are of special interest. He was apparently amazed, appalled, and amused by what he saw. ". . . Suffice it to say," he remarked at one point, "that the most seemingly extravagant accounts of their idolatry and superstition . . . may be safely credited. No people are more the sport of religious contingencies, or put greater faith in lucky days." Entering the "Joss-houses" where the Chinese worshiped, he had seen the "image of a fat, laughing old man" before whom worshipers were prostrating and knocking heads on the floor. He had also looked in larger temples, observing "various idols, in the form of men and women" which he described as "many times larger than life" and "of most terrific appearance."[39] Though he did not moralize on the bizarre scenes he witnessed—the standard practice in most Western travel accounts of the time—clearly Chinese religion did not impress him favorably. He confines his comments on Chinese social and religious practices to the first voyage; as he explained, there could be "nothing to remark, in a second voyage, respecting a people whose manners and customs may be considered like the laws of the ancient Medes and Persians, which altered not."[40] The persistent myth of an unchanging China had reached America.

During a second voyage to China in 1786 Shaw had the opportunity to visit Bengal—making him one of the earliest Americans to view both India and China firsthand. The time was short and contacts limited. Indeed, he seems to have spent most of his time with English officials of the East India Company, all too common among early American travelers to India. He concluded that the country was well governed by the English, commerce in a "flourishing condition," and the natives "easy and apparently happy."[41] Perhaps because of the confinement of his recent Chinese visit, he was dazzled by the hospitality, affluent life-styles, and brilliant social events of the upper-class English community. It was a sign of the changing times that while in Calcutta, he ran into an old Boston acquaintance, Benjamin Joy, America's first consul to India, who had come on a "private speculation." Shaw spent more than a month in the Calcutta area and an additional ten days in Madras.

He immediately grasped the centrality of religion in the lives of the Hindu people. As with the Chinese, he was particularly drawn to the more bizarre forms. "It is said," Shaw wrote, "that a Hindoo will sometimes, by way of penance, crawl on his belly the whole length of the Ganges; . . . another will extend his arm, and, vowing never to draw it in again, keep it in that position till his death; while a third, locking his hands together, will suffer the nails of each to penetrate the back of the other, and in that manner rivet them inseparably."[42] Though he confessed that he had not personally witnessed these oddities of human behavior, he noted that on two occasions he had observed devotees being swung around a pole from a hook that had been passed through the fleshy part of their backs.

Shaw's account presents one man's view; yet it seems fairly characteristic. Obviously, he wished to understand the Chinese and Hindus but felt repelled by much that he saw. His negative reactions are hardly surprising in view of the radical differences between American and Asian culture and the limited time he had for observation. Professor Stuart Miller, who has recently completed an impressive analysis based on fifty accounts recorded in the China trade between 1785 and 1840, concludes that while a few traders indicated positive attitudes toward Chinese life, the general reaction was unfriendly. By Miller's count only four of the fifty works he examined were "fully friendly" to China and the Chinese. There has been no comparable study for India, although Professor Bhagat devotes an impressionistic chapter to the reactions of early American travelers in his *Americans in India*, which suggests that the traders were so engrossed in their business that they rarely wrote of what they saw.[43] But considering the time and circumstances, it remains significant that a minority of American traders viewed the Asian cultures positively and that most accounts found something with which to sympathize.

One other testimony must be noticed, that of Amasa Delano, who went to China and India in the 1790s; his *Narrative of Voyages and Travels* deserves to rank alongside Shaw's *Journals* as a classic source concerning early American-Asian relations. It is interesting that Delano and Shaw were both aboard the *Massachusetts* in 1790 when it set out for Canton. Delano remained in Asian waters, serving on an English ship and a Danish East India Company ship; he visited Bombay, Calcutta, and Canton before returning to the United States in 1794.[44] He made subsequent voyages to China in 1801-1802 and in 1806-1807.

Delano was much more positive than Shaw toward the customs he encountered as well as more critical of Western mistreatment of Asian peoples. Meditating on the value of his travel, he would reach a remarkable conclusion:

In the voyage of survey and discovery among the oriental islands, I had an opportunity to learn much of the human character in various circumstances, and under various institutions. Virtue and vice, happiness and misery, are much more equally distributed to nations than those are permitted to suppose who have never been from home, and who believe, like the Chinese, that their residence is in the center of the world. . . .[45]

One of the most charming episodes recounted in the *Narrative* (reminding one of Swift's *Gulliver's Travels*) concerned Delano's meeting and discussions with Abba Thule, the ruler of a small Pacific kingdom. In warfare Thule always gave his enemies a full three-day warning when preparing to attack. When Delano remonstrated that this practice destroyed the possibility of surprise, Thule replied that war was "horrid enough" even when pursued in the "most open and magnamimous manner. . . ." Inevitably comparing such a policy with the ruthless warfare practiced by Christian nations of the West, Delano found himself forced to admit that, "However savage may be the exterior of such a man, his heart must be allowed to be richly furnished with affections and principles worthy of a christian discipline. If he is wanting in our forms of religion, he still has the substance and dignity of virtue."[46] Though brief, Delano also makes sympathetic remarks concerning Chinese society and Hindu religious practices.

Intellectually, the eighteenth-century movement that seemed to hold out the greatest promise of awakening American interest in Oriental thought was the Enlightenment, which was to have such profound influence on American thought and institutions generally. In Europe the Enlightenment's emphasis on religious toleration, the influence of environment in the formation of one's ideas, and the basic oneness of human nature all contributed to a more sympathetic attitude toward Asian thought. Voltaire would hail Confucius as one of history's greatest men, while English Deists placed Oriental religion on an equal footing with Christianity. It is true that by the 1740s a reaction had set in against such Sinophilism, but one wonders how much of it penetrated America.

To be sure, American Enlightenment leaders had little or no direct acquaintance with Asian thought, but they were familiar with the works of European writers who had. As Herbert Morais has pointed out, a number of Voltaire's works were circulated in America after 1763, as was the Comte de Volney's popular *Ruins: or a Survey of the Revolutions of Empires* (1791); both authors often referred to Oriental thought in their writings. Volney employed Indian as well as Islamic and Jewish speakers to ridicule Christian dogma in *Ruins*, arguing that since all religions appealed to the supernatural to justify their claim to truth, none—including Christianity—could support the claim.[47] Volney came to the United States in 1795 and lived here for two years. Another European Enlightenment figure whose writings might have introduced Americans to Oriental religious doctrine was Joseph Priestley, who came to America in 1794 and spent the last decade of his life here.

Benjamin Franklin provides an instructive early example of the American Enlightenment response. As an intimate of the French salons, it would have been curious had he entirely ignored Asian thought, since it was then so stylish among French intellectuals. He arrived in France in 1767, the very year in which Quesnay's *Despotism in China*, which held up Chinese government as a model for Europeans, was published; he sometimes visited Quesnay's home.[48] Apparently, he already had a nodding acquaintance with the Noble Sage, having published extracts of Confucius' sayings in the *Pennsylvania Gazette*; he had also extolled the Chinese sage's teachings to the evangelist George Whitfield.[49] Perhaps he also had something to do with the call for closer study of China that formed the preface of the first volume of the American Philosophical Society's *Transactions* (1771). Noting that America's soil and climate closely approximated China's, Franklin or an associate argued that the American economy might profit from borrowing the skills and products of China. If the United States could successfully "introduce the industry of the Chinese, their arts of living and improvements in husbandry, as well as their native plants," the preface declared, "America might in time become as populous as China. . . ."[50] Despite such pronouncements, the society showed little interest in Asia; Franklin did publish a note in the *Transactions* in 1783 recommending the Middle Kingdom's superior techniques for manufacturing paper. (Years later, in 1838, the society published the first monograph on the Chinese language ever printed in America.)

On one occasion, at least, Franklin also revealed literary interest in China. In a "Letter from China," published in a London magazine in 1788, the versatile Pennsylvanian tried his hand at an Oriental tale. The tale recounts the Chinese travels of two sailors who had left Captain Cook's expedition in Macao. The superficiality of the piece is obvious in the reference to Chinese religious practices; one of Franklin's sailors comments that the Chinese "have a sort of religion, with priests and churches, but do not keep Sunday, nor go to church, being very heathenish." However, the tale does have the Franklinesque touch. Asked why they did not go to church to pray as Europeans did, one of the Chinese replies that "they paid the priests to pray for them, that they might stay at home and mind their business; and that it would be a folly to pay others for praying, and then go and do the praying themselves. . . ."[51]

We have Jared Sparks's word that an intimate acquaintance of Franklin's told him that the great Pennsylvanian was "very fond of reading about China" and that Franklin had once confessed that if he were a young man again, he would like to go to China.[52] Only the Chinese seemed to attract his interest, which seems logical considering his humanistic orientation: Hindu mysticism would only have repelled him.

There is one tantalizing connection with India, however. For a number of years Franklin maintained a close friendship with Sir William Jones, the brilliant English Orientalist, who founded Western Sanskrit studies. Indeed, with Franklin's backing, Jones nearly emigrated to the United States. In the early 1780s, Jones had concluded that he should do one of two things: either go to India, where he had applied for a judgeship and where he could continue the language studies that had already established him as one of England's ablest Orientalists; or move to America, whose revolutionary ideals greatly excited him. He had actually made preparations to depart for America, when the granting of the judgeship diverted him to India.[53] America's loss was scholarship's gain, since Jones used the years in India to found the Asiatic Society of Bengal and to make seminal translations of the *Laws of Manu* and Kalidasa's *Sakuntala*.

In most cases Asia impinged very lightly or not at all. A considerable search of Jefferson's, Madison's, Hamilton's, and other writings failed to turn up more than fragmentary references. A good example is Benjamin Rush, the eminent physician whose wide scientific interests and humanitarian activities epitomize the Enlightenment man. Rush's practice was to invite interesting visitors who came to Philadelphia to dine with him, occasions he utilized to learn what he could. Several American traders and a number of European travelers who had traveled in Asia were among the steady of visitors who enjoyed his hospitality. He faithfully preserved the scraps of information gleaned during the talks in his "Commonplace Book." The following 1789 entry records a conversation with a prominent Philadelphia merchant: "Jonth. Mifflin, lately arrived from Canton, gave me the following facts respecting the Chinese. The labouring men are often bent and have large varices in their legs from carrying heavy burdens. They live chiefly on vegetables. He never saw but one Chinese angry. They are very ingenious in roguery. They count age honourable. . . ."[54] So much for the Chinese. A few years later, John Stewart of London filled him in on the religious life of India:

October 8 [1791]. This morning Mr. Stewart breakfasted with me. He spoke with horror of the religion of the Gentoo [Hindu] nation which admitted of women burning themselves on the same funeral pile with their husbands. . . . He saw one of these sights, and saw other Gentoos suspended by hooks in their flesh and swing for a great while in the air, by order of their priests. The sufferers bear these things without complaining. He thinks their vegetable diet calms down their feelings and prevents emotions. The religion of the Gentoos consists, he says, wholly in ceremonies. They comb their heads and put on their cloaths [*sic*] as a part of their religion. Morality is no part of their religion. They have neither probity, nor benevolence.[55]

Other entries indicate visits by a British doctor who had accompanied the Macartney expedition to China and who attempted to explain Chinese medicine to Rush, and by the Comte de Volney, who drew on the Japanese experience to defend suicide as an act of "just reasoning."[56] Rush was genuinely anxious to know more concerning the Chinese and Hindus, but no more so than the curious habits of the Hottentots or Eskimo. Men of the Enlightenment had immense appetites for obscure facts. The entries do underscore the significant role of the Western traveler as a source of early information concerning the Orient.

One can only conclude that if the Enlightenment view seemed conducive to a more sympathetic attitude toward Oriental ideas, the evidence does not suggest much awareness or influence. (The two major exceptions—Joseph Priestley and John Adams—are discussed in chapter 2.)

Finally, Hannah Adams's *A View of Religions*, a religious handbook published in 1801, suggests a new attitude toward the Oriental religions. Adams (1755-1831) has been hailed as the first woman in America to make writing a profession.[57] She was deeply influenced by her father, who was known among this neighbors as "Book Adams" because of his addiction to reading. Apparently, the father aided his daughter with her researches, for the Reverend William Bentley speaks of Mr. Adams visiting him in 1791 "to collect materials for a 'Dictionary of all Religions' " to be published by his daughter.[8] Hannah Adams did not have an easy life. Reading her autobiography, one finds personal tragedy striking again and again: the death of her mother when she was ten, the bankruptcy of her father, the death of a beloved sister, and the periodic failure of her own eyesight, which threatened her sole means of survival.

Hannah Adams devoted herself mainly to religion, an interest that she had turned to passionately at the age of twenty. Years later she would recall the effort to read everything written on the subject. The experience had been disillusioning. She wrote that she "became disgusted" with the "want of candor" on the part of the authors she consulted, who invariably gave the "most unfavorable descriptions of the denominations they disliked. . . ."[59] Concluding that she could do better, she began to compile her own account, an *Alphabetical Compendium of the Various Sects Which Have Appeared from the Beginning of the Christian Era to the Present Day*, which was first published in 1784 and reprinted in several enlarged editions. Others of her works include *A Summary History of New England* (1799), *The Truth and Excellence of the Christian Religion* (1804), and *History of the Jews* (1812). Mainly a compiler who created mosiacs from the works of other authors, Adams did have a knack for condensation; she also reveals an unusually broad viewpoint in handling religious questions. Writing in 1825, Jared Sparks, a man of considerable literary weight, would praise her as a well-known and "successful" writer on theological subjects whose fourth and latest revision of the *Alphabetic Compendium* provided the "best manual" available.[60]

Adams added a thirty-page sketch on the Asian religions in the third edition of the *Alphabetic Compendium* published in 1801. She changed the title to *A View of Religions*, or to be more accurate: *A View of Religions in Two Parts. Part I Containing an Alphabetical Compendium of the Various Religious Denominations which Have Appeared in the World, from the Beginning of the Christian Era to the Present Day. Part II Containing a Brief Account of the Different Schemes of Religion Now Embraced Among Mankind. The Whole Collected from the Best Authors, Ancient and Modern*—a typical title in a less-hurried age. One of the volume's most notable features was Adams's commitment to a fair presentation of the sects and religions summarized in the book. She wrote that she had sought to "avoid giving the least preference of one denomination above another. . . ."[61] On the whole, she achieved her objective, though she did not always succeed in concealing her personal reactions. One example was her reference to the "incredible tortures" that the Hindu yogi imposed upon himself. "A minute description of the voluntary sufferings of the Indian devotee," she shuddered, "fills the mind with increasing horror, and freezes the astonished reader to a statue, almost as immoveable as the suffering penitent."[62] Most of her information was culled from a random collection of histories, encyclopedias, and travelers' accounts, including Montesquieu's *Spirit of the Laws*, Middleton's *Geography*, Maurice's *History of the Antiquities of India*, and Sir William Jones's *Asiatic Researches*. She confessed immense difficulties with her research, noting that a considerable part of the new material in the *View* had been gathered in booksellers' shops because she could not afford the purchase of the books.[63]

The summaries of the Oriental religions are all extremely brief and reveal the strengths and weaknesses of the sources consulted. Hinduism is accorded the most pages. She observed that thanks to scholars such as Jones, the veil obscuring that ancient religion had been largely removed. She then proceeded to confound this optimistic assessment by tracing the origins of the Indian people back to the Flood when Noah or his descendant Shem had led a migration into western India. Their descendants had lived in a primitive state of innocence while practicing the purest rites of the Hebraic religion for many centuries. Unfortunately, Ham's descendants had subsequently conquered India, corrupting the ancient religion; Hinduism was the consequence.[64] In the course of her sketch she touches upon the Hindu concept of God, the Hindu "trinity," metempsychosis, the religious practices of *sannyasins* and yogis, the self-immolation of Hindu widows, and the proliferation of sects. There are also appreciative references to the magnificence of Hindu temples and Indian tolerance ("Theirs is the most tolerant of all religions. . . .")[65]

The treatment of Chinese religion is briefer and less knowledgeable—probably because Adams had no authority comparable to William Jones. "The present religion of this kingdom is Pagan," she wrote, "but it is said, there are almost as many sects as persons among them. For as soon as a Chinese expects the least advantage from it, he is, without any consideration, to-day of one religion, to-morrow of another, or of all together."[66] She noted that there were three principal "sects": the followers of "Laokium" (apparently Lao-Tzu), "Foe" (Buddha), and Confucius. Her comments on Buddhism are especially interesting, since it was much less well known than Hinduism until the end of the nineteenth century. There were two Buddhisms: the external teaching meant for the common people, emphasizing acts of charity and the building of temples; and the internal teaching, kept from the people, which taught a "pure unmixed atheism," which rejected rewards or punishments after death, providence, and the immortality of the soul and acknowledged "no other God but the *void*. . . ." Of the three religions Confucianism is treated most sympathetically. It was, she declared, a religion that consisted "in a deep inward veneration for the God, or King of heaven, and in the practice of every moral virtue." Confucians had "neither temples, nor priest[s], nor any settled form of external worship: every one adores the Supreme Being in the way he likes best."[67] Ancestor worship and the Jesuit missionary movement in China also receive comment. Finally, there are brief sketches of religious life in Japan, Siam, Ceylon, and Burma, but their brevity and inconclusiveness suggest that these areas were little more than names to her.

In 1905, climaxing twenty-five years of scholarly effort to develop a comparative approach to the study of the world's religions, Lewis Henry Jordan, one of the movement's first historians, sought to identify the "Prophets and Pioneers" who had made the late nineteenth-century advances possible. In the American scene he noted several "distant and shadowy" figures who had attempted studies, but he questioned whether any deserved inclusion as pioneers. There was, however, one exception, "one worker who, in the judgment of every one who will make himself intimately acquainted with her history" deserved to be added to the list of true pioneers.[68] He was, of course, referring to Hannah Adams, who deserves recognition, not because of her scholarship, but because of the approach she adopted toward the world's religions. She spells out her approach in a prefatory note to the *View of Religions*, which bears quotation at length:

> 1st. To avoid giving the least preference of one denomination above another: omitting those passages in the authors cited, where they pass their judgement on the sentiments, of which they give an account: consequently the making use of any such appellations, as Heretics, Schismatics, Enthusiasts, Fanatics, etc. is carefully avoided.
>
> 2d. To give a few of the arguments of the principal sects, from their own authors, where they could be obtained.
>
> 3d. To endeavour to give the sentiments of every sect in the general collective sense of that denomination.
>
> 4th. To give the whole as much as possible, in the words of the authors from which the compilation is made, and where that could not be done without too great prolixity, to take the utmost care not to misrepresent the ideas.[69]

It would be more than a hundred years before such procedures were widely accepted by American students of Oriental religion.

These were important beginnings, but one must remind oneself of the almost total darkness that still obscured American awareness of Oriental thought at the end of the eighteenth century. The lack of volumes dealing with Asia in libraries and the absence of references to the East in the periodicals and public writings of the time emphasis this. One historian who has made a recent examination of early American knowledge about China reports that an "exhaustive search of the lists of books in private libraries in colonial America" had "failed to turn up more than a handful of works on China."[70] There were impressive private libraries, but only a few contained even a single Oriental volume. James Logan, the Philadelphia Quaker who had one of the three greatest private collections of the period, was one of the few exceptions: he owned the works of Confucius. The same historian reveals that a careful check of twenty-eight American periodicals in the colonial era uncovered less than two dozen references to China—omitting advertisements for tea and porcelain.[71] Though no comparable investigation has been made concerning India, a similar conclusion seems probable.[72]

Notes

1. Mukhtar A. Isani, "Cotton Mather and the Orient," *New England Quarterly* 43 (March 1970): 46. See the whole article, pp. 46-58.

2. Ibid., 47-48.

3. Cf. Ernst Benz, "The Pietist and Puritan Sources of Early Protestant World Missions (Cotton Mather and A. H. Francke)," *Church History* 20 (June 1951):

28-55. Also see Kuno Francke, "Cotton Mather and August Hermann Francke," *Harvard Studies in Philology and Literature* 10 (1896): 56-67 and "Further Documents Concerning Cotton Mather and August Hermann Francke," *Americana Germanica* 1 (1897): 31-66.

4. Cotton Mather, *Diary of Cotton Mather*, 2 vols. (New York: Frederick Ungar, 1957), 2: 364. Also see: 2: 193. Mather did have some reservations concerning Pietism, however.

5. Ibid., 2: 348, 516.

6. Note his passing reference in Kenneth Silverman, ed., *Selected Letters of Cotton Mather* (Baton Rouge, La.: Louisiana State University Press, 1971), p. 138, which undoubtedly reflected his own opinion.

7. Heavy reliance throughout this section has been placed on Mukhtar A. Isani, "The Oriental Tale in America through 1865: A Study in American Fiction" (Ph.D. diss., Princeton University, 1962), which fills a crucial gap in the early history of Oriental ideas in America. Isani makes a systematic page-by-page survey of sixty magazines through 1865.

8. Martha P. Conant, *The Oriental Tale in England in the Eighteenth Century* (New York: Columbia University Press, 1908), pp. 226-27.

9. William W. Appleton, *A Cycle of Cathay: The Chinese Vogue in England during the Seventeenth and Eighteenth Centuries* (New York: Columbia University Press, 1951), p. 90.

10. Lyon N. Richardson, *A History of Early American Magazines, 1741-1789* (1931; reprint ed., New York: Octagon Books, 1966), pp. 170, 227, 229-30. Isani, "Oriental Tale," p. 24.

11. Isani, "Oriental Tale," pp. 47-48.

12. Ibid., pp. 135-36.

13. Ibid., p. 52.

14. For a detailed description of the Chinese trade, see Kenneth Scott Latourette's old but still ueful *The History of Early Relations between the United States and China, 1784-1844* (New Haven, Conn.: Yale University Press, 1917), pp. 10-84. Also see Foster R. Dulles, *The Old China Trade* (Boston: Houghton Mifflin, 1930).

15. See Goberdhan Bhagat's recent *Americans in India, 1784-1860* (New York: New York University Press, 1970), pp. 3-84; also Richard H. McKey, Jr., "Elias Hasket Derby and the Founding of the Eastern Trade," *Essex Institute Historical Collections* 98 (January 1962): 1-25 and ibid. 98 (April 1962): 65-83; and Holden Furber, "The Beginnings of American Trade with India, 1784-1812," *New England Quarterly* 11 (June 1938): 235-65.

16. Latourette, *History of Early Relations*, p. 48.

17. Bhagat claims that historians have overemphasized the Chinese trade at the expense of the Indian. He notes that American exports to India sometimes exceeded Chinese exports during the early years, while America's imports from India from 1790 to 1820 were "far higher" than imports from China. American ships were restricted to one Chinese port (Canton), while they were permitted a much wider coastal trade in India. No record was kept of this coastal trade, but it would considerably increase the true trade figures with India. Bhagat, *Americans in India*, pp. viii-ix, 73. However, the graphs on pp. 138-39 make it clear that if imports from

India ran well ahead of Chinese imports in most years from 1795 to 1820, U.S. exports to China ran far ahead of Indian exports in the same years.

18. Van Wyck Brooks, *The Flowering of New England, 1815-1865*, rev. ed. (New York: E. P. Dutton, 1937), pp. 49-50.

19. Cf. Ping Chia Kuo, "Canton and Salem: The Impact of Chinese Culture upon New England Life during the Post-Revolutionary Era," *New England Quarterly* 3 (July 1930): 420-42. See also Kenneth W. Cameron's "Notes on Massachusetts Orientalism," appended to Ralph Waldo Emerson, *Indian Superstition*, ed. Kenneth W. Cameron (Hanover, N.H.: The Friends of the Dartmouth Library, 1954), Appendix A, pp. 64-66.

20. Sydney and Marjorie Greenbie, *Gold of Ophir or the Lure That Made America* (Garden City, N.Y.: Doubleday, Page, 1925), p. 53, and Bhagat, *Americans in India*, pp. 54n., 79.

21. Both the Greenbies' *Gold of Ophir* and James Duncan Phillips's *Salem and the Indies: The Story of the Great Commercial Era of the City* (Boston: Houghton Mifflin, 1947) are good examples of popular romanticization.

22. Stuart C. Miller, *The Unwelcome Immigrant: The American Image of the Chinese, 1785-1882* (Berkeley, Calif.: University of California Press, 1969), p. 19.

23. Kuo, "Canton and Salem," p. 439.

24. See the sketches in Samuel A. Eliot, ed., *Heralds of a Liberal Faith*, 3 vols. (Boston: American Unitarian Association, 1910), 1: 149-59, and Joseph Waters, "A Biographical Sketch of Rev. William Bentley," in *The Diary of William Bentley, D.D. Pastor of the East Church, Salem, Massachusetts*, 4 vols. (Gloucester, Mass.: Peter Smith, 1962), 1: ix-xxi, a reprint of the 1905 Essex Institute edition. The "amen" story is recounted in Eliot, *Heralds of a Liberal Faith*, 1: 154.

25. See the description in the *North American Review* 6 (January 1818): 283-85, and Bentley's own entry, *Diary*, 2: 321. Also: Waters's comment in his "Biographical Sketch," *Diary*, 1: xvi.

26. Bentley, *Diary*, 3: 68.

27. Ibid., 1: 175, 228; 2: 235, 342.

28. Miller, *Unwelcome Immigrant*, p. 184.

29. Bentley, *Diary*, 4: 146, 160, 355, 356. See also 4: 543.

30. Dale Riepe, *The Philosophy of India and Its Impact on American Thought* (Springfield, Ill.: Charles C. Thomas Publishers, 1970), p. viin.

31. Hiram Bingham, *Elihu Yale: The American Nabob of Queen Square* (New York: Dodd, Mead, 1939) and S. M. P. [Stanley M. Pargellis], *Dictionary of American Biography*, 20: 590-91. (Hereafter cited as *DAB*.)

32. Bhagat, *Americans in India*, pp. xxiv, 117-18.

33. See the rather chilling summary of the fate of one crew in Amasa Delano's *Narrative of Voyages and Travels in the Northern and Southern Hemispheres: Comprising Three Voyages Round the World; Together with a Voyage of Survey and Discovery, in the Pacific Ocean and Oriental Islands* (Boston: E. G. House, 1817), pp. 27-29.

34. See Josiah Quincy's "Memoir" in Samuel Shaw, *The Journals of Major Samuel Shaw, The First American Consul at Canton* (Boston: William Crosby & H. P. Nichols, 1847), pp. 3-129 and the brief notice in the *DAB*, 9 (1957): 47-48.

35. *Journals of Shaw*, p. 183.

36. See, for example, Elma Loines, "Houqua, Sometime Chief of the Co-Hong at Canton (1769-1843)," *Essex Institute Historical Collections* 89 (April 1953): 99-108.

37. *Journals of Shaw*, p. 183.

38. Ibid., p. 199.

39. Ibid., pp. 195, 196-97.

40. Ibid., p. 227.

41. Ibid., p. 263.

42. Ibid., p. 287.

43. Stuart C. Miller, "The American Trader's Image of China, 1785-1840," *Pacific Historical Review* 36 (November 1967): 375-95. Eleven accounts are classified as very unfriendly, with the remaining accounts designated as marginal or defying classification. Bhagat, *Americans in India*, pp. 115-29.

44. *DAB*, 3 (1957): 217.

45. Delano, *Narrative of Voyages*, p. 256.

46. Ibid., pp. 60, 64.

47. Herbert M. Morais, *Deism in Eighteenth Century America* (1934: reprint ed., New York: Russell & Russell, 1960), pp. 48, 126-27.

48. H. G. Creel, *Confucius: The Man and the Myth* (New York: John Day, 1949), p. 274.

49. Alfred O. Aldridge, *Benjamin Franklin and Nature's God* (Durham, N.C.: Duke University Press, 1967), pp. 120-21.

50. Noted in William W. Lockwood, "Adam Smith and Asia," *Journal of Asian Studies* 23 (May 1964): 348.

51. Aldridge, *Franklin*, p. 140.

52. John Bigelow, ed., *The Works of Benjamin Franklin*, 12 vols. (New York: G. P. Putnams, 1904), 10: 311n.

53. S. N. Mukherjee tells the story most fully in *Sir William Jones: A Study in Eighteenth-Century British Attitudes to India* (London: Cambridge University Press, 1968), particularly pp. 49-72, but see also Garland Cannon, *Oriental Jones. A Biography of Sir William Jones (1746-1794)* (New York: Asia Publishing House, 1964), pp. 92, 163.

54. George W. Corner, ed., *The Autobiography of Benjamin Rush* (Princeton, N.J.: Princeton University Press for the American Philosophical Society, 1948), p. 175.

55. Ibid., p. 210. The first bracket added by the editor.

56. Ibid., pp. 245-46, 242.

57. *DAB*, 1: 61. The basic source is *A Memoir of Miss Hannah Adams, Written by Herself* (Boston: Gray & Bowen, 1832).

58. Bentley, *Diary*, 1: 238; see also 2: 324.

59. *Memoir of Hannah Adams*, p. 11.

60. Jared Sparks, "Letters on the Gospels," *North American Review* 20 (April 1825): 366.

61. Hannah Adams, *A View of Religions*, 3rd rev. ed. (Boston: Manning & Loring, 1801), p. vii.

62. Ibid., p. 409n.

63. *Memoir of Hannah Adams*, p. 28.
64. Adams, *View of Religions*, p. 406.
65. Ibid., p. 415.
66. Ibid., p. 400.
67. Ibid., p. 402.
68. Lewis Henry Jordan, *Comparative Religion. Its Genesis and Growth* (Edinburgh: T. & T. Clark, 1905), p. 145. Hannah Adams is treated on pp. 145-49.
69. Adams, *View of Religions*, p. vii.
70. Miller, *Unwelcome Immigrant*, p. 13.
71. Ibid., pp. 13-14.
72. However, see chapter 1 of Isani, "Oriental Tale," pp. 1-22.

2
Widening Contacts and Early Explorations

There is no dramatic break in moving into the nineteenth century, though American awareness of Asia steadily increased. Trade with India and China continued; increasing numbers of Americans traveled to Asia and returned to report their impressions; and the influence of the Enlightenment persisted—all preparing the way for a more sympathetic discussion of Oriental religion when the time was ripe. At the same time new movements appeared in the century's first decades that were to be decisive in the American transaction with Oriental thought—the most important being Unitarianism. New contacts and new literary channels that increased American interest in the Asian religions were also established. The deep mists that had enveloped Asia when fragmentary contacts were first made began to rise, revealing the dim outline and immense richness of Asian thought.

A memorable milestone as the century dawned was the publication of the first serious inquiry into the Oriental religions published in America: Joseph Priestley's *A Comparison of the Institutions of Moses with those of the Hindoos and other Ancient Nations*. Priestley, of course, was already a man of international reputation when he decided to emigrate to the United States in 1794. He had won an enduring place in the history of modern science by his isolation of oxygen and had done important work as well in electricity, encouraged by his friend Benjamin Franklin.[1] He had also taken an active part in the fierce political debates touched off by the French Revolution, writing in favor of revolution. A howling Birmingham mob, assailing him as a traitor, had burned his house and destroyed his library.

This trauma, coupled with the fact that three sons had already emigrated, convinced him to make his way to America.

Though science brought him fame, Priestley's first line of work, his choice of vocation, was the ministry; he was an outspoken exponent of "enlightened" Christianity and a founder of English Unitarianism.[2] One authority has judged that he was "beyond doubt the most influential figure in the earlier history of the Unitarian movement in England. . . ."[3] His *Institute of Natural and Revealed Religion* (1772-1773) and *History of the Corruptions of Christianity* (1782) became basic primers for all freethinking religionists. This needs emphasis because it was the religious—not the scientific or the political—vocation that was uppermost in America.

Since Priestley was already sixty-one and battle-scarred when he came to America, one would not anticipate his great activity during the ten years of life remaining to him. The move seemed to revive him. Two weeks after his arrival, he was rejoicing: "I feel as if I were in another world"; he spoke of living with a "sense of perfect security and liberty. . . ."[4] (Unfortunately, America has never quite lived up to its reputation as the Promised Land: a few years later, shaken by fear of the contagion of the French Revolution, there was an unsuccessful move to deport the aged exile under the terms of the Alien and Sedition Laws.) Turning down several offers to lecture, including a professorship of chemistry at the University of Pennsylvania, he joined his sons in Northumberland in rural Pennsylvania and began to write. Works that he had pushed aside or long wished to undertake were now published in rapid succession: a four-volume *General History of the Christian Church*, as well as *Unitarianism Explained and Defended, Socrates and Jesus Compared, Notes on All the Books of Scripture* (in four volumes), *The Doctrines of Heathen Philosophy Compared with Those of Revelation* —and, finally, the *Comparison of the Institutions of Moses with those of the Hindoos*. He did much of the writing at night before the parlor fire surrounded by his family.[5]

Priestley's treatment of Oriental religion can be understood only in terms of his larger religious view. Though regarded as a dangerous freethinker and skeptic, he always insisted that he was a believer in true Christianity. He emphasized that his attacks on orthodox Christianity were aimed only at "corruptions" of the original spirit. He claimed to be a materialist and supporter of determinism, but he also affirmed that the soul would be raised immediately after death by a miraculous act of God and that the second coming of Christ was imminent.[6] If his views were radical by contemporary standards, they seem tame and surprisingly Christian by modern ones. This is especially true of his American writings, which reveal more preoccupation with combating the views of freethinkers and agnostics than orthodox Christians. Summing up his views in the year of his death, he declared his belief in the existence, perfection, and guiding providence of God; in the miracles, death, and resurrecton of Jesus; and in a final judgment in which Jesus would return to earth and the dead would be raised from their graves.[7] These hardly seem the beliefs of an infidel.

The Comparison was his most extended analysis of Asian region, but Priestley also dealt with Oriental religions elsewhere in his published works. There is a brief discussion of Indian philosophy in his *Disquisitions Relating to Matter and Spirit* (the 1782 edition, revised and enlarged) and a several-page comparison of Christianity with Islam and Hinduism in the *Letters to a Philosophical Believer, Part II.*[8] Finally, his *Discourses Relating to the Evidences of Revealed Religion*, composed soon after his arrival in America, prefigures most of the arguments subsequently developed in the *Comparison*. He sharply condemned Paine, Volney, and Voltaire for anti-Christian bias and offered brief comparisons of Christianity and the "Heathen" religions meant to demonstrate the former's superiority. If brief, the references to Oriental religions nevertheless indicate that he had been looking in their direction. He revealed at one point that he had just seen the the third volume of the *Asiatic Researches*, the publication of the Asiatic Society of Bengal put out by William Jones, Colebrooke, and others, that was revolutionizing Western knowledge about India.[9] He treated the Hindu achievement with respect, observing, "This people was famed, in all ages, for their superior wisdom and civilization"; he noted that both Egyptian and Greek mythology had "been borrowed from theirs," or else "derived from the same source." This did not prevent a harsh dismissal of Hindu religion: "What absurd notions concerning the origin and constitution of the universe, and what a complicated *Polytheism* are the foundation of it!" Again: "How horrid were some of the rites of the Hindoo religion, and how abominable and disgusting were others of them!"[10]

Priestly had prepared the *Discourses* originally as public lectures, which he delivered in Philadelphia in 1796. They were a sensation. He spoke of delivering the first three discourses to "very crowded audiences, great numbers not being able to get into the place"; he was told "that the greater part of the members of Congress are my hearers, and intend to continue so." His fame and notoriety were undoubtedly the major attractions, though reports concerning the novelty of his lectures must have increased popular interest. Priestley sensed this. "What strikes my hearers most," he reported to a friend, "is the comparison I have at some length drawn between the religion of the Hebrews and that of the Heathens, and also of their philosophy. . . . Everything that I have advanced on these subjects seemed to be perfectly new to almost every body here."[11]

Priestley's most ambitious effort to confront Oriental thought appeared in 1799: *A Comparison of the Institutions of Moses with those of the*

Hindoos and other Ancient Nations. Where he had dealt with Asian doctrines in passing in the earlier works, he now gave them center stage. Though suggesting outwardly an intention to compare the Oriental and Western faiths from a disinterested viewpoint, the book is an apology for Christianity. But then Priestley believed that disinterested scholarship could come to no other conclusion. Testifying that he had long believed that a "fair comparison of the ancient Heathen religions" with the "system of Revelation" would establish the latter's superiority, he predicted that the resulting study would make his readers grateful "that they were born in a Christian country. . . ." As in earlier writings, he recognized that undoubtedly there were "some sentiments of just, and what may be called *sublime* devotion in the Hindoo writings," but he adamantly insisted that the "general character of the devotion of the Hindoos" was a "debasing superstition."[12]

Priestley cites an assortment of books as sources for Hindu religion, a good number authored by men who had spent time in India, including J. T. Phillipps's *An Account of the Religion, Manners, and Learning of the People of Malabar* (1717), Alexander Hamilton's *A New Account of the East Indies* (1727), La Croze's *Histoire du Christianisme des Indes* (1758), John Z. Holwell's *Interesting Historical Events Relative to the Provinces of Bengal and the Empire of Indostan* (1767), Alexander Dow's *History of Hindostan* (1768), Nathaniel B. Halhed's *A Code of Gentoo Laws* (1777), and Sir William Jones's *Institutes of Hindu Law; or, The Ordinances of Menu* (1796).[13] However, Herdotus and Plutarch are also cited and would have been much less authoritative.

One might wonder where Priestley found such books in America in the 1790s. For the most part, he did not. He repeatedly complained to English correspondents of his need for books, noting that he especially missed the older tomes to be found only in Europe. Much of the time he had to rely on the personal library he had brought from Europe, presumably much depleted by the Birmingham riots. Remarking to a friend in 1798, "If you would know and feel the value of books of literature, come hither, where they are not to be had," he observed that he had seen three college libraries since arriving in America and that "mine is three times more valuable than all." He did discover a "very valuable learned library" in Philadelphia, which he repeatedly used; but since he did most of his writing in Northumberland, he could not have consulted it very often. These difficulties slowed his work on *Comparison*; he confided to a friend, "I wrote it twice over in long hand, which I never did with respect to any thing before."[14]

Much of the discussion in *Comparison* was addressed to contemporary European writers, whose favorable comments concerning the Oriental religions raised questions concerning the superior claims of Christianity. It opened with the question of Hinduism's age, certainly a crucial matter, for if Hinduism were older than Judaism, as some European writers maintained, then one might question the biblical story of creation and the claim that religion first appeared in the ancient Middle East. In all disputed areas Priestley found reasons for Christian reassurance; thus, he concluded that Hinduism was not as old as many believed and that it was a degenerate form of an older worship of a single God.[15] In succeeding pages he considered the *Vedas* and other Hindu sacred writings, the general principles of Hindu philosophy, the caste system, the place of women in Indian society, and popular devotional practices.

The most original feature of the work was its comparative approach. While intent on accentuating differences between Christianity and the Oriental systems, he was willing to admit some remarkable similarities, including statements concerning the nature of God, an "unequivocal" tradition of a universal flood, and "some excellent moral maxims" that closely paralleled Christianity. However, the differences outweighed the similarities, and Christianity retained its superiority. If Hindus had once worshiped one Supreme Being, they were now polytheists and idolaters. He denied the claim that Hinduism was mild and tolerant, and he denounced it for its humiliation of women—a dominant theme in nineteenth- and twentieth-century discussions of Indian society. In the end he insisted, "Every system of Heathenism, ancient or modern, was formed on principles fundamentally different from those of the *Hebrew* Scriptures."[16]

Whatever its limitations, Priestley's *Comparison of the Institutions of Moses with those of the Hindoos* launched American exploration of Asian religious thought. He wrote not to praise but to diminish the Oriental religions, and he sought to reassert the claim of Christianity as the one true faith. One may read him as a rather narrow-minded bigot. Still, he was the first writer in America to take the Oriental religions seriously enough to seek to understand them. Despite his indictment, he revealed recognition of the splendor of the Asian achievement, a view that steadily grew over the century. And finally, by adopting a comparative standpoint, he pioneered an approach that would culminate in the comparative religions movement at the end of the century.

Priestley was too radical to have had any sizable influence in awakening American interest in the Oriental religions. Moreover, his American works were published in small editions in backwoods Pennsylvania, and the discussion of Asian religion occupied a small space. There is one important exception, who seems to have been directly provoked into serious reading about the Oriental religions by Priestley: John Adams, the only American Enlightenment thinker to indicate definite interest in Asian thought.

Adams had been in the throng that flocked to hear Priestley's Philadelphia lectures in 1796—where the famous émigré had compared the merits of the Hebrew and "Heathen" religions. Priestley described himself as "an old acquaintance and correspondent" of Adams's; when he subsequently published the Philadelphia lectures as *Discourses Relating to the Evidences of Religion*, he dedicated the volume to the vice-president. However, Priestley was greatly disappointed. Within a year, he was complaining that Adams, the typical politician, had deserted him because his lectures had become unpopular.[17] Adams became president, Priestley died, and the matter seemed closed.

But after 1812 Adams is to be found considering Priestley's views once again, and through him Oriental thought. This unexpected development may be followed in the series of remarkable letters he and Thomas Jefferson exchanged in their last years.[18] The two men had broken off relations during the troubled 1790s, but in 1812 became reconciled and began to exchange long, revealing letters. Philosophical by temperament and wide-ranging in their interests, their letters covered an immense spectrum. One topic was religion, which Adams kept introducing into their dialogue. The distinguished New Englander confessed to his friend, "For more than sixty Years I have been attentive to this great Subject."[19] Retirement from politics now gave him the opportunity to pursue the subject to his heart's content. In 1812 and 1813 Oriental thought became increasingly prominent. In one of the earliest references, Adams observed that Plato had borrowed most, if not all, of his doctrines from Indian and Egyptian philosophers. However, his brief summary of Oriental philosophy suggests that he had not yet made more than the most superficial acquaintance with Asian thought. This suspicion is corroborated by a subsequent letter in which, objecting to Jefferson's evaluation of Christianity, he commented, "That it is the most sublime and benevolent, I agree. But whether it has been more perverted than that of Mosse [Moses], of Confucius, of Zoroaster, of Sanchoniathan of Numa, of Mahomet[,] of the Druids, of the Hindoos etc. etc. etc. I cannot as yet determine; because I am not sufficiently acquainted with those Systems. . . ."[20] That he had resolved to become better acquainted becomes apparent in succeeding letters. Priestley was to be the major catalyst.

After Adams lamented that he knew of no work that compared Christianity's moral principles with those of other religions, Jefferson referred him to Priestley's *Doctines of Heathen Philosophy Compared with Those of Revelation* and had a copy forwarded from Philadelphia. Adams read the work and others by Priestley as well. He fumed at Priestley's unevenness and catalogued numerous instances of omission, unfairness, and distortion; nevertheless, he learned a good deal. By 1814, he was boasting to Jefferson, "You will perceive, by these figures that I have been looking into Oriental History and Hindoo religion. I have read Voyages and travels and every thing I could collect, and the last is Priestleys 'Comparison of the Institutions of Moses, with those of the Hindoos'. . . ."[21] Two years later he notified the Virginian that he had sent for Charles Dupuis's twelve-volume *Origine de tous les cultes,* which would consume much of his time in succeeding months. "Your undertaking the 12. volumes of Dupuis," Jefferson commented admiringly, "is a degree of heroism to which I could not have aspired even in my younger days." Adams found Dupuis one of the most fascinating works he had ever read: "Of all the Romanc[e]s, and true Histories I ever read, it is the most entertain[in]g And instructive. . . ." Not wishing to be misunderstood, he added, "Conclude not from all this, that I have renounced the Christian Religion, or that I agree with Dupuis in all his Sentiments. Far from it. I see in every Page, Something to recommend Christianity in its Purity, and Something to discredit its Corruptions." By late 1816 he confided that over the past two years he had completed fifteen volumes of Grimm, twelve volumes of Dupuis, four volumes of "Jesuitical History," as well as numerous other volumes. He denied that the reading had caused fundamental changes in his religious views, but admitted finding many new ideas, especially in Dupuis. "My Conclusion from all of them," he added, "is Universal Tolleration."[22]

The climax came in 1817. About the middle of the year Adams notified Jefferson that he had just received a new shipment of books, including Sir John Malcolm's *History of Persia* and Sir William Jones's *Works*. Amazed at his own industry, he interrogated himself: "What can I do with all this learned lumber? Is it necessary to Salvation to investigate all these Cosmogonies and Mythologies?" Jones's writings increased his respect for the achievements of ancient Indian civilization. The Englishman's discussion of the debate between materialists and spiritualists in ancient India emphasized how little originality there was in modern religious controversies: "We find that Materialists and Immaterialists existed in India and that they accused each other of Atheism, before Berkly or Priestley, or Dupuis, or Plato, or Pythagoras were born. Indeed Neuton himself, appears to have discovered nothing that was not known to the Antient Indians. He has only furnished more ample demonstrations of the doctrines they taught."[23] There is one last, tantalizing comment: "Now Sir! please to hear a modest Proposal. Let me go back to twenty. Give me a million of Revenue, a Library of a Million of Volumes, and as many more as I should want. I would devote my life to such an Oe[u]vrage as Condorcet tells us, that Turgot had in contemplation, all his Lifetime. I would digest Bryant, Gebelin, Dupuis, Sir William Jones and above all the Acta Sanctorum of the Bolandists."[24] An old man's fantasy, of course, but one that emphasizes the attraction that his reading exerted.

Several things stand out in Adams's letters. The most significant is his real fascination with Oriental thought; the second president of the United States was seriously attracted to the East. The letters also emphasize that by the first decades of the nineteenth century Oriental thought was coming within the reach of serious American readers, thanks to an increasing stream of books from European scholars. But finally there is the candor of the letters: since they were intended for Jefferson's eyes alone, Adams felt free to unburden himself. The result is a unique document for the first period of Oriental discovery.

No movement played a more significant role in bringing Oriental religion to public attention during the nineteenth century than the movement that Joseph Priestley helped launch—Unitarianism. Unitarians played a large, if not decisive role in many other movements: Transcendentalism, the Free Religious Association, Oriental scholarship, and the World's Parliament of Religions. Not all Unitarians, of course, indicated an interest in Asian religion, but an unusual number of Americans who did reveal such interest had Unitarian backgrounds. Considering the movement's small numbers, this feature is the more remarkable.

Despite Priestley's prominence in the history of early Unitarianism, he seems to have played little role in the rise of an American movement. He held Unitarian services in his home in Pennsylvania and noted the great opportunities America opened for Unitarianism's spread, but he did not seek to lead the way.[25] Instead American Unitarianism seems to have arisen independently of Unitarianism elsewhere in the world, evolving out of the liberal wing of New England Congregationalism. Led by Jonathan Mayhew and Charles Chauncy, the liberals were at first able to coexist with the orthodox party. But eventually relations deteriorated, climaxing in Henry Ware's election as professor of divinity at Harvard in 1805; the so-called "Unitarian Controversy" was underway. Over the next two decades, a sizable portion of New England's Congregational churches and the Harvard Divinity School were carried by the Unitarians.[26]

The special Unitarian interest in Asian thought seems to have begun with Rammohun Roy, a brilliant Hindu reformer who burst upon the West about 1820. Born into a wealthy Hindu family, Roy had held a high position in the Indian civil service. Retiring at the age of forty-two, he became a leader in reviving and reforming Hinduism. Between 1815 and 1820 he published *An Abridgment of the Vedant*, translations of several of the *Upanishads*, and a *Defense of Hindoo Theism*. In these tracts he called for a return to the pure monotheistic faith of early Hinduism and an end to the idolatry that had come to dominate later Hinduism. To implement these reforms he organized a new religious society, the Brahmo Samaj, which quickly became a major focus for reform Hinduism. Significantly, Roy was one of the earliest Hindus to travel to the West; he would die in England in 1833 during a visit.[27] He combined the old with the new and East with West. Fluent in English and deeply indebted to Western ideas, he yet defended ancient Hindu teachings.

American Unitarian attention was first drawn to Rammohun Roy by strange reports of his conversion to Unitarianism. In fact, he was strongly attracted to Christianity's ethical teachings. Early in his religious studies he had taken up the study of the Gospels, publishing a selection of the essential teachings in 1820, entitled *The Precepts of Jesus, The Guide to Peace and Happiness*.[28] Astonishingly, he adopted a "unitarian" perspective. Setting out to apply the same critical standards to Christianity that he had earlier applied to Hinduism, he had eliminated all suggestions of a trinitarian godhead and miracles. Christian missionaries in India were outraged and launched a bitter attack. He had responded by reminding the missionaries that a belief in three gods in one was no less polytheistic than the traditional Hindu belief in 330 million gods—a frequent point of attack by missionary polemicists.[29] The *coup de grace* was Roy's conversion of one of the missionaries to his "unitarian" viewpoint!

News of these astonishing developments began to reach America as early as 1818; for the next decade Unitarian periodicals would be buzzing with accounts of the remarkable Indian reformer. Both the *Christian Register* and *Christian Examiner*, the two most important American Unitarian organs, treated the story as a major event. There were more than one hundred references between 1821 and 1830 in the *Register* alone, many articles of length. Non-Unitarian publications also picked up the story: Adrienne Moore, who has made a meticulous count, concludes that nearly 50 percent of the religious journals in the eastern United States carried some reference to him.[30] Significantly, the attitude toward Roy in these pieces was almost uniformly laudatory. In a century when non-Westerners, and Asians in particular, were frequently dismissed as lesser races, Roy offered living proof that intellect and high ideals were not monopolies of Western civilization.

But Rammohun Roy's greatest significance was his translation and explication of the Hindu religious classics. If the translations of William Jones and other Western scholars were beginning to reach America, they were still hard to find. Meanwhile, Roy's tracts helped fill the gap. Modern scholars would surely debate his emphasis upon the monotheism of the *Vedas* as well as other interpretations, but in view of the vacuum that existed in America concerning Hinduism in the 1820s these faults seem minor. It seems clear that Roy wished to reach a Western audience: the very fact that he translated the Hindu works into English would suggest this. He also explains in the introduction of his *Translation of an Abridgment of the Vedant* that he had undertaken the work with the desire to "prove to my European friends, that the superstitious practices which deform the Hindoo religion have nothing to do with the pure spirit of its dicates."[31] How widely Rammohun Roy's translations circulated in America is difficult to determine; the fact that they had to be brought from India and that they were printed in small editions certainly limited their reach. On the other hand, extracts from the writings were included in a number of early articles that reached a much wider audience.

One of the earliest presentations was William Tudor's "Theology of the Hindoos, as Taught by Ram Mohun Roy," compiled from Roy's translations of the *Upanishads* and his *Defense of Hindoo Theism*. Tudor mentions that all three works were in his possession, indicating that some copies of Roy's translations were obviously reaching America. The primitive presentation of Hinduism—undoubtedly suited to unfamiliar American readers—is suggested by his opening lines:

> The scriptures, or sacred books of the Hindoos, are called the Vedas. These books they suppose to have been written, and bequeathed to them, by their great legislator, Brama. They are in the Sanscrit language, and of very remote antiquity. The period in which they were written has not been ascertained.[32]

Roy's contention that Hinduism's oldest records clearly taught an "enlightened worship of one God" was approved. Tudor observed that though no Christian, Roy's doctrine differed "very little from the christian doctrine respecting the nature and attributes of the Deity." He concluded that he had dwelled on the subject because "it is novel" and because "it is likely hereafter to attract much attention."[33]

In 1823 another writer presented a much longer account based on no less than sixteen of Rammohun Roy's works. He noted that all sixteen were in his possession. The history of Roy's controversies in India was reviewed and sizable extracts from his books reprinted. Translations of the *Upanishads* and Roy's view of ancient Hindu religion figure prominently. Like Tudor, the writer was struck by Roy's distinction between the higher Hinduism of the original scriptures and later popular Hinduism; however, he expressed reservations about the interpretation. He conceded that Roy had made his point concerning the monotheism of the *Vedas*, but declared he was "by no means equally satisfied, that the idolatry of the Hindoos has not abundant authority in the more modern at least of their sacred books."[34] The piece includes a two-page selection of sayings from the Hindu scriptures, which the commentator recommended for their purity.

The interest generated by Roy's writings seems to have awakened interest in other contemporary Hindu publications as well. In 1824 a *Christian Examiner* reviewer revealed that, in addition to one of Roy's books, he had just received another work by a Hindu author, Ram Doss's *A Vindication of the Incarnation of the Deity, as the Common Basis of Hindooism and Christianity*. Characterized as a "very singular production," the book was the result of letters exchanged between Ram Doss and an Englishman, in which the Hindu had sought to demonstrate that the "theology of Hindoos and of Trinitarian Christians" was "essentially the same." A Hindu magazine, *Brahmunical Magazine*, was also noticed which presented "Reasons of a Hindoo for rejecting the Doctrines of Christianity" and "A Reply to certain Queries directed against the Vedant."[35] Clearly, works on Hinduism by Hindu writers were reaching America early in the century.

It must be emphasized that the interest American Unitarians indicated in Rammohun Roy was not motivated by admiration for the revitalized Hinduism he championed, but rather by his surprising affirmation of views close to their own and the hope that his activities would lead to an Indian Unitarian movement. Interest in his work sharply increased interest in India and the new Hinduism, but the original excitement centered on the possible expansion of Unitarianism. Thus the immediate result of the discovery of Rammohun Roy was that American Unitarians decided to launch missionary work in India.[36]

The opening of missionary work in India in the 1820s was a sensitive matter for most Unitarians, and they undertook it with considerable hesitation. As champions of religious toleration and frequent critics of orthodox Christian missionaries, some members argued that Unitarians had no more business carrying the cross to the "heathen" than conventional missionaries, that the very idea of Unitarianism was incompatible with missionary activity. The resulting debate foreshadowed the much larger debate within orthodox Christianity later and produced a new rationale for missionary work.[37] Joseph Tuckerman, who played a leading role in establishing the India mission, provided one of the best defenses in an article published in 1824. While recognizing the legitimacy of earlier Unitarian coolness to missionary activity, Tuckerman explained why they must now support an Indian work. One of the basic objections to any missionary work was the conviction that as long as the non-Christian sought to live a virtuous life and follow his ideals, he would not be rejected by God. Tuckerman defended the superiority of this position over that of the Christian bigot who threatened that unless the "heathen" accepted Jesus as his personal savior, he must burn, but he insisted that Unitarians still had a responsibility to share Christianity's social benefits with less privileged peoples.

A second objection to missionary work for most Unitarians was the "injudicious manner" in which previous missions had been conducted, but Tuckerman argued that Unitarians need not repeat earlier mistakes. Instead of sending fifty missionaries to preach original sin, he suggested two or three well-educated men, trained in philosophy, who could converse with the non-Christians on their own terms.[38] He also emphasized the need to concentrate on the enlightened upper class—a proposal that recalls the missionary strategy adopted by Roman Catholic missionaries centuries earlier, led by Francis Xavier and Nobili.

The result was that in 1826 a Society for the Promotion of Christianity in

India was formally launched with Henry Ware as president and Joseph Tuckerman as corresponding secretary. The sizable sum of $7,000 was sent to India to inaugurate the mission, with an additional $600 a year promised for ten years to support the difficult first period. William Adam, the Scottish missionary who Rammohun Roy had converted to Unitarianism, was recruited to lead the effort.[39] However, the work never prospered. A chapel and school were established in Calcutta, but Adam eventually broke away to work along other lines. In 1839 the Scottish missionary was in the United States. A contemporary report notes that he was "solicited by the Divinity students at Cambridge" to impart some of the knowledge he had gathered in India, including information concerning the "theology of the Brahmins" and "especially" the activities of Rammohun Roy. He spoke twice. Subsequently, he is identified as professor of Oriental literature at Harvard, though the nature of the position is unclear.[40] In 1855 the effort was renewed, this time by C. H. A. Dall, who spent a number of years in India; parallel work was also begun in Japan. Neither succeeded, though the interest in India seems to have persisted: as late as 1913 Jabez Sunderland traveled to India once again to report upon new developments.[41] If the missionary hopes raised by Rammohun Roy were ultimately unfulfilled, nevertheless his writings provided many Americans the opportunity to hear Hinduism explained by an Asian—a unique experience in the early nineteenth century.

Magazines played a much larger role in the dissemination of ideas and in the general intellectual life of the country in the first half of the nineteenth century than they do today. Two were especially vital in expanding early American knowledge of Asian thought—the *Edinburgh Review* and the *North American Review*. Emerson and other early American students of Asian thought regularly dipped into their pages for information concerning Oriental religions.

The *Edinburgh Review* was one of the period's finest European magazines, an intellectual journal whose essay-length discussions of new books in all areas played a sizable role in many Americans' education. One of the magazine's most remarkable features was the serious attention it devoted to Asia. A close examination of its contents reveals that from its first appearance in 1802 until 1820, nearly every issue included some piece dealing with the Orient. (After 1820 the Asian emphasis tapers off somewhat, though important essays concerning the East continued to appear.) India received greatest attention, more indeed than all other Asian countries combined, because of Britain's extensive commitments there. Though most of the books reviewed were travelers' accounts, serious scholarship was not overlooked. Indeed, one of the *Review*'s most outstanding series comprised the essays devoted to successive volumes of the *Asiatic Researches*, the seminal publication put out by the Asiatic Society of Bengal. The man responsible for these authoritative pieces, a Scotsman named Alexander Hamilton, had spent more than a decade in India in the 1780s and 1790s; after returning to Europe, he led in launching Sanskrit studies in the West. Hamilton's reviews gave reading Americans access to the best contemporary European scholarship on India.[42]

Oriental scholarship, Sanskrit grammar, Indian social conditions, the missionary movement, Hindu astronomy, British relations with India, Hindu drama—these are only a sampling of the rich offering to be found in the *Review*.[43] One of the books reviewed was Thomas Moore's popular Oriental romance, *Lalla Rookh*, hailed as offering the "finest orientalism we have had yet," which would play a key role in Emerson's and other Transcendentalists' first Oriental readings.[44] India's religious experience came in for discussion at regular intervals, often in an article dealing with another subject. Three essays offered lengthy expositions: a review of Edward Moor's book *The Hindu Pantheon*; the discussion of the *Prabodh Chandrodaya*, a Hindu religious play; and a combined review of several new books on Hinduism.[45] After India, China received most attention,[46] with Ceylon, Burma, Vietnam, and Korea achieving occasional notices.[47]

The attitude that the *Edinburgh Review*'s contributors took toward Asian civilization is important to notice, since the European attitude helped mold early American attitudes. If the viewpoint in the *Review* tended to be more critical than that of earlier European Enlightenment writers, the general view was fairly sympathetic. A few contributors openly stated their distaste for the peoples and cultures of Asia. One example is the reviewer of John Barrow's *Travels in China*, who characterized the Chinese as a "mean and semi-barbarous race, distinguished by fewer virtues or accomplishments than most of their neighbors. . . ." The vaunted cultural acheivements of the Chinese are dismissed even more harshly: "Of the *sciences* and *arts* of the Chinese, it is unnecessary to say any thing. They have no science, and never seem to have had any; and all the arts they possess seem, though they have been practised for some thousands of years, to be still in their infancy."[48]

However, most writers in the *Edinburgh Review* adopted a more balanced stance. It was generally agreed that a flat condemnation of everything about Asia was as unjustified as an unqualified celebration. "The Chinese have not hitherto had very fair play in Europe," complained one writer, who proceeded to offer an able explanation of the European failure. He blamed the Jesuit missionary for first leading Westerners astray by giving a "most exaggerated account" of the attainments of the Asian societies; eighteenth-century philosophes had increased the distortion by transforming the Asians into "creatures of pure reason and enlightened beneficence." Inevitably, a negative reaction had resulted with detractors appearing who, not content with merely "denying the virtues and sciences of the Chinese," sought to represent them "as among the most contemptible and debased of the barbarians." The reviewer ended by extolling the emergence of men of more "moderate and rational opinions" as little inclined "to extol the Chinese, from childish admiration, or out of witty malice, as to detract from their real merits, because they appeared under an outlandish aspect, or had been overpraised by some of their predecessors."[49] Such evaluations helped American readers approach the strange Asian cultures with better perspective.

The same attitude appears in essays that deal with India. In a discussion of a series of books on Hindu religious life, the commentator lamented how unfortunate it was "that with all our opportunities of observation, our information on the subject should hitherto have been not merely imperfect, but incorrect." Early Western observers of Hindu society had been so struck by its "extraordinary aspect" that their accounts were "more marvellous than intelligible," tending "to increase our wonder at the peculiarities of the Hindu character" rather than explain it. Western opinion had run to extremes in both directions: on the one side, the Hindu "is extravagantly praised, and not only admired, but almost adored"; on the other, he was rejected "as exciting a deeper disgust, and a greater contempt and abhorrence, than that of any other portion of the race."[50]

Founded in 1815, the *North American Review* in many ways closely resembled the European review; its format and coverage were similar and its intelligence and sophistication nearly as impressive.[51] It also devoted significant attention to Asia, featuring a steady stream of reviews on new books, beginning with a notice of Anquetil Duperron's translation of the *Upanishads* in the second issue.[52] Memorable contributions abound over the next decades. These include Professor Edward Channing's essay on the *Lalla Rookh*, which was more critical than the review in the *Edinburgh Review*; William Tudor's already noted "Theology of the Hindoos," which included extracts from Hindu sacred writings; Theophilus Parsons's review of the newly published American edition of Abbé Dubois's *Description of the Character, Manners and Customs of the People of India*; Alexander Everett's sympathetic discussion of the Chinese language; a discussion of the American John White's report of voyages in the China Sea; Edward Everett's "Hindu Drama," which called attention to new translations of Hindu plays; and an analysis of "Chinese Manners" based on the French scholar Abel Rémusat's translation of a Chinese novel.[53] Briefer items also sprinkled the *North American*'s pages, including Chinese maxims reprinted from the *Peking Gazette*, a report on the Salem East India Marine Society's activities, and a description of Indian education based on an account from the *Calcutta Gazette*.[54] Though attention to Asia declined in the 1830s, important contributions continued to appear during the 1840s and 1850s. Notable later pieces include John Pickering's enthusiastic review of Du Ponceau's *Dissertation on the Nature and Character of the Chinese System of Writing*; Andrew Peabody's notice of *The Middle Kingdom*, the first important scholarly work on China by an American scholar; and William Alger's discourse on "The Brahmanic and Buddhist Doctrine of a Future Life."[55] Charles Eliot Norton, who had traveled to India as a youth, also contributed several articles on modern India.[56]

Perhaps because of greater unfamiliarity, Americans found it difficult to take the balanced view assumed by writers in the *Edinburgh Review*. Chinese civilization was found to be especially impressive. One of the most far-reaching testimonies came from Andrew Peabody: "We see there the highest stage of civilization which has as yet been attained by any nation independently of Christian institutions." One would have to reach all the way back to Jesuit and Enlightenment Sinophilists to find an appreciation as glowing as his enumeration of China's achievements:

> It has modified the theory of government, and rendered its institutions in form and pretence almost incapable of improvement. It has created and diffused a popular literature negatively pure, and endowed with many positive traits of moral excellence. It has established seminaries of education and incentives to the pursuit of knowledge, nominally within the reach of all. It has constructed and maintained routes of inland communication, both by land and water, surpassing those of any other country in their extent and costliness, and in scientific skill exceeding the capacity of the Western nations at the age when they were planned. It struck out, many centuries ago, mechanical discoveries and inventions still recent in Europe. It has brought agriculture and many of the arts of practical utility to a high degree of perfection.[57]

Admittedly, this was only one view and a late one, but there are other statements expressing the same appreciation. Writing in 1823, Alexander Everett urged that Westerners must assimilate the Chinese accomplishment if they were to avoid parochialism. China made up "about half of the inhabitants of the globe" and formed a "second civilized world." He emphasized that the "cultivated moral world" must include both East and West and that the "student of man" who confined himself to one had "examined but half his subject. . . ." He concluded that "however highly it may be estimated," the importance of Chinese literature could "hardly be overvalued."[58] The numbers, industriousness, and mechanical ingenuity of the Chinese people were most commonly emphasized, but their talent in art and literature were not forgotten.

The attitude toward Indian civilization was more ambivalent: the writers seemed both repelled and attracted by its strangeness. Theophilus Parsons reflected the dominant feeling in his exasperation at the "astonishing inconsistency" of the *Vedas*. Here was a scripture that proclaimed the "unity and infinite perfection of the Deity . . . not ambiguously or by implication, but openly and directly and without reserve"—and yet "in the next or the same page" the same book would describe the lives and actions of "deities without number," prescribing a "thousand unmeaning or mischievous ceremonies to their honour."[59] Tudor revealed the same split in his "Theology of the Hindoos." He insisted that the Vedic concept of God was "just, and calculated to lead the mind to true conceptions of his character and perfections," but went on to dismiss traditional Hinduism as an unsavory mixture of "barbarous sacrifices and idol worship."[60]

By the 1830s the first era of discovery was closing, preparing the way for Emerson and the Transcendentalists. Looking back over the first century of America's contact with Asia, New England's complete dominance is noteworthy. A large portion of the first ships and first travelers to the Orient came from there, and a large portion of the first Oriental goods and books returned there. Cotton Mather had first looked eastward in the 1720s; one hundred years later Unitarians from the same New England area were still in the vanguard. It seems only natural that the *North American Review*, which helped introduce literate Americans to Asian thought, should have been published in Boston. New England intellectuals and scholars would continue to lead until the end of the century.

Notes

1. John T. Rutt, ed., *The Theological and Miscellaneous Works of Joseph Priestley* (Hackney, England: George Smallfield, 1817), published in twenty-five volumes, still provides the indispensable source. Priestley's "Memoir" and selected letters are published in vol. 1, parts 1 and 2. I have also consulted Philip Hartog's *sketch in the Dictionary of National Biography* (DAB), 16: 357-76, and Frederick W. Gibbs, *Joseph Priestley: Revolutions of the Eighteenth Century* (Garden City, N.Y.: Doubleday, 1965).

2. See Sydney Ahlstrom, *Religious History of the American People* (New Haven, Conn.: Yale University Press, 1972), pp. 356-58 for a summary.

3. Earl M. Wilbur, *A History of Unitarianism in Transylvania, England, and America*, 2 vols. (Cambridge, Mass.: Harvard University Press, 1952), 2: 294. See the whole chapter, "The Liberal Dissenters Follow the Leadership of Joseph Priestley, 2: 293-315.

4. Rutt, *Works of Priestley*, 1: pt. 2, 255-56. It is impressive how often eminent European émigrés have been revitalized by the move to America: one thinks of Alfred Whitehead, Paul Tillich, and Mies van der Rohe in the twentieth century.

5. [John F. Fulton], *Dictionary of American Biography (DAB)*, 8: 226.

6. Wilbur, *History of Unitarianism*, 2: 314.

7. See the "Dedication" to Joseph Priestley, *The Doctrines of Heathen Philosophy, Compared with Those of Revelation* (Northumberland, Penn.: John Binns, 1804), p. ii.

8. Rutt, *Works of Priestley*, 3: 391-98 and 4: 499-503.

9. See ibid., vol. 16, particularly the discourses on the following pages: 6-13, 35-62, 90-117, and 197-200. The reference to the *Asiatic Researches* appears on p. 11.

10. Rutt, *Works of Priestley*, 16: 197, 198.

11. Ibid., 1: pt. 2, 334, 338.

12. Ibid., 17: 132, 133, 141.

13. A list of the books quoted in the *Comparison* is provided in the Appendix of Rutt, *Works of Priestley*, 25: 305-6.

14. Rutt, *Works of Priestley*, 1:pt. 2, 320, 357, 392, 423. Quotes on pp. 392, 423.

15. Ibid., 17: 141-52.

16. Ibid., 17: 161, 166, 204.

17. Ibid., 1: pt. 2, 336; 1: pt. 2, 391. Quote on p. 336. It is interesting that Hannah Adams had also dedicated her *A View of Religions* to the popular politician.

18. Reprinted in vol. 2 (1812-1826) of Lester Cappon, ed., *The Adams-Jefferson Letters: The Complete Correspondence between Thomas Jefferson and Abigail and John Adams*, 2 vols. (Chapel Hill, N.C.: University of North Carolina Press for the Institute of Early American History and Culture, 1959). Cappon has reprinted the letters exactly as written; hence the peculiarities of the quoted sections.

19. Cappon, *Adams-Jefferson Letters*, 2: 361.

20. Ibid., 2: 309, 359. My brackets. Quotation on p. 359.

21. Ibid., 2: 364, 368, 378, 410, 412-13, 427-28. Quotation on p. 427.

22. Ibid., 2: 491, 494, 499. The brackets are Cappon's.

23. Ibid., 2: 515, 517.

24. Ibid., 2: 518-19. Brackets added by Cappon.

25. Wilbur, *History of Unitarianism*, 2: 396.

26. Cf. ibid., 2: 166, and Conrad Wright, *The Beginnings of Unitarianism in America* (Boston: Beacon Press, 1955), the most authoritative discussion of the early evolution.

27. Sophia D. Collet, *The Life and Letters of Raja Rammohun Roy*, 3rd ed. (Calcutta: Sadharan Brahmo Samaj, 1962). Though first published in 1900, still a standard reference. I have also consulted the briefer sketches in John N. Farquhar, *Modern Religious Movements in India* (New York: Macmillan, 1915), pp. 29-39 and William T. DeBary, ed., *Sources of Indian Tradition* (New York: Columbia University Press, 1958), pp. 571-80.

28. For Roy's beliefs, see Collet, *Life of Roy*, pp. 97-99, 128-29, 190-91. However, note the comment of Dilep K. Biswas and Prabat G. Ganguli, "Though a believer in Universal Theism Rammohun's religious and philosophical thought remained firmly grounded in the *Vedánta.*" (p. 97) J. T. [Joseph Tuckerman], "Is Rammohun Roy a Christian?" *Christian Examiner* 3 (September-October 1826): 361-69 provides a good example of the debate over Roy's true views.

29. Collet, *Life of Roy*, chap. 4, 108-66.

30. Adrienne Moore, *Rammohun Roy and America* (Calcutta: Sadharan Brahmo Samaj, 1942), pp. vii, 2-3. Mainly a bibliographical study, Moore provides a

comprehensive list of articles concerning Roy published in American and British journals between 1816 and 1840.

31. William B. Stein, ed., *Two Brahman Sources of Emerson and Thoreau* (Gainesville, Fla.: Scholars' Facsimiles & Reprints, 1967), p. 4. A reproduction of the 2nd edition published in London in 1832.

32. [William Tudor], "Theology of the Hindoos, as Taught by Ram Mohun Roy," *North American Review* 6 (March 1818): 386.

33. Ibid.: 383, 393.

34. "Writings of Rammohun Roy," *Christian Disciple and Theological Review*, New Series 5 (September-October 1823): 370.

35. "Indian Pamphlets," *Christian Examiner* 1 (May-June 1824): 239-40.

36. See [Joseph Tuckerman], "Prospects of Christianity in India," *Christian Examiner* 1 (July-August 1824): 301-18.

37. For the arguments of one supporter, see the articles by F. W. P. Greenwood in the *Christian Examiner* 3 (March-April 1826): 109-20; 3 (May-June 1826): 177-85; 3 (July-August 1826): 265-77; and 3 (November-December 1826): 449-54. For the opposing view, see Francis Parkman in ibid. 6 (May 1829): 252-59 and 10 (May 1831): 220-38. Twenty-five years later, the arguments were restated in A. A. Livermore's "Unitarianism and Foreign Missions," ibid. 59 (July 1855): 18-37.

38. [Joseph Tuckerman], "On the Causes by Which Unitarians Have Been Withheld from Exertions in the Cause of Foreign Missions," ibid. 1 (May-June 1824): 182-96.

39. For the events leading up to the creation of the society, see ibid. 3 (May-June 1826): 261-62; 3 (November-December 1826): 521-22; 5 (March-April 1828): 175-77. Adam's letters and reports were regularly excerpted and printed. See particularly, ibid. 3 (July-August 1826): 337-52; 5 (July-August 1828): 353-61; and 5 (September-October 1838): 425-29. Also see George W. Cooke, *Unitarianism in America* (Boston: American Unitarian Association, 1902), p. 298.

40. *Monthly Miscellany of Religion and Letters* (Boston) 1 (April 1839): 47-48 and ibid. 4 (April 1841): 236-37. Quote on p. 47. Cooke, *Unitarianism in America*, p. 298, speaks of Adam being a professor of Oriental literature "for a few years," but I did not find evidence of this.

41. See "Missions to India and Japan," in Cooke, *Unitarianism in America*, pp. 295-309, and Ramlal B. Bajpai, "Dr. J. T. Sunderland Honored by Hindus in America," *Modern Review* (Calcutta) 43 (June 1928): 680-82.

42. For the reviews of *Asiatic Researches*, see *Edinburgh Review* 1 (October 1802): 26-43; 9 (October 1806): 92-101; 9 (January 1807): 278-304; 12 (April 1808): 36-50; 15 (October 1809): 175-89; and 16 (August 1810): 384-98. Cf. Rosane Rocher, *Alexander Hamilton (1762-1824): A Chapter in the Early History of Sanskrit Philology* (New Haven, Conn.: American Oriental Society, 1968).

43. For representative examples, see *Edinburgh Review* 1 (January 1803): 412-21; 13 (January 1809): 366-81; 48 (September 1828): 32-47; 6 (July 1805): 462-77; 10 (July 1807): 455-71; 29 (November 1817): 141-64; 15 (January 1810): 255-74; and 22 (January 1814): 400-409.

44. Ibid. 29 (November 1817): 1-35. Quote on p. 1.

45. Ibid. 17 (February 1811): 311-30; 22 (January 1814): 400-409; 29 (February 1818): 377-403.

46. Ibid. 5 (January 1805): 259-88; 14 (July 1809): 407-29; 16 (August 1810): 476-99; and 29 (February 1818): 433-53.

47. Ibid. 2 (April 1803): 136-47; 41 (October 1824): 123-42; 43 (February 1826): 373-94; and 29 (February 1818): 475-97.

48. Ibid. 5 (January 1805): 259-88. Quotes from pp. 262, 281; italics in the original.

49. Ibid. 16 (August 1810): 476-99. Quotes from p. 476.

50. Ibid. 29 (February 1818): 377-403. Quotes from p. 377.

51. Though an independent journal, it should be noted that the *North American* was dominated by Unitarians. According to Earl Wilbur, "it appealed largely to the Unitarian public, its contributors were very largely Unitarians, and for more than sixty years its editors were Unitarians." (*History of Unitarianism*, 2: 438n.)

52. *North American Review* 1 (July 1815): 212-13.

53. Ibid. 6 (November 1817): 1-25; 6 (March 1818): 386-93; 9 (June 1819): 36-58; 17 (July 1823): 1-13; 18 (January 1824): 140-57; 26 (January 1828): 111-26; and 27 (October 1828): 524-62.

54. Ibid. 4 (March 1817): 430-31; 6 (January 1818): 283-85; 6 (March 1818): 418-19.

55. Ibid. 48 (January 1839): 271-310; 67 (October 1848): 265-91; and 86 (April 1858): 435-63.

56. Ibid. 73 (July 1851): 135-52; 77 (October 1853): 439-66; 81 (October 1855): 531-43; 88 (April 1859): 289-312.

57. Ibid. 67 (October 1848): 270, 271.

58. Ibid. 17 (July 1823): 12.

59. Ibid. 9 (June 1819): 38.

60. Ibid. 6 (March 1818): 389, 386.

3
Emerson's Discovery of the East

Few Americans in the nineteenth century or since have spoken more warmly of Oriental thought than Ralph Waldo Emerson. He said, "The Indian teaching through its cloud of legends has yet a simple & grand religion like a queenly countenance seen through a rich veil. It teaches to speak the truth, love others as yourself, & to despise trifles. The East is grand,—& makes Europe appear the land of trifles."[1] Again: "Yes, the Zoroastrian, the Indian, the Persian scriptures are majestic, and more to our daily purpose than this year's almanac or this day's newspaper. . . ." And recalling his discovery of one of the masterpieces of Hinduism, he confessed: "I owed—my friend and I owed—a magnificent day to the *Bhagavat Geeta*. —It was the first of books; it was as if an empire spake to us, nothing small or unworthy, but large, serene, consistent, the voice of an old intelligence which in another age and climate had pondered and thus disposed of the same questions which exercise us. Let us not now go back and apply a minute criticism to it, but cherish the venerable oracle."[2]

Impressed by such affirmations, students of Transcendentalism have been prone to claim that Emerson and the Transcendentalists were the original American discoverers of Asian thought, the first to look upon the Orient sympathetically, and the first to write accounts that would introduce Americans to Asian thought. Arthur Christy, who did more than any other scholar to launch the modern investigation of Asian influences in American history, gave this view currency when he spoke of his *The Orient in American Transcendentalism* as a "study of the beginnings of American interest in

Oriental thought." Though noting earlier trade contacts, he observed, "It was not until about Emerson's time that the Oriental was more than a heathen and his religious literature more than foolishness. The tide turned with the growth of the Transcendental Movement. . . ."[3] More recently, Frederic Carpenter declares that Emerson "helped introduce the Western mind to Eastern thought. . . ."[4] The implication is that he was first in this. However, though Emerson was indeed a crucial figure, neither he nor any other Transcendentalist inaugurated America's serious interest in Asian thought. It is closer to the truth to claim that he was the first important American to incorporate strains of Oriental thought and to seek a reconciliation between Eastern and Western ideals.[5] As we have seen, the first awareness obviously dates back well before Emerson, and writers from a variety of perspectives had been reporting upon Eastern thought decades before Emerson's emergence.

In January 1820, during his junior year at Harvard, Emerson began to keep a journal and notebooks which he would continue into old age. They were crucial to his career as a writer, since they served as a kind of "memory bank" for his later essays and books. They contained quotes from his reading, thoughts on a wide variety of questions, lists, outlines, trivia. And, of course, they provide an indispensable record of his intellectual development, including the growth of his Oriental interests. Although he was clearly not a typical man, his detailed record offers an invaluable case study of the way Oriental religion penetrated American consciousness during the nineteenth century.

The record indicates fascination with the Orient almost from the first. As early as April 1820 he notes lectures by Edward Everett and Dr. John Warren and "much" reading in the *Quarterly Review*, all providing the opportunity for rich, deep thought. The entry ends tantalizingly with, "All tends to the mysterious east."[6] The sense of Oriental mystery was undoubtedly encouraged by some of his earliest reading concerning the East: the semi-Oriental tales of poets Thomas Moore and Robert Southey. We know that he withdrew Moore's *Lalla Rookh* from the Boston Library Society in 1819 and again in 1820. Years later he would remark, "Moore's Lalla Rookh was some of my best travelling."[7] Southey's *The Curse of Kehama* appeared on his reading list in 1820, and he consulted the notes on Indian mythology attached to the work in the preparation of a senior class poem. "As long ago as Menu enlightened morality was taught in India," Emerson quoted from the *Curse*.[8] Both works emphasized the picturesque and grotesque qualities that had strong appeal to the Romantic artist.

If the Oriental tale was one stimulus that helped awaken Emerson's interest in Asian thought, the American sensation created by Rammohun Roy was another (though as far as I could see, a slight one). As a Unitarian, young Emerson was aware of Roy's work and "conversion" to Unitarianism. He wrote to his remarkable aunt, Mary Moody Emerson, that he knew no "more about your Hindoo convert than I have seen in the Christian Register," but that he was "truly rejoiced that the Unitarians have one trophy to build up on the plain where the zealous Trinitarians have builded a thousand." Mary Emerson, who exercized a strong influence on her nephew, encouraged his Eastern interests; on one occasion she sent him a passage from Sir William Jones's "A Hymn to Narayana," lauding it as a "sweet morsel of Hindu poetry." Emerson replied that he was "curious to read your Hindu mythologies," but confessed finding the pages "as dark to me as the characters on the Seal Solomon. . . ." [9] The year was 1822, and the youth was nineteen.

Magazines provided a third source. During the 1820s and 1830s Emerson conscientiously read four periodicals—the *Edinburgh Review, North American Review, Quarterly Review,* and *New Jerusalem Magazine*. He looked to the four not only for information but as a guide to his reading, relying on their reviews in his selection of books. As we have seen, two of them printed a sizable number of articles on Asian thought. References to the magazines are frequently encountered in the *Journals* and *Notebooks;* occasionally the articles are extracted and quoted at some length. There are enough references to Asian articles to establish the importance of such reading in Emerson's Oriental education. In 1823, for example, he paraphrases essays on Hindu mathematics and religion he had just encountered in the *Edinburgh Review*.[10]

Most important, Emerson read a lengthening list of books over the years that offered more extended introductions to Oriental thought. One of the earliest was Priestley's *The Doctrines of Heathen Philosophy,* read in 1820; unfortunately, he did not record his reaction to the book.[11] In the early 1830s he discovered Marie Joseph de Gérando's *Histoire comparée des systèmes de philosophie,* a popular philosophical work that included sizable sections on Oriental philosophy. He filled his *Notebook* with quotations and outlines from the work that hint at some of his later themes: "First come the *Cosmogonies,* Indians, Chinese, Chaldeans, Egyptians, Phenicians [*sic*], Persians, have a striking sameness in them, but all these are an intellectual offspring. . . ."[12] Another work that awakened his enthusiasm was Victor Cousin's three-volume *Cours de philosophie,* which also included sections on Asian philosophy. Many years later, he credited the *Cours* with sparking his original enthusiasm for the *Bhagavad-Gita*: "I remember I owed my first taste for this fruit to Cousin's sketch. . . ," he wrote.[13] Cousin's discussion of Oriental philosophy was largely based on Colebrooke's writings in the *Transactions of the Asiatic Society of London*. One begins to understand the complexities of transmission: Cousin offered a French philosopher's interpretation of an English scholar's translation of the extremely difficult texts of an ancient Indian civilization. It is not surprising that Oriental notions were often misunderstood. Still another series that won Emerson's favor was A. H. L. Heeren's multivolume *Historical Researches*, which he praised for gathering "up all the facts of oldest India, Egypt, Persia, Phoenicia." He found Heeren's factual approach refreshing: "Such a book stimulates us to more thought than one where all is inferred & said for you."[14] Emerson had outgrown such volumes by the later 1830s; fortunately, full-scale translations of the major Oriental works were finally reaching America, and would offer more substantial fare.

As Emerson became more familiar with Asian thought, his attitude changed. His first reactions were quite critical, like the response of many Americans exposed to Asia's alien conceptions for the first time. His hostility may be attributed in part to the unsympathetic European sources he first encountered, but one also senses personal antagonism. This is pointed up by his "Indian Superstition," the recently rediscovered poem he submitted as a senior for the Bowdoin Prize. The very title of the poem proclaims a negative viewpoint. Instructed to write on the influence of weather on the mind, he had sketched the following outline: "Plan—The poor inhabitants of Indostan are distressed & degraded by the horrors of a flimsy & cruel Superstition. The iron hath entered into their souls, & their situation is in all respects abominable." In another entry he speaks of the "ostentatious rituals of India which worshipped God by outraging nature. . . ."[15] He apparently relied heavily on Southey's notes to the *Curse of Kehama*—which would explain the emphasis on the gross aspects of Hindu society.

In later years Emerson hailed the wisdom of Confucius, but one finds little such sympathy in the early *Journals*. If anything, he was more critical of Chinese than of Indian civilization. Though confessing, "I cannot accurately judge of the Chronicles of China since they are little accessible to many, and less so, to me," he did not allow a "vague knowledge" to soften his judgment:

> In the grave and never-ending series of sandaled Emperors whose lives were all alike, and whose deaths were all alike, and who ruled over myriads of animals hardly more distinguishable from each other, in the eye of an European, than so many sheeps' faces—there is not one interesting event, no bold revolutions, no changeful variety of manners & character. Rulers & ruled, age and age, present the same doleful monotony, and are as flat and uninteresting as their own porcelain-pictures.[16]

In a subsequent entry we find him complaining that earlier generations had greatly exaggerated the greatness of China. "The Celestial Empire—hang the

Celestial Empire! I hate Pekin. I will not drink of the waters of the Yellow Sea," he wrote petulantly. And again: ". . . I hate China. 'Tis a tawdry vase. Out upon China.' "[17] Later he would repeatedly emphasize that Americans might learn from the Orient, that the West needed the East. This certainly was not his view in the 1820s when he was declaring that he could see no "meaning in the venerable vegetation of this extraordinary people. They are not tools for other nations to use," he insisted. "Even miserable Africa can say I have hewn the wood & drawn the water to promote the wealth & civilization of other lands. But, China, reverend dulness! hoary ideot [*sic*]! all she can say at the convocation of nations must be—'I made the tea.' "[18]

The early 1830s marked a watershed in Emerson's life in more ways than one. He resigned his ministry at the Second Church and sailed to Europe on his first crucial visit abroad. He lost one wife, married another, buried a beloved younger brother, and began a new career as a Chautauqua lecturer. And finally, he ceased to be a Unitarian and became a Transcendentalist instead. He confided to his *Journal*, "I have sometimes thought that in order to be a good minister it was necessary to leave the ministry. . . . In an altered age, we worship in the dead forms of our forefathers. Were not a Socratic paganism better than an effete superannuated Christianity?"[19] These painful changes and new commitments seemed to deepen Emerson's compassion and widen his intellectual outlook. The alterations, together with a much better acquaintance with Oriental literature, may explain the new prominence of the Orient in his thought by the late 1830s.

As usual the *Journals* announce the change. There are more frequent and more appreciative references to more substantial Oriental volumes than before. His maturing tastes are suggested by the notation, "Many books are not so good as a few. Once, a youth at College, with what joy & profit I read the Edinburgh Review. Now, a man, the Edinburgh Review, & Heeren, & Blackwood & Goethe get a languid attention."[20] One prize discovery was David Collie's translation of the *Chinese Classical Works*, which he came upon in 1843. Extracting much of the work into his *Journal*, he informed Margaret Fuller that he now had the "best of Chinese Confucian books." This included the "book of *Mencius*," which was "wholly new" to him.[21] At this time he also first read Charles Wilkins's translation of the *Vishnu Sarma* and Horace Wilson's translation of the *Vishnu Purana*, works that his *Journal* indicates he came to value very highly.[22] In another place he copied out a Hindu hymn from an article by Colebrooke, which he encountered in a volume of the *Asiatic Researches*.[23] And there are still other references and quotations from the *Rig-Veda*, the *Upanishads*, the *Laws of Manu*, and the *Bhagavata Purana*—all crucial volumes in Indian sacred literature.

However, the work that most delighted Emerson was the *Bhagavad-Gita*, a volume he came back to again and again in the following years. He first announced the good news to his sister in 1845: "The only other event is the arrival in Concord of the 'Bhagvat-Geeta,' the much renowned book of Buddhism, extracts of which I have often admired but never before held . . . in my hands."[24] (The *Gita* is of course the renowned book of Hinduism, not Buddhism; it is strange that he should have confused it, but more about that later.) He borrowed the copy from his friend James Cabot and kept it for many weeks, apologizing for his slowness in returning it. However, he soon had his own copy, sent from London, and several years later requested a second one.[25] He quickly transmitted his new enthusiasm to friends, recommending it as essential reading, frequently loaning his own copy. One of the borrowers, the poet John Greenleaf Whittier, remarked, "It is a wonderful book—& has greatly excited my curiosity to know mōre of the religious literature of the East."[26] Though the novelty seemed to wear off after several years, as indicated by a declining curve in frequency of references, Emerson would continue to quote and praise the Oriental work into old age.

That Emerson came to admire the Oriental religious classics can hardly be denied in view of the record. What has been less clear is their impact upon his thought, and debate has raged since Emerson's contemporaries first recognized his attraction. William T. Harris, the Hegelian philosopher and friend of Bronson Alcott, who once directed the Concord School of Philosophy, believed that the Oriental strain was crucial. Noting Emerson's claim (in *Representative Men*) that Plato represented a balance between East and West, Harris observed, "What Emerson says of Plato we may easily and properly apply to himself. But he goes farther than Plato towards the Orient, and his pendulum swings farther West into the Occident." Harris asserts that perhaps "nowhere in our literature" could one find "so complete a characterization of the East Indian philosophy" as in Emerson's poem, "Brahma."[27] However, until the 1930s when Frederic Carpenter and Arthur Christy reexamined the matter, most writers tended to minimize the Oriental dimension.

In an 1897 article, "Emerson, Sixty Years After," John Jay Chapman neatly formulated the anti-Oriental view. He suggested that if one had to admire Emerson's cosmopolitanism for his insistence on the value of the Eastern poets, that was as far as one needed to go. "The East added nothing to Emerson, but gave him a few trappings of speech," Chapman claimed. "The whole of his mysticism is to be found in Nature, written before he knew the sages of the Orient. . . ."[28]

Theodore Parker, who should have known, expressed serious doubts that Emerson understood the East at all. Significantly, Parker not only knew Emerson, but shared his Transcendental enthusiasm and had also studied

Oriental thought. In an 1850 article noting the "allusions to the ancient oriental literature" in Emerson's writings—including "some hard names and some valuable thoughts"—he insisted that the Concord poet had been "led astray" and that it was "plain" that he did "not understand" the "curious philosophy" he so often quoted. Parker believed that Emerson's major error was his habit of forcing "his oriental allies" to defend modern conceptions.[29] The three views represent positions that still agitate discussions of Emerson.

The charge that Emerson's frequent quotation from Oriental sources was external and superficial may be considered first because it is easiest to dismiss. Emerson's writing habits do provide some basis for such a complaint: throughout his long career it was his practice to keep extensive journals where he deposited the siftings of his wide readings. As he wrote, he went back to the journals to cull out quotations and illustrations that seemed appropriate. The result often suggests a mosaic of bits and pieces loosely tied together. References to the *Laws of Manu,* Confucius, or *maya* crop up in essays that are totally unrelated to Oriental thought. Hence, a number of students have concluded that Emerson's Oriental interest was almost entirely literary; when at a loss for an example or in need of a touch of mystery or color, he simply inserted one of the Oriental pieces from his ever-ready *Journal.*

But this will not do. To begin with, it quite misunderstands Emerson's seriousness as an artist. The way one says something and what one says are nearly inseparable, particularly in a highly self-conscious writer. Emerson would explain: "My best thought came from others. I heard in their words my own meaning, but a deeper sense than they put on them. . . ."[30] The Oriental allusions were adornments perhaps, but functional adornments, not mere "trappings." Examining the references, it becomes clear that they serve one purpose again and again: to universalize a point under discussion, which underscored one of Emerson's deepest convictions. As an idealist and Transcendentalist, he believed that Reality was spiritual and that this spirituality permeated all peoples. "There is one mind common to all individual men. Every man is an inlet to the same and to all of the same," he once explained.[31] Further, he believed that this universal spirit appeared in purest form in highly developed geniuses who from time to time emerged to renew the divine element. He wrote, "In all ages, souls out of time, extraordinary, prophetic, are born, who are rather related to the system of the world than to their particular age and locality. These announce absolute truths. . . ."[32] It is surely no coincidence that the concept closely approximated the Hindu concept of the "avatar." His conclusion was that ancients and moderns, Easterners and Westerners, Hindus and Americans, were all linked together by an identical spirituality.

Once he had hit upon the formula—that he might use an ancient Hindu or Chinese (or Persian or Egyptian) quotation whenever he wished to universalize his point—the device became one of the identifying marks of his prose. He declared, "The largest is always the truest sentiment, and we feel the more generous spirit of the Indian Vishnu,—'I am the same to all mankind.' "[33] Appearing before the senior class at the Harvard Divinity School in 1838, where he spoke on the moral sentiment, he explained his frequent reliance on quotation: "The sentences of the oldest time, which ejaculate this piety, are still fresh and fragrant," he told his student listeners. "This thought dwelled always deepest in the minds of men in the devout and contemplative East; not alone in Palestine, where it reached its purest expression, but in Egypt, in Persia, in India, in China. Europe has always owed to oriental genius its divine impulses. What these holy bards said, all sane men found agreeable and true."[34] Significantly, he employed the device from the first, as one discovers in *Nature*, his earliest publication. Analyzing the difficult relationship between mind and matter, Emerson interpolated: "It is the standing problem which has exercised the wonder and the study of every fine genius since the world began; from the era of the Egyptians and the Brahmins to that of Pythagoras, of Plato, of Bacon, of Leibnitz, of Swedenborg."[35]

How far Emerson went toward embracing Oriental thought presents a far more difficult question. One point that is obvious is that the influence cannot be gauged by his published writings alone. In fact, only a small part of his total published works reveals incontrovertible evidence of his Asian interests. Besides the occasional quotations and references that may be encountered throughout the published record, the major exhibits are the following: the "Ethnical Scriptures," which appeared in the *Dial* between 1842 and 1844; the poems "Brahma" and "Hamatreya"; and several essays, most notably "Plato," "Fate," and "Illusions." Only when the many revealing statements in his *Journals* and letters are added can one accurately evaluate the depth and seriousness of his interest. It is also likely that Emerson consciously downplayed the seriousness of his Oriental interests. The most far-reaching testimonials, for example, are almost always concealed in the *Journals* or communicated privately to close friends—not revealed to the general public. It should be remembered that after 1833 his livelihood depended on public lectures and that the United States was still very much a Christian country. An open affirmation of Oriental doctrine could cause difficulty—as he learned from the harsh criticisms and snide jokes that greeted the publication of his "Brahma" in the *Atlantic Monthly* in 1857. (Emerson's response bears recalling. He wrote his daughter, "If you tell them to say Jehovah instead of Brahma they will not feel any perplexity."[36]) Another indication of his sensitivity concerned the *Bhagavad-Gita*, the Oriental scripture he admired above all others. While strenuously urging the book upon his friends in conversation and by letter, when urged to sponsor an American edition, he refused, explaining lamely that it would not do "to publish our prayers" in the daily paper. His further justification that "students who were ripe" would "rather take a little pains, & search for it, than find it on the pavement" also seems unconvincing.[37] (On the other hand, he did agree to provide a preface for the first American edition of the Persian poet Saadi's *Gulistan*, brought out in 1865.)

Obviously Emerson was deeply attracted by Asian thought or more precisely by the religious thought of India; whenever he spoke of Asia, he usually meant India. Though quite explicit about what he disliked in Indian religion—its "endless ceremonial nonsense" and caste restrictions—his general attitude was overwhelmingly positive. Describing the feelings generated in him by the *Vedas*, he wrote, "In the sleep of the great heats there was nothing for me but to read the Vedas, the bible of the tropics, which I find I come back upon every three or four years. It is sublime as heat and night and a breathless ocean. It contains every religious sentiment, all the grand ethics which visit in turn each noble and poetic mind. . . ."[38] This fervent testimony was confided to a friend by private letter in 1840.

Several things drew him toward Indian thought, one of the most important being its mystical emphasis. Although Emerson may never have had a deep mystical experience himself, *Nature* and such pieces as the Swedenborg essay in *Representative Men* leave little doubt that he was deeply drawn to the unitive experience proclaimed by mystics. He seemed to accept the notion of a *philosophia perennis*, a "perennial wisdom" handed down by the saints and seers of all ages. Mysticism represented one current in Western religious thought; it practically subsumed the whole message in Hinduism. Emerson's high regard for Hinduism's disciplined approach to mystical union is evident in the following entry: "In the history of intellect no more important fact than the Hindoo theology, teaching that the beatitude or supreme good is to be attained through science: namely, by the perception of the real and unreal, setting aside matter, and qualities . . . as Maias [*Mayas*] or illusions, and thus arriving at the contemplation of the one eternal Life. . . ."[39]

A second attraction was Hinduism's monism, a difficult conception in Emerson's thought because he sometimes identified the One with the unity of all creation, sometimes with the unity that stood behind creation. (On other occasions, he affirmed both the One and the Many, insisting that plurality was also real!) Let us say that to the extent that he was a monist, he was drawn to Hinduism. He wrote, "In all nations there are minds which incline to dwell in the conception of the fundamental Unity. . . . This tendency finds its highest expression in the religious writings of the East, and chiefly in the Indian Scriptures, in the Vedas, the Bhagavat Geeta, and the Vishnu Purana."[40]

Finally, he was drawn by the largeness, cosmic sweep, and rich speculative powers of Indian thought. ". . . If there is anything grand and daring in human thought or virtue, any reliance on the vast, the unknown; any presentiment, any extravagance of faith, the spiritualist adopts it," he wrote in "The Transcendentalist." "The oriental mind has always tended to this largeness."[41] Spirituality, unity, universality, mysticism, contemplation —these were all magical words for Emerson, and all were associated with India.

In addition, Emerson also seems to have been attracted by specific Hindu doctrines, although here the evidence is less decisive, depending upon what one makes of the suggestive parallels between a number of his most cherished beliefs and Hindu conceptions. Practically all students familiar with Oriental thought have been impressed by the close correspondences, in particular between his conception of the "Over-Soul" and the Hindu conception of *Brahman*, his notion of a Higher Self and the Hindu *atman*, his "illusion" and the Hindu *maya*, and his conceptions of "compensation" and "fate" and the Hindu doctrines of karma and reincarnation.[42] Thus, like the Hindu, Emerson tended to view God as an impersonal, universal, and absolute Being, as "that Unity, that Over-Soul, within which every man's particular being is contained and made one with all other. . . ."[43] Paralleling the Hindu distinction between the external self and the higher spiritual Self, the latter (*atman*) corresponding to Ultimate Reality (*Brahman*), he wrote, "We live in succession, in division, in parts, in particles. Meantime within man is the soul of the whole . . . the eternal One."[44] Like the Hindu, he emphasized the pervasive role of deception (*maya*) in obscuring the Ultimate Reality: "I find men victims of illusion in all parts of life," he observed in his essay on "Illusion." This time the Oriental parallel is made explicit: he refers to Hindu thought at several points, mentioning Yoganidra, the "goddess of illusion" and commenting that "in their sacred writings" the Hindus had revealed an intense feeling for both the "essential identity" and the "illusion" of the world. In 1861 he would go even further: "The doctrine of the Imagination can only be rightly opened by treating it in connection with the subject of Illusions. And the Hindoos alone have treated this last with sufficient breadth in their legends of the successive Maias of Vishnu."[45]

Finally, there are the important essays on "Compensation" and "Fate," which strongly suggest the Hindu doctrines of karma and reincarnation. Karma may be explained as the belief that one's destiny is a result of one's good and bad actions, that one reaps what one has sown; reincarnation as the belief that the moral consequences of one's actions pass from generation to generation until the individual achieves release (*samadhi*). Emerson defined "compensation" as "polarity" or "action and reaction." It was the principle that "Cause and effect, means and ends, seed and fruit, cannot be severed; for the effect already blooms in the cause, the end preexists in the means, the fruit in the seed." Though he does not mention karma in the essay, he does observe that "The Indian mythology ends in the same ethics. . . ."[46]

The "Fate" essay emphasizes both the inexorable operation of law and the creative counterforce of man's thought and moral sentiments. "If we must accept Fate," Emerson wrote, "we are not less compelled to affirm liberty, the significance of the individual. . . ." He cites Indian thought several times and approvingly quotes the Hindu saying, "Fate is nothing but the deeds committed in a prior state of existence."[47] His attitude toward reincarnation is much more ambivalent than to the idea of karma; the notion of endless rebirths was too pessimistic to win his unconditional approval. However, at times he did seem to accept it. "*Transmigration* of Souls: that too is no fable. I would it were; but look around you at the men & women, & do you not see that they are already only half human," he meditated in 1840. He also spoke of transmigration as "easy of reception" where the mind was "not preoccupied."[48] The entries make it clear that the Indian conceptions were often vague in his mind.

The parallels are impressive, but one cannot entirely dismiss the possibility that Emerson drew them from other non-Oriental sources. Several studies have, indeed, suggested that much of the influence usually attributed to the Orient probably stemmed from Platonist and Neoplatonist sources.[49] There are also important differences between the Emersonian and the Hindu concepts that should not be blurred: his Over-Soul is more theistic than the Hindu *Brahman*, his concept of Self more voluntaristic than the *atman*, his Illusions less binding than *maya*, and his Compensation less deterministic than the Hindu karma and reincarnation. Since he drew from so many sources, the question of formative influences will probably remain a matter for debate. However, the evidence of Hinduism's influence is much too extensive to ignore; if Indian thought did not form his thought, it certainly widened and deepened it.

Though much less important than Indian thought, Confucianism also attracted Emerson's sympathies. The Transcendental mystic found refuge in Hinduism, but the Yankee realist could appreciate the practicality of the Noble Sage. It was characteristic that he could approve two such divergent viewpoints. He admired Confucius, but did not feel the same toward Chinese religion generally; at one point he dismissed Chinese religious observances as a worship of "crockery Gods which in Europe & America our babies are wise enough to put in baby houses. . . ."[50] He made this statement early, when he was lashing out against all aspects of Chinese civilization, but there is no indication that he changed his mind later. By contrast, he ranked Confucius with Plato, Manu, Socrates, and Muhammad as the great men to whom all mankind looked for spiritual leadership. He emphasized Confucius' special role as mediator, as a man who had maintained balance between the Real and the Ideal: "Confucius [,] glory of the nations, Confucius[,] sage of the absolute East, was a middleman," he remarked. "He is the Washington of philosophy. . . ."[51] (But he also jibed, "Ah thou evil two-faced half & half!" suggesting that occasionally he felt the Chinese Sage had carried compromise too far.[52]) He always came back to the wisdom and durability of the great Chinese philosopher, remarking in 1863 that "I am reading a better Pascal" and again that Confucius "anticipated the speech of Socrates, and the *Do as be done by*, of Jesus."[53]

Finally, there is Theodore Parker's charge that, despite frequent quotation, Emerson did not really understand Oriental thought. The Concord poet's remarks concerning Buddhism, which he occasionally noticed in his writings, are most damaging on this point. A man who could laud the *Bhagavad-Gita* as the "much renowned book of Buddhism," or who spoke of the "Hindoo Buddhism" represented in the "prayers of the Bhagavata Purana" could hardly have had a very clear conception of that religion.[54] He ranged over a wide area in his reading, but there is almost no record that he consulted Buddhist works. The exception is one late reference to Edward Upham's *The History and Doctrine of Buddhism*, which he withdrew from the Harvard Library in 1846.[55] The *Journal* suggests that in his mind Buddhism was less a religious system than a metaphor for the dark aspects of human life. He wrote, "*Buddhism*. Winter, Night, Sleep, are all the invasions of eternal Buddh, and it gains a point every day." The emphasis is not on doctrine, but on a kind of dark and ghostly spirit that seemed to hover mysteriously around all people. Again: "The man wriggles this way & that[,] then dives to ecstasy & abandonment & that is Buddism." Occasionally, he was a bit more specific: "Buddhism read literally is the tenet of Fate. . . ."[56] Emerson was not unique in his ignorance; Americans generally remained almost totally uninformed about Buddhism until after the Civil War.

Parker also expressed unhappiness with Emerson's approach to Asian thought, particularly his tendency to force "his oriental allies" to defend novel conceptions. The charge is well founded. Emerson had read extensively in ancient Indian literature but tended to assimilate the reading to preconceived notions. All Oriental doctrines were viewed as harmonious and consistent statements in a single, unchanging, universal tradition—a gross simplification. He quoted Confucius frequently but with no concern for the context or meaning intended by the Chinese philosopher. As he observed in his *Journal*, "If the picture is good, who cares who made it? . . . The authorship of a good sentence, whether Vedas or Hermes or Chaldaean oracle, or Jack Straw, is totally a trifle for pedants to discuss."[57] If the passage served his purpose, that was all that mattered. He also revealed unconcern toward historical change and shifts in doctrine: Hinduism was Hinduism, whether ancient or modern. James Eliot Cabot, Emerson's close friend and literary executor, suggested that the "wide range" of Emerson's quotations and the "unhesitating way" in which he used them encouraged the notion that the Concord poet had a deeper knowledge of most subjects than he actually did. "He had a quick eye for a good sentence, and never forgot one," Cabot noted, "but the quotations, I think, are sometimes all that he cared to know of the book. . . ."[58]

The limitations are numerous, and yet Emerson should not be judged too harshly. At a time when most Americans were still completely unaware of Oriental thought, he was investigating it seriously. His reading preferences indicate excellent judgment: Wilkins's translation of the *Bhagavad-Gita*, Wilson's translation of the *Vishnu Purana*, Jones's translation of the *Laws of Manu*, and Legge's translation of the writings of Confucius—the best contemporary sources.

Obviously, Emerson's special place in this history does not rest on a deep knowledge of the Oriental religions or on a seminal work that changed American understanding. Nor was he a significant popularizer: he declined to sponsor an American edition of the *Bhagavad-Gita* and utilized Oriental thought sparingly in his elegant essays. Neither scholar nor popularizer, he may be best remembered as a prophet, the pre-Civil War American, who most fully realized the philosophical significance of Asian thought and the first to seek to reconcile Oriental ideas with Western thought.

Other Americans had looked forward to a single world civilization—but a Christian one, or, in the case of the Enlightenment, a civilization based on reason and the Newtonian laws of nature. He was first, so far as I have been able to discover, to envision this as a fusion of East and West. The raw idea may be found in the *Journals*, but the fullest presentation is offered in his "Plato" essay published in *Representative Men* in 1850. Confined to a few pages in an essay on a Western philosopher, the sketch offers little more than a suggestion.

Emerson initiates his analysis by distinguishing the two "cardinal facts" at the base of all philosophy: what he speaks of as "the one, and the two," or Unity and Variety. The split had appeared and reappeared in many variations: as the one and the many, being versus intellect, necessity versus freedom, rest versus motion—and, finally, East versus West. The key passage follows:

> The country of unity, of immovable institutions, the seat of a philosophy delighting in abstractions, of men faithful in doctrine and in practice to the idea of a deaf,

unimplorable, immense fate, is Asia; and it realizes this faith in the social institution of caste. On the other side, the genius of Europe is active and creative: it resists caste by culture; its philosophy was a discipline; it is a land of arts, inventions, trade, freedom. If the East loved infinity, the West delighted in boundaries.[59]

Several references in the passage deserve comment. He speaks of "Asia" but thinks of India as indicated by his references to a "philosophy delighting in abstractions" and the "social institution of caste." East and West are defined in intellectual terms; the difference is not political or economic, but a difference in minds that distinguishes the two worlds. This is characteristic: Emerson and the Transcendentalists generally looked upon the East not as a place but as an idea. But the most interesting point revealed by the quote is the revelation of Emerson's Western bias: he speaks of "immovable institutions" and a "deaf, unimplorable" fate in characterizing the Asian mind, but emphasizes the "active" and "creative" genius in characterizing the Western mind. Though paired, the Western mind clearly stands higher. The pro-Western preference is more overt in the *Journal*: "Orientalism is Fatalism, resignation: Occidentalism is Freedom & Will./ We occidentals are educated to wish to be first." And again: "We read the Orientals, but remain Occidental."[60]

He proceeds to suggest a synthesis, or, more accurately, to claim that the synthesis had already been achieved at the very beginning of Western civilization. He writes, "The unity of Asia and the detail of Europe; the infinitude of the Asiatic soul and the defining, result-loving, machine-making, surface-seeking, opera-going Europe,—Plato came to join, and, by contact, to enhance the energy of each."[61] In Emerson's mind Plato was the world's greatest philosopher; by linking the ancient Greek thinker to the reconciliation of East and West, he reveals the high place East-West synthesis occupied in his own mind. Indeed, as William T. Harris first observed, Emerson's remarks better describe his own intellectual position than Plato's: the champion of the One and the Many, unity and variety, infinity and limits, idealism and realism, he was also the prophet of Eastern spirituality and Western intellectuality.

Emerson's concern for East-West reconciliation fed an interest in compiling a "world bible." He emphasized the radical antithesis between East and West in the "Plato" essay, but elsewhere dismissed the differences in favor of the essential identity of truth the world over. (He did not seem troubled by such discrepancies. "I need hardly say to any one acquainted with my thoughts that I have no System," he confessed in his *Journal*. He had hoped to reduce the "great topics" of human concern to a "sort of Encyclopaedia," but now recognized "that my curve was a parabola whose arcs would never meet. . . ."[62]) His interest in a "world bible" may be documented as early as

1836: "Make your own Bible," he had commanded himself.[63] He seems to have first conceived this as a compilation of Western sources, but soon expanded coverage to include the East. By 1838 the Oriental references had so increased that he found it necessary to justify himself. He explained that "we fly to the pagans & use the name & relations of Socrates, of Confucius, Menu, Zoroaster" not because these were "better or as good as Jesus & Paul," but because they provided "good algebraic terms" that were less likely to be confused than more familiar Christian passages.[64] Though he continued to speak of the superiority of the Christian revelation, he increasingly applied the word "bible" to Oriental as well as Western scriptures. By 1841 he was remarking, "How easily these old worships of Moses, of Zoroaster, of Menu, of Socrates, domesticate themselves in the mind. I cannot find any antiquity in them. They are mine as much as theirs."[65]

The culmination of this rising interest was the "Ethnical Scriptures," which Emerson inaugurated in the *Dial* in July 1842 with selections from the *Vishnu Sarma*. Over the next two years he and Thoreau offered additional selections from Jones's *Laws of Manu*, Marshman's *Works of Confucius*, Collie's *Chinese Classical Work*, and the sayings of Buddha.[66] Emerson prefaced the first installment by explaining that "each nation" had "its bible more or less pure," but that none had "been willing" to "collate its own with those of other nations. . . ." He went on to suggest that this could best be achieved by eliminating the "civil-historical" and "ritual portions" in favor of the moral message.[67] The "Ethnical Scriptures" could not have reached a wide audience because of the *Dial*'s limited circulation. Nevertheless, the idea of a "world bible" remained alive; eventually Moncure Conway, one of Emerson's ardent disciples, published such a work.

Emerson's early and deep sympathies with Oriental thought, his fragmentary but seminal conception of the fusion of East and West, and his enthusiasm for a "world bible" all place him in the vanguard of America's discovery of the Oriental religions. He did not advocate Asian thought as a replacement for Western conceptions, but as its complement. When pressed, he came back to the superiority of the West—as one sees in a revealing piece published in *Century Magazine* in 1882, the year of his death. The call for closer acquaintance with Eastern thought remains, but the assertion of Western superiority is much stronger than earlier. He lauds the "breadth and luxuriance of Eastern imagery and modes of thinking" and affirms, "There is no writing which has more electric power to unbind and animate the torpid intellect," but concludes that if forced to choose concerning their "final superiority," it was "too plain" that the "star of empire rolls West. . . ."[68] Later in the century some would go much further, dismissing crass Western materialism in favor of a more profound Oriental idealism. Emerson would not have approved. He could hail the East without abandoning the West.

Notes

1. William Gilman, et al., eds., *The Journals and Miscellaneous Notebooks of Ralph Waldo Emerson*, 14 vols. (Cambridge, Mass.: Belknap Press of Harvard University Press, 1960-), 9: 322. Note that the complex editorial symbols and cancelled portions have been omitted in this as well as in all succeeding quotations from these volumes. Gilman's edition supercedes Emerson's and Forbes's earlier edition (next note); the Emerson and Forbes edition will be used only for the years not treated in the Gilman edition.

2. Edward Waldo Emerson and Waldo Emerson Forbes, eds., *Journals of Ralph Waldo Emerson*, 10 vols. (Boston: Houghton Mifflin, 1909-1914), 7: 241-42 and 7: 511. All three quotations come from the unpublished journals—a significant point that will be returned to in the text.

3. Arthur E. Christy, *The Orient in American Transcendentalism: A Study of Emerson, Thoreau, and Alcott* (1932; reprint ed., New York: Octagon Books, 1963), p. vii.

4. Frederic I. Carpenter, *Emerson Handbook* (New York: Hendricks House, 1953), p. 111. The same view is to be found in his earlier *Emerson and Asia* (Cambridge, Mass.: Harvard University Press, 1930), pp. 254-55.

5. Aside from Christy's and Carpenter's works, which remain indispensable, the following should also be consulted: Man M. Singh, "Emerson and India," (Ph.D. diss., University of Pennsylvania, 1946); Kurt F. Leidecker, "Emerson and East-West Synthesis," *Philosophy East and West* 1 (July 1951): 40-50; K. R. Chadrasekharan, "Emerson's Brahma: An Indian Interpretation," *New England Quarterly* 33 (December 1960): 506-12; and Dale Riepe, "Emerson and Indian Philosophy," *Journal of the History of Ideas* 28 (January-March 1967): 115-22.

6. Gilman, *Journals and Notebooks of Emerson*, 1: 12.

7. Ibid., 7: 257. "Travelling" underscored in the original.

8. Ibid., 1: 340. In addition, see Singh's chapter "Emerson's Reading," pp. 5-11, in "Emerson and India," and the series of articles by Kenneth W. Cameron, the most persistent investigator of the sources of Emerson's first awareness of the Orient: "Young Emerson's Orientalism at Harvard" in Ralph Waldo Emerson, *Indian Superstition*, pp. 13-47; "Emerson and Southey's Oriental Books" in *The Transcendentalists and Minerva*, 3 vols. (Hartford, Conn.: Transcendental Books, 1958), 2: 433-37; "More Remarks on 'Indian Superstition' and Emerson's Oriental Resources while at Harvard," ibid., 3: 829-54; "More Notes on Orientalism in Emerson's Harvard," *Emerson Society Quarterly*, no. 22 (1st Quarter 1961): 81-90; and " 'Indian Superstition' and Orientalism in Emerson's Harvard," *Emerson Society Quarterly*, no. 33 (4th Quarter 1963): 7-16.

9. Ralph L. Rusk, ed., *The Letters of Ralph Waldo Emerson*, 6 vols. (New York: Columbia University Press, 1939), 1: 116-17. Years later he met William Adam, the Scottish missionary whom Roy had converted from trinitarianism. Cf. Gilman, *Journals and Notebooks of Emerson*, 7: 213, and *Letters of Emerson*, 2: 201.

10. Gilman, *Journals and Notebooks of Emerson*, 1: 399; 2: 195.

11. Ibid., 1: 350n. Emerson's father owned Priestley's *A Comparison of the Institutions of Moses with those of the Hindoos*, which would also have been accessible until 1822 when it was sold. Cf. Kenneth W. Cameron, "More Notes

on Orientalism in Emerson's Harvard," *Emerson Society Quarterly*, no. 22 (1st Quarter 1961): 81-90.

12. Gilman, *Journals and Notebooks of Emerson*, 3: 362.

13. Rusk, *Letters of Emerson*, 6: 246. Also: 1: 322-23.

14. Ibid., 2: 154. Also: 2: 158 and 2: 174-75.

15. Gilman, *Journals and Notebooks of Emerson*, 1: 50; 1: 210. See also the reference in ibid., 2: 195.

16. Ibid., 1: 83.

17. Ibid., 2: 229.

18. Ibid., 2: 379. He made later amends as is revealed by his appreciative "Speech at the Banquet in Honor of the Chinese Embassy," printed in Edward W. Emerson, ed., *The Complete Works of Ralph Waldo Emerson* [*Centenary Edition*], 12 vols. (Boston: Houghton Mifflin, 1903-1904), 11: 471-74.

19. Gilman, *Journals and Notebooks of Emerson*, 4: 27.

20. Ibid., 7: 65-66.

21. Rusk, *Letters of Emerson*, 3: 179. For other references, see Gilman, *Journals and Notebooks of Emerson*, 8: 354, 366-67.

22. Gilman, *Journals and Notebooks of Emerson*, 8: 14, 356, 444, 485, 489, 491-92.

23. Ibid., 8: 478.

24. Rusk, *Letters of Emerson*, 3: 290. See also 3: 288.

25. Ibid., 3: 293, 299, 303, 343, 479.

26. Ibid., 4: 248, 336, and 350-51. Quote is on p. 336.

27. William T. Harris, "Emerson's Orientalism," in *The Genius and Character of Emerson. Lectures at the Concord School of Philosophy*, ed. Franklin B. Sanborn (Boston: James R. Osgood, 1885), pp. 372, 373. Also see his "Emerson's 'Brahma' and the 'Bhagavad Gita,' " *Poet-Lore* 1 (June 1889): 253-59.

28. John Jay Chapman, "Emerson, Sixty Years After," *Atlantic Monthly* 79 (January 1897): 40.

29. [Theodore Parker], "The Writings of Ralph Waldo Emerson," *Massachusetts Quarterly Review* 3 (March 1850): 211-12.

30. Emerson and Forges, *Journals of Emerson*, 8: 528.

31. Emerson, *Complete Works of Emerson*, 2: 3.

32. Ibid., 6: 205.

33. Ibid., 4: 139.

34. Ibid., 1: 126.

35. Ibid., 1: 34. The notion that Emerson had already arrived at his basic philosophy, as expressed in *Nature*, before coming into contact with the Orient has been discredited by research since World War II. Cf. Singh, "Emerson and India," pp. 1-34.

36. Emerson, *Complete Works of Emerson*, 9: 467.

37. Stanley T. Williams, ed., "Unpublished Letters of Emerson," *Journal of English and Germanic Philology* 26 (October 1927): 484. See also Rusk, *Letters of Emerson*, 1: lxi, 4: 350-51; Carpenter, *Emerson and Asia*, pp. 22-23.

38. Charles Eliot Norton, ed., *Letters from Ralph Waldo Emerson to a Friend, 1838-1853* (1899; reprint ed., Port Washington, N.Y.: Kennikat Press, 1971), pp. 28-29.

39. Emerson and Forbes, *Journals of Emerson*, 10: 162.

40. Emerson, *Complete Works of Emerson*, 4: 49.
41. Ibid., 1: 337.
42. See Christy, *Orient in American Transcendentalism*, pp. 73-123; Carpenter, *Emerson and Asia*, pp. 103-46; and Riepe's more recent "Emerson and Indian Philosophy," pp. 115-22.
43. Emerson, *Complete Works of Emerson*, 2: 268.
44. Ibid., 2: 269.
45. Ibid., 6: 313, 324 and Emerson and Forbes, *Journals of Emerson*, 9: 302.
46. Emerson, *Complete Works of Emerson*, 2: 96, 103, 106.
47. Ibid., 6:4, 12.
48. Gilman, *Journals and Notebooks of Emerson*, 7: 385; 9: 263.
49. See John S. Harrison, *The Teachers of Emerson* (New York: Sturgis & Walton, 1910) and Carpenter, *Emerson and Asia*, pp. 39-102. However, both works see Western sources preparing the way for the later Oriental influence.
50. Gilman, *Journals and Notebooks of Emerson*, 2: 378; see also 2: 224.
51. Ibid., 9: 318. Brackets added by the editor.
52. Ibid., 9: 317.
53. Emerson and Forbes, *Journals of Emerson*, 9: 533, 535. Emerson was also drawn to Persian writings, which have been excluded. See Christy, *Orient in American Transcendentalism*, pp. 137-54; Carpenter, *Emerson and Asia*, pp. 161-94; and the two articles by J. D. Yohannan, "Emerson's Translations of Persian Poetry from German Sources," *American Literature* 14 (January 1943): 407-20 and "The Influence of Persian Poetry upon Emerson's Work," *American Literature* 15 (March 1943): 25-41.
54. Rusk, *Letters of Emerson*, 3: 290; Emerson and Forbes, *Journals of Emerson*, 10: 242. Carpenter, *Emerson and Asia*, pp. 146-50, recognizes his confusion, but emphasizes that he had very definite ideas about Buddhism.
55. Rusk, *Letters of Emerson*, 3: 360.
56. Gilman, *Journals and Notebooks of Emerson*, 8: 383; 9: 277, 313. Brackets added by the editor.
57. Emerson and Forbes, *Journals of Emerson*, 8: 570.
58. James E. Cabot, *A Memoir of Ralph Waldo Emerson*, 2 vols. (Boston: Houghton Mifflin, 1899), 1: 288.
59. Emerson, *Complete Works of Emerson*, 4: 52.
60. Gilman, *Journals & Notebooks of Emerson*, 10: 90; Emerson and Forbes, *Journals of Emerson*, 9:116.
61. Emerson, *Complete Works of Emerson*, 4: 53-54.
62. Gilman, *Journals & Notebooks of Emerson*, 7: 302.
63. Ibid., 5: 186.
64. Ibid., 7: 104.
65. Emerson, *Complete Works of Emerson*, 2: 28.
66. Roger Mueller provides a detailed examination in "The Orient in American Transcendental Periodicals (1835-1886)," (Ph.D. diss., University of Minnesota, 1968) pp. 6-138.
67. [Emerson], "Veeshnoo Sarma," *The Dial* (Boston) 3 (July 1842): 82.
68. Emerson, *Complete Works of Emerson*, 10: 179. It should be noted, however, that elements of this article were composed as early as 1847.

4
Further Transcendental Explorations: Thoreau, Alcott, and Parker

"I delight much in my young friend, who seems to have as free & erect a mind as any I have ever met," Emerson wrote in his *Journal* in 1838, heralding his fateful friendship with young Thoreau.[1] Thoreau had read and greatly admired *Nature* while at Harvard. It seems paradoxical that a man as intransigently independent and as much a "loner" should have accepted a relationship of such intimacy. Recognizing Emerson's profound influence, for many years critics underestimated the younger man's achievement. James Russell Lowell observed in 1838, "I met Thoreau last night and it is exquisitely amusing to see how he imitates Emerson's tone and manner. With my eyes shut, I shouldn't know them apart."[2] The relationship cooled as Thoreau cast out on his own, but for a number of years the two men were in constant contact; Thoreau actually moved in with the Emersons in 1841, and lived with them for two years.

Though one recent biographer claims that Thoreau had already come to know Asian thought before his friendship with Emerson,[3] the older man's role in stimulating and directing Thoreau's Oriental interests appears crucial. Plodding forward on his own, with occasional suggestions from his Aunt Mary, it had taken Emerson almost twenty years to begin to appreciate the profundity of Oriental thought. Thoreau, who did not check out a single Oriental book during four years at Harvard, was swept away in one year. "How thrilling a noble sentiment in the oldest books,—in Homer, the Zendavesta, or Confucius! It is a strain of music wafted down to us on the breeze of time, through the aisles of innumerable ages," he wrote in 1838 after coming into the older man's orbit.[4] With Emerson's encouragement, Thoreau moved directly to the Oriental sources and was soon extolling the *Bhagavad-Gita* and *Laws of Manu,* the latter affecting him much more powerfully than it had Emerson. Coming upon the East more suddenly and more completely than Emerson had in his first encounters, Thoreau seemed more intensely moved:

> That title, "The Laws of Menu with the Gloss of Culluca," comes to me with such a volume of sound as if it had swept unobstructed over the plains of Hindostan; and when my eye rests on yonder birches, or the sun in the water, or the shadows of the trees, it seems to signify the laws of them all. They are the laws of you and me, a fragrance wafted down from those old times, and no more to be refuted than the wind.
>
> When my imagination travels eastward and backward to those remote years of the gods, I seem to draw near to the habitation of the morning, and the dawn at length has a place. I remember the book as an hour before sunrise.[5]

Two months later he was still intoxicated: "I cannot read a sentence in the book of the Hindoos without being elevated as upon the table-land of the Ghauts. It has such a rhythm as the winds of the desert, such a tide as the Ganges, and seems as superior to criticism as the Himmaleh Mounts."[6] Emerson's appreciations seem almost restrained next to such effusions. Considering Thoreau's acid views on so many questions, the affirmations are all the more impressive.

Thoreau not only telescoped Emerson's twenty-year pilgrimage into a year, he also bypassed the older man's early negativism. With a few reservations, he seemed ready to embrace the Orient whole, right from the beginning. Thus, where the young Emerson had been contemptuous of the conservatism of Chinese civilization, complaining of its "doleful monotony" and "reverend dullness," young Thoreau found a preference for permanence to be one of the East's many attractions. "The inhabitants of those Eastern plains seem to possess a natural and hereditary right to be conservative and magnify forms and traditions," he wrote of the ancient Hindu, approving Manu's declaration that "Immemorial custom is transcendent law." Thoreau quipped, "The fault of our New England custom is that it is memorial." Transferring and transforming the passage in *A Week on the Concord and Merrimack Rivers,* he would rhapsodize, "It is a sublime conservatism; as wide as the world, and as unwearied as time. . . ."[7] (It is true that a few pages later he finds Hindu teaching less practical than the New Testament: "The Brahman never proposes courageously to assault evil, but patiently to starve it out. His active faculties are paralyzed by the idea of caste, of impassable limits of destiny and the tyranny of time."[8] However, this is almost the only criticism, and he immediately softens it by recommending the need for both contemplation and activity.)

Yoga seems to have been the key to Thoreau's deep attraction to Hinduism and the area of most obvious Oriental influence—another divergence from Emerson, who ignored the yogic disciplines. He refused to be dismayed by the extreme behavior often linked to the disciplines. He offers a detailed list of the oddities in the opening pages of *Walden*—but note his conclusion:

> What I have heard of Bramins sitting exposed to four fires and looking in the face of the sun; or hanging suspended, with their heads downward, over flames; or looking at the heavens over their shoulders "until it becomes impossible for them to resume their natural position" . . . or dwelling, chained for life, at the foot of a tree; or measuring with their bodies, like caterpillars, the breadth of vast empires; or standing on one leg on the tops of pillars,—even these forms of conscious penance are hardly more incredible and astonishing than the scenes which I daily witness.[9]

He is, of course, leading up to his famous proposition that "The mass of men lead lives of quiet desperation." The intellectual disciplines associated with *jnana yoga,* rather than the unusual austerities, most attracted him.[10] More ascetic in personality, more driven to act on his beliefs than Emerson, he found natural attraction in yoga's promise that one could achieve higher consciousness by actively undertaking disciplines to yoke the mind.

The most astonishing evidence of Thoreau's acceptance of yoga is the much-quoted, often debated passage from an 1849 letter:

> "Free in this world, as the birds in the air, disengaged from every kind of chains, those who have practiced the *yoga* gather in Brahma the certain fruit of their works."
>
> Depend upon it that rude and careless as I am, I would fain practice the *yoga* faithfully.
>
> "The yogin, absorbed in comtemplation, contributes in his degree to creation: he breathes a divine perfume, he hears wonderful things. Divine forms traverse him without tearing him, and united to the nature which is proper to him, he goes, he acts, as animating original matter."
>
> To some extent, and at rare intervals, even I am a yogin.[11]

The quotes from Hindu reading are immediately followed by his personal affirmations. Arthur Christy, a careful scholar who devoted a lifetime to the study of the Transcendental-Oriental connection, was convinced that Thoreau *did* in fact think of himself as a yogi. The retreat to Walden may be interpreted as the yogi's abandonment of the world.[12]

Christy exaggerates perhaps—but not by much. The *Journal* certainly suggests a personal interest: "The very austerity of these Hindoos is tempting to the devotional as a more refined and nobler luxury." Again: "One may discover the root of a Hindoo religion in his own private history, when, in the silent intervals of the day or the night, he does sometimes inflict on himself like austerities with a stern satisfaction."[13] Such interests would explain his special attraction to the *Laws of Manu*. "The sublime sentences of Menu carry us back to a time when purification and sacrifice and self-devotion had a place in the faith of men, and were not as now a superstition," he wrote. The passages quoted from Manu repeatedly focus on the disciplines of yoga; at one point, he speaks of the *Laws* as a "manual of private devotion. . . ."[14]

One other key difference between Thoreau and Emerson stemmed from differing attitudes toward Christianity. Emerson was a harsh critic of organizational Christianity, but the Bible and Jesus were still sacred. He honored the Oriental religions, but in the end preferred Western belief. Thoreau was more hostile to Christianity and less willing to accept reconciliation in later years; in the end he seemed more inclined toward Oriental religion. He wrote in *A Week on the Concord*, "The reading which I love best is the scriptures of the several nations, though it happens that I am better acquainted with those of the Hindoos, the Chinese, and the Persians, than of the Hebrews. . . . Give me one of these bibles, and you have silenced me for a while."[15] In comparisons of the Oriental and Judeo-Christian faiths, he inevitably came down in favor of the East. "What extracts from the Vedas I have read fall on me like the light of a higher and purer luminary, which describes a loftier course through a purer stratum," he remarked in 1850. "The religion and philosophy of the Hebrews are those of a wilder and ruder tribe, wanting the civility and intellectual refinements and subtlety of the Hindoos."[16] It is true that he also praised Jesus, but not above the great Oriental sages; he speaks of "my Buddha," never of "my Jesus."[17]

There were important differences between Thoreau's and Emerson's responses to the Orient, but there were also basic similarities. Like Emerson, Thoreau was most attracted to Hinduism, but was also charmed by the writings of the ancient Chinese and Persians.[18] Like Emerson, he usually mined the Oriental writings for their "lusters"—to embellish and universalize an idea; he had little interest in exploring and mapping the Oriental systems. Ellery Channing, one of Thoreau's closest friends, remarked, "If there was the one good line, he took it." The reading mainly served to lubricate his writing; he "did not stop in a book" and "rarely or never read them over."[19] Like Emerson, Thoreau was excited by the conception of a world bible and the wider faith such a book might induce; he declared in *A Week on the Concord* that it "would be worthy of the age" to gather a "Scripture of mankind."[20] Above all, both approached the Orient as writers and poets, not as philosophers, historians, or even amateur scholars and popularizers. As usual, Thoreau was blunt about this: "As for the tenets of the Brahmans," he wrote, "we are not so much concerned to know what doctrines they held, as that they were held by any. . . . It is the attitude of these men, more than any communication which they make, that attracts us."[21]

Both may also be criticized for the same failing: despite their fervent testimonies, neither read the Oriental works nor handled the Asian conceptions very carefully. If so much was to be learned from the ancient East, one would think the sources deserved closer study. Thoreau recognized the dangers of misinterpretation, commenting after he consulted Wilson's translation of the *Rig-Veda* in 1856 that he sometimes felt inclined to wonder whether the "translator has not made something out of nothing. . . ." However, he generally disparaged the preoccupations of scholars. Thus, he grandly announced that while "commentators and translators" were "disputing about the meaning of this word or that," he intended to hear only the "resounding of the ancient sea," that he did "not the least care where I get my ideas, or what suggests them."[22] Some conflict is inevitable perhaps: too much scholarship may degenerate into pedantry just as excessive concern with literary style may result in distortion. However, neither concern deserves contempt; it seems surprising that Emerson and Thoreau both dismissed the scholarly ideal.

Thoreau's life was short, and so was his involvement with Asian thought. It is largely concentrated in the early 1840s when he rapidly explored the Eastern writings and then compiled the results. Aside from the *Journal* where references abound, his conclusions may be found scattered among his writings, beginning with the "Ethnical Scriptures," which he and Emerson presented in the pages of the *Dial*. It is significant that, with the exception of the opening piece from the *Vishnu Sarma,* all the East Asian selections—including Confucius, Mencius, the sayings of Buddha, and Manu—were compiled by the younger man; Emerson provided the Zoroastrian and Chaldean selections. (Comparing the two men's handling of sources, a recent study concludes that Thoreau's versions were much closer to the original texts and revealed much greater concern for the context and coherence of the quotes.[23]) The preparation of the "Ethnical Scriptures" must have contributed a great deal to Thoreau's Oriental education. Thoreau also made translations of two Buddhist works from French to English: "The Preaching of Buddha," a translation of Eugène Burnouf's *Saddharmapundarika,* a Northern Buddhist work, and "The Transmigration of the Seven Brahmans," a fable translated from Alexandre Langlois's *Harivansa.* (The "Transmigration" was not discovered until long after his death and not published until the 1930s.[24]) Though it is difficult to gauge the extent of his Buddhist interests, the translations suggest enough interest to take the trouble to convert them into English. Finally, there are the two published books—*A Week on the Concord and Merrimack Rivers* and *Walden*—both containing numerous references to the Orient. The *Week* especially stands out, including extended passages that reveal deep personal commitment to Asian conceptions.

Thoreau's affirmation of Oriental ideas probably had something to do with his contemporary literary reputation. His lack of recognition during his life and for a generation after provides a classic example of greatness unrecognized. When James Munroe Company of Boston pressed him to do something about the unsold volumes of *A Week on the Concord,* Thoreau found himself the owner of 706 of the original 1,000 copies, leading to his dry claim that he now had a "library of nearly nine hundred volumes, over seven hundred of which I wrote myself."[25] His lack of success stemmed in part from unfavorable reviews of his books; one major reason seems to have been his touting of Oriental thought. (Emerson, it is true, also enthused about the Orient—and was criticized for doing so—but he did not go as far in attacking Christianity or proclaiming the superiority of the Orient.) This was a major factor in George Ripley's displeasure, for example, in his review of the *Week* in the *New York Tribune*. He particularly complained of Thoreau's "misplaced Pantheistic attack on the Christian Faith." Thoreau's reference to "my Buddha" and assertion that he considered "the Sacred Books of the Brahmins in nothing inferior to the Christian Bible" led Ripley to explode that he found Thoreau's treatment "revolting alike to good sense and good taste." If also hostile to Thoreau's Transcendental philosophy, which he dismissed as "second-hand, imitative, often exaggerated" and a "bad specimen of a dubious and dangerous school," the statements in favor of Hinduism most antagonized him.[26]

The most damaging reviews came from the pen of James Russell Lowell, whose cruel barbs have been credited with delaying Thoreau's recognition for decades. Lowell's criticisms were primarily aesthetic rather than philosophical—he particularly complained of the formlessness and many distracting diversions in Thoreau's writing—but once again the young poet's Oriental references seemed to cause special offence. "What . . . have Concord and Merrimack to do with Boodh?" Lowell sharply demanded at one point, citing the many "digressions on Boodh," Anacreon, Persius, and Friendship as "snags" that jolted the reader. Attacking Thoreau's unfortunate proclivity for dark utterances, Lowell quipped that "it must be this taste that makes him so fond of the Hindoo philosophy, which would seem admirably suited to men, if men were only oysters."[27] One of the rare favorable reviews, that of an obscure Harvard undergraduate whose comments so raised Thoreau's drooping spirit that the next time he traveled to Cambridge, he sought him out to give him a gift copy, was also critical of the Orientalism. "Their Christ," "my Buddha!" "Shakespeare youthfully green" beside the "cosmogonal philosophy of the Bhagvat Geeta!" he disapprovingly quoted Thoreau. "O where the end of this eternal Eastern business,—this

Buddha and Brahm panegyric!" Defending the superiority of Christianity while flailing Indian thought, the fledgling critic complained that Thoreau had played "too long upon that one string,—we get too much of that heathenish music, when we have as good or better of our own."[28] Significantly, this was the only area of criticism in an otherwise laudatory review.

In his last years Thoreau's attention shifted almost entirely to the nature studies that had always consumed much of his energy. Signaling the shift, he wrote in his *Journal* in 1856, "The most interesting domes I behold are not those of Oriental temples and palaces, but of the toadstools."[29] References to Asian thought are rare henceforth. There is one final footnote involving a superb collection of Oriental books that came into Thoreau's possession in 1855. The books arrived too late to affect his views, but his enthusiasm suggests that though his interests were shifting elsewhere, the Orient remained high in his esteem to the end. The donor was a young Englishman, Thomas Cholmondeley, who had visited Thoreau in Concord. Friendship had resulted, and upon his return home Cholmondeley had the books sent from England. Informing a friend of his good fortune, Thoreau announced, "I send you information of this as I might of the birth of a child." There were forty-four volumes in all, most of them classics of Indian religious thought: Wilson's *Rig-Veda Sanhita*, the *Upanishads*, the *Vishnu Purana*, Haughton's *Ordinances of Menu*, the *Sankhya Karika*, the *Bhagavad-Gita*, Monier Williams's *Shakuntala*, Colebrooke's *Miscellaneous Essays*, and Spence Hardy's *Eastern Monachism* and *Manual of Buddhism*.[30] Thoreau was genuinely excited, writing back to thank Cholmondeley for his "princely gift"; he described how he had immediately spread them out on his floor, "wading knee deep in Indian philosophy. . . ." "I begin to think myself learned for merely possessing such works, . . ." he confessed.[31] He stored the books lovingly in a case he constructed from driftwood and river boards gathered on his walks. Emerson inherited most of the collection after Thoreau's death.

Like his friends Emerson and Thoreau, Bronson Alcott was also sympathetic to the Oriental religions, although Asian thought did not play the role in his life it did in theirs. In a sense Alcott was the natural Transcendentalist—born to the rarefied view that others labored so hard to develop. Naive, trusting, idealistic, and impractical, he was a pure type. Unlike Emerson and Thoreau, he was a self-made philosopher. Exposed to minimal schooling, he had spent his youth peddling almanacs, tinware, and scissors in the South. After many shifts, he won fame in the mid-1830s for his educational innovations at the Temple School in Boston. Soon after he joined the Transcendental fellowship at Concord.[32]

Emerson would play the crucial role in stimulating Alcott's interest in

Asian religion, but the foundations were in place before their friendship. Raised an Episcopalian, Alcott had already arrived at a very broad outlook before his acquaintance with Emerson. An 1827 diary entry, in which he complains of the tendency to idolize Jesus, reveals his view. While recognizing that Jesus had "unquestionably" been a "great and good man" and that his teachings embodied the "best system of ethics" yet known, he nevertheless questioned whether such ancient ideas were "equally well adapted to the present state." And in another passage he remarks, "I hold that the Christian religion is the best yet promulgated, but do not thence infer that it is not susceptible of improvement; nor do I wish to confound its doctrines with its founder. . . ."[33] He eventually became a Unitarian, but even Unitarianism was too sectarian: "I am dissatisfied with the general preaching of every sect, and with the individuals of any sect," he wrote in 1828. "The style of preaching among the Unitarians, as regards thought and manner, approaches nearest my views; but even this . . . is very objectionable. There is too much merely doctrinal. . . ."[34] He heard Emerson speak in 1828—significantly, on the "Universality of the Notion of the Deity"; however, their friendship developed only after 1835.[35]

The best source for gauging the extent and nature of Alcott's Oriental interests is his *Journal*, a massive enterprise that eventually ran to fifty volumes (approximately *five* times the size of Emerson's effort! The neatly bound volumes constituted most of Alcott's personal library; Ellery Channing suggested they be christened "Encyclopédie de Moi-Même, en cent volumes."[36]) Though he had previously read both Confucius and De Gerando, whose *Histoire comparée des systèmes de philosophie* included a sketch of Oriental philosophy, his allusions to Oriental thought practically all date after 1840 and his friendship with Emerson.[37] Many of these concerned the *Bhagavad-Gita*—every Transcendentalist's favorite Oriental reading. It seems surprising that Alcott read it for the first time only in 1846, since Emerson and Thoreau had been praising it as a masterpiece since 1841. "In the evening I had an hour's quiet reading of the oriental wisdom in the Chapters of the *Bhagvat Geeta*," he remarks, proceeding to enter several pages of extracts from its pages in his *Journal*.[38]

Once he had dipped into its pages, however, he was as entranced as Emerson and Thoreau. "I read more of the *Bhagvat Geeta* and felt how surpassingly fine were the sentiments," he wrote later in 1846, proclaiming it superior to any of the other Oriental scriptures, the "best of all reading for wise men," and the "best of books—containing a wisdom blander and far more sane than that of the Hebrews, whether in the mind of Moses or of Him of Nazareth." Already a controversial figure, he was drawn to a use for the *Gita* that would surely have increased his well-established reputation as a heretic: "Were I a preacher," he speculated, "I would venture sometimes to take from its texts the mottos and moral of my discourse. It would be healthful and invigorating to breathe some of this mountain air into the lungs of Christendom."[39] For a brief time anyway Oriental thought was a passionate concern. One final testimony may be quoted, which emphasizes Emerson's vital role in his enthusiasm:

> Evening: I saw Emerson and had full discourse, mostly on the *Geeta* and the genius of the Oriental faith. I know of no literature more purely intellectual. Its philosophy and poesy seem to me superior to, if not transcending greatly, all others.
>
> Almost all moral teaching has been oppressive, but I think this sweetly pure, and spiritually sane.[40]

There are few references to any Oriental work after 1847, although a decade later he was borrowing the *Gita* from Thoreau's new collection. Reporting the visit to Cholmondeley, Thoreau noted that Alcott had taken a "special interest in the oriental books"; he savored Alcott's appreciation: "And then that he should send you a library! Think of it!"[41] Appropriately, Alcott received the *Bhagavad-Gita* after Thoreau's death.

Alcott's special project with regard to the Oriental scriptures was to bring them together with other sacred writings in a universal bible—an *idée fixe* among the Transcendentalists. Though Emerson refers to making a bible as early as 1836, it is by no means certain that he launched the notion among Transcendentalists. The idea seemed to be in the air. Thus, Convers Francis wrote to Theodore Parker in 1839, "We might have (Might we not?) what I should call a *World Bible,* which if we had now our choice to make would be better than the Jewish and Christian Bible,—I mean a combination of the essentially true and wise, which lies scattered among the sages of all times and nations. . . .Wouldn't it be a noble, a truly God-sent Bible?"[42] The scheme especially appealed to Transcendentalists because it so nicely exemplified their belief in the universality of spiritual ideas. Alcott did not originate the idea, but he became one of its most persistent backers. A crucial entry in his *Journal* in 1839 deserves full quotation:

> Emerson passed the afternoon with me. We had desultory conversation on Swedenbourg, Bruno, Behmen [Boehme], and others of this sublime school. I proposed that some measures should be taken to put English readers in possession of the works of these great minds. Confucius, Zoroaster, Paracelsus, Galen, Plato, Bruno, Behmen, Plotinus, More, Swedenbourg, etc., should be in the hands of every earnest student of the Soul. Had I the means, I should like to collect these works and set scholars upon translating them into our tongue. It would be a noble enterprise, worth living to execute. We should have access to the fountains of truth through the purest channels.[43]

Alcott comes back to the project several times in his *Journal*. At one point, he contemplates the idea of collecting and publishing the works as an anthology, or even an entire library to be called the "Mankind Library." He apparently got no further than a sketch:

MANKIND LIBRARY

The Sacred Scriptures, with Mythological and Biographical elucidation, first collected and edited: being the Lives, works and times of

Moses	Plato
Confucius	Christ
Zoroaster	Mahomet
Pythagoras	Behmen
Socrates	Swedenbourg

Mythology

I. Hebrew and Egyptian	III. Greek and Roman
II. Oriental and Indian	IV. Christian and Cosmic[44]

At another point, he projected a series of public "conversations" on the teachings of the Oriental sages and began collecting the sacred writings. Two years later he was still gathering materials, as indicated by his notations that he had brought home "Marshman's Confucius," "Morals of Confucius," and "Oracles of Zoroaster," with the intention of obtaining other volumes from friends, the Harvard Library, and his personal collection. The first conversation was held, but there is no record of others.[45] In 1866 he mentions the scheme once again: "Emerson spends the evening with me. The Oriental Scriptures, we agree, are to be given to the people along with the Hebrew books, as a means of freeing their faith from the Christian superstitions."[46] The sacred writings were eventually made available to the American public—but not by Alcott.

Emphasis on the equality of the world's religions was bound to raise questions about the claim of Christian superiority, and indeed the relative standing of the Oriental faiths and Christianity became a sensitive point among Transcendentalists. There seemed to be two Alcotts. Much of the time he placed Christianity above the Asian religions and seemed to take his stand with Jesus. Appearing before an 1842 "Bible Convention," for example, he declared that the religious writings of Brahmins and Muslims "were inspired in like manner as the Christian Scriptures," but that "no books contain so full and faithful an exposition of eternal truth as do the Old and New Testaments."[47] Significantly, Thoreau became indignant when Alcott declared that Jesus "stood in a more tender and intimate nearness to the heart of mankind than any character in life or literature."[48] Alcott both spoke of Christianity as "the religion of the most advanced nations" and closely associated with orthodox Christian leaders. Noting his intimacy with Boston's the Reverend Joseph Cook, an outspoken champion of evangelical Christianity, Thomas Wentworth Higginson charged that he was abandoning his earlier religious radicalism to return to the "historical Christianity" of his childhood.[49]

On other occasions, he championed the equality of the world's religions. Following a distressing meeting of the Radical Club, a gathering place for Boston's advanced religious thinkers, Alcott complained that it was "discreditable to a company like this to be bandying Puritan or even Christian epithets" while "exaggerating our real differences." "The revelation was One. . . . All religions were partial forms of the Absolute Religion, and we should no longer set Christianity above the rest."[50] In response to the charge that he had fallen under Cook's influence, he declared, "I have striven to reconcile the different religious beliefs with an underlying universal faith, and if I must be classed, prefer to belong to the *Church Universal*, not to any particular *Sectarian body* of Christians."[51]

How significant were Alcott's Oriental interests? Arthur Christy, who has made the most extensive survey, concludes, ". . . In his time Alcott probably had no equal as a popularizer of Orientalism." He also asserts that Alcott's Oriental involvement was "essentially no less important" than Emerson's and Thoreau's.[52] Both claims are excessive. It is true that he talked of compiling a universal bible, but talk was all he did. There is really no serious comparison with Emerson and Thoreau. An examination of the *Tablets*, one of his most important publications, reveals one quotation from the *Bhagavad-Gita* and a few passing references to the East. *Concord Days* makes several tantalizing allusions to a coming spiritual revolution, but says little about Eastern thought. ("Plainly, the drift of thinking here in New England, if not elsewhere, is towards a Personal Theism, inclusive of the faiths of all races, embodying the substance of their Sacred Books. . . ."[53]) Both the number and the quality of the references to Oriental thought are much higher in Emerson's and Thoreau's writings. While they were consulting a sizable part of the available Hindu religious literature, Alcott was content with the *Bhagavad-Gita*. While Emerson delved into the doctrines of transmigration and *maya* and Thoreau into yoga, Alcott remained content to extol the *Gita*.

Theodore Parker proves that Transcendentalists were not all rhapsodic enthusiasts concerning Oriental thought. He recognized positive elements in the Eastern religions, but was no advocate of the Wisdom of the East. He emphasized the need for closer study, not so much as a means to spiritual enlightenment, but as a means to improve man's knowledge. Where Emerson and Thoreau approached the Orient as devotees, Parker insisted on the need for a critical mind; where they idealized the Eastern faiths, he viewed the Asian religions as a lower stage in the evolution of Absolute Religion. One of the earliest Americans to call for a comparative approach to religion, he stands out as an important precursor of the later comparative religions movements.

As all his biographers have emphasized, Parker is to be remembered as a great preacher and reformer.[54] His ability to simplify complex issues and to act on them as well as his willingness to take advanced positions and to fight for them made him one of the most controversial spiritual figures in midnineteenth-century America. His famous sermon on "The Transient and Permanent in Christianity" added to his reputation as a disturber of the peace. There was another Parker who concerns us here: Parker the scholar, the man who wished to be remembered as a diligent researcher and scientific worker who projected an ambitious scholarly work, never finished, that would have given major attention to the Oriental religions.

Parker unquestionably had the talent and prodigious energy necessary to become a great scholar. His self-discipline and industry were already legendary before he entered the Harvard Divinity School in 1834. Too poor to go to college, he completed the requirements for the BA degree by studying at home after work, appearing at Harvard only to take the exams. He was a good student because he was an insatiable reader; during one brief fourteen-month period he read 320 volumes, many in foreign languages.[55] Once he began to earn a good income, he launched one of the most impressive personal libraries in nineteenth-century America, a mammoth collection of more than 11,000 volumes and 2,500 pamphlets that gradually overran every room of his house. These included such formidable works as Moreri's *Dictionnaire historique* in four volumes, Semler's *Welthistorie* in seventy-two volumes, Ersch and Gruber's *Allgemeine Encyclopödie* in one hundred fifty volumes, and Hammer-Purgstall's seven-volume history of Arabian literature.[56] Finally, he had the requisite gift for languages, achieving some degree of proficiency in more than twenty, including Icelandic, Chaldaic, Persian, Coptic, and Arabic.[57]

Though soon to be diverted by controversy and demands on his time as a popular preacher, for several years after leaving divinity school he was able to spend a good deal of his energy on research and writing. He rapidly completed a two-volume translation of De Wette's *Introduction to the Old Testament* and began to compose *A Discourse of Matters Pertaining to Religion*, published in 1842. According to Octavius Brooks Frothingham, his mind literally "teemed with literary projects" during this period: "Studies in primitive Christianity; studies in church-history; studies in the development of doctrine; studies in the dynasties of Egypt . . . studies in mythology, —Persian, Semitic, Christian; studies in philosophy. . . ."[58] One of these would force him to a serious consideration of Oriental religions.

The work was to be called a "History of the Progressive Development of Religion among the Leading Races of Mankind." Parker did not complete the book; however, he did manage an outline and 190 pages of manuscript, which his first biographer, John Weiss, includes in his early biography. Weiss explains Parker's intent "to establish a historical and philosophical ground for pure theism, by marking the different epochs of religious development in the races of mankind, so that the divine premeditation might be discovered. . . ."[59] The title as well as Weiss's explanation emphasize Parker's plan to offer a comprehensive history of religion. One would expect a significant treatment of the East in such a work and in fact the outline reveals that Eastern religions were to figure prominently in several chapters. Chapter 3 of Book Two, for example, was to focus on the "National Form of Religion in India," while chapter 4 would analyze the "National Form of Religion in Persia." Strangely, China is omitted, Parker explaining in the manuscript that he would "neglect the forms of religion" which had had "little influence on the people of the world," including the "religion of the savage" and the "religion of the Chinese."[60] The historical sketches of the world religions were to be followed by several comparative chapters, including one on the "Generic Agreement of Christianity and Other Forms of Religion" and another on "Specific Difference between Christianity and Other Forms of Religion." Parker explained why a comparative approach was necessary: "To understand the religious history of mankind, we must study these various forms of religion. . . . No one must be neglected. To understand any one phase thereof, we must see it in its relation to the whole."[61]

Parker did not live to complete his magnum opus, but he did present a statement of his general views in a series of lectures in Boston in 1841-1842, published as *A Discourse of Matters Pertaining to Religion*. His attitude toward the Oriental faiths grew out of his general view of religion. Though he favored a more critical and more systematic approach to religion than Emerson and his circle, Parker wrote the *Discourse* as a Transcendentalist. He emphasized that man had an inborn religious faculty and that religion was universal. Like other Transcendentalists, he affirmed that the shapes assumed by historic religions were merely local variations of the universal religion. "There is but one Religion, though many theologies," he declared.[62] (In his most famous formulation, he characterized the difference as that between "the Transient" and "the Permanent.") At the same time, he saw a progression of the historic religions toward ultimate Religion. From such an evolutionary perspective all religions—Eastern as well as Western—represented positive steps in the emergence of a higher religious consciousness. But Parker was most Transcendental in his insistence on the independent validity of every individual's view of religion: "As all men are at bottom the same, but as no two nations or ages are exactly alike . . . so therefore, though the religious element be the same in all, we must expect to find its manifestations are never exactly alike in any two ages or nations. . . ." His conclusion was stunning: "From the difference between men, it follows, that there must be as many different subjective conceptions of God, and forms of religion, as there are men and women who think about God. . . ."[63] The radical implication was that every religious viewpoint was equally valid —a blasphemy to most of his contemporaries.

Though clearly on his mind, Oriental religion is barely mentioned in the *Discourse* and usually only in footnotes. However, the references do emphasize his awareness of Eastern thought. At one point, he recommends Priestley's *Comparison of the Institutions of Moses with those of the Hindoos*. Describing pantheism, he remarks that this "mystical tendency" had especially prevailed in the "ancient religions of the East. . . ." At another point, he complains, "It is difficult to determine accurately the date of events in Chinese history, such are the pretensions of Chinese scholars on the one hand, and such the bigoted scepticism of dogmatists on the other. . . ."[64] Obviously, the *Discourse* is memorable not for its extensive treatment of the Oriental religions, but for its attempt at a systematic defense of a universal religious viewpoint; not because it embraces the Oriental perspective, but because it provides a philosophic rationale for adopting a more sympathetic attitude toward Oriental religions. The *Discourse* points up Parker's special significance as a Transcendentalist: while Emerson, Thoreau, and Alcott flaunted intuition and subjective judgment, Parker emphasized the value of systematic inquiry.

If the record indicates that Parker deserves to be remembered as one of America's earliest proponents of a comparative religious viewpoint and as one of the few first-generation Transcendentalists to attempt a systematic inquiry concerning the nature of religion, the question remains: What, if anything, did he know of Oriental thought? He had chastized Emerson for his inadequate knowledge of Oriental literature, complaining that it was "plain" that the Concord thinker had not really understood the "curious philosophy" that he often quoted.[65] May the same judgment be brought against Parker?

He seems to have undertaken the study of Oriental religion while in divinity school, for he mentions that he had "studied the historical development of religion and theology amongst the nations not Jewish or Christian, and attended as well as I then could to the four other great religious sects —the Brahmanic, the Buddhistic, the Classic, and the Mahometan." He also remarks that, "as far as possible" he had "studied the sacred books of mankind in their original tongues, and with the help of the most faithful interpreters."[66] Unfortunately, he does not reveal what he read or his reactions. German scholarship was the most probable source of his knowledge of the Eastern religions. If all Transcendentalists were to some extent Germanophiles, no one equaled Parker's wide acquaintance with German scholarship. German scholars were very prominent in comparative and Oriental studies by the midnineteenth century; an omnivorous reader with proficiency in German as well as other languages, Parker was well equipped to assimilate these studies. Several other early sources are certain: we know that in the 1830s, like other Transcendentalists, he read Cousin's *Cours de philosophie*, which includes a sketch of Indian philosophy. It apparently left a deep impression, for many years later he recommended the work very highly. He also discovered Moore's "Lalla Rookh," commenting in 1835, "I have not lately been so much delighted with any poem as with this little treasury of sweets. It is full of the East. . . ."[67] The reaction is interesting, since Moore conveyed the romantic image of the East that Parker would later repudiate.

Much of the evidence of Parker's acquaintance with Oriental thought is to be found in his correspondence with Convers Francis, a man who deeply influenced his intellectual development. Unitarian minister, scholar, and student of German culture, Francis would soon be called to teach at the Harvard Divinity School. Recognizing Parker's remarkable intellectual promise, Francis became his mentor—loaning him books, advising him on his reading, and listening to his ideas. Indeed, according to one biographer, Francis gave Parker his "first initiation" into Transcendentalism.[68] The ease with which references to Eastern religions crop up in their letters suggests that the topic was a familiar one between them. Parker often sought the older man's reactions to his religious speculations. "Is Revelation at an end? Is the Bible better than the soul? The Hindoo says that of his Veda, the Mohammedan of his Koran," Parker observed in one early letter. On another occasion he wrote, "In the history of religions, which do you take to be the true notion: was this the order in which the human race 'evolved' itself, viz.—1, Fetichism; 2, Polytheism; 3, Monotheism; or was a part of mankind monotheistic from the beginning?"[69] The most revealing exchange should be quoted in full:

> I don't remember any rationalistic explanations of the absurdities in the Indian Vedas. It would be contrary to the genius of the people. It seems to me that fancy predominated over all else with them. They revelled in the improbable; the grotesque took the place which the beautiful takes with us. The scientific-true, it seems to me, they cared little about. I seldom open their works without disgust. Their historians lacked both geography and chronology, . . . and their philosophers were *grannies*, I think. Emerson has come upon them *late*, and both exaggerates their merits, and misleads himself by their *bizarreries*.[70]

If negative, his reaction indicates considerable acquaintance with Oriental thought. It is unusual to find a leading Transcendentalist speaking of Indian religion and civilization so harshly.

There are other indications of Parker's serious interest in Oriental thought. One is the pages of the *Massachusetts Quarterly Review*, the journal he founded in 1847. Though formally listed as coeditor, Parker dominated its operations from the first, writing a sizable proportion of its articles and determining its emphasis. If political and social concerns receive greatest coverage, considerable attention is devoted to Asia. One finds several reviews of books on China, a long, sympathetic review of a Chinese novel, and James Eliot Cabot's important full-length article on "The Philosophy of the Ancient Hindoos"—one of the earliest such pieces to be printed in any American magazine.[71]

Other scattered references that point up a genuine interest include an undated letter thanking a correspondent "for calling my attention to an article on 'Buddhism,'" a subject he had been "studying"; an appreciation of an excellent series of articles on Asian civilization that had been appearing in the *Christian Examiner*; and a tantalizing reference to a meeting with "Salisbury the Orientalist" during an 1848 visit to Yale.[72] An Arabic specialist and writer on Buddhism, Salisbury might have told him much about Eastern religions. Finally, there is an 1851 letter in which he speaks familiarly of Colebrooke's and Schlegel's writings on Indian philosophy, followed by the significant remark: "We are a little too early to learn the Hindoo philosophy. Ten years hence it will be easier. Burnouf is at work on something . . . that will help a good deal."[73] What one misses here is evidence of the close reading in the Oriental classics carried out by Emerson and Thoreau. He perhaps read more widely on the Oriental religions, but not as deeply.

He also took a dimmer view of the Orient. The negativism seems to have increased in his last years, as indicated in a significant 1858 essay on Thomas Buckle's *History of Civilization in England*. Hailing the book as one of the great works of the century, to be compared with Bacon's *Novum Organum* and Newton's *Principia*, he sent Buckle the review and a testimony of his admiration; the men subsequently exchanged appreciative letters. Though he encountered Buckle's ideas late, they seem to have had considerable influence on his thought.[74] This is astonishing in view of Parker's Transcendental commitments.

Much of the essay is devoted to a summary of Buckle's familiar argument that physical factors—food, soil, and climate—explained the differences between civilizations. The Englishman believed that material factors had been the dominant forces in history. Parker was especially fascinated by Buckle's interpretation of the effects of such physical factors on Asian societies, which figure prominently in the essay. One is offered a very unflattering view of Indian civilization. Buckle argued that a tropical climate had encouraged an uncontrolled imagination with the most unfortunate effects. Parker explained,

> The same characteristics appear in the Indian religion. Its mythology, like that of every tropical country, is based upon terror of the most extravagant kind. The most terrible deities are also the most popular. The same thing appears in the Indian art, which is an expression of the monstrous.[75]

One must remember that Parker is summarizing Buckle's view; it seems clear, however, that these were Parker's views as well. He assured his readers that if the Englishman had made mistakes both in fact and interpretation, that Buckle's "grand inductive generalization" remained "secure." He accepted Buckle's "terrible portrait of the destructive deities of the Hindoos," but insisted that Hindu conceptions of God were "less hideous than the Deity set forth by our own Jonathan Edwards."[76] That is, he agreed that the Hindu deities were hideous, but they were *less* hideous than some conceptions found in the West. The views are almost identical with those Parker had used in the letter to Convers Francis quoted earlier, in which he dismissed the "absurdities" of the *Vedas* and characterized the Indians as a people in whom "fancy predominated over all else" and in whom the "grotesque" had prevailed.[77]

Parker offers a fascinating variation on the Transcendental theme. He insisted on the existence of an Absolute Religion, yet affirmed that every person must be the judge of religious truth. He championed a universal religion, yet claimed that Christianity stripped of transient elements represented the true religion. He favored the study of the Eastern religions, yet dismissed Oriental absurdities. He remained an apologist for Christianity, yet went further than most of his contemporaries in affirming the truths to be found in the Oriental religions.

The Transcendentalists were unquestionably the first Americans to approach Asian thought sympathetically and to assimilate Oriental ideas into their world view. Priestley had investigated the Oriental religions earlier, but had not been receptive. He recognized Asian ideas as a position to be rebutted, not incorporated. Most of the Transcendentalists preferred Christianity (this is not clear in Thoreau's case), but none would have disagreed that a better acquaintance with Oriental thought would be beneficial. There seem to be three stages in the assimilation of any new idea or intellectual system—first, hostility, often combined with apathy; next, insistence on the truth of one's own system combined with a willingness to accept complementary truths to be found in other systems; and finally, outright acceptance of some part or all of the new system. Transcendentalism led the way from the first into the second stage.

At the same time the Transcendental view created problems. Trusting in intuition, in the heart rather than the head, Transcendentalists blurred all distinctions in the conception of a universal religion; all religions, including the Oriental religions were viewed as one. The very belief in a uniform human nature and universal religion that promoted a positive view of the Oriental religions tended to obscure recognition of the immense differences between Asian religions. The soaring idealism of the Transcendental faith made differences seem unimportant. The awareness of differences awaited the growth of a more empirical perspective and the rise of Oriental scholarship in the latter decades of the century.

The Transcendental approach was also selective. Emerson, Thoreau, Alcott, and Parker all indicated serious interest in Oriental religion, but Asian thought was only one intellectual concern among many. Transcendentalists were supreme eclectics, drawing freely on many intellectual systems. In focusing on the influence of Asian ideas on the four men, there has been no thought of denying the even greater influence of other elements —Plato and NeoPlatonism on Emerson, Pythagoras on Alcott, or German scholarship on Parker. The intensity of interest in Oriental thought also varied over time. The 1840s was the decade of greatest concern, but references to Asian conceptions continue much later. To sum it up, there is a great deal of evidence that all four men felt real interest in Asian thought at certain points in their lives; however, it is difficult to go further and demonstrate that Oriental thought in fact transformed their thinking. Alcott was the least and Thoreau the most affected, perhaps because Alcott began to read Oriental literature so late and Thoreau at a much younger age than the others.

Finally, other Transcendentalists must not be forgotten. There could have been no movement without Emerson, Thoreau, Alcott, and Parker, but they were not the whole movement. If one recalls the other prominent spokesmen who indicated little or no interest in the East—including George Ripley, Elizabeth Peabody, Orestes Brownson, Frederick Hedge, Ellery Channing, and Margaret Fuller—it becomes apparent that the Orient touched only a minority of Transcendentalists. Nor should the second-generation Transcendentalists be forgotten; they would emerge after the Civil War to broaden the earlier Oriental explorations. I refer to Samuel Johnson, who published a massive three-volume study of *Oriental Religions and their Relation to Universal Religion*; Moncure Conway, who edited the *Sacred Anthology*; and James Freeman Clarke, who contributed the popular *Ten Great Religions*. Indeed, one could argue that Transcendentalism's most significant contributions toward the introduction of Oriental ideas in America came after the Civil War, not before.

Notes

1. William Gilman, et al., eds., *The Journals and Miscellaneous Notebooks of Ralph Waldo Emerson,* 14 vols. (Cambridge, Mass.: Belknap Press of Harvard University Press, 1960-), 5: 452.

2. Leon Edel, *Henry D. Thoreau* (Minneapolis: University of Minnesota Press, 1970), p. 13.

3. Sherman Paul, *The Shores of America: Thoreau's Inward Exploration* (Urbana, Ill.: University of Illinois Press, 1958), pp. 69-71.

4. Thoreau, *Journal*, 1: 55. The *Journal* is published as vols. 7-20 in *The Writings of Henry David Thoreau*, ed. Bradford Torrey and Francis H. Allen, 20 vols. (Walden ed., 1906; reprint ed., New York: AMS Press, 1968). Note that the *Journal* is also numbered separately; vol. 7 of the *Writings* may be also cited as vol. 1 of the *Journal*. Following the practice of other scholars, all *Journal* citations will be listed separately. A citation to the *Writings* will be reserved for published works, poems, and familiar letters, which appear as vols. 1-6 in the full series.

5. Thoreau, *Journal*, 1: 261.

6. Ibid., 1: 266.

7. Ibid., 1: 263; Torrey and Allen, *Writings of Thoreau*, 1: 140.

8. Torrey and Allen, *Writings of Thoreau*, 1: 146.

9. Ibid., 2: 4-5.

10. Several recent students have focused on Thoreau's interest in yoga. See Winfield E. Nagley, "Thoreau on Attachment, Detachment, and Non-Attachment," *Philosophy East and West* 3 (January 1954): 307-20; Sreekrishna Sarma, "A Short Study of the Oriental Influence upon Henry David Thoreau with Special Reference to his *Walden*," *Jahrbuch für Amerikastudien* (Heidelberg) 1 (1956): 76-92; and Frank Macshane, "Walden and Yoga," *New England Quarterly* 37 (September 1964): 322-42.

11. Walter Harding and Carl Bode, eds., *The Correspondence of Henry David Thoreau* (New York: New York University Press, 1958), p. 251.

12. Arthur Christy, *The Orient in American Transcendentalism: A Study of Emerson, Thoreau, and Alcott* (1932; reprint ed., New York: Octagon Books, 1963), p. 199.

14. Ibid., 1: 280, 279. See also ibid., 2: 191, for quotes from the *Harivansa*, that seem to express his deepest thoughts.

15. Torrey and Allen, *Writings of Thoreau*, 1: 72.

16. Thoreau, *Journal*, 2: 4.

17. Torrey and Allen, *Writings of Thoreau*, 1:68. According to Paul, *Shores of America*, p. 219n. the popularity of the *Week* suffered as a result of Thoreau's attack on Christianity.

18. Cf. Harding and Bode, *Correspondence of Thoreau*, p. 447. Lyman V. Cady evaluates the Chinese interests in "Thoreau's Quotations from the Confucian Books in Walden," *American Literature* 33 (March 1961): 20-32.

19. William Ellery Channing, *Thoreau the Poet-Naturalist*, rev. ed., ed. F. B. Sanborn, (Boston: Charles E. Goodspeed, 1902), pp. 49, 50. The original edition was published in 1873.

20. Torrey and Allen, *Writings of Thoreau*, 1: 150.

21. Ibid., 1: 159.

22. Thoreau, *Journal*, 8: 135.

23. Roger Mueller, "The Orient in American Transcendental Periodicals (1835-1886)," (Ph.D. diss., University of Minnesota, 1968), pp. 10-11.

24. Ibid., pp. 99-101, and Arthur Christy, ed., *Transmigration of the Seven Brahmans: A Translation from the Harivansa of Langlois* (New York: W. E. Rudge, 1932).

25. Thoreau, *Journal*, 5: 459.

26. George Ripley, "H. D. Thoreau's Book," *New York Tribune*, June 13, 1849, reprinted in [Samuel A. Jones, ed.], *Pertaining to Thoreau* (Detroit: Edwin B. Hill, 1901), pp. 1-10. Quotes on pp. 6, 8, 1.

27. James Russell Lowell, "A Week on the Concord and Merrimack Rivers," *Massachusetts Quarterly Review*, December 1849, reprinted in [Jones], *Pertaining to Thoreau*, pp. 13-31. Quotes on pp. 24, 25, 26.

28. Edwin Morton, "Thoreau and his Books," *Harvard Magazine*, January 1855, reprinted in [Jones], *Pertaining to Thoreau*, pp. 51-72. Quotes on pp. 67, 68.

29. Thoreau, *Journal*, 8: 464.

30. Harding and Bode, *Correspondence of Thoreau*,p. 403. The original shipping list is published in ibid., pp. 395-96. These have been checked against the books listed in Walter Harding's *Thoreau's Library* (Charlottesville, Va.: University of Virginia Press, 1957). Franklin Sanborn first described the gift in "Thoreau and his English Friend Thomas Cholmondeley," *Atlantic Monthly* 72 (December 1893): 741-56.

31. Harding and Bode, *Correspondence of Thoreau*, pp. 397, 398.

32. Cf. F. B. Sanborn and W. T. Harris, *A. Bronson Alcott. His Life and Philosophy*, 2 vols. (Boston: Roberts Bros., 1893), a crucial source because of the authors' firsthand acquaintance and inclusion of long extracts from Alcott's *Journals*. The standard modern biography is Odell Shepard, *Pedlar's Progress. The Life of Bronson Alcott* (Boston: Little, Brown, 1937).

33. Sanborn and Harris, *Alcott*, 1: 99, 100.

34. Ibid., 1: 137-38.

35. Ibid., 1: 136-37, and chap. 6, pp. 235-302 in the same volume.

36. Ibid., 2: 474.

37. Ibid., 1: 165, and Odell Shepard, ed., *The Journals of Bronson Alcott* (Boston: Little, Brown, 1938), p. 109.

38. Shepard, *Journals of Alcott*, p. 178. Shepard observes, "This appears to be the first recorded instance of Alcott's reading in the literature of India. . . ." See p. 178n.

39. Ibid., p. 180.

40. Ibid., p. 181.

41. Harding and Bode, *Correspondence of Thoreau*, p. 43. See also Shepard, *Journals of Alcott*, pp. 282, 349.

42. Clarence L. F. Gohdes, *The Periodicals of American Transcendentalism* (Durham, N.C.: Duke University Press, 1931), p. 190.

43. Shepard, *Journals of Alcott*, pp. 136-37. The *sic* has been omitted.

44. Cited in Christy, *Orient in American Transcendentalism*, p. 241.

45. Ibid., pp. 242-44.

46. Shepard, *Journals of Alcott,* p. 383. There is still another reference in 1867; cf. ibid., p. 388.

47. Sanborn and Harris, *Alcott,* 1: 332.

48. Franklin B. Sanborn, *Henry D. Thoreau,* rev. ed. (1882, Boston: Houghton Mifflin, 1910), p. 191.

49. Thomas Wentworth Higginson, *Contemporaries* (Boston: Houghton Mifflin, 1899), pp. 29-30.

50. Shepard, *Journals of Alcott,* pp. 402-3.

51. Richard L. Herrnstadt, ed., *The Letters of A. Bronson Alcott* (Ames, Iowa: Iowa State University Press, 1969), p. 767.

52. Christy, *Orient in American Transcendentalism,* p. 238.

53. Bronson Alcott, *Concord Days* (Boston: Roberts Bros., 1872), p. 265. See also pp. 266, 267. For references in *Tablets* (Boston: Roberts Bros., 1868), see pp. 16, 135, 142-43, 162.

54. Any treatment of Parker's life must begin with his own retrospective account, "Experience as a Minister," included in *Autobiography, Poems and Prayers,* published in *The Works of Theodore Parker* [*Centenary Edition*], 14 vols. (Boston: American Unitarian Association, 1907-1911), 13: 275-413. Equally indispensable are three contemporary lives by devoted admirers: John Weiss, *Life and Correspondence of Theodore Parker,* 2 vols. (1864; reprint ed., New York: Bergman Publishers, 19679); Octavius B. Frothingham, *Theodore Parker: A Biography* (Boston: James R. Osgood, 1874); and John W. Chadwick, *Theodore Parker, Preacher and Reformer* (Boston: Houghton Mifflin, 1900). Weiss is especially useful because he reprints so many of Parker's letters. The standard modern life is Henry Steele Commager's *Theodore Parker: Yankee Crusader,* 2nd ed. (1947; paperback reprint, Boston: Beacon Press, 1960).

55. Weiss, *Life of Parker,* 1: 95.

56. Thomas W. Higginson, "Report to the Trustees of the Boston Public Library on the Parker Library," in *Bibliography and Index to the Works of Theodore Parker,* published in *Works of Theodore Parker,* 15: 1-10.

57. Chadwick, *Parker,* 44.

58. Frothingham, *Parker,* p. 177.

59. Weiss, *Life of Parker,* 2: 48.

60. Ibid., 2: 56.

61. Ibid., 2: 55. The outline is on ibid., 2: 50-52.

62. Parker, *A Discourse of Matters Pertaining to Religion,* reprinted in *Works of Theodore Parker,* 1: 35n.

63. Ibid., 1: 37-38.

64. Ibid., 1: 58-59n. Quotes on pp. 79n. and 87n.

65. Parker, "Ralph Waldo Emerson," *The American Scholar* (Boston: American Unitarian Association, 1907), reprinted in *Works of Theodore Parker,* 8: 69-70.

66. Parker, "Experience as a Minister," in *Works of Theodore Parker,* 13: 300.

67. Weiss, *Life of Parker,* 1: 64. Theodore Parker, "A Letter Concerning a Plan of Reading," *Saint Bernard and Other Papers* (Boston: American Unitarian Association, 1911), reprinted in *Works of Theodore Parker,* 14: 225. Quote in Frothingham, *Parker,* p. 59.

68. Chadwick, *Parker*, p. 29. See also Commager, *Parker*, p. 24.

69. Weiss, *Life of Parker*, 1: 119, 174.

70. Ibid., 1: 364.

71. *Massachusetts Quarterly Review* 1 (December 1847): 126; 1 (March 1848): 265-66; 2 (December 1848): 129-34. James Eliot Cabot's article appears in *Massachusetts Quarterly Review* in ibid. 1(September 1848): 401-22.

72. Weiss, *Life of Parker*, 1: 389, 267, 275 and 2: 354. Quotes on pp. 275, 389.

73. Ibid., 1: 381.

74. Theodore Parker, "Buckle's History of Civilization," *The American Scholar*, reprinted in *Works of Theodore Parker*, 8: 364-418. See Parker's comment quoted in Weiss, *Life of Parker*, 1: 463, and George Willis Cooke's statement appended to the Buckle review, *Works of Theodore Parker*, 8: 523.

75. Parker, *Works of Theodore Parker*, 8: 381.

76. Ibid., 8: 378, 414.

77. Quoted in Weiss, *Life of Parker*, 1: 364. That Parker had read Buckle some months earlier is indicated in his letter of December 29, 1857, to Professor Henry D. Rogers. Cf. *Works of Theodore Parker*, 8: 522.

5
The Missionary View

In tracing the dawning American consciousness of Oriental religion in the first half of the nineteenth century, one other movement that had special reasons for getting to know the East must be considered. This was the missionary movement, or more accurately, the Protestant missionary movement, since American Catholicism played little role in Asian missions before 1900. Its view was profoundly negative: where the Transcendentalist ignored the blemishes and celebrated the higher truths, the missionary magnified the blemishes and denounced the delusions promoted by the Asian faiths. Indeed, the darkest, most unpleasant portraits ever drawn of Asian religions originated with the nineteenth-century missionary. The missionary view is important as the major source of the negative view that many Americans held in the nineteenth century.

The impulse to establish missions in Asia after 1810 represented a sudden and unexpected movement in American Protestantism. Though John Eliot and David Brainerd had labored among the Indians and Cotton Mather had written in support of a mission in the West Indies, most early American Christians had shown indifference and even hostility toward establishing foreign missions.[1] In New England, where the movement was to rise and first flourish, Puritan theology stood in the way. The doctrine of predestination promoted the belief that salvation was, after all, God's doing, not man's, since only His intervention could provide salvation. Moreover, the doctrine of the elect emphasized that only a small number should expect salvation. It was easy to conclude that if He desired the conversion of the "heathen," He would ordain it—at His time and in His own way. Besides, a raw, new society had enough problems in mere survival, without permitting a diversion of energies to the other side of the world.

Several factors promoted a more positive view as the eighteenth century advanced. Theologically, the most important development was the increasing emphasis on the human role in the drama of salvation, a profound shift caused by the decline of the older Calvinism, the growth of Arminianism, and the powerful evangelical impulse encouraged by the Great Awakening and Second Awakening. The philosophical rationale was provided by Samuel Hopkins (1721-1803), a disciple of Jonathan Edwards, who argued for the doctrine of "Disinterested Benevolence": that as a matter of duty, the true Christian must be willing to work for improvement in his fellowmen's condition for the greater glory of God.[2] The opportunity for a missionary effort was opened by the new commercial ties inaugurated by the voyage of the *Empress of China*, which established Asian contact and drew the attention of evangelical Christians to the millions in China and India who had never heard of Jesus.

The immediate stimulus came from evangelicals in Great Britain, who not only deeply influenced the creation of a missionary movement in this country, but directed early American attention toward India. In the last decade of the eighteenth century missionary groups were sprouting in Britain, including the English Baptist Missionary Society, founded in 1792, London Missionary Society (1795), Scottish Missionary Society (1796), and Church Missionary Society (1800). These missionary organizations became models for similar bodies in America. Perhaps the greatest British stimulus was the magnificent example of William Carey, a former cobbler who inaugurated the so-called Serampore Mission in India in 1792. Carey's *Enquiry into the Obligations to Use Means for the Conversion of the Heathens* had immense influence in persuading Americans to take up the cross.[3]

Circumstances in India promoted an especially intimate relationship between the Serampore missionaries and American Christians. Until 1833 the British East India Company sought to prevent missionary activity, so that for several decades English missionaries bound for India came to America to book passage on American ships. Placed in regular contact, pious Americans were drawn to the cause and were soon contributing financial support for the English effort. Recognizing the importance of this support, Carey took pains to keep American sympathizers informed of the progress of the work through regular letters to America.

A significant body of Americans must have gained their first impression of India's people and religions through these communications, which were widely reprinted in American periodicals. India and Indians were portrayed in the worst possible light. In a typical 1800 letter, Carey suggested that no people had "more completely surrendered their reason than the Hindoos"; their books were filled with the "most abominable stories" and the "characters of their gods" were so "black that even the father of wickedness himself" would have disowned them.[4] India's "Black legend"—the standard interpretation among nineteenth-century evangelical Christians—was underway. Thanks to *The Panoplist*, the most important early American missionary journal, Americans were kept well informed concerning the Serampore missionaries' work. In one typical letter, dated in 1808, the English missionaries lamented the "number of perishing souls" in Calcutta and noted the "multitudes" who had lately come to hear them preach—obviously a challenge to American readers.[5] The impression that Hindus were hungering for Christianity and that mass conversions would quickly result from missionary effort pervaded the early communications. Americans were already girding themselves to join the cause.

In 1810 the American Board of Commissioners for Foreign Missions (ABCFM), the most important American missionary body in the first half of the century, was formed, and two years later the first missionaries were dispatched to India. The group included five devout young men who had come together at Andover Theological Seminary—Samuel Newell, Adoniram Judson, Samuel Nott, Gordon Hall, and Luther Rice.[6] Twenty years would pass before a similar effort was made in China. Despite incredible hardships and many setbacks—including harassment by local government officials, frequent sickness, early deaths, and very slow progress in making converts—the missionary enterprise in Asia steadily expanded. If the ABCFM led the way, most denominations soon established their own work. The Reformed Church began to send its own missionaries to India as early as 1819; it was followed by the Presbyterians in 1833, Baptists in 1835, Lutherans in 1841, and Methodists in 1856. Though the first American missionaries were not sent to China until 1830, there were eighty-eight American missionary workers present by 1860, making China the main focus and showcase of later nineteenth-century American activity.[7]

In discussing the attitudes of nineteenth-century American missionaries toward Oriental religions, one must constantly remember the deep Christian commitment that led the missionary to give up a secure life in America for the hardships and uncertainties of life in the Far East. Clearly, the missionary went to Asia to give, not to receive. Jesus' command made this perfectly clear: "Go therefore and make disciples of all nations, baptising them in the name of the Father and of the Son and of the Holy Spirit, teaching them to observe all that I have commanded you; and lo, I am with you always, to the close of the age."[8] The command was to go and to teach, and the early missionary tended to follow the injunction literally.

Placed in a more favorable position than most nineteenth-century Americans to study Oriental religions, the missionary rarely utilized the opportunity. Since his view had already been established before going to Asia, his reports concerning Eastern religions are for the most part similar and unaffected by residence in the country.

The physical and cultural limitations under which the missionary worked should also be recalled. Under the best of conditions any American traveler faces immense difficulty in assimilating radically different conceptions and experiences to be encountered in the Orient. Conditions in the first decades of the missionary's work made understanding especially difficult. Until the Opium Wars of the 1830s and 1840s, the only areas in China open to American missionaries were sections of Canton. A port city that confined foreign traders and merchants to a small area, it hardly provided a suitable observation point to study Chinese religion and civilization. It should be added that most missionaries entered China or India ignorant of the country's languages. Some made strenuous efforts to acquire proficiency, but the missionary rarely understood either the language or the culture of the country in which he labored. Finally, the typical missionary was young, usually in his early twenties, had never traveled outside the United States, and had grown up on a farm.[9] Such a background did little to prepare him for the multiple culture shocks experienced upon entering the very old, very complex societies of Asia.

A survey of the ordination sermons preached as the young missionary recruit completed his religious training and prepared to depart for a distant station, a popular ceremonial event in the decades after 1810, suggests that a negative view toward Oriental religions had already been instilled before the missionary left American shores. The sermon of Professor Leonard Woods, Abbot Professor of Christian Theology at the Andover Theological Seminary, who preached at the ordination of the original contingent of Newell, Judson, Nott, and Rice in 1812, offers an excellent example. A passionate appeal and justification of the inauguration of missionary work among the "heathen" of Asia, the sermon painted a pathetic scene: "See the poor, degraded Africans. See the thousands of children sacrificed in the Ganges. See the throngs of miserable pilgrims pressing forward to devote themselves to the impure and sanguinary worship of Moloch." However, he emphasized that *"The souls of all these are as precious as your own."*[10] The "heathen"—or perhaps one should say the "heathen soul"—was dear to God; his religion was an abomination.

Moses Stuart, also of Andover Seminary, was even more blunt in an 1818 sermon. He called attention to the need for Christianity by a comparison of the non-Christian faiths. "Compare the followers of Brahma and Mohammed, with the real disciples of Jesus!" he exhorted his listeners. "Compare them in their most holy things—the sacred rites of their religion. Juggernaut will tell you how to estimate the Hindoos. . . . *Impurity* and *blood* is written on the banners of Brahma, through all the East. . . ." The ultimate test of any faith was the attitude toward suffering and the kind of society that resulted from adopting its doctrines. The failure of the non-Christian religions was overwhelming: "Walk in the suburbs of Canton, of the temple of Juggernaut, of Constantinople—and see thousands of miserable wretches, every year, absolutely perishing with hunger and nakedness, while not a single hand is moved, or heart touched for them." Finally, Stuart emphasized that the evils were not partial but all-pervasive and the abuses no aberration but central to "heathen" religion. "The gods of India, and of the whole heathen world, almost without exception, are of the very basest character, which the imagination can form; and as religion always consists in a resemblance of the worshipper to his god, a heathen devotee, of *necessity* is a bad man," he declared.[11] Such a conclusion seemed to repudiate Woods's admonition that the souls of Asians were also precious to God.

Most of the early missionaries to India were sent by the American Board of Commissioners for Foreign Missions and were concentrated in two areas: the Mahratta Mission in northwest India, founded in 1813, and the Madura Mission in south India, established in 1834. An auxiliary effort was opened in Ceylon (Sri Lanka) in 1834, with frequent rotations of missionary workers between India and Ceylon.[12] From the first, Hindu religious life came in for comment. The mission was to spread the Gospel, but a certain fascination with the exotic was natural. Indeed, some acquaintance with Oriental religions was necessary, since the enemy needed to be known to be vanquished.

What did the missionary say of Hinduism? One immediate answer is a good deal. The *Missionary Herald*, the successor of *The Panoplist* and official organ of the ABCFM, is literally filled with communications concerning Indian religious practices. Perhaps because American missionaries went to India first and in greater numbers than to other Asian countries, Hinduism received much greater attention than the other Oriental religions.

In almost every case the Hinduism that was discussed was the popular Hinduism encountered in the streets and temples of nineteenth-century India, not the more philosophical religion that the Transcendentalists had discovered in the sacred literature. The distinction is crucial and explains the radical divergence in early accounts of Indian religion. To a large extent, the Western admirer has always identified Hinduism with the lofty ideals embodied in the *Upanishads* while the detractor has associated it with its popular forms and aberrations. Thus, while Emerson and Thoreau extolled the timeless truths revealed in the *Upanishads* and the *Bhagavad-Gita*, the missionary indicted the fresh excesses perpetuated daily in the name of Siva and the god Jagannath. The emphasis on Hinduism's more sensational features, of course, served the missionary strategy of identifying Hinduism with its least attractive aspects.

One motif running through practically every missionary account was the importance of austerities and self-torture in all forms of Hinduism. Indeed, most of the early ordination sermons alluded to such practices; the result was that the typical missionary seems to have come east expecting to be shocked. Occasionally one even senses the new arrival's actual disappointment that the practices observed were not more horrible. Thus, Luther Rice, one of the earliest Americans to gain admission to India, observed that he had "seen but one instance of self-torture" since his arrival in Calcutta and "that of so moderate a character, compared with some others, that here it would be scarcely noticed."[13] The reported incident seems astonishing enough—a Hindu stretched out on the ground and rhythmically beating himself with a brick—but Rice had apparently expected more.

Many forms of self-torture were described—the yogi who gazed at the sun until blinded, the ascetic who had himself closed off in a cave and never came out, or the *fakir* who stood on one leg or held up an arm so continuously that it became paralyzed in that position. (That many Westerners still automatically associate Hinduism with the notorious yogi on his bed of nails testifies to the continuing impact of the missionary literature.[14]) Judged by the frequency with which it is mentioned, "hook-swinging" seemed to be the missionary favorite. Reading the accounts, one might easily conclude that it was the popular pastime of most Hindus. The practice involved the insertion of hooks in the fleshy parts of the body, particularly the back; the hooks were tied to a pole and the devotee was twirled about it. During the rotations the Hindu might pantomime a battle scene, smoke, eat, or merely eye the crowd gathered to witness his act.[15] The principle behind such austerities was the demonstration of indifference to pain and the subjugation of the body, viewed as prerequisites to spiritual advancement, but in many cases the practice had clearly degenerated into exhibitionism. Perhaps the closest Western analogy would be the feats performed in circus sideshows.

While the missionary expressed appropriate horror, he obviously relished describing hook-swinging as a powerful witness to Hinduism's low state. After minutely describing one such demonstration, the missionary sadly confessed that, "I retired with more abhorrence of paganism, and more pity for deluded pagans, than I have ever before felt." The point made over and over was that such practices defined authentic Hinduism, that self-torture represented the very essence of Hindu teaching. Another missionary warned readers that they must not think such austerities were limited to a few worshipers. On the contrary, "All their principal gods" had "festivals annually celebrated in their honor, some of which last several days" during which "self-torture of some kind or other" was "inflicted."[16] Most missionaries should have known that such austerities were hardly unique to Hinduism, as indicated by the prominence of hair-shirts and self-flaggelation among Christian ascetics. Later Hindu apologists would protest that such aberrations may be found in all religions and that the philosophic monism of *Vedanta*, representing Hinduism's highest expression, has little to do with such practices.

However misguided, the practice of hook-swinging did not usually cost the devotee his life. The same could not be said of the worship of the god Jagannath (usually referred to as "Juggernath" in contemporary Western accounts), which was believed to cost hundreds and even thousands of lives annually. The special ceremonies, held annually at Puri in Orissa, always attracted hundreds of thousands and even millions of pilgrims from all over India. The high point of the celebration involved pulling a huge statue of Jagannath through the streets on a massive cart. As the immense crowd moved, participants frequently fell under the cart's wheels or were trampled. The missionaries insisted that many crazed devotees actually threw themselves under the cart as sacrifices. (The modern English word "juggernaut," of course, derives from the festival; significantly, it is defined as an overpowering, destructive force.)

Despite expressions of intense repugnance—one viewer describing the Jagannath statue as "probably the coarsest image in the country"[17]—missionary observers flocked to the annual display of the god. Indeed, it became one of the country's major tourist attractions, drawing Western travelers of all types. Like hook-swinging, it was meticulously described in the *Missionary Herald*. One classic description was penned by the Reverend Claudius Buchanan, an English missionary whose writings were highly esteemed in American missionary circles. In a dramatic 1806 report, he wrote as one lucky to survive to tell the story: "I have seen Juggernaut. . . . No record of ancient or modern history can give, I think, an adequate idea of this valley of death. . . ."[18] The account would have done honor to a Romantic poet: the exotic appearance of the crowd, the gorgeous trappings of the procession, the awful appearance of Jagannath, and the frenzied reactions of devotees are all evoked in the most expressive language. Shuddering at the experience, Buchanan expressed a feeling of "doing wrong" in witnessing the event; "appalled at the magnitude and horror of the spectacle," he confessed that he "felt like a guilty person, on whom all eyes were fixed. . . ." At one point he had actually moved to withdraw, but drawn back, witnessed the horrifying spectacle of a devotee who had lovingly lain down before the cart to be crushed to death. Returning to the grounds the following day, he discovered the bones of still another victim. Contemplating the grisly remains, he meditated: "And this, thought I, is the worship of the brahmins of Hindoostan! And their worship in its sublimest degree! What then shall we think of their private manners, and their moral principles!"[19] Although other reports lack Buchanan's dramatic intensity, they almost always emphasize the sacrifice of worshipers and the excesses of the ceremonies.[20]

The Jagannath observances were condemned not only for their bloodshed, but also for their immorality, another theme emphasized in the usual presentation of Hinduism. Practically every missionary who described the Jagannath ceremony made some reference to "indecent" or "immoral" practices. Buchanan not only mentioned "lascivious" gestures; he actually described one in a fleeting reference. The editor of one account observed that he had been forced to excise a paragraph from an eyewitness report because of its lasciviousness.[21] The charge was soon broadened to include all aspects of Hinduism. Explaining cuts in Gordon Hall's account of Hinduism, the editor declared, "Some of the passages, though perfectly proper to be communicated to the officers of a missionary society, would be quite improper to be published." He also noted that "amusements" were frequently presented at festivals before mixed audiences that were so "scandalously obscene" that they did not "admit of description in a Christian country."[22] The sexual explicitness of Hindu religious art was also frequently condemned.

Fifty years later, Hindu writers were still bitterly protesting missionary misrepresentations of the Jagannath ceremonies, objecting that if worshipers occasionally lost their lives, this was not a matter of human sacrifice but of uncontrolled mob behavior. The presence of so many worshipers in a confined area would inevitably lead to accidents.[23] Even if no Hindu had ever lost his life and the procession had been completely controlled, Jagannath would probably have still figured prominently in missionary accounts. The whole ceremony reeked of idol worship, which the missionary was committed to extirpate. By identifying Hinduism with the worship of idols, missionaries found it easy to justify the destruction of Indian religion. If the Jagannath celebration had not existed, the nineteenth-century missionary would have been tempted to invent it. To some extent he did.

Hinduism as portrayed by the missionary was not only to be condemned for its religious failings, but also for its harmful social consequences. It was declared over and over that the relative merits of Christianity and Hinduism could be best determined by a comparison of the societies in America and India. The wretchedness of India, the incredible poverty, the disease, and suffering were consequently viewed as direct affects of Hinduism.

Two practices came in for special condemnation: *sati*, or "suttee" as it was known in the West, and female infanticide. In *sati* the widow of a recently deceased husband was burned on the funeral pyre with her mate; the act was said to be the highest tribute a grieving widow could pay her husband's memory. Though the British government had strenuously worked to suppress the practice, missionary observers insisted that it was still widely observed, one account revealing that between 1815 and 1824 in the Bengal presidency alone a total of 6,000, or an average of nearly 600 women a year, were its victims. The *Missionary Herald* published several vivid accounts of such burnings, portraying the wives as pitiful, unwilling victims who had to be physically forced to carry out the act.[24] Female infanticide was also portrayed as a widespread practice, indicating the inhumanity of Hindu parents toward their children. Missionary writers hammered the point that both evils were direct consequences of Hindu religious belief. "These evils are not things that *were*, but things that *now are*," one writer emphasized. "They result directly from the religious systems now adhered to by, perhaps, 150,000,000 of people; religious systems, whose direct and powerful tendency is to pollute, rather than purify mankind. . . ."[25] Both practices were also interpreted as assaults against women. This was a very serious charge in a time of rising sensitivity, which would culminate in a full-scale woman's rebellion in the decades before the Civil War. The widely embraced claim that Hinduism mistreated its women soon became a standard complaint.

Recognizing that the future of missions depended upon the country's youth, in the 1830s the editors of the *Missionary Herald* introduced a special monthly series designed to educate young readers about "heathen" religious practices. Written in a simplified style and supplemented by vivid pictures, the series suggests the "Weekly Readers" used in modern schools. Typically, each installment focused on one area of "heathen" belief and included a page-size engraving of the rite or practice to be discussed, followed by a three- or four-page description culled from missionary writings. A sizable number were devoted to Oriental religious practices, the very first one focusing on hook-swinging. The second number described the worship of the Hindu triad—Brahma, Vishnu, and Siva. Later installments offer illustrated accounts of the incarnations of Vishnu, the life of Buddha, missionary work in Siam, the worship of Jagannath, Hindu self-torture, and the worship of the Hindu god Indra. The most terrifying piece for young readers must have been a description of the sacrifice of children in Sri Lanka; in the illustration two women are shown handing over their children to be devoured by a ferocious goddess.[26] It is impossible to guess how widely the series was read; however, the strange engravings and vivid descriptions were well designed to reach young people and undoubtedly had something to do with perpetuating the dark image of Oriental religions.

If the typical missionary account was marked by a relentless hostility, the mission worker who spent much time in India was often forced to make concessions as he recognized that the realities of Asian life were more complex than he had first thought. The softening foreshadows a more sympathetic attitude toward Oriental religions that emerged among increasing numbers of missionaries in the century's last decades. One of the earliest and most unhappy revelations was the discovery that the Hindu was not eagerly awaiting conversion as many had been led to believe. As one disgusted missionary lamented, most Hindus did not indicate the "least desire" to know the truth. "You may convince a Hindoo of a truth an hundred times, and make him confess it," he complained, but if it served his purposes "he will as often deny it." The difficulty was often attributed to the Hindu's singular moral obtuseness. In the field longest, the Baptist missionaries at Serampore should have known Hinduism best. If so, they could give little encouragement to those who expected a rapid Christian victory. Warning against expectations that the "great edifice of Hindoo superstition" was about to fall, one wrote, "We are too well acquainted with its strength and solidity, to interpret the opening of an arch or two, or the decay of part of its foundation, into any indication of immediate dissolution. Enough, alas, of the system still remains, and is likely long to remain, to retard the progress of improvement."[27] Though hardly sympathetic, such views reflected a new and grudging respect for Hinduism as a system of belief.

Another realization that soon dawned upon many missionaries was the recognition that the Hindu was not inevitably the benighted, uninformed believer most had expected. How was a Christian to deal with the sophisticated rejoinder noted by William Ramsey in a conversation with several Hindus? After listening politely to his arguments, one had replied that "they thought my religion was good for me, and theirs for them."[28] Hinduism has, of course, long been noted for its broad tolerance and cosmopolitan spirit: unable to ignore a competing system, it has characteristically incorporated it. Acquaintance with the sacred literature of Hinduism also helped moderate missionary biases. Such reading became fairly widespread among the more literate missionaries, serving both to improve language skills and to acquaint one with the system to be overthrown. The results could be unsettling. Ramsey, who has just been cited, revealed that he had been reading the *Bhagavad-Gita*, helped by his pandit who explained the more obscure passages. Ramsey confessed that he had "been struck with the resemblance many of its parts bear to the Scripture history. It does seem to me that the writer, whoever he may have been, had some knowledge of the word of God."[29] Such a recognition made it difficult to view Hinduism with the same contempt as before.

The dramatic transformation that could develop from living in an Asian culture over a number of years is suggested by a fascinating letter written by Henry Scudder in 1848, after nearly four years in the Madras area. The letter opens with a list of the things Scudder had come to admire in Hindu life—in itself a radical shift in missionary perspective. "I love India.

I love her soil; I love her people," Scudder rhapsodized. "I repudiate as a calumny many things that have been said of this country." Bypassing the standard denunciations, he insisted that India was a pleasant land, that its languages and literature were rich and interesting, and that the Hindu people were extremely attractive. Most remarkable for a missionary, he argued that the Hindu people had shown wonderful forbearance in the face of repeated Christian attacks and deserved high praise for their civility. He particularly defended Hindu intellectual powers, warning that missionary trainees in America who looked upon India as an intellectual backwash were "sadly deceived." On the contrary, he affirmed that during his years in India the "heathen" had taught him a "vast deal" and on many occasions "set all my wits agog. . . ."[30] To be sure, Scudder went on in the same letter to condemn the Hindus for holding false religious doctrines and to castigate the awful consequences of the Hindu social system, but the attacks do not conceal a new spirit. If appreciations are rare before the Civil War, they are increasingly common after.

Beginning in the 1830s American missionary efforts in the East were focused increasingly on China, providing contact with Buddhism, Confucianism, and Taoism. The attitude was as hostile as that toward Hinduism. The degree to which nearly identical reactions were expressed toward each of the Asian religions suggests that in the first generation the missionary did not so much perceive as confirm negative images brought from America. Though "heathenism" might take endless shapes and conceal itself behind many masks, the inner core always seemed to be the same.[31]

Active American interest in China as a missionary field goes back at least to 1807 when Robert Morrison, the first English Protestant missionary to China, began operations at Canton. As already noted in connection with William Carey's work in India, Anglo-American cooperation was the keynote in the early ventures. Morrison originally made his way to China by way of the United States, stopping long enough to get a letter from Secretary of State James Madison requesting the American consul in Canton to assist him.[32] Once in China, the Englishman kept Americans informed of his work through occasional letters in *The Panoplist*. Pressed to provide some idea of China and Chinese religion, Morrison offered brief resumes in letters published in *The Panoplist* in 1809, among the earliest presentations of Chinese religion to appear in an American journal. He noted the large number of gods worshiped in China, but observed that they were not taken seriously. On the other hand, Confucius' writings were greatly esteemed. Though the typical advocate of missions was a congenital optimist, Morrison warned that the missionary recruit should expect a prolonged labor before expecting even a small success.[33]

Finally in 1830—surprisingly late when one recalls that the original

American contact went all the way back to 1784—Elijah Bridgman and David Abeel departed as the first American missionaries to China. They were soon joined by Samuel Wells Williams, Ira Tracy, Edwin Stevens, and Peter Parker. For years the survival of the original beachhead owed a great deal to D. W. C. Olyphant, a devout American trader who provided free boat passage and a considerable part of the expenses. The Americans worked closely with Morrison and subsequently with his son.[34] Restricted at first to Macao and Canton, the missionaries suffered the same isolation faced by early missionaries in India. In the absence of direct contacts, they concentrated on literary activities, the study of native languages, and translation of the Bible into Chinese. In 1832 the *Chinese Repository* was initiated; published for the next twenty years, its pages provide a crucial source concerning early missionary attitudes toward Chinese religion.

Like his coworker in India, the missionary to China usually arrived with firm preconceptions. Days after his arrival young Samuel Wells Williams wrote to his father, "I have been here a week, and in that short time have seen enough of idolatry to call forth all the energies I have."[35] David Abeel, who was forced to return to the United States within a year because of failing health, discerned a pervasive "moral debasement. Their temples are numerous, their gods without number," he wrote "One idol, and frequently more, are seated in state, in every temple. . . . Some of these are frightful looking figures; all are gross in form. . . ."[36] The same language is to be found in a hundred other accounts: idolatry, degradation, immorality, idolatry, degradation, immorality. A modern reader quickly develops battle fatigue reading the reports.

Since the opinions closely parallel similar judgments of Hinduism, there seems little point in repeating the denunciations. The attempt to generalize the missionary's response to each of China's traditional religions seems more promising. Indeed, despite some confusion, most missionaries quickly grasped the fact that China presented a society of not one, but three major religions: Confucianism, Buddhism, and Taoism. Considering the fact that few Americans could distinguish Hinduism from Buddhism (including a literate man such as Emerson), this was an accomplishment. Of the three, Taoism received such cursory treatment that it will be passed over. It was to remain the least known of the Oriental religions until the twentieth century.

Buddhism came under much discussion, undoubtedly because of its large following and immense influence, but also because of the growing recognition bestowed on it by European scholars. Very much aware of the work of Western scholars, the China-based missionary indicated increasing irritation at the glossing of Buddhism's failings.[37] Charles Gutzlaff charged that, out of a misplaced desire to "discover a rational system of idolatry," the scholars were correcting Buddhism's "moral deficiencies" out of their "own stores of knowledge" and then presenting the result as the "most commendable and rational" of systems.[38] (German by birth, Gutzlaff worked closely with the Anglo-American mission; his attempt to get Bibles into the hands of the Chinese people by illegal sorties up and down the coast of China made him a popular hero in America.[39]) The typical scholar drew his picture at second hand, accepting a highly idealized literary account in place of the real thing; Gutzlaff insisted that there was no alternative to direct experience. It was not that Buddhism lacked all appeal, and a number of writers in the *Chinese Repository* recognized redeeming features, Gutzlaff conceding that it was the "least degrading" of the Oriental systems and that in China it appeared in its "least objectionable form." In the end, however, it was pervaded by "atheism" and "gross idolatry."[40] Although ranked a little above Hinduism, the religion of Buddha was still judged a cruel and false system.

Though Confucianism is regularly mentioned in the pages of the *Chinese Repository*, little attempt was made to examine the great master's teachings.[41] Most of the missionaries recognized that the ancient philosopher's teachings pervaded Chinese society, exercizing an even greater impact than Buddhism. His influence was regarded as the common source of both the negative and positive features of Chinese life: the origin of the Chinese people's haughty attitude toward outsiders and mindless adherence to tradition, but also of their rational, down-to-earth character. Confucius' greatest legacy was that he freed the Chinese people of the cant found in other Oriental peoples. Extolling Confucian man, Edwin Stevens characterized the typical Chinese as a "man of business" and "prudent foresight," who had avoided the "established and pampered priesthood" and "unnatural and absurd superstitions" of "weaker or more debased nations." His sympathies are clear: "We suppose there remains in the Chinese mind in general an unusual share, for a pagan people, of the elements of right reasoning and sound judgment."[42] Several writers specifically compared Chinese and Hindu civilization, indicating that the key difference was China's Confucian avoidance of the heavy metaphysics and pervasive religiosity of India.[43]

The evidence is clear. While rigidly opposed to Chinese religion and deeply committed to the conversion of the Chinese, the missionary developed real affection and admiration for the Chinese people and their achievements. Elijah Bridgman sums up the view: ". . . All in all, we suspect the Chinese will not, in natural endowments, suffer in comparison with the inhabitants of any other equal portion of the globe."[44] A people who made common sense and hard work a philosophy of life, Americans inevitably admired the same traits in other peoples. China's achievements as a civilization were also recognized. Comparing Chinese literature to that of Greece and Rome,

Bridgman argued that if one did not find the same beauties of style, the Chinese nevertheless had "their own claim to excellence. . . ." Their books abounded in "ingenious expressions, striking illustrations, curious comparisons, and bold metaphors."[45] J. R. Morrison emphasized that in the growing contact between China and the West, the West would benefit as well as China. The manufacture of porcelain and cultivation of tea were only two examples.[46] Like the missionaries in India, American missionaries who spent much time in China soon recognized that they were confronting an ancient civilized people.

But one must not allow sincere but occasional affirmations to obscure the only possible conclusion: in general, early Anglo-American missionaries viewed Chinese religion and Chinese civilization very darkly. Admirable among Orientals, the Chinese achievement hardly deserved comparison with that of a higher Christian civilization. Consider Robert Morrison's comparison of the Bible with the Chinese classics: "When contrasted with the sacred books of China, how poor in conception, how mean in execution, do the latter appear!" Or his comparison of Jesus and Confucius: "The sage of China who has been honored and idealized more than twenty centuries, is utterly insignificant, when put in competition with the herdmen and fishermen of Galilee."[47] Finally, one may return to Elijah Bridgman, whose warm appreciations of the Chinese have already been quoted. He wrote, "So far as I have been able to ascertain, the Chinese have *no knowledge of God*. . . ." And further on, "Gross and carnal, their moral and religious sense is dull. They are almost without a conscience. . . ."[48] In noticing affirmative remarks, the intention has not been to conceal the sweeping denunciations, but to call attention to the seeds of another view that lurked beneath the surface.

One final consideration remains, namely the large role played by the China missionary in launching American Sinological studies. When the American Oriental Society was inaugurated in 1844, missionaries were heavily counted upon and, on the whole, played a major role.[49] The new Oriental scholarship would have immense significance for subsequent American explorations of Asian ideas by providing key texts and explications of the great Eastern religious writings. The Anglo-American missionaries led the way as one can see by returning to the *Chinese Repository*.

As the new journal's editor and dominating spirit, Elijah Bridgman explained the *Repository*'s raison d'être in a long note appended to the first issue. Expressing "astonishment" that there had been "so little commerce in intellectual and moral commodities" over the long period of the West's intercourse with Asia, he indicated the desire of the *Repository* to close the gap between the West and China. China, he explained, offered the "widest, and the most interesting field of research under heaven."[50] Thus, from the beginning, Bridgman and his coworkers embraced the ideal of scholarship and the advancement of knowledge as a major objective. For the next twenty years, the *Chinese Repository* reflected this commitment.

A brief examination of the *Repository* suggests the great value and wide range of research carried out by the Anglo-American group. There are articles on bordering countries, but most focus on China. There are contributions on the geography, plant and animal life, government, military organization, history, artistic achievement, literature, economic life, and foreign relations of the Chinese empire. Representative articles include Bridgman's "Penal Laws of China," Ira Tracy's "Condition of Females among the Chinese," S. Wells Williams's "Agriculture in China," J. R. Morrison's "Structure of the Chinese Government," Gutzlaff's "Remarks on the Japanese Language," and W. M. Lowrie's "Readings in Chinese Poetry."[51] As we have seen, Chinese religious life also received much attention. In addition to pieces already noted, one encounters such articles as Edwin Stevens's "Chinese Theology," S. Wells Williams's "Worship of Ancestors among the Chinese," Robert Morrison's "Metempsychosis," and G. H. Burger's "Religious Worship of the Japanese."[52] Though practically all the contributions are permeated by missionary bias, much general information is communicated. Considering the richness of its coverage, the suspension of the *Repository* at the end of 1851 for lack of funds was a major setback for serious students of Chinese civilization. No nineteenth-century American publication gave China so much attention.

Notes

1. James S. Udy, "Attitudes Within the Protestant Churches of the Occident towards the Propagation of Christianity in the Orient: An Historical Survey to 1914" (Ph.D. diss., Boston University, 1952). See particularly chap. 2, pp. 25-45.

2. See Oliver W. Elsbree, "The Rise of the Missionary Spirit in New England, 1790-1815," *New England Quarterly* 1 (July 1928): 295-322.

3. Kenneth S. Latourette, *The History of Early Relations between the United States and China, 1784-1844* (New Haven, Conn.: Yale University Press, 1917), pp. 85-87.

4. Leighton and Mornay Williams, eds., *Serampore Letters Being the Unpublished Correspondence of William Carey and Others with John Williams, 1800-1816* (New York: G. P. Putnam's, 1892), p. 61.

5. "East Indies," *The Panoplist* 4 (October 1808): 237. For other communications from Carey and his coworkers, see ibid. 2 (August 1806): 138; 2 (April 1807): 530-33; 3 (July 1807): 86-88; 3 (February 1808): 421; 4 (January 1809): 378-80; 5 (May 1810): 568-69; 6 (June 1810): 36-45; 6 (May 1811): 569-72; and 8 (June 1812): 43-44.

6. Clifton J. Phillips, *Protestant America and the Pagan World: The First Half Century of the American Board of Commissioners for Foreign Missions, 1810-1860* (Cambridge, Mass.: Harvard East Asian Monographs no. 32, 1969).

7. Bernard S. Stern, "American Views of India and Indians, 1857-1900" (Ph.D. diss., University of Pennsylvania, 1956), pp. 7-8, and Foster R. Dulles, *China and America: The Story of their Relations since 1784* (Princeton, N.J.: Princeton University Press, 1946), p. 42.

8. Matthew 28: 19-20 (Revised Standard Version).

9. Phillips, *Protestant America and the Pagan World*, pp. 30-31.

10. Leonard Woods, *A Sermon Delivered at the Tabernacle in Salem, Feb. 6, 1812* . . . (Boston: Samuel T. Armstrong, Cornhill, 1812). p. 12.

11. Moses Stuart, *A Sermon Preached in the Tabernacle Church, Salem, Nov. 5, 1818* . . . (Andover, Mass.: Flagg & Gould, 1818), pp. 14, 15, 16.

12. "Historical Sketch of the American Board of Commissioners for Foreign Missions," *Missionary Herald* 73 (January 1877): 1-7.

13. "American Missionaries," *The Panoplist* 8 (January 1813): 374.

14. Examples are cited in "Hindoo Devotees," printed separately as no. 12 in the "Monthly Paper" series and bound at the back of the *Missionary Herald* 29 (June 1833): 45-48 (Yale University Library copy). Also see *The Panoplist* 12 (November 1816): 509. The *Panoplist* merged with the *Massachusetts Missionary Magazine* in 1808 and was renamed the *Missionary Herald* in 1820. Cf. *Missionary Herald* 75 (January 1879): 4-5. To avoid confusion, the *Panoplist* and *Missionary Herald* have been cited separately. For a modern analysis, see Harold R. Issacs, *Images of Asia: American Views of China and India* (New York: Capricorn Books, 1962), pp. 249-58. The book was originally published as *Scratches on Our Minds*.

15. See the description extracted from William Ward's *View of the History, Literature, and Religion of the Hindoos*, reprinted in the "Monthly Paper" series, bound at the back of the *Missionary Herald* 28 (April 1832): 2. See also "Swinging at the Festival at Gangamma," ibid., 25 (April 1829): 131, and "Mahrattas. Journal of Mr. Allen at Bombay," ibid. 37 (August 1841): 343-44.

16. "Bombay Mission. Ahmednuggur. Extracts from the Journal of Mr. Read," *Missionary Herald* 30 (March 1834): 93 and no. 1 in the "Monthly Paper" series, bound at the back of ibid. 28 (April 1832): 3.

17. "Idolatry of the Hindoos, Account of Juggernauth," ibid. 20 (April 1824): 115.

18. See the extract in "Juggernaut and his Worship," no. 11 in the "Monthly Paper" series bound at the back of ibid. 29 (May 1833): 43.

19. Ibid., p. 44.

20. Cf. "India," *The Panoplist* 3 (August 1807): 136; "Idolatry of the Hindoos, Account of Juggernauth," *Missionary Herald* 20 (April 1824): 114-18; and "Juggernaut," *Missionary Herald* 63 (June 1867): 166-67.

21. "Juggernaut and his Worship," no. 11 in "Monthly Paper" series, bound at the back of *Missionary Herald* 29 (May 1833): 44 and "Dr. Buchanan's Christian Researches in Asia," *The Panoplist* 7 (October 1811): 222, 223.

22. "American Missionaries," *The Panoplist* 12 (November 1816): 505.

23. See Purushotam Rao Telang, "Christian Missions as Seen by a Brahmin," *Forum* 18 (December 1894): 485-86 and Virchand R. Gandhi, "Christian Missions in India," *The Arena* 11 (January 1895): 164.

24. See the description in "Madras. Letter from Mr. Winslow, Nov. 18, 1843," *Missionary Herald* 40 (April 1844): 125-26. Also: "Burning of Widows in India,"

ibid. 25 (March 1829): 99-100. The figures are reported in "Burning of Widows in India," ibid. 25 (April 1829): 131.

25. "Burning of Widows in India," ibid. 25 (April 1829): 130.

26. Published separately and bound at the back of the volumes held by Yale University Library. Cited in order of publication: ibid. 28, no. 1 (April 1832): 1-3; 28, no. 2 (May 1832): 5-8; 28, no. 7 (October 1832): 25-28; 29, no. 9 (March 1833): 33-36; 29, no. 10 (April 1833): 37-40; 29, no. 11 (May 1833): 41-44; 29, no. 12 (June 1833): 45-48; 29, no. 15 (September 1833): 57-60; 30, no. 17 (March 1834): 65-68; and 30, no. 18 (June 1834): 69-72.

27. "Bombay Mission. Ahmednuggur. Extracts from the Journal of Mr. Read," ibid. 30 (March 1834): 91, and "Bengal. The Hindoo Priesthood," ibid. 23 (July 1827): 216.

28. "Bombay. Extracts from the Journal of Mr. Ramsey," ibid. 30 (April 1834): 118.

29. Ibid.

30. "Madras. Letter from Mr. H. M. Scudder, March 11, 1848," ibid. 44 (August 1848): 257.

31. Stuart Miller provides an excellent analysis in "The Protestant Missionary Image, 1807-1870," chap. 4 in his *The Unwelcome Immigrant* (Berkely, Calif.: University of California Press, 1969), pp. 57-80. See also James M. McCutcheon, "The American and British Missionary Concept of Chinese Civilization in the Nineteenth Century," (Ph.D. diss., University of Wisconsin, 1959).

32. Kenneth S. Latourette, *A History of Christian Missions in China* (1929; reprint ed., New York: Russell & Russell, 1967).

33. "Religious Intelligence," *The Panoplist* 6 (September 1810): 186-88, and "A Letter from Mr. Morrison. . . . " 6 (October 1810): 227-28.

34. Several older histories provide the basic story. For a participant's account, see S. Wells Williams, *The Middle Kingdom*, 2 vols. (New York: Wiley & Putnam, 1848), 2: 339-57. Also: Latourette, *History of Early Relations*, pp. 85-88, and George H. Danton, *The Culture Contacts of the United States and China: The Earliest Sino-American Culture Contacts, 1784-1844* (New York: Columbia University Press, 1931), pp. 34-71.

35. Frederick Williams, *The Life and Letters of Samuel Wells Williams, LL.D.: Missionary, Diplomatist, Sinologue* (New York: G. P. Putnam's, 1889), p. 64.

36. David Abeel, *Journal of a Residence in China, and the Neighboring Countries, from 1829 to 1833* (New York: Leavitt, Lord, 1834), p. 68.

37. See Robert Morrison's complaints in the *Chinese Repository* 1 (June 1832): 75, and ibid. 14 (September 1845): 435.

38. Philosinensis [Charles Gutzlaff], "Remarks on Buddhism," ibid. 2 (September 1833): 214.

39. Originally covered in ibid. and reprinted in the *Missionary Herald* 29 (April 1833): 143-47 and 30 (February 1834): 60-68.

40. Philosinensis, *Chinese Repository* 2 (September 1833): 214. See also Charles Gutzlaff, "The Buddhism of Siam," ibid. 1 (November 1832): 274-76.

41. For an exception see W. [S. Wells Williams], "Sketch of the Life of Confucius, the Chinese Moralist," ibid. 11 (August 1842): 411-25.

42. [Edwin Stevens], "Promulgation of the Gospel in China," ibid. 3 (January 1835): 435.

43. Philosinensis [Charles Gutzlaff], "Remarks on the Religion of the Chinese," ibid. 4 (October 1835): 271.

44. [Elijah C. Bridgman], "Intellectual Charcter of the Chinese," ibid. 7 (May 1838): 1-2.

45. [Elijah C. Bridgman], "The Chinese Language," ibid. 3 (May 1834): 7.

46. [J. R. Morrison], "Second Report of the Society for the Diffusion of Useful Knowledge in China," ibid. 5 (March 1837): 509.

47. [Robert Morrison], "The Bible," ibid. 1 (July 1832): 101.

48. "Canton. Letter from Mr. E. C. Bridgman, August 25, 1848," *Missionary Herald* 45 (February 1849): 52.

49. See chap. 10.

50. [Elijah C. Bridgman], "Introduction," *Chinese Repository* 1 (May 1832): 1.

51. Ibid. 2 (May 1833): 10-19, continued in 2 (June 1833): 61-73 and 2 (July 1833): 97-111; 2 (November 1833): 313-16; 3 (July 1834): 121-27; 4 (July 1835): 135-51; 6 (July 1837): 105-13; and 16 (September 1846): 454-62.

52. Ibid. 2 (November 1833): 310-12; 18 (July 1849): 363-84; 1 (July 1832): 102-3; and 2 (November 1833): 318-24.

6
The Free Religious Association and the Orient

Emerson had prophesied, "Calvinism rushes to be Unitarianism, as Unitarianism rushes to be Naturalism."[1] Reacting against this tendency, Transcendentalism sought to revive the spiritual realm by an appeal to intuition. By the century's later decades, it had become evident that the movement toward naturalism went far beyond Unitarianism. The authority of science was rising everywhere, Darwin and Spencer were being hailed as the age's new prophets, and positivism and naturalism proclaimed as the new religions.[2] Younger Transcendentalists as well as Unitarians found themselves swept along by the naturalist current. One result was the Free Religious Association, organized in 1867. Made up primarily of Unitarians, it also drew the support of such diverse figures as Robert Dale Owen, Lucretia Mott, Rabbi Isaac Wise, and Felix Adler. Many surviving Transcendentalists became associated with it. No American religious movement in the 1870s and 1880s gave the Oriental religions a larger role in its discussions.

The event that sparked the establishment of the Free Religious Association (FRA) was a move by organization-minded Unitarians to consolidate all Unitarians into a National Conference of Unitarian Churches. Conservatives had been concerned that Unitarians were straying at least since Emerson's Divinity School Address; by 1865 they had apparently concluded that to survive, Unitarianism would have to emphasize doctrinal consensus more. In the end this meant greater emphasis on Unitarianism's Christian viewpoint. The blowup occurred when the conservatives proposed a constitution that spoke of all members as disciples of the "Lord Jesus Christ."[3]

Failing to get the affirmation deleted, a rump group led by Octavius Brooks Frothingham, William James Potter, and Francis Ellingwood Abbot split away to form the Free Religious Association. Instead of an avowal to follow Christ, the association's constitution pledged the new body "to promote the interests of pure religion, to encourage the scientific study of theology, and to increase fellowship in the spirit. . . ."[4] Though always small, the association remained active into the late 1880s. Two journals served the body as semiofficial organs: *The Index*, founded by Francis Ellingwood Abbot, and *The Radical*, edited by Sidney H. Morse.

Free Religionists believed that science provided the only valid foundation for sound religious belief: not biblical faith, not a simple Transcendental trust in intuition, but systematic inquiry based on the facts. The ideal as described by a number of writers was a "science of religion." Theology approached religious questions from an a priori viewpoint; the science of religion preferred an inductive and empirical approach.[5]

Beyond faith in science, Free Religionists were united by a strong commitment to a comparative viewpoint. William Potter described this as a "science of comparative theology," in which the world's religions would be "brought side by side to be impartially studied. . . . Only in this way," he observed, "can a scientific comprehension and statement of the religious development of mankind ever be reached."[6] Francis Ellingwood Abbot envisioned a series of studies, beginning with "comparative biography" focused upon the lives of Jesus, Buddha, and Mohammed, and proceeding to similar comparative studies focused on whole nations. He correctly predicted that "at no distant day" every major university in the country would "be compelled to establish special schools for the study of this science. . . ."[7] It was, of course, as students of comparative religion that Free Religionists turned to the Oriental religions.

The frequency and approval with which the great Orientalist Max Müller's writings are cited suggests that his works were particularly influential in shaping Free Religious views on comparative and Oriental religion. German by birth, Müller spent most of his career in England; his professional reputation was mainly built on studies in the *Rig-Veda*. However, he was also a founder of comparative religion, publishing an *Essay on Comparative Mythology* (1856) and an *Introduction to the Science of Religion* (1873) and editing a multivolume translation of the *Sacred Books of the East*, launched in the 1870s. His books and lectures were regularly reported in the Free Religious periodicals. Hailing the *Sacred Books of the East*, a writer in the *Radical* glowed, "We greet these volumes with somewhat of the same pleasure with which Columbus welcomed the birds and the sweet odors that floated out to his ship from the new lands he was approaching."[8] Such admiration was typical. Another writer declared that Müller's translation of the

Dhammapada had so pleased him that he had "read it through . . . last year in our regular Sunday meetings, as the best series of 'Scripture lessons' at hand."[9] Pleased by the praise, Müller exchanged a series of cordial letters with Abbot, *The Index*'s editor. Abbot printed several of the letters in the magazine, proclaiming Müller "one of the most distinguished scholars of modern times" and praising his role in transmitting the "wonderful treasures of Oriental literature and Oriental religion. . . ."[10] Ultimately, Müller sent *The Index* several pieces for publication, including "A Chapter of Accidents in Comparative Theology," a "Lecture on Missions," and a lecture on "The Sacred Books of the East."[11] Such articles from one of Europe's most famous Orientalists emphasize the pioneering role played by Free Religion.

The best indication of Free Religious interest in Asian thought is the pages of its journals. *The Index* particularly stands out for its thorough coverage: one recent investigator has tabulated that over the seventeen years of its existence it published more than five hundred separate items relating to the Orient.[12] There are expositions of Oriental doctrine, articles comparing the Asian faiths and Christianity, reports of new developments in Oriental scholarship, accounts of Christian missionary activity in the Far East (very unfriendly), reports on Chinese immigration to the United States, selections from the Oriental classics, and reviews of new books on the East. It is significant that much more attention is devoted to Buddhism and Confucianism than Hinduism, reflecting the ethical and practical preferences of most Free Religionists. Mysticism was frowned upon. Transcendentalists had admired Confucius but reserved their highest praise for the Hindu classics. Though brief, the Asian pieces would have provided a helpful introduction to Asian religion.

Abram W. Stevens's article, "Confucius and his Religion," offers a good example of the emphasis and presentation in the more informative pieces. Readers were presented with a compact summary of Confucius' life, character, and main doctrines, followed by a selection of his maxims. Confucius had been a "strict and high-toned moralist" and a "reformer and a philosopher, rather than a prophet or a seer." He had been "simple and natural" in his life and method of instruction.[13] Though not a radical distortion, it is obvious that in presenting Confucius as a moral reformer Stevens emphasized the aspect most likely to appeal to Free Religionists. Indeed, Stevens's Confucius must have struck many readers as a very modern man: he had said little about either God or a future life, though Stevens was certain he had accepted both. Stevens expressed special appreciation of the Sage's emphasis upon the goodness of human nature, which he contrasted to the harsh doctrine of evangelical Christians. Though critical of evangelical Christianity, most Free Religionists remained admirers of Jesus, and a mark of Stevens's high esteem is that he would finally rank the Chinese Sage alongside the founder of Christianity. "In ethical teachings," he held, "Jesus was not more wise that Confucius; while in matters of practical reform . . . Confucius left a far deeper impress upon his day and nation than Jesus did upon his. What the great Chinese teacher, in comparison with the Judean, may have lacked in spirituality, he more than made up in practicality."[14] The piece represents one of the earliest American accounts of Confucianism.

Of the Asian religions, however, Buddhism, not Confucianism, commanded greatest attention. Representative pieces include Thomas Wentworth Higginson's "The Character of Buddha," Dyer Lum's "Buddhism Notwithstanding," and "The Whole Duty of the Buddhist Layman," a translation of one of Buddha's sermons.[15] The articles indicate considerable acquaintance with the newest European scholarship. "The English Buddhist literature multiplies so fast," Higginson wrote, "that the three latest translations seem really to throw more light on the actual teachings of Buddha than did all their predecessors."[16] He mentions Max Müller's translation of the *Dhammapada*, Henry Alabaster's *Wheel of the Law*, Samuel Beal's *Catena of Buddhist Scriptures from the Chinese*, and Bishop Bigandet's *Life of Buddha from Burmese Sources* in the course of the article. Free Religionists generally treated Buddha as a religious reformer. Writing of his life in the *Atlantic Monthly*, Felix Adler would entitle his piece, "A Prophet of the People." Just as Catholicism had "called forth a Luther," he observed, Brahmanism had raised a Buddha, "an earlier protestant" and "no less powerful reformer."[17] Formerly, Buddha had been almost unknown in America.

Dyer Lum's contribution stands out for its call for an inside view of Buddhism; he subtitles his presentation "An Attempt to Interpret Buddha from a Buddhist Standpoint." Such a view would not win general acceptance until the twentieth century. While recognizing the ideal of objectivity, Lum emphasized that "to be earnest and effective, the heart must glow with sympathy towards the subject under investigation. To understand Buddha, we must bring to our task a mind fully in sympathy with his central ideas. . . ."[18] The Lum account is also exceptional for its emphasis on Buddhism's philosophical side, usually passed over in favor of Buddha's ethical teachings. He briefly analyzes the Buddhist conception of mind and the doctrines of karma and nirvana. He denied the common charge that Buddhism was nihilistic, emphasizing it affirmative spirit and beneficial results. Indeed, because of a greater compatibility with science, Buddhism actually excelled the Christian viewpoint.

Several other articles deserve comment. Perry's opening of Japan in 1853 awakened serious American interest in Japanese religion for the first time. Carolyn Dall provided one of the first American discussions of Shintoism in the course of a series on Japan.[19] In another series, "The Secret of the East," Felix Oswald argued for the Buddhist origins of Christianity—a notion that enjoyed surprising popularity in the latter part of the century. Though ultimately discredited, the theory was seriously debated.[20] Aside from articles, book reviews kept readers informed of new works on the Asian religions, especially popular expositions suited to a general audience. Among books reviewed were Sir Edwin Arnold's *Light of Asia*, James Freeman Clarke's *Ten Great Religions*, C. D. B. Mills's *The Indian Saint*, A. P. Sinnett's *Esoteric Buddhism*, and Ram Chandra Bose's *Hindu Philosophy Popularly Explained*. Ednah Cheney explained, "For a long time the study of these Eastern religions has been the employment of *savans* [*sic*[, but it had no influence upon popular thought. Now, however, the faithful work done in the darkness so long has risen to the surface. . . ."[21] Free Religious publications played a key role in this.

As advocates of a more universal religion, Free Religionists were quick to embrace the idea of a world bible—the Transcendentalist dream. *Index* contributors repeatedly referred to the need for such a work. Noting in 1870 that he had "recently" heard of new efforts to produce a "Bible of Universal Religion," William Potter commented, "Such a book is greatly needed, and the age is fast ripening for it. It would be immediately adopted by many religious societies for devotional reading in their public services."[22] He explained the value of such a volume in a subsequent article, observing that it would, of couse, be a "great help in overthrowing the exclusive and arrogant claims of specific faiths" and that it would "set an excellent lesson in spiritual freedom and fellowship"; it might also produce a "more appreciative reading" of the Christian Bible as well.[23] Shortly, four such anthologies were published: Moncure Conway's *Sacred Anthology* (1874), Lydia Maria Child's *Aspirations of the World* (1878), C. D. B. Mills's *Pebbles, Pearls, and Gems of the Orient* (1882), and Martin Schermerhorn's *Sacred Scriptures of the World* (1883). Significantly, all four compilers had close ties with Free Religion.

Meanwhile, *The Index* launched an "Essence of All Faiths" series in 1880, and it ran weekly through the first half of 1881.[24] Recalling the earlier "Ethnical Scriptures" series in *The Dial*, *The Index* series included selections from Hindu, Chinese, and Persian sources from Confucius, Mencius, Lao-Tzu, Buddha, and King Asoka. Plato, Marcus Aurelius, Jesus, Saint Paul, Goethe, Voltaire, and Carlyle were also represented, as well as a number of writers closely identified with Free Religion—Abbot, Frothingham, David Wasson, John Weiss, and Felix Adler. The selections were apparently used in Free Religious services for devotional purposes.[25] A few readers were unimpressed by the Oriental offerings. Thus, reviewing Conway's *Sacred Anthology*, W. C. Gannett noted that though the compilation revealed the essential unity of all religions, it also "attested" to the "general preeminence of the Hebrew and Christian Scriptures."[26] B. W. Ball was more vehement, observing that as far as he was concerned, Gibbon's judgment of the Koran—an "endless, incoherent rhapsody of fable and precept and declamation"—applied to all bibles. He traced the obscurities and mystifications back to the "Oriental mind," which he described as "emotional, fanatical, ejaculatory, incoherent. . . ."[27]

In its 1870 statement of principles the Free Religious Association had proclaimed itself as "broader than anything before attempted" and went on to envision an "ultimate union, not simply of all sects in Christendom, but of all religions, Christian and non-Christian. . . ."[28] At its 1870 annual convention it took a dramatic step to demonstrate its universality by staging a special presentation of non-Christian faiths. Samuel Johnson opened with an ecumenical statement in favor of "The Natural Sympathy and Unity of Religions," Rabbi Isaac Wise presented the tenets of Judaism, Thomas Wentworth Higginson spoke on Islam, and William Henry Channing commended the religions of China.[29] The unusual event pointed forward to the more celebrated 1893 World's Parliament of Religions, where Asians would present their own faiths.

Another avenue toward achieving universal religion involved cooperation with broad-minded religionists elsewhere. One of the bodies that most excited Free Religious interest in the early 1870s was the Brahmo Samaj, the Indian religious society whose founder, Rammohun Roy, had drawn American curiosity a half century earlier.[30] The memory of Rammohun Roy had rapidly receded after his death in 1833; however, the Samaj had not broken up but continued to flourish under a succession of notable leaders —Debendranath Tagore (father of the great Indian poet, Rabindranath Tagore), Keshub Chunder Sen, and Protap Chunder Mozoomdar.[31] Sen caught the eye of Free Religionists, rekindling American interest in the Brahmo Samaj's work. Under Roy and Tagore the society had sought to reform Hinduism by a return to the original spirit of the *Vedas*; Sen seemed more radical. He championed a whole series of advanced social reforms and reorganized the Samaj as the Church of the New Dispensation to promote a universal religion based on harmonizing all religions. He went so far as to incorporate scriptures and rites from other religions, including Christianity, into New Dispensation services—exactly what many Free Religionists favored.

The Free Religious Association opened official contact with the Samaj as early as 1867, shortly after the association's formation. Hearing of Keshub Chunder Sen's work through C. H. A. Dall, the Unitarian missionary in India, Potter had written to the Indian, enclosing a copy of the association's constitution. When Sen reciprocated with a summary of the Samaj's teachings, Potter read the letter at the association's annual meeting in 1868 and subsequently published it in *The Index*. Ecstatic, Potter hailed the Samaj as "pure Theism."[32] If Free Religionists welcomed the Samaj in a spirit of universal brotherhood, their special enthusiasm arose from a recognition of remarkable similarities between the two movements. Just as Unitarians had earlier hailed the Samaj as Indian Unitarianism, so Free Religionists now proclaimed it Indian Free Religion. A week after the publication of Sen's letter, Potter introduced a synopsis of the Brahmo Samaj's key doctrines with the caption, "Free Religion in India."[33] Sen, to be sure, encouraged this view when he spoke of the Samaj as a "revival of the unitarian faith and worship" within Hinduism, which had since evolved into a theistic organization standing "precisely in the same relation to its old creed as the 'Free Religious Association' does to Unitarian Christianity."[34] Further letters followed, with each of Sen's communications published in full in *The Index*.

Excited by their remarkable discovery, the association began to pressure Sen to come to America. A visit seemed especially feasible in 1870, when he traveled to England to seek support for the Samaj's social reforms. Free Religious officials were optimistic; it was announced that Sen had been "officially invited" to be present at the association's annual meeting and that he would "probably come."[35] There were also plans to include him in a series of religious lectures sponsored by the association.[36] Unfortunately, Sen was unable to come. He explained that he had "almost made up" his mind "to visit America after making a short stay in England," but that illness and the urgency of the English mission had compelled him to abandon the project.[37]

The Indian reformer never visited America, but his work continued to be followed closely; extracts from the Samaj newspaper, the *Indian Mirror*, were regularly printed in *The Index*. Though deeply touched by Western influence, Sen was viewed as a superb embodiment of authentic Asian religion. One reader wrote to Abbot, "If any *Christian* Missionary from our country, or from any Christian country to any heathen country, has ever delivered to them as good and as true a discourse as the sermon of the Indian missionary, Brother Sen, in the last INDEX, I have not seen it in print. . . . In some things they and their books are wiser than we and our books."[38] The attitude was characteristic of most Free Religionists. Abbot worried about this and found it necessary to warn Sen's admirers that there was a critical difference between Free Religion and the Brahmo Samaj. The Samaj, he wrote, "has a *Theistic creed* as its bond of union; the F.R.A. has its bond of union in the simple principle of *Freedom of Fellowship*." The American body was broader, more universal. While Free Religionists "cannot but feel the liveliest sympathy for the Hindu reform movement," Abbot continued, "they would be false to their own fundamental ideas, if they abandoned the principles of absolute freedom of thought for any creed, however true in itself. . . ."[39]

The feeling toward Keshub Chunder Sen cooled in later years as the result of his increasingly mystical preoccupations, close relations with traditional Hindu holy men, and claims to divine revelation—the side of India that always made Free Religionists uneasy. However, he was not forgotten. When he suddenly died in 1884, the association sponsored an elaborate service commemorating his work, including testimonials by Potter, Higginson, Julia Ward Howe, and others. Potter did not pass over the disappointments of the later years, complaining that Sen's "extravagances" had weakened the Samaj's influence. However, he insisted that Free Religionists had been correct to support the Indian and he took pride in the fact that the association had been the "agency by which Keshub Chunder Sen was first introduced . . . to the American public."[40] The claim is fully justified. Though there had been vague reports of Sen in the American religious press, Free Religious periodicals made his work known.

The prominence of Oriental thought in the Free Religious movement owed much to the advocacy of a group of younger, second-generation Transcendentalists, who combined Free Thought and Transcendental idealism. Key names include Octavius Brooks Frothingham, Thomas Wentworth Higginson, Moncure Conway, Samuel Johnson, Samuel Longfellow, and William Henry Channing. There is considerable arbitrariness in the list as well as in the selection of people for discussion. Actually a first-generation Transcendentalist, Channing lived long enough and participated actively enough in the Free Religious Association to deserve inclusion. Emerson was courted by the association, signed up as its first member, and was made one of its vice-presidents, but he did not play an active role, and he has not been included.[41] Conway and Johnson are so important that their role has been reserved for fuller discussion in another chapter. All shared strong sympathies for Oriental thought and Free Religion.

Octavius Brooks Frothingham played the largest role in the Free Religious Association and also moved furthest beyond Transcendentalism. His intellectual development mirrored the times: the son of a distinguished Unitarian leader, he began as a Unitarian, moved on to Transcendentalism, and then converted to scientific theism, or what he called the "Religion of Humanity."[42] At the end of his life, he became one of Transcendentalism's first historians, composing a series of works on the movement and leaders that has been indispensable ever since.

Though he notes that his father's library had included Oriental works, Frothingham's serious investigation of Eastern thought followed his conversion to Transcendentalism. The Oriental religions apparently played a significant role in his adoption of a universal religious viewpoint. Affirming the belief that a common spiritual nature united people everywhere, he explained that he found support for universal religion in the "great religions of the world," the "substantial agreement of all sacred books," and the "spontaneous homage paid" saints and prophets in past ages. He regularly incorporated Oriental scriptural readings into his services as minister of a "free" church in New York.[43] As a founder and first president, Frothingham also played a key role in establishing the Free Religious Association's favorable stance toward the comparative study of Oriental religions. Explaining "Why Am I a Free Religionist," he strongly supported the Association's openness to non-Christian religions, and on several occasions took up his pen to defend the study of these religions.[44]

As a scientific theist, Frothingham emphasized the need to know something about Oriental religion; at the same time he saw no purpose and considerable harm in going further. In view of later developments, his reservations are important. Aware of the growing interest in Buddhism, he noted that sooner or later some Westerners would prefer the Eastern religions to Christianity. He opposed such conversions as a serious mistake, since "there would be no advantage in substituting one corrupted and decaying faith for another corrupted and decaying faith." What gain could there be in exchanging one "formalism," one "species of dogmatism" for another he asked. His statement deserves quotation:

> In Buddhism I have small interest and smaller faith. That it will ever have a large following,—will ever make disciples in any considerable numbers among the cultivated or the uncultivated classes . . . of earnest or thoughtful minds in the Western world, I do not in the faintest degree believe, hope or desire. . . . But if the publication and dissemination of Buddhist writings . . . could convince "Christians" . . . that they enjoy no monopoly of moral or religious truth; that their best ideas and purest principles are shared by older and equally impressive faiths; that some of their most exalted beliefs are borrowed from people whom they call heathen and torture with ineffuctual missionary work . . . that the very story of their Founder and Head is paralleled almost word for word and incident for incident in the wonderful legend of Buddha; and that the historical development of their religion was faithfully and literally rehearsed in Asia long before the drama of their own church began or was meditated;—if, we say, effects like these could follow, as they will, and must, and do follow from an acquaintance with these crude and strange, but most interesting and impressive Scriptures, a long stride would be taken. . . .[45]

The quotation makes it clear that Frothingham's study of Oriental religion was inspired as much by the desire to combat orthodox Christian claims as by personal interest.

William Henry Channing came to Oriental thought with much the same background as Frothingham, but otherwise their paths diverged sharply. Both were active in the Free Religious Association and both had been Transcendentalists, but while Frothingham looked forward to scientific theism, Channing looked back toward a revitalized and transcendentalized Christianity.[46] Few had better Transcendental credentials: he had grown up with most of the movement's founders, participated in the discussions that led to Brook Farm, written for *The Dial,* and helped compose his friend Margaret Fuller's *Memoir.* He also ministered to a "Free Christian" church and spoke often before the Free Religious Association's annual conventions. Though he moved to England in 1854 to succeed James Martineau as head of a Unitartian society in Liverpool, he frequently returned to the United States and persisted in regarding this country as his home.

Channing could hardly have failed to be aware of Oriental thought considering his active participation in the Transcendental movement during the 1830s and 1840s. He edited a series of short-lived periodicals during these years that confirm his acquaintance. One was the *Western Messenger,* which published several brief pieces on Asia and Oriental religion, including an article reprinted from the *Canton Register* on the "History of Early Christian Missions in China." The article is not particularly sympathetic, but includes a brief analysis of Chinese religion—the area that attracted Channing's greatest interest.[47] Tantalizing references are also sprinkled through *The Present* and *The Spirit of the Age,* which Channing edited in the 1840s. "The Piety of All Ages" series published in *The Spirit of the Age* is most notable; resembling *The Dial*'s earlier "Ethnical Scripture" series, it included selections from the *Bhagavad-Gita* and Wilkins's translation of the *Hitopades.*[48] Other articles worth noting include "The Tooth of Buddha" and "Oriental Faiths," the latter a synopsis of Oriental religion culled from the *Christian Inquirer.*[49] Though hardly evidence of deep acquaintance, these scattered pieces demonstrate Channing's awareness of Oriental thought before he became associated with the Free Religious Association.

Channing's active interest in the Oriental religions bloomed in the late 1860s and 1870s. In 1869 he made one of his frequent returns to America to deliver a series of lectures on the "Progress of Civilization" before Boston's Lowell Institute. Spread over twelve Friday evenings, he presented lectures on "History, Aryan and Hindu," "China," "Buddhism," and "Persia," as well as on Greece, Rome, Egypt, ancient Israel, and medieval Christianity. Though especially committed to Christianity, his universal outlook is evident throughout the lectures. He affirmed that "all the religions of the earth" were "essentially the same,—communications to men of divine truth, revelations from the Eternal Spirit." Christianity had the advantage of being the most recent and thus the most modern system, but it brought no truths that could not be found in other faiths. "The older faiths did not lead up to Christianity, as precursors and preparatives," he declared, "they, as originally given, contained all its fundamental conceptions."[50] Channing was eager to present the lectures to a wider audience, and in 1872 broached the idea of publishing the extracts in a sacred anthology.[51]

Channing's special interest was Chinese religion, a subject he first presented at the FRA's 1870 annual convention and subsequently expanded upon in pamphlet form. The pamphlet presentation is disappointing. Instead of a summary of Taoism, Confucianism, and Chinese Buddhism, one finds a string of loosely joined quotations laboriously culled from ancient Chinese sources. References to James Legge, Abel Rémusat, Klaproth, Stanislas Julien, and Samuel Beal suggest that he had consulted the important works of Oriental scholarship; however, he made little attempt to digest his reading. All three Chinese systems, it seemed, echoed Channing's personal beliefs: he asserted that the "Central, Universal Principle" of Chinese religion was "Sincerity of Heart" and that Confucius had been no "mere expounder" of ethical precepts, but "pre-eminently a Religious and Social Reformer." If the interpretation may be doubted, the spirit was right. After citing numerous quotations from the *Shih King*, he concluded that such sentiments might be "multiplied without end," but that enough had been offered "to prove the ignorance or unfairness of all who scoff at the religion of the ancient Chinese."[52]

Channing maintained an interest in Asia right up to his death: he helped launch the American edition of Edwin Arnold's *Light of Asia* (Arnold had married his daughter) and delivered four lectures on "Oriental and Mystical Philosophy" before the Concord School of Philosophy in 1880. Moncure Conway recalled the occasion when Channing's enthusiastic remarks on "True Buddhism" so impressed his listeners that the following day they called on him to demand another lecture to explain why they should not become Buddhists![53] He regularly incorporated Oriental scripture into his devotions; he confessed that ever since childhood he had begun the day by reading favorite spiritual authors—including selections from Confucius, Lao-Tzu, the *Bhagavad-Gita*, and the *Dhammapada*.[54]

Thomas Wentworth Higginson penned the most influential Free Religious statement concerning non-Christian religions, a frequently cited piece entitled "The Sympathy of Religions." Young Higginson's father had been an East Indian trader until Jefferson's Embargo had ruined him. Entering divinity school in the same class as Frothingham, Samuel Johnson, and Samuel Longfellow, Higginson had been a Transcendentalist, antislavery leader, and man of letters.[55] Today he is mainly remembered as the famous commander of a black regiment during the Civil War and father-confessor to Emily Dickinson, the well-known poet. His pioneering role as a popularizer of Oriental religion should also be remembered.

Among Free Religionists Higginson was widely respected as one of the movement's most knowledgeable students of non-Christian religions. He was lecturing on Muhammad as early as 1852 (Thoreau, who heard the lecture, asked himself "Why did I not like it better? Can I deny that it was good?");

he also spoke for Islam at the 1870 Free Religious presentation on non-Christian religions.[56] In addition, he lectured on Buddhism and reviewed books dealing with comparative religions and Eastern religions in the *Atlantic Monthly* and *Radical*. He even presumed to show Thoreau a new translation of the *Vishnu Sarma*.[57]

Buddhism was especially attractive to him. He published two essays on that religion, the more important a summary of Buddha's life and teachings published in *The Index* in 1872. He hailed Buddha as both a supreme religious teacher and great reformer, who, like Jesus, had broken away from a narrow creed to proclaim the brotherhood of men. Buddhism was made a spiritual equal of Christianity: he hailed Jesus and Buddha as the world's two "greatest religious teachers" and as the founders of the "two great religions of the world."[58] The other contribution, a review-essay of Max Müller's translation of the *Dhammapada*, consisted largely of quotations and paraphrases of Buddha's teachings. Higginson closed the essay with the observation that he did "not envy" the man who did not "find the depth of his soul stirred by a book like this."[59]

Most important by far was "The Sympathy of Religions," originally published in *The Radical* in 1871. Higginson got a great deal of mileage out of the piece, reprinting it several times in journal and pamphlet form; according to one authority, it was the "most widely distributed document of free religion."[60] Higginson called on the lecture as late as 1893, when he appeared before the Chicago Parliament of Religions. He argued that all religions were alike in fundamentals; all pointed toward a universal religion. Acceptance of these truths dictated a policy of "sympathy" toward other religions. "Every year," he wrote, "brings new knowledge of the religions of the world, and every step in knowledge brings out the sympathy between them." All revealed the "same aim, the same symbols, the same forms, the same weaknesses, the same aspirations." The result was "one religion under many forms"; the "essential creed" the "Fatherhood of God, and the Brotherhood of Man."[61] The only real difference between Christianity and Buddhism or Hinduism or Islam was that each filled "some blank space in its creed with the name of a different teacher." Each and every religion was no more than "Natural Religion *plus* an individual name."[62] There was only one unpardonable sin—the claim to exclusive truth. Higginson supported his argument with copious quotes from ancient Greek and Roman writers, modern European scholars, the Talmud, Koran—and of course the *Vedas*, *Vishnu Sarma*, Confucian *Analects*, and *Dhammapada*. The greater the diversity, the more impressive the testimony to unity.

The strength and weakness of Higginson's view are at once apparent: the broad generous estimate that promoted a more positive view of the Oriental religions but also the persistent blurring of differences in the name of a universal religion that would make a deeper understanding of the Asian religious experience difficult. There was little originality in Higginson's argument; what he proclaimed, others had been saying for years. Samuel Longfellow had expressed almost the same views in "The Unity and Universality of the Religious Ideas" three years earlier.[63] However, Higginson's statement attracted much greater attention. Repeatedly hailed and attacked in subsequent years, a Christian critic warned readers of the *Homiletic Review* as late as 1896 of its persuasive but misleading arguments in favor of the equality of religions.[64]

Though not a Transcendentalist, Lydia Maria Child should also be included in this group.[65] She knew most of the Transcendentalists, corresponded with Emerson, contributed to *The Dial,* and attended Transcendental meetings—but resisted inclusion with her associates.[66] (She was deeply influenced by her brother, Convers Francis, who is usually counted as a Transcendentalist and who also displayed a certain coolness toward the movement.) Her credentials as a Free Religionist are not in doubt—a vice-president of the FRA for eight years, she was recognized as a leader.[67]

Child compiled the most extensive American survey of Oriental religions before the Civil War, a pioneering study entitled *The Progress of Religious Ideas through Successive Ages* published in three volumes in 1855. Her close ties to Transcendentalism stand out: she insisted that feeling rather than thought was the essence of religion, that all historic religions embodied the same universal religious impulse, and that the proper attitude toward other religions was sympathy. Her approach might still serve as a model for students of religion:

> I have treated all religions with reverence, and shown no more favour to one than to another. I have exhibited each one in the light of its own Sacred Books; and in giving quotations, I have aimed in every case to present impartially the beauties and the blemishes. . . . I have not declared that any system was true, or that any one was false. I have even avoided the use of the word heathen; for though harmless in its original signification, it is used in a way that implies condescension, or contempt. . . . I have tried to place each form of worship in its own light; that is, as it appeared to those who sincerely believed it to be of divine origin.[68]

Despite her promise of equal treatment, her allotment of pages clearly favored the Western religions: the religious histories of India, Egypt, China, Chaldea, Persia, Greece, Rome, the Celtic tribes, and the Jews were all sketched in volume one, while later Judaism, Christianity, and Islam were assigned volumes two and three.

Child's discussion of the Oriental religions in the *Progress of Religious Ideas* is fairly superficial, her strength lying in a sympathetic approach rather than her grasp of the intricacies of Oriental religion. She did better by Indian than Chinese religion, devoting 138 pages to India and only 50 pages to China and Tibet, but both sketches are unsatisfactory. (Japanese religion is barely mentioned.) She emphasized Hinduism's great antiquity and mystical bent, discussed the *Vedas*, *Laws of Manu*, and *Mahabharata*, and included sections on Jainism, Buddhism, and the later reforms of Rammohun Roy. Turning to China, she outlined Confucianism, offered a brief and inaccurate discussion of Taoism (Lao-Tzu is identified as a Hindu teacher!) and skimmed over the rise of Chinese Buddhism and Tibetan Lamaism. She epitomized Chinese morality as "unquestioning obedience to superiors"—an untimely statement considering that the Taiping Rebellion, one of the most far-reaching revolts in Chinese history, had just begun. Though an amateur, her acquaintance with the scholarly literature was respectable. For Indian religion she indicated indebtedness to Sir William Jones, Heeren's *Historical Researches*, Maurice's *History of Hindostan*, Rammohun Roy's translation of the *Vedas*, and several of Joseph Priestley's works; for Chinese religion to Huc's *Travels in Tartary, Thibet, and China*, Du Halde's *China*, Pauthier's *Confucius et Mencius*, and David Collie's *Chinese Classics*.[69]

Child described her eight years of labor on *Progress of Religious Ideas* as a "real pilgrimage of penance with peas in my shoes, walking over rubble-stones most of the way." Unfortunately, her labor went largely unappreciated. She sent one of the first sets to Emerson, who praised the volumes warmly; he remarked that though he had "only taken a survey & a few soundings here & there," he had found it a "noble piece of work to spend summers on. . . ." A Free Religious writer testified that the volumes had opened his eyes to the equality of religions and perfectly expressed the Free Religious viewpoint. However, most readers ignored the book; according to a recent biographer, the volumes "barely paid for the paper and ink" required to write them.[70] Too radical for orthodox believers, too labored for the general reader, too simplified for scholarly readers, the volumes missed their mark.

Though active in many causes, Child continued to write on Oriental religions in later years. In the early 1870s she published a short article on the "Resemblances Between the Buddhist and the Roman Catholic Religions," pointing up the remarkable parallels between the two faiths; and in "The Intermingling of Religions," she hailed Buddha as a "great reformer and a benevolent, holy man" and predicted the future merging of the world's religions into an "Eclectic Church."[71] At seventy-six she produced a final statement, *Aspirations of the World* (1878), a brief compilation from the scriptures of the world's religions brought together with the intention of showing that there was "much in which all mankind agree." In a fifty-page essay preceding the scriptures, she argued that all religions agreed on three fundamental propositions: the existence of "One Supreme Being" who created and sustained the world, the belief in the existence of an immortal soul, and the belief in a "Natural Law of Justice" which provided the "basis of all other laws."[72] 'It was a modest effort, for Child had examined few Oriental sources in the preparation of the volume, drawing the Eastern selections almost entirely from other edited collections. To a considerable extent, the result was a compilation of compilations.

Though joined in the name of freedom and a more universal religion, there was always a certain tension within the Free Religious Association between the rationalists led by Francis Ellingwood Abbot and William Potter, and those with Transcendental backgrounds led by Frothingham and Higginson. Where Abbot and Potter insisted on a strictly scientific approach, the Transcendentalists appealed to intuition—though insisting that science would confirm the intuition. Where the hard-nosed rationalist favored an agnostic stance with regard to questions of God's existence and immortality, the Transcendentalist professed an unshakable faith in God and immortality.[73] Inevitably, the differences were also reflected in the view of Oriental religions: the rationalists were less sympathetic toward the Eastern faiths than the Transcendentalists and preferred a more disinterested stance. Though the differences were minimized, periodically the tensions came to the surface.

Shortly after the novel presentation of non-Christian religions at the 1870 convention, Potter worried that the association's heavy emphasis on these religions was being misunderstood. He lamented that some had apparently concluded that the association proposed to "establish the Universal Religion by simply leaving out the peculiar features of all the specific religions and *mechanically* combining them on the ground of their common elements." Such a notion was nonsensical, since "Religions grow; they are not made."[74] However, the doubt seems to have lingered, as he came back to the matter the following month. He complained that because of its attempt "to do justice to all religions," some had wrongly concluded the Free Religious Association had "seriously set itself" the task of reviving the "old religions." In fact, the association had focused attention on the non-Christian religions—not with the desire to synthesize a new religion or to revive an old one—but to "show the relationship of the religions to one another as phases and expressions of one spiritual *substance*. . . ."[75] He insisted that the order of religious development must not be reversed; the older religions had had their day.

Francis Ellingwood Abbot spoke openly of differences, suggesting that the association had always been split between those who took a "sentimental" and those who took a "scientific" view of religion. Supporters of the sentimental view had emphasized the acceptance of all religions in a spirit of fellowship; they had sought to substitute a policy of "fraternal and catholic fellowship" for the old spirit of "rivalry and ill-will." Though he does not mention "The Sympathy of Religions," Higginson's views fit the specifications exactly. By contrast, the more tough-minded "scientific" view required a "complete and total separation" from all historic religions since the essence of universal religion involved opposition to "those special claims of supremacy" which every historic religion had emphasized.[76]

If generally favorable, then, the attitudes of Free Religionists toward the Oriental religions showed definite variations. Some, led by the Transcendental group, came close to championing the superiority of Eastern religions. Others admitted certain truths in non-Christian religions, but insisted that purified Christianity incorporated the best elements of all religions. And still others looked upon all earlier religions as steps in the evolution of a higher religious consciousness; earlier religions were obsolescent in the face of science.

Previous studies of America's discovery of Oriental thought have usually presented a very incomplete picture of nineteenth-century developments. Most accounts dwell on Transcendentalism in the 1840s and then skip to the end of the century, to describe the popularity of Arnold's *Light of Asia*, the rising interest in scientific religious studies, and the Parliament of Religions. Almost completely ignored, the Free Religious Association provides the crucial link between the two periods. Its promotion of comparative religion and the new Oriental scholarship, the wide attention it gave Eastern religions in its journals, its advocacy of a more sympathetic attitude toward non-Christian religion, and its role in publicizing the work of the Brahmo Samaj all contributed significantly to America's growing awareness of Asian thought.

Notes

1. Edward Waldo Emerson and Waldo Emerson Forbes, eds., *Journals of Ralph Waldo Emerson*, 10 vols. (Boston: Houghton Mifflin, 1909-1914), 10:9.

2. See Richard Hofstadter, *Social Darwinism in American Thought*, rev. ed. (1944; Boston: Beacon Press, 1955); Paul Boller, *American Thought in Transition: The Impact of Evolutionary Naturalism, 1865-1900* (Chicago: Rand McNally, 1969); and Sidney Warren, *American Freethought, 1860-1914* (New York: Columbia University Press, 1943).

3. Stow Persons, *Free Religion: An American Faith* (1947; paperback reprint ed., Boston: Beacon Press, 1963). pp. 1-2, 13-17; Octavius B. Frothingham, *Recollections and Impressions, 1822-1890* (New York: G. P. Putnam's, 1891), chap. 9, pp. 115-32; and chap. 4 in Warren, *American Freethought*, pp. 96-116.

4. *The Index* 1 (January 1, 1870): 8.

5. William J. Potter, "Religion and the Science of Religion," ibid. 5 (March 26, 1874): 146.

6. [William J. Potter], "Progress, Not Regression," ibid. 1 (July 16, 1870): 7.

7. [Francis Ellingwood Abbot], "The Scientific Study of Religion," ibid. 10 (October 23, 1879): 510.

8. *The Radical* 7 (March 1870): 254.

9. *The Index* 3 (March 23, 1872): 94. There were occasional complaints that Müller conceded too much to the opinions of orthodox Christians. See Potter's remarks, for example, in ibid., 1 (August 27, 1870): 7.

10. "A Letter from Max Mueller," ibid. 11 (April 1, 1880): 163.

11. Ibid. 3 (November 9, 1872): 357-59, 363; 5 (February 5, 1874): 62-64; and 7 (June 15, 1876): 280-81.

12. Roger C. Mueller, "The Orient in American Transcendental Periodicals 1835-1886" (Ph.D. diss., University of Minnesota, 1968), p. 202n. Mueller's count includes references to western Asia as well as East Asia.

13. Abram W. Stevens, "Confucius and his Religion," *The Index* 6 (September 2, 1875): 410.

14. Ibid. 412.

15. Ibid. 3 (March 16, 1872): 81-83; 6 (April 29, 1875): 194-96; 6 (May 6, 1875): 206-8; and 7 (August 31, 1876): 410-11.

16. Thomas Wentworth Higginson, "The Character of Buddha," ibid. 3 (March 16, 1872): 81.

17. Felix Adler, "A Prophet of the People," *Atlantic Monthly* 37 (June 1876): 680.

18. Dyer D. Lum, "Buddhism Notwithstanding: An Attempt to Interpret Buddha from a Buddhist Standpoint," *The Index* 6 (April 29, 1875): 194.

19. Caroline H. Dall, "Kami No Michi, or 'The Way of the God,'" ibid. 13 (November 24, 1881): 247-48 and 13 (December 1, 1881): 259-60.

20. Felix Oswald, "The Secret of the East," ibid. 14 (March 1, 1883): 410-11; 14 (March 22, 1883): 447-48; 14 (April 12, 1883): 482-84; 14 (April 19, 1883): 495-96; 15 (August 2, 1883): 52-53; 15 (October 25, 1883): 198-201. For a fuller discussion, see chap. 8.

21. E. D. C. [Ednah C. Cheney], "Home Missionary Work," *The Index* 3 (April 20, 1872): 125.

22. [William J. Potter], "A Universal Bible," ibid. 1 (April 9, 1870): 7.

23. W. J. P. [William J. Potter], "A Universal Bible," ibid. 2 (November 4, 1871): 350.

24. The first in the series appeared in ibid. 12 (July 1, 1880): 1 and the last in 12 (June 30, 1881): 625. A new series, "Live Thoughts Old or New," began in the thirteenth volume; however, Oriental selections were much more rare.

25. See ibid. 1 (April 9, 1870): 7 and 3 (March 23, 1873): 94.

26. Ibid. 5 (April 9, 1874): 176.

27. B. W. B. [B. W. Ball], "Bibles," ibid. 12 (May 19, 1881): 555.

28. [William J. Potter], "Department of the Free Religious Association," ibid. 1 (February 12, 1870): 7.

29. "The Annual Convention," ibid. 1 (June 11, 1870): 7.

30. See chap. 2.

31. Cf. William T. DeBary, ed., *Sources of Indian Tradition* (New York: Columbia University Press, 1958), pp. 602-20 and D. S. Sarma, *Studies in the Renais-*

sance of Hinduism in the Nineteenth and Twentieth Centuries (Benares, India: Benares Hindu University, 1944), pp. 71-116.

32. *The Index* 1 (January 22, 1870): 7.

33. [William J. Potter], "Free Religion in India," ibid. 1 (January 29, 1870): 7.

34. Ibid. 1 (January 22, 1870): 7.

35. "Keshub Chunder Sen," ibid. 1 (May 21, 1870): 7.

36. [William J. Potter], "The Boston Lectures," ibid. 1 (December 3, 1870): 7.

37. "Letter from Chunder Sen," ibid. 1 (December 24, 1870): 7.

38. Ibid. 1 (August 27, 1870): 6.

39. [Francis Ellingwood Abbot], "A Vital Difference," ibid. 1 (December 24, 1870): 4.

40. "Commemoration of Keshub Chunder Sen and of the Brahmo Somaj," ibid. 15 (February 14, 1884): 387, 386.

41. Octavius B. Frothingham, *Recollections and Impressions, 1822-1890* (New York: G. P. Putnam's, 1891), p. 168, suggests that after a short time, Emerson's enthusiasm dimmed and he ceased to play any role in association affairs.

42. Most crucial is Frothingham's own *Recollections*, but also see the sketches by J. P. Quincy, "Memoir of Octavius Brooks Frothingham," *Proceedings of the Massachusetts Historical Society*, Second Series, 10 (March 1896): 507-39 and Paul Revere Frothingham, "Octavius Brooks Frothingham, 1822-1895," in Samuel A. Eliot, ed., *Heralds of a Liberal Faith*, vol 3: *The Preachers* (Boston: American Unitarian Association, 1910), pp. 120-27. Edmund C. Stedman penned a laudatory contemporary intellectual portrait in *Octavius Brooks Frothingham and the New Faith* (New York: G. P. Putnam's, 1876).

43. Frothingham, *Recollections*, pp. 3, 59, 127-28. Quote on p. 59.

44. Octavius Brooks Frothingham, "Why Am I a Free Religionist?" *North American Review* 145 (July 1887): 9-10. O. B. F. [Octavius Brooks Frothingham], "The Sin of Monotony," *The Index* 2 (March 11, 1871): 77-78 and "The Hospitalities of Faith," ibid. 2 (June 21, 1871): 21.

45. O. B. F. [Octavius Brooks Frothingham], "The Rival Faiths," *The Index* 2 (November 18, 1871): 365.

46. The beginning point is Octavius B. Frothingham's *Memoir of William Henry Channing* (Boston: Houghton Mifflin, 1886), but see also Thomas W. Higginson's sketch in Samuel A. Eliot, *Heralds of a Liberal Faith*, 3: 59-66, and Frothingham, *Transcendentalism in New England: A History* (New York: G. P. Putnam's, 1876), pp. 335-40. For Channing's religious views, see Frothingham, *Memoir of Channing*, pp. 113-14, 172-73, 285, 344-45, 356-59.

47. "History of Early Christian Missions in China," *Western Messinger* 6 (March 1839): 328-33. Also see "Chinese Rules of Conduct," ibid. 6 (April 1839): 389-90.

48. "The Piety of All Ages," *Spirit of the Age* 1 (August 11, 1849): 83; 1 (August 25, 1849): 116; 1 (September 29, 1849): 197-98; 1 October 6, 1849): 211-12; and 1 (November 17, 1849): 311-12.

49. "The Tooth of Buddha," ibid. 2 (February 9, 1850): 95-96, "Oriental Faiths," 1 (August 11, 1849): 87.

50. Frothingham, *Memoir of Channing*, p. 390.

51. Ibid., pp. 392-94.

52. William Henry Channing, *Religions of China. Address before the Free Religious Association. Boston, May 27, 1870* (Boston: John Wilson, 1870), pp. 3, 9, 11.

53. Moncure Conway, *My Pilgrimage to the Wise Men of the East* (Boston: Houghton Mifflin, 1906), p. 127.

54. Arthur Christy, *The Orient in American Transcendentalism: A Study of Emerson, Thoreau, and Alcott* (1932; reprint ed., New York: Octagon Books, 1963), pp. 247-53; Frothingham, *Memoir of Channing*, 394, 458.

55. See Higginson's autobiography, *Cheerful Yesterdays* (Boston: Houghton Mifflin, 1898). Anna M. Wells, *Dear Preceptor: The Life and Times of Thomas Wentworth Higginson* (Boston: Houghton Mifflin, 1963) focuses on the relationship with Emily Dickinson.

56. *Journal*, 3: 213 in Bradford Torrey and Francis Allen, *Writings of Henry David Thoreau*, 20 vols. (Walden ed., 1906; reprint, New York: AMS Press, 1968); *The Index* 1 (June 11, 1870): 7.

57. For the book reviews, see *Atlantic Monthly* 17 (July 1866): 779 and 23 (June 1869): 771-72; *The Radical* 7 (June 1870): 509-11. *Journal*, 7: 102 in Torrey and Allen, *Writings of Thoreau*.

58. Thomas Wentworth Higginson, "The Character of Buddha," *The Index* 3 (March 16, 1872): 81, 83.

59. Thomas Wentworth Higginson, "The Buddhist 'Path of Virtue,' " *The Radical* 8 (June 1871): 362.

60. Persons, *Free Religion*, p. 23. For the successive editions, see the "Preliminary Note" to the pamphlet edition, Thomas Wentworth Higginson, *The Sympathy of Religions*, rev. ed. (Boston: Free Religious Association, 1876), n.p.

61. Thomas Wentworth Higginson, "The Sympathy of Religions," *The Radical* 8 (February 1871): 2.

62. Ibid. 3, 4.

63. Samuel Longfellow, "The Unity and Universality of the Religious Ideas," ibid. 3 (March 1868): 433-57.

64. William C. Wilkinson, "The Sympathy of Religions," *Homiletic Review* 31 (February 1896): 109-14.

65. Lydia Maria Child, *The Letters of Lydia Maria Child* (1883; reprint ed., New York: Negro Universities Press, 1969) is a good beginning point. See also Helene G. Baer, *The Heart Is Like Heaven: The Life of Lydia Maria Child* (Philadelphia: University of Pennsylvania Press, 1964) and Milton Meltzer, *Tongue of Flame: The Life of Lydia Maria Child* (New York: Thomas Y. Crowell, 1965). Neither author gives Child's pioneering role as a writer on Oriental religion the attention it deserves.

66. See *Letters of Lydia Child*, pp. 34, 56-57, 169. George Willis Cooke, *An Historical and Biographical Introduction to Accompany "The Dial,"* 2 vols. (1902; reprint ed., New York: Russell & Russell, 1961) comments that it is "evident that Mrs. Child was a transcendentalist," although she did not closely affiliate with the school. (2: 166)

67. Cf. "Lydia Maria Child," *The Index* 12 (October 28, 1880): 211.

68. Lydia Maria Child, *The Progress of Religious Ideas through Successive Ages*, 3 vols. (New York: C. S. Francis, 1855), 1: vii-viii. See the entire "Preface," pp. vii-xi.

69. For Taoism, see ibid., 1: 213-15 and for the reference to Chinese morality, ibid., 1: 200. The "List of Books Used in the Preparation of These Volumes" in ibid., 3: 463-64.

70. *Letters of Lydia Child*, p. 78. Stanley T. Williams, ed., "Unpublished Letters of Emerson," *Journal of English and Germanic Philology* 26 (October 1927): 482-83. *The Index* 12 (October 28, 1880): 211. Baer, *Heart Is Like Heaven*, p. 225.

71. Lydia Maria Child, "Resemblances Between the Buddhist and the Roman Catholic Religions," *Atlantic Monthly* 26 (December 1870): 660-65, and "The Intermingling of Religions," ibid. 28 (October 1871): 385-95. Quoted material on p. 395.

72. Lydia Maria Child, ed., *Aspirations of the World. A Chain of Opals* (Boston: Roberts Bros., 1878), pp. 1, 13. A portion of the introduction was published in *The Index*. Idem., "Christianity and Other Religions," *The Index* 9 (August 8, 1878): 374-77, 380.

73. Persons, *Free Religion*, 36-37.

74. [William J. Potter], "Universal Religion," *The Index* 1 (June 4, 1870): 7.

75. [William J. Potter], "Progress, Not Regression," ibid. 1 (July 16, 1870): 7.

76. [Francis E. Abbot], "Two Views of Free Religion," ibid. 10 (February 20, 1879): 90.

7
Later Transcendentalists and Oriental Thought: The Culmination

In many ways the Transcendental exploration of Asian religion climaxed in the early 1870s with the efforts of three men—James Freeman Clarke, Samuel Johnson, and Moncure Conway. In 1871 Clarke published *Ten Great Religions*; in 1872 Johnson offered the first volume of his *Oriental Religions and their Relation to Universal Religion*; and in 1874 Conway presented his *Sacred Anthology*. All three were serious students of Eastern thought. Their careers provide an excellent point at which to close the Transcendental role in America's discovery of Asian thought.[1]

Born the same year as William Henry Channing, James Freeman Clarke shared Channing's distinction of participating in both prewar and postwar Transcendentalism. An original member of Hedge's Club, close friend of Margaret Fuller's, and frequent contributor to *The Dial*, he lived on to participate in the stormy controversies that surrounded the birth of the Free Religious Association. Clarke began his career as a Unitarian minister in Louisville, Kentucky, but soon moved to Boston to found the Church of the Disciples, his base of operations for the next fifty years. In time, he became one of the city's leading lights: a famous Unitarian minister, Harvard lecturer, reformer, and prolific author of many articles, sermons, and books.[2]

Before turning to Clarke's interest in Oriental religion, something needs to be said concerning his religious views and special position in the Transcendental movement. No other Transcendentalist approached the Eastern religions from so Christian a perspective. At the crucial 1865 Unitarian convention where the affirmation of discipleship to Jesus caused dissidents to break away to form the Free Religious Association, Clarke sided with the conservative majority. He wrote important books and articles on the Oriental religions, but he also wrote the *Christian Doctrine of Prayer, The Ideas of the Apostle Paul,* and *Steps of Belief; or, Rational Christianity Maintained Against Atheism, Free Religion, and Romanism*—all revealing strong Christian commitments. Unlike the radicals, he accepted the need for organization and denominational authority, and he affirmed that Jesus and the Christian tradition should retain their place. He maintained some ties with the radicals and on several occasions sought to persuade Free Religionists that their differences were insignificant, but in the end he aligned himself with conservative Unitarianism.[3]

His conservatism not only placed him at odds with Free Religionists, but also put a certain distance between him and other Transcendentalists. Bronson Alcott, who attended one of his services in 1865, expressed the sense of unease: "Hear Freeman Clarke at his Church of Disciples. Louisa goes with me. Earnest, devout, sensible, the services, the sermon, good doubtless for the pastor and people, but for me, formal, and far too Hebrew, touched beyond truth and nature with numerous allusions to Jesus. . . ."[4] And yet Clarke always affirmed an intuitive philosophy; he is perhaps best classified as a Christian Transcendentalist. Octavius Frothingham summed it up well when he declared that if Clarke's interests had not been "confined" to Transcendentalism and if the "technicalities or details of the transcendental movement" had not concerned him, nevertheless, "a Transcendentalist he was, and an uncompromising one."[5] His sensitivity to Asian thought offers one of the best arguments in favor of such a judgment.

Many years after the event, Clarke still fondly recalled the beginnings of his lifelong interest in Oriental thought. As a boy he had been browsing in his grandfather's library one summer afternoon when he had stumbled upon Kalidasa's *Sakuntala*, serialized in the *Monthly Anthology*. (Emerson's father had briefly edited the journal.) Gathering an armful of the magazines, he recalled that he had carried them to a platform study he had built in a large chestnut tree, where he spent the rest of the afternoon immersed in the ancient Hindu drama.[6] For a long time his interest remained quiescent. When he edited the *Western Messenger* in the late 1830s, he included occasional notices of Asia, but the view is unsympathetic.[7] His serious urge to examine the Eastern religions seems to have bloomed in the 1840s; he states in *Ten Great Religions* that he had first made the study of world religions his "specialty" more than twenty-five years before. Preparing a series of public "conversations" on the teachings of the Oriental sages in 1849, Bronson Alcott turned to him for help. Clarke had responded with a list of works —including the writings of Confucius, the *Vedas*, and the *Vishnu Purana* —that suggests acquaintance. By 1854 he was lecturing on comparative religion at the Harvard Divinity School.[8]

The first fruit of these investigations was an article, "Comparative Theology of Heathen Religions," published in the *Christian Examiner* in 1857. The piece previewed most of the arguments that he would expound more fully in *Ten Great Religions*. Despite the negative tone suggested by speaking of the non-Christian religions as "heathen," Clarke makes a strong plea for a more positive approach toward other religions. He particularly questioned the traditional Christian approach of classifying the world's faiths into "true" and "false" religions, with all except Christianity and Judaism dismissed as rankest superstition. He made the telling point that the acceptance of such a view raised doubts concerning God's providence. If most of the world had always lived in darkness, what became of the belief in a progressive direction in history? Even more telling was the objection that such a view did not square with the observed "facts" presented by other religions. Whatever their limitations, the non-Christian religions' good features outweighed the bad. "In their essence," Clarke claimed, they were "not superstitions, but religions"; their doctrines conveyed "truth rather than falsehood"; and "in the main" their moral tendency was "good rather than evil."[9] He concluded that intelligent Westerners would admit virtues in the non-Christian religions—with the virtues to be seen as preparations for the coming of Christ.

A four-year appointment in 1867 as lecturer on non-Christian religions at the Harvard Divinity School gave Clarke the opportunity to extend his studies. Two years later he published the first results in the *Atlantic Monthly*, including separate essays on Hinduism, Buddhism, and Confucianism.[10] Revised, they became chapters in *Ten Great Religions*, published in 1871.

One of the most influential American books of the second half of the nineteenth century, *Ten Great Religions* stands out not merely as a pioneer work in historical and comparative religious studies, but as the century's most popular American treatment of Oriental religions. The work made an ideal primer for the beginner: clearly written, tightly organized, with all complexities sacrificed to bold generalization, each religion was compactly summarized from standard European authorities. Readers obviously approved: it went through nineteen editions over the next thirty years. Countless Americans got their first glimpse of the "mysterious" East through Clarke's attractive work.

In a number of respects Clarke approached his subject in much the same way as the Free Religionists. First, he intended to be scientific: he promised to pursue his analysis impartially and in the spirit of a "positive science" and spoke of providing a "natural history" of the world's religions. Like the Free Religionists, he especially commended the comparative method, calling for a "comparative theology" parallel to such existing disciplines as comparative anatomy, comparative geography, and comparative philology. He also called for a new, nonnormative classificaion of the world's religions into "ethnic" and "catholic" religions. Rejecting the older, moralistic categories of Christian apologists, he would classify religions in much the same way the botanist classified plants: either as "ethnic" religions, non-missionary religions restricted to a specific race and territory; or as "catholic" religions, actively missionizing religions that transcended racial and geographical boundaries.[11] Though less offensive than the older distinction between "true" and "false" religions, the new classification was hardly value-free.

Clarke's treatment of Oriental religion is concentrated in three long chapters on Hinduism, Buddhism, and Confucianism. He emerges as a temperate and appreciative, though not uncritical judge; positive and negative features are carefully balanced. If he points out the limitations of the Oriental religions, he also cites examples where the West could learn from the East. The major weakness is a proneness to facile overgeneralization: he differentiates all religions too sharply, neatly lining them up for contrast and comparison. It is much too tidy.

Thus, Hinduism was quintessentially the religion of spirit. Above all other religions it had sought the spiritual over the material, eternity over time, the infinite over the finite, and substance over form. Its greatness was its profound spirituality; its failure its otherworldliness, denial of moral responsibility, and essential negativism. Clarke's evaluation reveals a profound ambiguity. The Hindus had "sacred books of great antiquity, and a rich literature extending back twenty or thirty centuries; yet no history, no chronology, no annals." They had a "philosophy as acute, profound and, spiritual as any in the world," but one "associated with the coarsest superstitions."[12] The discussion is noteworthy for its recognition of the differences between schools of Indian philosophy—indicated by his separate treatment of the *Vedanta, Sańkhya,* and *Nyaya* schools—and for the familiarity he demonstrates with both the classic texts and major European commentaries.

Buddhism was the polar opposite of Hinduism; it emphasized the finite rather than the infinite, man rather than God, morality rather than religion. Hinduism was spiritualistic and pantheistic, Buddhism humanistic and rationalistic. Clarke was intrigued by the analogy between Buddhism's revolt against Hinduism and Protestantism's revolt against Roman Catholicism; he entitled the chapter, "Buddhism or the Protestantism of the East." He noted the parallels in their common rejection of sacramentalism, hierarchical organization, and excessive ritualism as well as their common emphasis on the individual's responsibility for salvation. "The human mind in Asia went through the same course of experience, afterward repeated in Europe," he suggested.[13] Certain features in Buddhism obviously attracted Clarke, including its tolerance, rationalism, and concern for humanity. He noted that it was the one Oriental religion that had expanded into new areas, revealing certain attributes of a "catholic" rather than "ethnic" religion.

However, like Hinduism, it was ultimately judged one-sided: it had carried revolt too far. "In asserting the rights of nature against the tyranny of spirit, Buddhism has lost God," he observed. "There is in Buddhism neither creation nor Creator."[14]

No book that pretended to completeness could omit Confucianism. In fact, Clarke devoted most of his space to the peculiarities of Chinese civilization, the nature of Chinese government, and the patterns of Chinese life; Confucianism was more a way of life than a "great religion." He observed that in Confucianism one missed the flights of fancy and imagination usually associated with the East; instead one found "worship of order, decency, propriety, and peaceful commonplaces."[15] The Chinese thought in prose rather than poetry; there was a "Quaker style" to their philosophies. Clarke applauded the permanency, cultural achievements, and ingenious methods of government of Chinese civilization. Assessing Chinese civil service examinations, he burst out: "What an immense advantage it would be to our own country if we should adopt this institution of China!" He hailed Confucius as "one of the master minds of our race" and as a member of that "small company of select ones whose lives have been devoted to the moral elevation of their fellow-men."[16] But Confucianism was also flawed; it lacked the supernatural element and embodied a conservative spirit that froze social progress. Taoism is mentioned, but the discussion is unsatisfactory and fragmentary; Lao-Tzu would remain a mystery for some decades yet.

Ten Great Religions made a persuasive case for a more positive attitude toward non-Christian religions, but Christianity was not forgotten. Indeed, much of the charm and attraction of the book to Christian readers must have been the claim that by adopting a more sympathetic view of non-Christian religions, Christianity would actually advance its claim. Christians need not fear comparison, since an objective evaluation would accentuate Christianity's superiority. Clarke warned that short-sighted apologists who persisted in an unfair presentation of the Oriental religions were actually having the opposite effect—causing some Americans to exaggerate the virtues of those religions. The *Vedas* were "talked about as though they were somewhat superior to the Old Testament" and Confucius "quoted as an authority quite equal to Paul or John," he lamented. The result in some cases was that an "ignorant admiration of the sacred books of the Buddhists and Brahmins" had replaced "former ignorant and sweeping condemnation of them."[17] Clarke's admonition indicates that despite the claim to offer a scientific, nonnormative study, *Ten Great Religions* actually presents an apology for Christianity. It is revealing that in the end he concluded that only Christianity qualified as a fully "catholic religion," that it alone incorporated all the good elements to be found in other great religions.

One of Clarke's major criticisms of earlier treatments of non-Christian religions concerned the defect in their scholarship. Noting the absence of citations to German and French works, he observed that any writer "unable to go to the original fountain in the ancient and Oriental languages" should turn to the "profound and thorough labors of modern Continental scholars."[18] This was one of the major pluses of his volume: no scholar himself, he made a serious attempt to read and synthesize the major works of European Orientalists, a task that need to be done. His work must ultimately be judged as popularization rather than scholarship; nevertheless, it was of a high order and performed a useful service.

Critics of *Ten Great Religions* condemned Clarke's sectarianism. Thomas Sergeant Perry, who reviewed the volume in the *North American Review*, complained of an almost schizophrenic quality in the book. "At one moment it strives to be cool, impartial, scientific, and at the next moment we are bidden, not, indeed, to detest the heathen, but to rejoice with the Christian," Perry complained. Lafcadio Hearn was even more severe: ". . . I do not like James Freeman Clarke's work,—immense labour whose results are nullified by a purely sectarian purpose." He charged, "Mr. Clarke sat down to study with the preconceived purpose of belittling other beliefs by comparison with Christianity. . . ."[19] What such critics overlooked was that by presenting a sympathetic view of the Oriental religions from a broad Christian view, Clarke was performing a special service. American popular culture was still very much a Christian culture; most Americans still viewed the world from a Christian perspective. An average American might have felt that here was a book that could be trusted, unlike other works that approached the subject from an anti-Christian bias. (This was a frequent complaint brought against Free Religious writers.) In short, Clarke's Christian preferences actually made him more effective in delivering the book's message that Christians should take a more sympathetic view toward non-Christian religions.

Finally, one needs to go all the way back to Emerson and Thoreau to understand Clarke's particular contribution in the Transcendental exploration of Asian thought. Clarke's interest in Oriental thought was not as personal or as deep as Emerson's and Thoreau's had been; yet, it was more significant in terms of broad influence. To a large extent, Emerson and Thoreau had explored Oriental thought privately; scattered references in their journals and occasional appreciations in their published writings provide the main evidence of their deep interest. Neither approached Oriental ideas systematically or attempted to offer popular expositions. Though both were deeply impressed by Oriental thought, only a handful of contemporaries were able to share in their excitement. Clarke, on the other hand, preferred a more systematic, more factual perspective; he was also deeply interested in presenting the Oriental religions to general readers. Though less attracted to the Asian religions, he was much more successful in communicating their basic doctrines. Indeed, he was the first American to present Oriental ideas successfully to a general American audience.

In 1872, just a year after the appearance of *Ten Great Religions,* Samuel Johnson published the first volume of his *Oriental Religions and their Relation to Universal Religion*. Clarke had managed to condense his explanation of the Oriental religions into three chapters; Johnson required three mammoth volumes. In sheer bulk his work stands out as one of the most ambitious efforts ever made by an American to master the Oriental mind.

Johnson lived most of his life in Salem; he was educated at Harvard Divinity School and ordained a Unitarian minister. Unlike Clarke, he soon cut his official ties with Unitarianism, breaking away in 1853 to found a nonsectarian Free Church in Lynn, Massachusetts.[20] Though close to the Free Religious movement and a frequent contributor to its publications, he refused to join the association. His divinity school classmate and lifelong friend Octavius Frothingham remembered him as a supreme individualist: "He attended no conventions, joined no societies, worked with no associations, had confidence in no parties, sects, schemes, or combinations, but nursed his solitary thought, delivered his personal message, [and] bore his private witness. . . ."[21]

It is plausible to trace Johnson's first awareness of the Orient to his childhood in Salem. Though by the 1820s the East Indies trade had already peaked and declined, there were still many reminders of that era left, including the quaint collections of the East India Museum. The mystery and legends surrounding the East Indies trade would surely have piqued the curiosity of a young boy. He read Cousin in college and was soon avowing his Transcendentalism. By mid-century he had obviously become a serious student of Asian thought: in 1854 he speaks of presenting the Oriental religions to his Free Church congregation, commenting to his friend Samuel Longfellow, "I have been putting the Oriental Lectures into a more sermonic form, to awake, if possible, some desire for a broader culture in the people." His viewpoint is suggested by an 1858 comment concerning the Swiss-American biologist Louis Agassiz, whom he had been reading: "It will take more than Agassiz to prove that *our* classifications are God's actual thinking, rather than man's conception of the universe. This anthropomorphism, I confess, shocks me. I like my old Brahmins better who only said, *God Is*."[22] In the introduction to his 1872 volume on the Oriental religions he wrote of the work as the "outgrowth of studies pursued with constant interest for more than twenty years," and he noted that his studies had "served substantially to confirm the views" he had presented two decades earlier in a series of lectures on the "Universality of Religious Ideas, as illustrated by the Ancient Faiths of the East."[23] From the 1860s until his death in 1882, he labored almost continuously on the Oriental studies, offering the volume on India in 1872 and a volume on China in 1877. The final volume on Persia, nearly finished at the time of his death, was published posthumously in 1884.

Johnson's analysis in *Oriental Religions* is dominated by his religious philosophy, a combination of Transcendentalism and evolutionism.[24] "I have written," he explained in a key statement of the first volume, "not as an advocate of Christianity or of any other distinctive religion, but as attracted on the one hand by the identity of the religious sentiment under all its great historic forms, and on the other by the movement indicated in their diversities and contrasts towards a higher plane of unity. . . ." Assuming the existence of an "Infinite Mind," which permeated all phenomena, he held that all religions were to a large degree identical. No religion could claim an exclusive hold on truth, as all embodied it.[25]

If the "identity of the religious sentiment" explained the similarities between religions, how was one to explain the many differences between religions? Johnson's answer was that, immediately, the differences were the result of variations in race and environment; ultimately, they merely reflected stages in the evolution of Infinite Mind. Infinite Mind had been evolving from the first, but race and environment determined the rate and direction of evolution; the differences between one religion and another reflected the degree to which Infinite Mind had evolved. He concluded that "there are differences of higher and lower in the forms of revelation; but there is no such thing as a revealed religion in distinction from natural religion." The climax of this evolutionary process would be the emergence of a "Universal Religion" which incorporated and yet transcended all previous religions. It could never be "any one, *exclusively*, of the great positive religions of the world," but it would be "what is best in each and every one of them. . . ."[26]

The differences between Clarke's and Johnson's attitude toward Oriental thought are significant. While Clarke conceded much of value in the Oriental religions, his perspective remained Christian. Like Johnson, he believed that all religions were evolving toward a universal religion; however, he believed that the universal religion would be a reformed Christianity, which would embrace the good elements in other religions. Ultimately, Christianity is different from other religions. Johnson insisted that Christianity was no different. Subject to the same evolutionary laws as the other religions, its fate would be the same. "The Christian ideal is but a single force among others, all equally in the line of movement," he observed.[27] Unlike Clarke, he believed that Oriental religion would play a large role in the transformation of the Western viewpoint. "The time has arrived," he announced, for a "mutual interchange of experience between the East and the West. . . ." He affirmed that "these *oldest* religions have an exceedingly important function to fulfil in the present transformation of the *latest* into a purer Theism. . . ." Recalling the past contributions of the East to the ancient Greeks, Romans, and early Christians, he exulted, "'*Ex Oriente Lux!*' Light from the East once more!"[28]

Johnson's analysis in *Oriental Religions* was dominated by the assumption that each of the Asian civilizations had produced a distinctive "mind." All peoples revealed a mixture of tendencies, but each—as the result of racial and environmental differences—showed a dominant tendency. He summarized the difference between Indian, Chinese, and Persian civilization as follows:

> The Hindu mind is subtle, introversive, contemplative. It spins its ideals out of its brain substance, and may properly be called *cerebral*. The Chinese—busy with plodding, uninspired labor, dealing with pure ideas to but little result, yet wonderfully efficient in the world of concrete facts and uses—may be defined as *muscular*. And the Persian, made for mediating between thought and work, apt alike at turning speculation into practice, and raising practice to fresh speculation, so leading out of the ancient form of civilization into the modern, no less plainly indicates a *nervous* type.[29]

The objections to such a typing of Oriental thought are obvious: the approach is excessively intellectual, and the assumption of a unified mind-set blurs crucial differences. The practical difficulties are illustrated in Johnson's tortured explanation of why Buddhism, the child of Indian cerebrality, had gained such wide acceptance in muscular China. It is significant that he ignored the Japanese mind, which had emerged from borrowed Chinese and native elements. Despite the limitations, the effort is impressive in its attempt to encompass and classify the whole range of Oriental thought; in a number of ways it foreshadows F. S. C. Northrop's later *Meeting of East and West*.[30]

Johnson's position that the Oriental religions must be judged in their own terms is one of the methodological strengths of his books. A standard assumption of twentieth-century religious studies, the idea was still quite novel in nineteenth-century America. Clarke had dismissed the bias of earlier Christian apologists, but still viewed the Oriental religions as precursors to universal Christianity. Johnson protested that Christianity "was in fact but a single step in a for ever unfolding process" and that "earlier beliefs are disparaged when they are made to point to it as their final cause. They stand, as *it* has stood, in their own right; justified, as it has been, by meeting, each in its own day and on its own soil, the demands of human nature."

It was a mistake to view any religion as a "forerunner" of a later faith; special pleading should be discontinued. He concluded, "It is time the older religions were studied in the light of their own intrinsic values."[31]

In *Oriental Religions* Johnson attempted to practice what he preached. The most unsympathetic features in Asian religion are treated as natural and functional adaptations of a different religious environment. His treatment of ancestor worship, polytheism, child marriage, and caste—practices almost universally condemned in the West—is notably sympathetic. Insisting on cultural perspective, he cited parallel cases from Western life that must appear as irrational and grotesque in Eastern eyes.

In an undertaking of such magnitude it is not surprising that Johnson relied heavily on the scholarship of others. He had studied Sanskrit, but for the most part his understanding depended on English, French, and German translations of the Oriental sources. Anticipating attack, he quipped that he was "prepared for the evil fame of attempting so much without knowledge of the forty thousand characters of the Chinese script." His defense was, "If I knew these, I should know nothing else."[32] (Indeed, much nineteenth-century scholarship now seems excessively concerned with mechanics, distracting the reader from the meaning and larger implications of the material under scrutiny.)

If his work was largely derivative, Johnson demonstrated an impressive acquaintance with Oriental scholarship. Whatever his limitations, he was the most scholarly Transcendental student of Oriental religion. An examination of his footnotes indicates that he had read most of the authorities of his time: Wilson, Müller, Roth, Rémusat, Lassen, Rosen, Schlegel, Julien, Burnouf, Colebrooke, Legge, Wilkins, Saint-Hilaire, Pauthier, Beal, Hardy, and Whitney. He not only read but compared his sources. Evaluating various translations of the *Rig-Veda*, he analyzes the relative strengths, weaknessess, omissions, discrepancies, and literary qualities of each. He apparently sought out all available translations in order to find the most authoritative. He declared that he had "avoided quoting texts for which there is but one authority" and warned that quotations from popular works "must be received with great caution," since they were often based on "very imperfect versions."[33] His analysis of the major sources (*Vedas*, *Bhagavad-Gita*, and *Four Books*) as well as detailed discussion of Indian and Chinese institutions and social life suggest considerable familiarity with his subject.

Johnson's intellectual powers, dedication, and long years of reading in the Oriental classics obviously impressed his friends; there was distress that his achievement was not more widely recognized. "Were Mr. Johnson more known," Octavius Frothingham wrote, "were his thoughts less interior, his genius less retiring, his method less private, his form of statement less close and severe, he would be one of the acknowledged and conspicuous leaders of the ideal philosophy in the United States, as he is one of the most discerning, penetrating, sinewy, and heroic minds of his generation."[34] Writers on the religious left, particularly those close to the Free Religious persuasion, were his warmest supporters. Thomas Wentworth Higginson hailed his volume on India as a rare event, a "really good book on the religious faiths of mankind" that one might shut oneself up with for six months. Contrasting Johnson's book with Clarke's *Ten Great Religions*, Higginson charged that Clarke had relied on outdated scholarship and "imprisoned" his treatment in a Judeo-Christian straitjacket; Johnson's work, by contrast, was informed and broad in spirit, providing a book "of which an American may speak with pride." He especially lauded Johnson's handling of Buddhism, which presented the "most admirable picture of Buddhism that I have ever had the good fortune to meet. . . ."[35] Several reviewers outside the Free Religious camp also commended Johnson's effort. Samuel Beal wrote in *The Nation* that the second volume on China was a "marvel of labor and research," while Thomas Sergeant Perry praised the India volume as an "invaluable" introduction for those unable to study original authorities.[36] Perry had been much more critical of Clarke's *Ten Great Religions* in a review two years earlier.

Despite such praise, Johnson's *Oriental Religions* never approached the impact of Clarke's *Ten Great Religions*. In letters to his close friend Samuel Longfellow, Johnson revealed a deepening pessimism as he observed the poor reception of his lifework. Completing a chapter in his projected volume on China, he wrote, "There is no encouragement for printing another volume in the sale of the first." Two years later: "I sent the last proofs [of the China volume] in from Boston yesterday, and came home with a sense of lifted cares, till I began to think of the probable fate of the heavy craft I was launching. . . ."[37] The volume on China did no better than the one on India: within a year Johnson decided to sell his extra copies to help pay off expenses incurred in producing it. A stubborn man, he went ahead with the third volume on Persia. The volumes received occasional notices over the next two decades, but for the most part were ignored. Their great bulk, esoteric subject matter, and treatment of the Oriental religions on a plane of equality with Christianity undoubtedly drove away many readers.

Unfortunately, the volumes also failed to win the approval of the scholars who might have been expected to favor such an effort. Such scholars complained of Johnson's lack of linguistic skills, frequent reliance on untrustworthy sources, and a straining of evidence to support his own ideas.[38] At Johnson's death in 1882, Max Müller revealed that the American had written him and sent his books, obviously hoping to enlist the great man's support. Müller confessed that he had not responded and that, perhaps, he had been unfair to Johnson. His defense was that the "man who breaks stones on the road, as I have been doing nearly all my life, has not always a very kindly feeling toward those who drive by in a carriage over the road that he has made or mended." Johnson, Müller concluded, was an honest man who had worked conscientiously within his limitations.[39] Johnson's ultimate misfortune was that his work failed to find an audience: too scholarly for the general reader, it was not sufficiently so for professionals.

Only four years old when Emerson's *Nature* appeared and destined to live into the twentieth century, Moncure Conway may be said to have concluded the long Transcendental affair with the Orient. His final testament, *My Pilgrimage to the Wise Men of the East*, was published in 1906. He had drawn deeply from Transcendentalism and particularly from Emerson. His original interest in Oriental ideas had been sparked in 1853, when, as a student at the Harvard Divinity School, he had traveled to Concord to meet Emerson. The event, often recalled in later years, had changed his life. Emerson had chatted with him for a while and then taken him to meet Thoreau. Thoreau, he reported, "received me pleasantly, and asked what we were studying at Cambridge." Answering, "The Scriptures," Thoreau had countered, "Which?" Emerson explained, "You will find our Thoreau a sad pagan."[40] If Thoreau felt irritation at the young man's eagerness, he seems to have quickly forgiven him, going so far as to show him "his bibles." Dazzled, young Conway moved to Concord during the summer vacation to be closer to his heroes. Emerson allowed him to join his afternoon walks and loaned him Oriental works from his personal library. Conway always remembered that he had first read Wilkins's translation of the *Bhagavad-Gita* in Emerson's house, a book which "became part of my canon."[41]

Conway's background was unusual for a future Transcendentalist. The son of a Virginia slave owner, he had begun life as a Methodist minister. Following a religious crisis, he moved north, entered Harvard Divinity School, and became a Unitarian minister. He spent most of his career as leader of the South Place Chapel, a nondenominational society in London. Despite long absences, he retained close American contacts throughout the later years, returning periodically for visits.[42]

Conway's exposure to Oriental thought in Concord in the 1850s inaugurated a lifelong interest. From an early date he made it his habit to compile favorite passages from his Oriental reading for use in Sunday services. He also included Oriental extracts in "The Catholic Chapter" when he revived *The Dial* in 1860. (Confessing to Emerson that the series was directly inspired by the earlier "Ethnical Scripture" series, he sought to get Emerson and Thoreau to contribute Oriental selections as they had for the original *Dial*.[43]) Moving to London in 1864, Conway found many opportunities to expand his Eastern acquaintance. At the height of its world imperial power, England attracted a steady flow of Asian visitors; Conway saw to it that a good number spoke at his South Place Chapel. He noted with pride that Keshub Chunder Sen, the Brahmo Samaj leader, delivered his second English address at his chapel. Another lecturer was a "brilliant" young Hindu professor who defended India's high philosophical and intellectual achievements. Conway was so taken with the address that he sent it on to readers of *The Radical*, suggesting that it should "open the eyes" of those who fancied that missionaries sent to India only had a "number of ignorant idolaters to deal with."[44]

One of Conway's most important contacts was Max Müller, the famous Orientalist. Conway courted the German insistently, repeatedly inviting him to speak at the South Place Chapel and soliciting his advice concerning literary projects. Müller seemed cool at first, but he came to appreciate Conway's value as an American intermediary. In fact, Conway seems to have first drawn Müller's attention to *The Index*, which published a number of the German scholar's earliest American pieces; he also relayed digests of Müller's lectures and books to American readers.[45] Upon reading Conway's abstract of his Hibbert Lectures, Müller cheered: "Bravo! Bravo! Bravo! that is an excellent abstract, the very marrow from beginning to end." Lamenting that the abstract had not also appeared in an English paper, Müller observed, "You know there is no greater satisfaction than to feel and see that one has been really understood. . . ."[46] Situated at an East-West crossroads, Conway performed a crucial role by bringing new developments and scholarship to the attention of American readers.

Conway informed his friend Francis Ellingwood Abbot of the good news in early 1874: "My *Sacred Anthology* is out. It is a volume of near five hundred pages . . . and contains seven hundred and forty selections from the Scriptures and classic authors of the East. It has been liberally subscribed for, and is already paid for. A very handsome volume!"[47] The book fulfilled a Transcendental fixation that went back to the 1830s. Compiled from Western as well as Eastern sources and gathered topically under such headings as "Wisdom," "Charity," "Man," "God," and "Nature," the *Anthology* proclaimed universal religion. Like earlier Transcendentalists, Conway chose to ignore crucial differences between religions. He confessed that in selecting the scriptures, he had sought to separate the "more universal and enduring treasures" from the "rust of superstition and the dross of ritual." Ultimately, he hoped that his work would pave the way for a "comparative Science of Religion" and beyond that for a "Religion of Humanity."[48] The echoes of Free Religion as well as Transcendentalism are unmistakable. Though denying any claim to critical scholarship, Conway revealed that he had employed several Hindus and Persians in the research and that "great masses of unpublished translations" had been consulted. The work went through several editions.[49]

In 1883 Conway sailed for the Orient on a journey that would carry him around the world and would include major stops in Sri Lanka and India. Transcendentalists had long idealized the Orient; Conway was the first of them to view it close up. He called the resulting book, *My Pilgrimage to the Wise Men of the East*. Arriving in Sri Lanka first, he visited religious leaders, lectured before curious audiences, and sought out the island's famous temples and shrines. He was much impressed by the spirituality and wide learning of the Buddhist leaders he encountered: "To find philosophers living in thatched cottages with earthen floors was an astonishment."[50] He discussed Emerson, Carlyle, and Max Müller with one village philosopher, who had known all their works by heart.

In India in early 1884, Conway visited Madras, Calcutta, Delhi, and Allahabad, detouring to Adyar to interview Helena Blavatsky, the seeress of the Theosophical movement—another Western pilgrim to the wise men of the East. He was delighted by her performance, but dismissed her Mahatmas as fraudulent. He came away satisfied that he had come off best in their exchange: "I felt that madame was a genius in her own way, and a moral phenomenon to be studied, but she made no pretenses with me."[51] He made a special trip to Buddh Gaya, where the young prince Siddhartha had experienced nirvana. Analyzing his sensations at that holy spot, he reflected that where Buddha had always seemed an obscure figure before, at Buddh Gaya the "thought of that young prince," burdened by man's sorrows, had "touched some subconscious source of tears and love for the man"; he had "longed to clasp his knees."[52] He was back in London in early 1884.

Despite his testimonials, Conway's book suggests that a closer encounter with the Orient caused a decisive alteration in the way he looked upon the East. He had apparently gone—the book's title and opening pages suggest this—in search of an idealized Orient: the spiritual East of mystical wisdom embellished by romantics for over a century. His comments indicate that he found much to support such a view; however, he also discovered quite another Orient. The recognition had dawned upon him as he observed a gathering of Hindu ascetics in Calcutta. He recalled that "in early life" he "used to find a certain romance in reading about *yogis*," a memory deeply indebted to Kalidasa's *Sakuntala*. After peering at the group, he recognized that the "*yogi* is much more attractive in the verse of Kalidasa than when seen near to."[53]

What he discovered—and the experience has been archetypal in the West's encounter with the East—was that there was a great difference between the Western idea of the East and the observable reality, between the literary conception and the complex reality. "One feels at every step the vast distance of the popular worship from the wit and wisdom of the ancient books," he declared late in the book, summing up in a few words what months of travel had revealed to him.[54] He complained repeatedly that Western students had distorted Oriental thought. Still the advocate of Oriental wisdom, he came back from the pilgrimage much more aware of the Orient's limitations.[55]

Well before Conway's final rendering of accounts, the Transcendental movement had dissipated. Emerson, Alcott, and most of the remaining founders had died by the 1880s; members of the second generation were also beginning to die or turning their energies elsewhere. The decade of the 1870s—the years that produced Clarke's *Ten Great Religions*, Johnson's *Oriental Religions*, and Conway's *Sacred Anthology*—marked the final decade in which Transcendentalists led in the American discovery of the Orient. At the same time, it is astonishing how often a Transcendental root is to be found in later movements: the Concord School of Philosophy, the Buddhist vogue surrounding Sir Edwin Arnold's *Light of Asia*, comparative religions, and the New Thought movement are all examples. Long after it had supposedly disappeared, subterranean Transcendental currents continued to nourish interest in Oriental thought.

Notes

1. This chapter is an enlarged and revised version of the author's "The Orient in Post-Bellum American Thought: Three Pioneer Popularizers," *American Quarterly* 22 (Spring 1970): 67-81.

2. The most important source has been Edward Everett Hale, ed., *James Freeman Clarke. Autobiography, Diary and Correspondence* (Boston: Houghton Mifflin, 1891), but see also Andrew P. Peabody, "Memoir of James Freeman Clarke, D.D.," *Proceedings of the Massachusetts Historical Society*, 2nd Series 4 (March 1889): 320-35 and Lilian F. Clarke's sketch in *Heralds of a Liberal Faith*, ed. Samuel Eliot, 3 vols. (Boston: American Unitarian Association, 1910), 3: 67-75. Two modern biographies should also be consulted: John W. Thomas, *James Freeman Clarke. Apostle of German Culture to America* (Boston: John W. Luce, 1949) and Arthur S. Bolster, Jr., *James Freeman Clarke: Disciple to Advancing Truth* (Boston: Beacon Press, 1954). Both barely mention Clarke's Oriental interests.

3. James F. Clarke, "Why I Am Not a Free-Religionist," *North American Review* 145 (October 1887): 378-83, a response to Octavius B. Frothingham's "Why Am I a Free Religionist?" in the July 1887 issue.

4. Odell Shepard, ed., *Journals of Bronson Alcott* (Boston: Little, Brown, 1938), p. 370.

5. Octavius Frothingham, *Transcendentalism in New England: A History* (New York: G. P. Putnam's, 1876), p. 343.

6. [James Freeman Clarke], "Brahmanism: According to the Latest Researches," *Atlantic Monthly* 23 (May 1869): 548-49.

7. *Western Messenger* 1 (May 1836): 718-21; 2 (September 1836): 135-39; 3 (July 1837): 807, 811, 836; 6 (March 1839): 328-33; and 6 (April 1839): 389-90.

Bernard Whitman, "A Letter to Unbelievers," ibid. 3 (June 1837): 738-39, is a good example of the lack of sympathy.

8. James F. Clarke, *Ten Great Religions: An Essay in Comparative Theology* (Boston: James R. Osgood, 1871), n.p.; Arthur Christy, *Orient in American Transcendentalism: A Study of Emerson, Thoreau, and Alcott* (1932; reprint ed., New York: Octagon Books, 1963), p. 243. The 1854 lectures are mentioned in M. A. DeWolfe Howe, ed., *Later Years of the Saturday Club, 1870-1920* (Boston: Houghton Mifflin, 1927), p. 112.

9. James F. Clarke, "Comparative Theology of Heathen Religions," *Christian Examiner* 62 (March 1857): 186-87.

10. James F. Clarke, "Brahmanism: According to the Latest Researches," *Atlantic Monthly* 23 (May 1869): 548-62; Idem, "Buddhism; or, the Protestantism of the East," ibid. 23 (June 1869): 713-28; and Idem, "Confucius and the Chinese, or the Prose of Asia," ibid. 24 (September 1869): 336-51.

11. Clarke, *Ten Great Religions*, pp. 3, 11ff.

12. Ibid., p. 82.

13. Ibid., p. 142.

14. Ibid., p. 143.

15. Ibid., p. 32.

16. Ibid., pp. 41, 44, 45.

17. Ibid., p. 13.

18. Clarke, "Comparative Theology of Heathen Religions," p. 189.

19. [Thomas Sergeant Perry], "Clarke's Ten Great Religions," *North American Review* 113 (October 1871): 428, and Elizabeth Bisland, *The Life and Letters of Lafcadio Hearn*, 2 vols. (Boston: Houghton Mifflin, 1906), 1 : 345.

20. O. B. F. [Octavius Brooks Frothingham], "Introduction," *Oriental Religions and their Relation to Universal Religion. Persia* (Boston: Houghton Mifflin, 1885), vii-xxiv, and Samuel B. Stewart, "Samuel Johnson, 1822-1882," in *Heralds of a Liberal Faith*, ed. Samuel Eliot, 3: 185-90. Roger C. Mueller's recent "Samuel Johnson, American Transcendentalist: A Short Biography," *Essex Institute Historical Collections* 115 (January 1979): 9-60, meets the need for a more detailed, modern study. Mueller is excellent on Johnson's Oriental interests. See particularly pp. 43-60.

21. Frothingham, *Transcendentalism in New England*, p. 347.

22. Samuel Longfellow, "Memoir," in Samuel Johnson, *Lectures, Essays, and Sermons* (Boston: Houghton Mifflin, 1883), pp. 47, 52. Extending over pp. 1-142, Longfellow's invaluable memoir includes numerous selections from Johnson's correspondence.

23. Samuel Johnson, *Oriental Religions and their Relation to Universal Religion. India* (Boston: James R. Osgood, 1872), p. 1.

24. See his "Transcendentalism" in *Lectures*, pp. 416-60. Octavius B. Frothingham, *Recollections, 1822-1890* (New York: G. P. Putnam's, 1891), pp. 208-24 provides an excellent summary of his ideas.

25. Johnson, *Oriental Religions. India*, pp. 2ff.

26. Ibid., pp. 5, 6.

27. Ibid., p. 4.

28. Ibid., pp. 29, 30, 32. The two men exchanged a series of letters in *The Radical*

that point up differences. Cf. *The Radical* 1 (December 1865): 148-52; 1 (February 1866): 218-26; 1 (May 1866): 342-47; and 2 (October 1866): 116-23.

29. Johnson, *Oriental Religions. India*, pp. 58-59.

30. F. S. C. Northrop, *The Meeting Of East and West: An Inquiry Concerning World Understanding* (1946; paperback reprint ed., New York: Macmillan, 1960).

31. Johnson, *Oriental Religions. India*, pp. 7, 13. See also Samuel Johnson, "The Piety of Pantheism. As Illustrated in Hindu Philosophy and Faith," *The Radical* 5 (June 1869): 487-98, an important early article.

32. Frothingham, "Introduction" to Johnson, *Oriental Religions. Persia*, pp. ix-x.

33. Ibid., p. 99n. For another good example, see the discussion of Mencius in Samuel Johnson, *Oriental Religions and their Relation to Universal Religion. China* (Boston: James R. Osgood, 1877), p. 637n.

34. Frothingham, *Transcendentalism in New England*, p. 347.

35. T. W. H. [Thomas W. Higginson], "Johnson's 'Oriental Religions,'" *The Index* 3 (November 9, 1872): 361.

36. [Samuel Beal], "Johnson's Religion of China," *The Nation* 29 (August 7, 1879): 97-98, and [Thomas S. Perry], Book review, *North American Review* 116 (January 1873): 210-12.

37. Johnson, *Lectures*, pp. 114, 119. Brackets added by Longfellow.

38. See Frothingham's summary in Johnson, *Oriental Religions. Persia*, pp. ix-xiii.

39. Max Müller, "Samuel Johnson," *The Index* 13 (April 20, 1882): 498.

40. Moncure D. Conway, *Autobiography. Memories and Experiences of Moncure Daniel Conway*, 2 vols. (Boston: Houghton Mifflin, 1904), 1: 140-41.

41. Ibid., p. 143. Also see Conway's testimony in *Emerson at Home and Abroad* (London: Trübner, 1883), pp. 3-4, 289-93.

42. In addition to the *Autobiography*, see Mary E. Burtis, *Moncure Conway. 1832-1907* (New Brunswick, N.J.: Rutgers University Press, 1952).

43. Ralph Rusk, *The Letters of Ralph Waldo Emerson*, 6 vols. (New York: Columbia University Press, 1939), 5: 181, and Walter Harding and Carl Bode, *The Correspondence of Henry David Thoreau* (New York: New York University Press, 1958), pp. 564-65. See *The Dial* (Cincinnati) 1 (April 1860): 252-57 and 1 (May 1860): 321-23.

44. See the reference in Moncure Conway, "Memories of Max Müller," *North American Review* 171 (December 1900): 886. A. Jayram, "The State of Scientific Thought in England," *The Radical* 10 (March 1872): 183.

45. Georgina M. Müller, ed., *The Life and Letters of the Right Honourable Friedrich Max Müller*, 2 vols. (New York: Longmans, Green, 1902), 1: 407, 475 and 2: 35, 213.

46. Ibid., 2: 53. See Conway's testimony in "Memories of Max Müller," *North American Review* 171 (December 1900): 884-93.

47. *The Index* 5 (January 8, 1874): 19.

48. Moncure D. Conway, ed., *The Sacred Anthology. A Book of Ethnical Scriptures*, 5th ed., (London: Trübner, 1876), pp. iii-xiv. The volume was originally published in 1873. Quotes on pp. xiii, xii.

49. Conway, *Autobiography*, 2: 330.

50. Moncure D. Conway, *My Pilgrimage to the Wise Men of the East* (Boston:

Houghton Mifflin, 1906), p. 109. He took the trip in 1883-1884, but did not publish his account until 1906. He apparently kept a journal of his travels.

51. Ibid., p. 200. However, see his later attack: "Madame Blavatsky at Adyar," *The Arena* 4 (October 1891): 579-90. For a fuller account of Blavatsky, see chap. 9.

52. Conway, *My Pilgrimage*, p. 263.

53. Ibid., p. 240.

54. Ibid., p. 315.

55. Reports of disillusionment were made and hotly denied. See the *Christian Register* 63 (May 15, 1884): 312 and Conway, *My Pilgrimage*, pp. 308-9.

8
The Vogue of Buddhism

Buddhism, still largely unknown at the century's midpoint, became almost fashionable in the nineteenth century's last two decades. Traveling in India in early 1883, Phillips Brooks, the well-known minister of Boston's historic Trinity Church, wrote his sister-in-law that he had that day made a "delightful excursion" to Buddh Gaya, the sacred site where Buddha had meditated under the Bo tree. Brooks explained, "In these days when a large part of Boston prefers to consider itself Buddhist rather than Christian, I consider this pilgrimage to be the duty of a minister who preaches to Bostonians. . . ."[1] Though spoken half in jest, the statement is a remarkable testimony to how much things had changed. Once taken up, a Buddhist vogue swept the country, leading to a general discussion of the relative merits of Buddhism and Christianity.

The strangely delayed American discovery of Buddhism deserves explanation. While Emerson and Thoreau were eagerly examining the *Bhagavad-Gita* and *Laws of Manu* in the 1830s, practically no mention is made of Buddhism until after the Civil War. There were undoubtedly a number of reasons for this, but the most important was the ignorance of European scholars to whom Americans habitually looked for guidance. A recent study emphasizes, "In fact, only since the beginning of the nineteenth century has Buddhism been the subject of intensive studies in Europe. The veritable encounter with Buddhism as both idea and historical datum is even younger—only about a hundred years."[2] Another obstacle was Buddhism's many shapes: fanning out from India, it varied a great deal from country to country. Tibetan Buddhism was different from Japanese Buddhism, which in turn differed from Buddhism in Sri Lanka. Western students became confused. Moreover, Buddhist scholarship required a mastery of Pali as well as other Oriental languages. While Sanskrit studies were already fairly advanced by the early 1800s, the study of Pali had just commenced.

A sprinkling of articles in the 1860s and 1870s signaled the rising interest. Not surprisingly, most of these first notices came from proponents of Unitarianism and Free Religion. A writer in the *Christian Examiner* was one of the first to notice Buddhism's rising appeal. Much of the article is given over to a summary of Buddhist doctine, with references to Burnouf, Spence Hardy, and Barthélemy Saint-Hilaire suggesting some acquaintance with the new European scholarship. Despite favorable comments concerning Buddha's moral stature and contributions to the reform of Indian religion, the writer made no attempt to conceal a deep distaste for Buddhism's negations—the usual objection of optimistic Americans. He expressed amazement that anyone could accept Buddhism—a viewpoint that purported to be religious, yet proclaimed that there was no God, that the phenomenal world did not exist, and that man's goal was ultimate extinction. He concluded that such a religion would never interest Americans. A "worn-out political society" such as that in Europe might find consolation in Buddhism's "grim despair," but the "genius of the New World" would "permit no such pollution."[3] In fact, the Buddhist vogue was already underway.

James Freeman Clarke and Samuel Johnson both included sympathetic sketches of Buddhism in their pioneering studies in the early 1870s. Clarke's concept of Buddhism as the "Protestantism of the East" was especially influential. Several European writers had already offered a "Catholic" interpretation, emphasizing that Buddhism's emphasis upon monasticism, worship of saints, and use of incense, rosaries, and relics closely paralleled Roman Catholicism.[4] Clarke objected that Buddhism's revolt from Hinduism, rejection of caste, and concern with individual salvation were much more fundamental. It hardly needs to be said that both interpretations represented gross oversimplifications; it was natural that early students should attempt to place Buddhism within a more familiar frame of reference. Clarke's interpretation made Buddhism more acceptable in a dominantly Protestant country.

The first book-length treatment of Buddha's life by an American, Charles D. B. Mills's *The Indian Saint*, appeared in 1876, one of the unnoticed but symbolic events of the centennial year. The case offers an excellent illustration of the way in which Transcendentalism continued to fuel later interest in Oriental religion. The link was Bronson Alcott, who served as Mills's intellectual and spiritual adviser, encouraging his study of Pythagoras and passing on tips concerning the arrangement of public lectures. After Mills completed the Buddhist manuscript, Alcott approached Boston publishers to help him get it into print.[5] Mills went on to write for *The Index*, publishing a selection of "Buddhistic Scriptures" and a piece on "The Mystic Piety of the Orient." In 1878 he was lecturing in the Middle West on "The Wisdom of the Orient" and in 1882 published *Pebbles, Pearls, and Gems of the Orient*, an anthology of Oriental selections that further linked him to Transcendentalism.[6]

The Indian Saint's most notable quality was its open advocacy of Buddhism, despite assurances that the account would be unbiased. "We are outgrowing the Jewish narrowness that has from the beginning been upon all Christendom," Mills declared in a characteristic statement. He expressed unqualified admiration for Buddha, who was ranked with the ultimate spiritual heroes: "Placed side by side with other great masters, he compares not unfavorably; none wrestled more strongly with the problems of being, none . . . sacrificed greater for man, none aspired more yearningly to the goal of the infinite peace." Mills confessed that he had written his work out of "love and admiration" for the Indian saint.[7] Readers were troubled by this. A reviewer in the *Atlantic Monthly* complained that in his enthusiasm he had drawn a "very rose-colored picture" and that there was "another side to the picture"; another reviewer speculated whether Mills was "not actually a Buddhist," in view of his close identification with the Buddhist position.[8] Mills did admit that Buddha's elevated teachings had been subsequently debased and that as a religion it suffered many of the limitations of other religions.

The quickening awareness of Buddhism by the early 1870s opened the way for Sir Edwin Arnold's *The Light of Asia*, which burst upon the public like a bombshell in 1879. A new life of Buddha rendered in free verse, it became an instant success and one of the literary events of the late nineteenth century. It has been estimated that it went through sixty English and eighty American editions and that between five hundred thousand and one million copies were sold in Great Britain and the United States.[9] Enthusiastically reviewed and widely quoted, hotly attacked and passionately defended, perhaps no work on Buddhism has ever approached its popular success. Certainly, no event in the late nineteenth century did more to rivet attention on Buddhism.

What is the explanation for the *Light of Asia*'s amazing popular reception? Appearing only three years earlier, Mills's sympathetic portrayal in *The Indian Saint* was barely noticed. One of the most important factors was Arnold's literary skill. A much better writer than Mills, he was able to make Buddha's search for religious truth more believable to his readers. He had gone to such standard works as Samuel Beal's *Abhinishkramana Sutra*, Spence Hardy's *Manual of Buddhism*, and Max Müller's *Dhammapada*, but had skillfully reworked the materials to eliminate the more incredible elements in the Buddha story. A brief experience as a teacher in India enabled him to add the small details and local color that made his version seem so authentic. At the same time, he expanded the dramatic and romantic chapters in Buddha's life—a sure formula for success.[10]

No less important than literary grace was Arnold's presentation of key Buddhist doctrines, which were adapted to appeal to Western preferences. Rejecting the claim of many scholars that nirvana entailed a literal extinction of being, he offered the more comforting view that it represented the soul's final liberation. He ignored the controversial question of Buddha's supposed atheism, while emphasizing his compassion for all living things and opposition to caste. And perhaps most important, he dwelled on the Buddhist elements that most closely paralleled the traditions of Christianity, creating the impression of a fundamental similarity between Christian and Buddhist experiences. Critics charged, with some justification, that he had tampered with the true Buddhist message.[11]

Finally, Arnold had excellent American contacts who promoted his book. Following the death of his first wife, he had married William Henry Channing's daughter (still another Transcendental connection.) Channing launched *Light of Asia* in America, writing his friends to ask assistance in promoting the volume. Bronson Alcott was particularly helpful. Working from a copy sent by Channing, he oversaw the first American edition and arranged for the book's first reviews by Franklin Sanborn, George Ripley (and probably Oliver Wendell Holmes). Channing's letter and the favorable reviews were included in the first American edition.[12]

Holmes set the tone of the American reception with his enthusiastic review in the *International Review*. His opening lines posed the question that most intrigued Western readers. Suppose that one were told that many centuries ago a sleeping woman had had a strange dream; that soothsayers had interpreted the dream as a sign of the birth of a wondrous child; that upon the infant's birth angels had appeared and merchants had come from afar bearing gifts; that in his eighth year the boy had confounded his teachers; and that, grown to manhood, he had renounced the world and begun to gather disciples whom he sent out to spread his doctrines—"of whom," Holmes closed, would the reader "think this wonderful tale was told?" Few Americans would have had trouble in answering. Holmes: "Would he not say at once that this must be another version of the story of the One who came upon our earth in a Syrian village, during the reign of Augustus Caesar, and died by violence during the reign of Tiberius?"[13] What would he say when he discovered in *Light of Asia* that the correct answer was

Buddha rather than Jesus and that the Buddha narrative predated the Jesus story by five or six centuries? The strange parallels would be intensely debated for the next two decades. Curiously, Holmes evaded the whole question with the remark that he meant to enjoy the poem and so would not ponder such "strange questions." He ended by endorsing the work extravagantly, recommending that it be read widely and characterizing it as a presentation of "one of the world's greatest ideal characters," embodying "some of the most striking legends of the story-telling East, . . . woven together in the richest and most effective phrases of an affluent English vocabulary."[14]

Everyone seemed to be reading it over the next decade. "*The Light of Asia* is giving a good deal of light to America," William H. Spencer wrote in 1880. "Who has not read this charming poem? People who five years ago had hardly heard of Lord Buddha, and could not be induced to read a prose history of the 'Christ of India,' are now completely fascinated with the story as sung by Edwin Arnold." Writing in *Old Testament Student*, Justin Smith commented, "Attention has been very much drawn, of late, to the person and teachings of . . . Prince Siddhartha, otherwise named Buddha. . . . Recent writings, especially those of Edwin Arnold, have invested Buddha with a species of interest which should make readers desirous of studying him and his teaching more at first-hand. . . ."[15] Far away in India, the Reverend Phillips Brooks found himself experiencing Buddha's homeland through Arnold's eyes: "We had to drive ten miles, and as we went the sun rose just as it did on Buddha in the same landscape in the fifth book of the 'Light of Asia,' which, as you see, I have been reading with the greatest interest." Many years later, Andrew Carnegie still recalled the pleasure of his first discovery of the book: "'The Light of Asia,' by Edwin Arnold, came out at this time and gave me greater delight than any similar poetical work I had recently read. I had just been in India and the book took me there again." Arnold later presented the great industrialist with the poem's original manuscript, which Carnegie ranked as "one of my most precious treasures."[16]

Few observers failed to note the explosive questions raised by the poem. Francis Ellingwood Abbot hailed the book's assault on orthodoxy as the "deadliest blow ever struck at the sole supremacy of the Christian religion." He emphasized that the claims made for Buddha were "every whit as lofty and unconditional" as those made for Jesus and that the claims were embraced "by a much larger body of believers in the former case than in the latter." Under such circumstances "even dull brains will put the question —*what really constitutes the superiority of Christianity over Buddhism?*"[17] Not that Abbot was on the verge of becoming a Buddhist; he believed that both Buddhism and Christianity would ultimately give way to rationalism. Quick to sense danger, Christian writers like Justin Smith insisted on the need for further investigation: "The conception given of him [Buddha] in such poems as 'The Light of Asia,' and in the writings of those who would gladly disparage Christianity by comparing it with Buddhism, should be tested by the actual facts of his career. . . ." Smith expressed confidence that such inquiry would reveal Jesus' superiority. However, Arnold's poem had raised important questions: "Correspondence, here and there, between Buddhistic teachings and those of the Bible, and similarities in what is related of Buddha himself with incidents in the life of Christ are very remarkable. How can we account for them?"[18]

Writers were already rushing to offer their theories as Justin Smith wrote, launching a far-reaching debate concerning the relationship and relative merits of Buddhism and Christianity that would extend over the next two decades. As one of America's early students, James Freeman Clarke had impressive credentials to speak. He considered the parallels in a judicious article in 1883. Granting that there were striking resemblances, he concentrated on discovering an explanation for the parallels. Three possibilities seemed to exist: that Christianity had derived from Buddhism, that Buddhism had arisen from Christianity, or that both stemmed from a common source. Clarke preferred a fourth explanation: that each had grown up separately from distinct religious trunks. The resemblances were to be explained as "homologies," that is, as the consequence of the "same law working out similar results under the same conditions, though under different circumstances."[19] *All* religions revealed certain resemblances because all reflected a common human nature. At the same time, he traced several of the most sensational parallels—the account of Buddha's virgin birth, the salutation by angels, the disputation with scholars, and the temptation in the wilderness—to the *Lalita Vistara*, a later Buddhist work composed as much as a thousand years after Gautama's death. One must distinguish between authentic parallels and late additions.

If Clarke occupied the middle ground, others were soon taking more extreme positions. W. L. Courtney not only affirmed essential similarities between Buddha and Jesus, but added Socrates for good measure. Treating the three as "great ethical reformers," he suggested that all religions followed the same evolution: beginning in awe, they inevitably ended in dogma, which produced reformers. He ignored doctrinal differences to emphasize similarities in background and general message. "Absolutely different as were the local circumstances in the midst of which the three reformers appeared," he observed, "it is curious . . . how many parallel points there were in their lives." All three had lived within a few hundred years of one another; all three rejected metaphysical theories in favor of a more practical, ethical message; all three taught an "essential humanism." Even their methods of teaching had been remarkably similar: rejecting arid speculation, all had relied on analogies or parables drawn from everyday life, using what had been too narrowly termed the "Socratic method."[20]

Dismayed by such comparisons, writers such as William M. Bryant objected that differences must not be glossed. He hammered on the unbridgeable differences between Buddhism and Christianity throughout the article: they had emerged out of "wholly different scenes," producing "radically different convictions." Sprung out of the prolific Hindu imagination, Buddhism tended to "endless mystification"; nurtured by the shrewd, practical experience of the ancient Hebrew, Christianity had developed the "utmost clearness and simplicity." Buddhism had emphasized nirvana, leading to a "religion of *Pessimism*"; Christianity had centered on the Beatitudes, creating a "religion of *Optimism*." Buddhism had acquiesced to pain as an objective reality; Christianity had subordinated it, transforming it into a force for good. Christianity had been permeated by "Reason"; Buddhism had always been dominated by "superstition."[21] Pro-Christian and anti-Christian writers shared a tendency to rely on overstated, oversimplified formulations.

In the article's final pages, Bryant turned to the *Light of Asia*. He protested that while one might reverence the sublime ideal presented in Arnold's poem, one could not overlook that Buddha fell far short of the ideal. To accept Arnold's portrayal as a historical representation, one would have to accept the "complete abandonment" of "critical methods of investigation" that had made modern advances possible. ". . . Mr. Arnold writes as a poet, not as a historian," he reminded his readers. "We might, indeed, as well take Milton's 'Paradise Lost' as a historical document for Christianity as to accept 'The Light of Asia' as a historical document for Buddhism." Instead of an authentic life of Buddha, the *Light of Asia* should be read as a Christian work. "Indeed," he claimed, "one has but to make careful analysis of the poem to recognize that its real substance is just Christianity itself. . . ." "It is scarcely to be wondered at, then, that Buddhism, viewed in this camera, should present so many startling analogies with the finest sentiment of Christianity!"[22]

No one was more agitated by the sensation generated by Arnold's poem than well-known missionary-scholar Samuel Henry Kellogg. In *The Light of Asia and the Light of the World,* he launched an emotional counterattack. He seemed especially troubled by the backsliding of many Christians. "There is reason to believe," he complained, that a "large class even of Christian people" had developed a "most exaggerated idea of the excellence of the great non-Christian religions" as well as the "extent to which their teachings agree with those of the Gospel of Christ." This was especially true of Buddhism, which had attracted the "special interest" of "many intelligent people, of every variety of religious opinion." As a missionary in India for eleven years, Kellogg claimed to know better: "However admirable many things in the Buddhist and other ethnic religions may seem to some," he observed, he had "seen too much of the practical working of these heathen systems to be deeply in love with them."[23] It is not clear how missionary experience in India—where Buddhism had died out many centuries earlier—qualified him to speak at first hand of the religion of Buddha. Most of the book's space is devoted to a detailed consideration of resemblances between Buddhism and Christianity, with Christianity emerging as superior in every case. Weighing the comparative reliability of Buddhist and Christian scriptures, he contended that while the Gospel record had been authenticated, the legends surrounding Buddha's life remained uncertain. Evaluating the supposed similarities between Buddha's and Jesus' lives, he concluded that not only was there "no coincidence which would impress any one," but, on the contrary, a "striking contrast."[24] The same was true of the much-discussed parallels between Christian and Buddhist doctrine: the similarities were largely mythical.

The most extravagant claims with regard to the strange parallels between Buddhism and Christianity were pressed by Felix Oswald, a medical doctor who lived in Tennessee. Claiming to reveal a closely guarded secret known to the church for many centuries, he disclosed that no one should be surprised at resemblances in view of the fact that Jesus had been a Buddhist! He offered this revelation in 1883 in the pages of *The Index*; it was then published in book form as *The Secret of the East*. He referred to Jesus as a "Galilean Buddhist," Buddha's "West-Asian apostle," and the "Galilean avatar." He claimed to document the undeniable East Indian elements in the New Testament in a subsequent 1891 article, "Was Christ a Buddhist?"[25]

Bizarre as Oswald's claims now seem, his theory was seriously debated. James T. Bixby, who wrote intelligently on questions of comparative religion, conceded that he had offered a "very bold, ingenious, and plausible argument. . . ."[26] So many surprising discoveries had already been announced during the century that nothing seemed impossible. Several respected European scholars had, in fact, provided some ground for accepting such a theory. The eminent French Orientalist Eugène Burnouf had hypothesized in the 1840s that Buddhist ideas had filtered into the Mediterranean world, influencing the Essenes, a mystical sect active in Palestine in the first century A.D. The philosopher Ernest Renan had adopted the view in his controversial *Vie de Jesus*, emphasizing that through the Essenes, Jesus had been influenced by Buddhism. The theory achieved further credibility as the result of work by Rudolf Seydel, who located no less than 223 parallels between passages in Gospel and Buddhist sources. In a sense Oswald merely carried a well-known hypothesis to its logical conclusion.

The difference was that Oswald went further and adopted a more sensational style. Where others hedged, he declared outright that the "Prophet of Nazareth was a Buddhistic emissary" and that he had preached "in the name of Buddha Sakyamuni."[27] Adding further controversial claims, he traced the original source of the Christ story behind Buddhism to the legend of Krishna, the popular Hindu deity. Well established long before Jesus, the Hindu tradition included all the familiar elements: Krishna's birth of a virgin, his precocious performance before the temple scholars, his temptation in the wilderness, and even his subsequent crucifixion. (The greatest difficulty with this theory is that most scholars agree that the Krishna cult is a later development in Hinduism, appearing after the ministries of both Buddha and Jesus.) Oswald claimed that Buddhists had superimposed the legend on Buddha's life, which had then passed to Palestine. Surprisingly, Oswald expressed intense distaste for Buddhism, lamenting that its life-denying philosophy of pessimism was poisoning the West. He wrote as a rationalist and humanist who opposed the influence of all religions.

A Russian journalist, Nicholas Notovitch, may be said to have carried the controversy to its ultimate *reductio ad absurdum* in his *La vie inconnue de Jesus Christ*, published in Paris in 1894. He claimed that Jesus had actually lived in India for a number of years, where he had studied Buddhism at its source. The response was immediate: three separate translations of *The Unknown Life* were brought out in the United States within a year, including one from the well-known novelist F. Marion Crawford.[28] Still another edition was published in 1907, introduced by a visiting Indian lecturer, Virchand Gandhi, who confessed astonishment that Christian theologians had not considered the work more seriously.[29]

Like Oswald's account, *The Unknown Life* gained some credibility from the discussions of contemporary scholars. Biblical students had been struck by the strange fact that Jesus' life between the time of his visit to Jerusalem at twelve and the beginning of his preaching when he was about thirty was almost entirely unknown. Surprisingly, the Gospel accounts had skipped fifteen of the most critical years of his life. The unknown years offered fertile ground for speculation, which Notovitch hastened to exploit. The Russian claimed that during travels in central Asia in 1887, he had learned of an ancient life of a "Saint Issa, Best of the Sons of Men," which had miraculously survived in Tibet. Traveling to the lamasery at Himis, he had persuaded the chief lama to allow him to see the ancient work. Immediately realizing its significance, he gained permission to copy the manuscript, which he carried to Russia and then to France where it was finally published.

Notovitch hailed the "Life of Issa" as a lost memoir of Jesus written by a contemporary witness within three of four years of his crucifixion—which would have made it both earlier and more authentic than New Testament accounts. Most exciting of all, the volume filled in Jesus' lost years. It seemed that at thirteen Jesus had accompanied a caravan of merchants from Palestine to India, where he spent the next six years studying the *Vedas* and other sacred Hindu works. Falling out with the Brahmins, he sought out Buddhist teachers, with whom he spent the next six years learning Pali and mastering Buddha's teachings. He had finally returned to Palestine, where, as the world knew, he had preached and been crucified. In view of such circumstances, the parallels between Jesus' teachings and Buddhism were easily explained.

One would think that by the time of Notovitch's publication, the American public would surely have been jaded by such revelations; this does not seem to have been the case, however. Noting the "precipitate haste" with which Americans were purchasing *The Unknown Life*, one unhappy *Biblical World* observer lamented that Notovitch's "worthless volume" had already run through eight editions in France and that it was finding "large sales in this country."[30] Disturbed by the book's popular success, several well-known figures sought to combat its claims. Edward Everett Hale offered one of the most hostile reviews; he suggested that Notovitch's work had many of the same qualities as Oswald's "Cossack attack" and Arnold's "pretty stories" of Buddha the decade before. Observing in a mocking voice that it seemed odd that a work of such momentousness had never been mentioned to previous travelers to Tibet, he dismissed *The Unknown Life* as a forgery and not a very good one at that. "It is Russo-French, and almost without a trace of Eastern habit," he concluded. Max Müller followed with a blast in *Nineteenth Century*, charging not only that the work was fraudulent but that it seemed improbable that Notovitch had ever traveled in Tibet.[31] Despite denunciations, *The Unknown Life* continued to be cited well into the twentieth century, particularly by followers of such groups as Theosophy and Rosicrucianism.

If Arnold's *Light of Asia* seems to have opened the door to the crank, it also stimulated more intelligent evaluations of Buddhism. Numerous treatments in the period reveal both sophistication and accuracy. There was more concern with the dangers of easy generalization about the Asian religions, a needed corrective. One writer observed: ". . . We talk foolishness when talking of Oriental religions, without having lived among Orientals long enough to understand them, and to know that their ways are not our ways, nor their thoughts of religion our thoughts. This being so, let us shake our heads distrustfully and move our lips doubtfully when we talk of Buddhist intellect, freedom, hope, religion, philanthropy, righteousness."[32] There was also greater recognition of the complexity of Buddhism. Writing from Japan, the Reverend Marquis Gordon concluded an account of

Japanese Buddhism with the observation, "We have found not Buddhism, but 'Buddhisms'; not one religion, but several."[33] (The piece includes a brief discussion of Zen Buddhism, which was to become so stylish a half-century later—one of the earliest notices in America.) Distinctions between the northern or Mahayana Buddhism of China, Japan, and Korea and the southern or Theravada Buddhism of Sri Lanka, Burma, and Siam were increasingly recognized.[34] Expositions by William Davies and James T. Bixby provide good examples of the more balanced, better informed accounts that were appearing in American magazines by the 1890s.[35]

Despite increasing sophistication, the best of the popularizers lacked the authority acquired through long years of research. Fortunately, several distinguished European Orientalists stepped forward at this time to instruct American readers concerning Buddhism. The most influential, perhaps, was the English scholar T. W. Rhys Davids, who was repeatedly quoted in the period. A resident of Sri Lanka for several years, he had returned to England to establish the Pali Text Society, which published nearly a hundred volumes of southern Buddhist texts over the next forty years.[36] Rhys Davids lectured in America in 1894-1895; the lectures were published in 1896 as *Buddhism: Its History and Literature*, which went through several editions. Throughout all his writing, the English scholar emphasized the importance of the Pali texts in establishing Buddha's authentic teachings. His comparison of Buddhism and Christianity was one of the sanest offered in the period.[37] The indefatigable Max Müller and J. Estlin Carpenter also offered scholarly expositions of Buddhism for the American public.[38] (American scholars like Henry Clarke Warren were also making significant contributions by the century's last decade, but their story has been reserved for another chapter.)

In the midst of the debate that *Light of Asia* sparked, Edwin Arnold continued to work. He came to lecture in America in 1889; impressed by his reception, he returned in 1891 for a much more ambitious tour arranged by James B. Pond, the lecture bureau impresario. He had agreed to give fifty readings from his works, but was so gratified by the eager response he found that he agreed to another hundred appearances. Unfortunately, his health broke under the strain. Andrew Carnegie took over his convalescence, sending his personal physician to oversee his recovery.[39]

Meanwhile, Arnold had shifted to Hinduism, seeking to do for the *Bhagavad-Gita* what he had already done in the life of Buddha. A free translation of the *Gita, The Song Celestial*, appeared in 1885. American readers again flocked to buy the book, though it never approached the *Light of Asia*'s popularity. He published a portion of the new *Gita* translation in the *International Review*, dedicating it to the American public "with all gratitude and attachment."[40] There was still a third phase to come.

Following the death of his wife, he moved to Japan, married a Japanese woman, and embraced Japanese culture. Drawing upon his experiences, he subsequently presented a series of sketches of Japanese life and manners in *Scribner's Magazine*.[41]

It is hard to exaggerate Arnold's role in increasing American popular interest in Buddhism and Oriental thought generally. Other writers had presented Eastern conceptions with some success—James Freeman Clarke most effectively—but none approached his ability to reach a general audience. As one writer would suggest, he took Buddhism out of the study and into the parlors and workshops. In the barbershop recently, his barber had "suddenly poised his shears and comb" and "confounded" him with the question: "What do you think of *The Light of Asia*?" Any writer whose work is discussed in a barbershop must be said to have attained some popular following. Writing twenty-five years later, Benjamin Flower, editor of *The Arena*, still looked back on Arnold's *Light of Asia* as "one of the most remarkable poetical successes of the century." Scholars like Max Müller had done splendid work in opening the riches of India, but their work had only reached a few; Arnold had brought those riches "to the people."[42] Almost forgotten today, Arnold and his poem were important in late nineteenth-century America.

One of the earliest American observers to notice the rising interest in Buddha concluded in 1865 that Buddhism would never make any inroad in America.[43] Few Americans then would have disagreed. By 1900, even the skeptics were referring to a "Neo-Buddhist" craze. If Buddhism's popularity could no longer be denied, critics continued to question the American understanding of Buddhism. Edward Washburn Hopkins, one of America's first professional Oriental scholars, dismissed Western-style Buddhism as a "very unreal Buddhism," amounting to little more than the "adoption of an altruistic creed." He declared that he knew no one "among the many" who professed themselves Buddhists who had "really adopted Buddhistic principles," and only a "few" who understood the principles.[44] Significantly, the talk was no longer about the impossible doctrines of an inscrutable Oriental faith, but the distortions of Western-style Buddhism and whether American champions understood what they were affirming. A very significant alteration.

One is forced to ask how it was that a religion as alien as Buddhism made so much headway in such a short time. Completely unknown in America barely fifty years before, by the 1890s it was being favorably compared to Christianity. The answer, it seems to me, has to do with the peculiar religious climate of late nineteenth-century America. Several historians have pointed to a widespread crisis of religious belief in the last quarter of the century.[45] Adjusting with difficulty to the shift from the farm to the city, beleaguered by the challenge of evolution and the new science, and undercut by the Higher Criticism and comparative religions, Christianity seemed to be declining. Liberal Americans increasingly rejected orthodox Christianity as intolerant, overly dogmatic, and unscientific. The way was opened to alien Oriental faiths.

To put it another way, the vogue of Buddhism in the late nineteenth century is to be explained as much by attitudes toward Christianity as by attitudes toward Buddhism. In numerous cases, the sympathy represented less a vote for Buddhism than a vote against Christianity. Throwing off the old-time religion, many were searching for a more universal viewpoint; the Oriental religions seemed more universal. The pattern recurs again and again, right down to the present: alienated by Western religion, Americans have looked to the East. This is not to minimize the intrinsic attractions of Eastern religion. Westerners who looked East on the rebound from Christianity often found far more than they had expected.

Observers familiar with the post-World War II vogue of Zen Buddhism will recognize certain parallels with the late nineteenth-century enthusiasm. Both periods were characterized by a mood of restlessness and deep dissatisfaction with the received religious tradition. In both, Oriental religion was only one of many options considered. Many who championed the ancient Eastern religions in both periods were modernists who rejected traditional Western forms. In both, anti-Christian feeling was a frequent factor in the search for religious alternatives. Even the critics seem to echo one another—in both periods the complaint was that ill-informed enthusiasts were misunderstanding the Eastern philosophies and overlooking their darker side. Writing in 1871 as the Buddhist vogue was just surfacing, Octavius Brooks Frothingham observed,

> In a London book-store I found myself standing at a counter on which lay several of the recently published works on the Buddhist religion. There were Alabaster's "Wheel of the Law," containing his interesting little book, "The Modern Buddhist;" Samuel Beal's "Catena of Buddhist Scriptures from the Chinese;" "Buddhagosha's Parables" [*sic*], with Max Mueller's translation of the "Dhammapadam" as an introduction; the "Pand-namah," or "Book of Counsels," and other specimens of the literature that is now interesting the modern religious world. The bookseller, an intelligent man well acquainted with his wares, in reply to my remark on the revival of interest in the ancient faith, said—"Yes, it is remarkable what a stir it makes. It seems as if Buddhism was to be the religion of the future. . . ."[46]

Visiting a bookshop after World War II, one would have found different titles and paperback rather than hardcover editions, but one can easily imagine a similar meditation.

Notes

1. Phillips Brooks to Mrs. Arthur Brooks, January 30, 1883, reprinted in Alexander V. G. Allen, *Life and Letters of Phillips Brooks*, 2 vols. (New York: E. P. Dutton, 1900), 2: 393.

2. Guy R. Welbon, *The Buddhist Nirvana and its Western Interpreters* (Chicago: University of Chicago Press, 1968), p. 1.

3. [Herman J. Warner], "The Last Phase of Atheism," *Christian Examiner* 78 (January 1865): 88.

4. James F. Clarke, "Buddhism; or the Protestantism of the East," *Atlantic Monthly* 23 (June 1869): 713-28 and idem, *Ten Great Religions* (Boston: James R. Osgood, 1871), chap. 4. Lydia Maria Child presented the Catholic view in "Resemblances Between the Buddhist and the Roman Catholic Religions," *Atlantic Monthly* 26 (December 1870): 660-65.

5. Cf. Richard Herrnstadt, ed., *Letters of A. Bronson Alcott* (Ames, Iowa: Iowa State University Press, 1969), pp. 260, 403, 559.

6. *The Index* 1 (October 1, 1870): 6; 8 (July 26, 1877): 355. *Unity* 1 (March 1, 1878): x; 1 (March 15, 1878): vii.

7. Charles D. B. Mills, *The Indian Saint; or, Buddha and Buddhism: A Sketch, Historical and Critical* (Northampton, Mass.: Journal and Free Press, 1876), pp. iii, iv, 188.

8. [Thomas S. Perry], Book review, *Atlantic Monthly* 37 (June 1876): 752, and William M. Bryant, Book review, *The Western*, New Series 3 (August 1877): 503.

9. Arthur E. Christy, ed., *The Asian Legacy and American Life* (New York: John Day, 1942), p. 43.

10. Brooks Wright, *Interpreter of Buddhism to the West: Sir Edwin Arnold* (New York: Bookman Associates, 1957), pp. 86-88. I have drawn heavily on Wright's excellent study.

11. Ibid., pp. 90-97.

12. Arthur E. Christy, *The Orient in American Transcendentalism: A Study of Emerson, Thoreau, and Alcott* (1932; reprint ed., New York: Octagon Books, 1963), pp. 248-53.

13. Oliver Wendell Holmes, "The Light of Asia," *International Review* 7 (October 1879): 345-46.

14. Ibid., 372.

15. W. H. S. [William H. Spencer], "The Light of Asia," *The Index* 12 (October 14, 1880): 188, and Justin A. Smith, "Sacred Books of the East," *Old Testament Student* 4 (November 1884): 140.

16. Allen, *Life of Phillips Brooks*, 2: 394, and Andrew Carnegie, *Autobiography of Andrew Carnegie* (Boston: Houghton Mifflin, 1920), p. 207.

17. [Francis Ellingwood Abbot], "The Light of Asia," *The Index* 11 (April 22, 1880): 198.

18. Smith, "Sacred Books of the East," p. 140. Brackets added.

19. James F. Clarke, "Affinities of Buddhism and Christianity," *North American Review* 136 (May 1883): 469.

20. W. L. Courtney, "Socrates, Buddha, and Christ," *North American Review* 140 (January 1885): 64, 72.

21. William M. Bryant, "Buddhism and Christianity," *Andover Review* 2 (September 1884): 262, 266, 267. He continued the article in 2 (October 1884): 365-81.

22. Ibid. 2 (October 1884): 374, 375. For other viewpoints see: Charles Schroeder, "Christianity and Buddhism," *The Arena* 5 (March 1892): 458-63; Frederick F. Kramer, "Jesus Christ and Gautama Buddha as Literary Critics," *Biblical World* 3 (April 1894): 252-59; George H. Palmer, "Similarities and Contrasts of Christianity and Buddhism," *The Outlook* 56 (June 19, 1897): 443-50; and J. Wesley Johnston, "Christ and Buddha: Resemblances and Contrasts," *Methodist Review* 80 (January-February 1898): 32-40.

23. Samuel H. Kellogg, *The Light of Asia and The Light of the World. A Comparison of the Legend, the Doctrine, and the Ethics of the Buddha with the Story, the Doctrine, and the Ethics of Christ* (London: Macmillan, 1885), pp. v, vi.

24. Ibid., p. 63.

25. Felix Oswald, "The Secret of the East," serialized in *The Index*, beginning with 14 (March 1, 1883): 410-11 and concluding with 15 (October 25, 1883): 198-201. Oswald, "Was Christ a Buddhist?" *The Arena* 3 (January 1891): 193-201.

26. James T. Bixby, "Buddhism in the New Testament," *The Arena* 3 (April 1891): 555.

27. Oswald, "The Secret of the East," *The Index* 14 (March 22, 1883): 448. Italics in original.

28. Edgar J. Goodspeed includes a chapter on the Notovitch episode in *Strange New Gospels* (Chicago: University of Chicago Press, 1931), 10-24. The editions are listed on pp. 10-11.

29. Nicholas Notovitch [Nicolai Notovich], *The Unknown Life of Jesus Christ* (Chicago: Indo-American Book Co., 1907), "Translator's Introduction." Another edition was brought out as late as 1926.

30. *Biblical World* 4 (August 1894): 147, 149; see also [Jabez Sunderland], "Editorial Notes," *The Unitarian* 9 (May 1894): 226.

31. Edward Everett Hale, "The Unknown Life of Christ," *North American Review* 158 (May 1894): 597, 598, 601, and Max Müller, "The Alleged Sojourn of Christ in India," *Nineteenth Century* 36 (October 1894): 515-22. See also J. Archibald Douglas, "The Chief Lama of Himis on the Alleged 'Unknown Life of Christ,'" *Nineteenth Century* 39 (April 1896): 667-77. Archibald sought out the chief lama, who indignantly denied that any life of Issa had ever existed.

32. C. H. A. Dall, "The Buddha and the Christ," *Unitarian Review* 18 (September 1882): 240-41.

33. M. L. Gordon, "The Buddhisms of Japan," *Andover Review* 5 (March 1886): 309. See also his "Buddhism's Best Gospel," ibid. 6 (October 1886): 395-403. Both articles reveal a strong missionary bias.

34. Cf. Annie E. Cheney, "Mahayana Buddhism in Japan," *The Arena* 16 (August 1896): 439-44; Warren G. Benton, "Chinese Buddhism," *Popular Science Monthly* 38 (February 1891): 530-37; and N. G. Clark, "Primitive Buddhism: A Study," *Andover Review* 12 (August 1889): 185-200.

35. William Davies, "The Religion of Gotama Buddha," *Atlantic Monthly* 74 (September 1894): 334-40, and James T. Bixby, "The Buddha's Path of Salvation," *Biblical World* 12 (November 1898): 307-17.

36. Cf. Welbon, *Buddhist Nirvana*, pp. 223-40.

37. T. W. Rhys Davids, *Buddhism. Its History and Literature*, 3rd rev. ed. (New York: G. P. Putnam's, 1896). See also his articles: "Buddhism and Christianity," *International Quarterly* 7 (March-June 1903): 1-13 and "Buddhism," *North American Review* 171 (October 1900): 517-27.

38. Max Müller, "Buddhist Charity," *North American Review* 140 (March 1885): 221-36 and J. Estlin Carpenter, "The Theistic Evolution of Buddhism," *New World* 1 (March 1892): 89-106.

39. Cf. Wright, *Interpreter of Buddhism*, pp. 130-33, 142-46, and Joseph F. Wall, *Andrew Carnegie* (New York: Oxford University Press, 1970), p. 426.

40. Sir Edwin Arnold, "A Book from the Iliad of India," *International Review* 10 (January 1881): 36-51, continued in 10 (April 1881): 297-306. Quote on p. 41.

41. Sir Edwin Arnold, "Japonica," *Scribner's Magazine* 8 (December 1890): 663-82, continued in 9 (January 1891): 17-30; 9 (February 1891): 165-76; and 9 (March 1891): 321-40. Quote on p. 323.

42. *The Index* 12 (December 30, 1880): 334 and Benjamin Flower, "Sir Edwin Arnold and Nineteenth Century Religious Concepts and Ideals," *The Arena* 32 (July 1904): 80.

43. [Herman J. Warner], "The Last Phase of Atheism," *Christian Examiner*, 88.

44. E. Washburn Hopkins, *The Religions of India* (Boston: Ginn & Co., 1895), p. 562.

45. See Paul A. Carter's recent *The Spiritual Crisis of the Gilded Age* (DeKalb, Ill.: Northern Illinois University Press, 1971), and Arthur Schlesinger, Sr.'s earlier "A Critical Period in American Religion, 1875-1900," *Proceedings of the Massachusetts Historical Society* 64 (June 1932): 523-47.

46. O. B. F. [Octavius Brooks Frothingham], "The Rival Faiths," *The Index* 2 (November 18, 1871): 365.

9
Theosophy

The Theosophical Society originated in New York City in 1875, the outgrowth of a small gathering assembled to hear George Felt lecture on "The Lost Canon of Proportion of the Egyptians." In the audience were some fifteen people, including Madame Helena Blavatsky, Colonel Henry Steel Olcott, and William Quan Judge, three key figures in the subsequent movement. According to recollection, during the discussion that followed, Olcott passed a note to Judge bearing the words, "Would it not be a good thing to form a society for this kind of study?" Judge surveyed the note, passed it on to Madame Blavatsky who nodded in assent, whereupon Judge stood to propose the formation of the organization.[1] Some weeks later the Theosophical Society was formed, with Olcott as first president, Blavatsky corresponding secretary, and Judge legal counsel.

The society was to have a sensational history. Spreading from the United States to India and then to Europe, it became embroiled in one controversy after another. Unlike the Transcendentalists, most Theosophical leaders traveled in the East and could report on Oriental religions at first hand. The first Western body to proclaim its adherence to Asian thought and the most zealous Western propagandizer for the acceptance of Eastern wisdom, the Theosophical Society did a great deal to popularize Asian religions; at the same time, its unseemly squabbles did much to discredit Eastern thought through association with occultism and religious chicanery. A blend of Hinduism, spiritualism, Buddhism, occultism, and rationalism, it presented an extraordinary amalgam of the new and old, the West and East, the parochial and universal.

Much of the controversy that has always surrounded Theosophy may be traced to the mysterious and fascinating Helena Petrovna Blavatsky, the central figure in the movement. Born in southern Russia in 1831, she experienced a difficult childhood, moving about between her father's army camp, the country estate of her grandparents, and various parts of Europe.[2] Quarrelsome, passionate, and unruly, she seems to have been virtually uncontrollable. Her marriage to the middle-aged General Nicephore V. Blavatsky at seventeen was the culminating disaster: she promptly deserted her husband and fled to Constantinople. Over the next twenty-five years she wandered widely over Europe and the Middle East, turning up in Cairo in the 1870s where she practiced spiritualism. In 1873 she immigrated to the United States where she became an American citizen. She moved on to India in 1878, back to Europe in the 1880s, and finally to London where she died in 1891.

Even her harshest critics agree that Madame Blavatsky was an unforgettable character. She is regularly described as a coarse, neurotic, profane woman who may be best remembered as a charlatan; and at the same time as a witty, astonishingly frank, and brilliant woman whose notoriety may be explained by her refusal to conform to the conventional conception of proper female behavior. Her coworker Henry Steel Olcott doubted whether there had ever been anyone "who was a greater conglomeration of good and bad, light and shadow, wisdom and indiscretion, spiritual insight and lack of common sense. . . ." And William Butler Yeats, the great Irish poet, described her affectionately as a "sort of female Dr. Johnson. . . ."[3] Close to Theosophy for a number of years, Yeats often visited her after she relocated in London in the 1880s. If she attracted cranks, she attracted distinguished men as well. Besides Yeats, these included noted British men of science Alfred Russel Wallace and William Crookes and American inventor Thomas Edison, who all became members of the society. William T. Stead, the well-known editor of the *Review of Reviews*, testified at her death that "Madame Blavatsky was a great woman, whom I am proud to have known. . . ." He declared that she had made it possible for the "most cultivated and skeptical men and women" of his generation to believe in an invisible world inhabited by higher beings.[4] Even her most devoted followers admitted that her faults were too evident to ignore.

If Blavatsky was the inspired voice and theoretician of Theosophy, Henry Steel Olcott was the chief organization man. Priding himself on common sense and practicality, a plodding but indefatigable worker, he was in many ways Blavatsky's antithesis. Born in 1832 in New Jersey, Olcott might have been remembered as a pioneer in the movement for scientific agriculture had he not met the Russian woman. He founded one of the country's first model scientific farms, and his early writing was devoted not to Buddhism, but to explaining the cultivation of sorghum (*Sorgho and Imphee, The Chinese and African Sugar-canes*). He served as agricultural editor for the *New York Tribune*, practiced law, and dabbled in spiritualism.[5]

Olcott's fateful first meeting with Blavatsky occurred at the Eddy farmhouse in Vermont in 1874, where he had come to investigate sensational reports of spiritualistic phenomena. Blavatsky had also come and immediately attracted Olcott's attention, thanks to a scarlet Garibaldian shirt and "massive Calmuck face." An incessant smoker, she was just preparing to light up as Olcott stepped forward. "*Permettez-moi, Madame*," the colonel gallantly offered. Recalling the moment many years later, he observed: ". . . Our acquaintance began in smoke, but it stirred up a great and permanent fire."[6] His life was wrenched from its course: middle-aged, the father of three children, and an established lawyer, Olcott abandoned everything to collaborate with Blavatsky in exciting investigations into spiritualistic phenomena.

They sometimes called themselves the "Theosophical Twins"; their alliance was certainly the single most important event in the history of the movement. There were rumors of sexual involvement, but the colonel always insisted that their relationship was platonic.[7] Despite growing tensions, they maintained an uneasy but productive collaboration for at least a decade. Blavatsky philosophized, the colonel managed the finances; she attracted public attention with seances and table-rappings, he signed up the on-lookers; she proclaimed the esoteric doctrine, he looked after the external detail. "She was the Teacher, I the pupil; she the . . . messenger of the Great Ones, I the practical brain to plan, the right hand to work out the practical details," the colonel explained.[8] It was a remarkable relationship as long as it lasted, but in time it soured. Expressing open contempt for the colonel's petty-mindedness and preoccupation with externals, Blavatsky eventually broke away to create her own Esoteric Section. The colonel continued to defend her genius, though warning against the tendency of later followers to deify her.

The beginnings were shaky. Blavatsky had made several earlier attempts to organize a society. She had briefly sponsored a "Société Spirité" in Cairo, which was advertised in spiritualist journals in London and Paris. After arrival in America, she had persuaded Olcott to initiate a similar spiritualistic society in New York called the "Miracle Club," but it, too, quickly disintegrated. The Theosophical Society represented the third effort, and it almost foundered as well. Olcott would later confess that it became "comparatively inactive" after 1876, with meetings held infrequently; conversion from an open-member to a semisecret society after several months failed to reverse the trend.[9] However, it rallied strongly in the 1880s.

Aside from launching the society, the most notable achievement of the early American years was the publication in 1877 of *Isis Unveiled*, Blavatsky's massive two-volume philosophical treatise. Rambling and often obscure, the work came to be regarded as one of the classic statements of Theosophic belief. In her preface, Blavatsky spoke of the volumes as the "fruit of a somewhat intimate acquaintance with Eastern adepts," powerful men of "mysterious powers" and "profound knowledge" to be found in the Orient.[10] For most readers, this was the first introduction to the *Mahatmas* or *Masters* who were to play such a crucial role in subsequent Theosophical history. Powerful, spiritually perfected beings supposed to reside in the Himalayas, these Masters were believed to be the guiding force behind the Theosophical movement. (Many of the society's later troubles would arise from claims and counterclaims concerning reputed communications from the Mahatmas.)

Isis Unveiled proclaimed a universal religion, or what Blavatsky still referred to as the "Hermetic philosophy"—an "anciently universal Wisdom Religion" which supplied the "key to the Absolute in science and theology." Both modern science and traditional theology are harshly indicted; she argued that the ancient sages and philosophers had known far more about ultimate reality. Unfortunately, the volumes say little about the doctrines of the new-old Wisdom Religion; the common teachings underlying the historic religions are frequently referred to but left unidentified. She obviously believed that the Oriental religions, especially Hinduism and Buddhism, represented the Wisdom Religions's original and purest form. All religions, including Christianity, are traced back to the original Indian seed: "What has been contemptuously termed Paganism," she wrote, "was ancient wisdom replete with Deity; and Judaism and its offspring, Christianity and Islamism, derived whatever of inspiration they contained from the ethnic parent. Pre-Vedic Brahmanism and Buddhism are the double source from which all religions sprung. . . ."[11] Occultism and spiritualism pervade the volumes.

Though immediately hailed by her followers as a masterpiece, *Isis Unveiled* was open to a number of criticisms that damaged its credibility. The writing manifested an obsessive anti-Christian viewpoint. Critics noted the incongruity of repeated attacks made on Christian doctrine in a work pretending to offer a universal message. Indeed, one modern commentator suggests that the volumes might have been more appropriately entitled *The Horrors of Christianity Unveiled and the Excellencies of Hinduism Praised*.[12] Blavatsky's methods of work also came under attack. After a meticulous examination and comparison of passages, William Emmette

Coleman, who became one of Blavatsky's most relentless critics, reported massive plagiarism. Coleman claimed that practically everything in the two volumes could be traced to one hundred standard works, with an astounding 134 and 107 passages respectively taken from two sources alone, Dunlap's *Sod: The Son of Man* and Ennemoser's *History of Magic*.[13] Olcott and other defenders responded that Blavatsky was a sloppy worker and that she took liberties in her writing, but that these were minor limitations in a person of genius.

How much did Blavatsky and Olcott know of the Oriental religions prior to their departure for India in 1878? And how central was Oriental thought in the movement's early history? Recalling their first meeting at the Eddy farmhouse, Olcott would later declare, "It was not as an Eastern mystic, but rather as a refined Spiritualist that she talked. For my part I knew nothing then, or next to nothing, about Eastern philosophy, and at first she kept silent on that subject." The colonel also notes that Blavatsky had not emphasized the doctrine of reincarnation in their first years of collaboration, a significant omission considering its centrality in her later writings. "When we worked on *Isis* it was neither taught us by the Mahátmás, nor supported by her in literary controversies or private discussions. . . ."[14] It is true that Blavatsky championed ancient Hinduism and Buddhism in *Isis Unveiled*, but the writing suggests no more than a cursory knowledge.

On the other hand, there is considerable evidence that in its first years Theosophy was dominantly a Western spiritualist society. Indeed, a Theosophical writer in the 1890s comments that it was a "matter of history" that the society's earliest adherents had been drawn "from the ranks of Spiritualism."[15] When Olcott delivered his inaugural presidential address to the new society in November 1875, he devoted much more attention to the organization's spiritualistic goals than to Eastern religions. India and Oriental religion are mentioned, but most of the references are to Neo-Platonists, Kabbalists, and Hermeticists, suggesting a dominantly Western viewpoint. His statement of the society's future work also suggests spiritualist preoccupations: "Mesmerism, Spiritualism, Od, the astral light of the ancients (now called the universal ether) and its currents—all these offer us the widest and most fascinating fields of exploration."[16] Until 1878, psychic phenomena and mediums were much more central in Theosophy than Oriental religion.

The decision to go to India was crucial in the development of the full-blown Orientalism of later years. Olcott recalled that, "In 1877 our correspondence with India and Ceylon began"; and that he and Blavatsky decided "to go to India and take up residence in, what to all students of Oriental philosophy and occult science, is a sort of 'Holy Land.' "[17] Through a chance Indian acquaintance, Olcott established contact with representatives of the Arya Samaj, one of the numerous Hindu reform movements then sprouting up in India, which would figure prominently in Theosophy's first years in Asia. Led by the dynamic Swami Dayananda Saraswati, the society called for purification of Hinduism by a return to the *Vedas*. A partial merger of Theosophy and the Samaj was carried out, and for several years Blavatsky and Olcott worked closely with the Indian organization. However, differences with Dayananda eventually led to separation.[18] Aside from the failure of the merger there were other discouragements in the first months. Plans for an export-import business, based on the shipment of tiger skins and carved ivory to the United States, fell through. There were also difficulties with the British government. Because of Russian-English tensions, Blavatsky's Russian ancestry was viewed with suspicion, and the two were shadowed for weeks as possible Russian spies. (In fact, Olcott was supplying the American government with information concerning the British army's tents and equipment, a point confirmed by documents in the National Archives.[19])

Despite difficulties, the two made a considerable splash in India as well as in Sri Lanka. Their defense of the ancient truths of Hinduism and Buddhism made headlines everywhere, and numerous converts among Hindus and Sinhalese flocked in to join the Theosophical movement. Societies were rapidly established in most of India's major cities and throughout Sri Lanka, and headquarters for the world movement—for Theosophy was soon spreading to Europe—was opened at Adyar, near Madras. A movement journal, *The Theosophist*, was established in 1879. The following evaluation by J. N. Farquhar, a prominent missionary for many years in India who published a pioneer study of modern Indian religious movements, will suggest the extent of Theosophy's early successes:

> By the year 1884 the Theosophical Society had attained great proportions. There were over a hundred branches in India, and Hindus everywhere rejoiced in its work. Nor is their enthusiasm hard to understand. Theosophy provided a new defence of Hinduism for the thousands of educated men whose Western education had filled them with shivering doubts about their religion. It condemned Christian missionaries as impudent and ignorant intruders, who dared to criticize Hinduism and Buddhism, the two faiths which alone among all the religions of the world still taught clearly the truths of the Ancient Wisdom.[20]

Alarmed by the movement's inroads, Christian missionaries throughout India and Sri Lanka unleashed a furious attack.

One of the most significant developments of these years was Olcott's and Blavatsky's formal announcement of their affiliation with Buddhism.

As leaders of a society committed to a universal religious viewpoint, the decision seems surprising; it would cause serious problems later. The occasion was their tour of Sri Lanka in 1880 when they publicly took *pansil*, a ritual approximating the Christian ceremony of confirmation, and proclaimed their adherence to the principles of Buddha. Olcott suggests that they already considered themselves Buddhists before departing America, though neither seems to have had much acquaintance with that religion before 1878.[21] Responding to the charge of sectarianism, Olcott insisted on the difference between his and Blavatsky's Buddhism and a debased sectarian Buddhism. Their Buddhism "was that of the Master-Adept Gautama Buddha," identical with the "Wisdom Religion of the Aryan Upanishads," the "soul of all the ancient world-faiths." In a few words, their Buddhism was "a philosophy, not a creed."[22] Thereafter, Olcott always spoke of himself as a Buddhist.

In many ways over the next decades Theosophy exercised greater influence in Asia than in either the United States or Europe, providing a powerful impulse to the revival of Hinduism and Buddhism in their home countries. Weakened by inner decay and overwhelmed by foreign rule and missionary attacks, both Hinduism and Buddhism were at a low point by the late nineteenth century, with educated youth rapidly breaking away. One of the period's most dramatic developments was an astonishing resurgence by both. Though internal pressures and indigenous Hindu and Buddhist reformers were the major influences, the Theosophical Society played a considerable role in sparking the desire for renewal.

Olcott deserves fullest credit for Buddhism's revival in Sri Lanka, which became a personal crusade. Reading accounts of a debate between Buddhists and Christian missionaries in Sri Lanka while still in New York, he had corresponded with Sinhalese Buddhist leaders. At the first opportunity after their arrival in Asia, he and Blavatsky journeyed to Sri Lanki to meet with Buddhist spokesmen and to judge the situation for themselves. Apparently, they were received as heroes, and the *Maha-Bodhi*, a pioneer Buddhist revival organ, reported that their arrival "was heralded all over Ceylon, and no king ever received the homage of a devoted people as these two when they landed on the shores. . . ."[23] The colonel found the situation even more dismaying than he had expected, with village children knowing next to nothing about their religion. Convinced that the future of Buddhism depended on a Buddhist education, he began to promote Buddhist schools. By 1900 three colleges and more than two hundred schools had been started, with much of the credit going to the colonel.

Olcott soon came to realize that schools were not enough; there must also be proper Buddhist texts. The result was his *Buddhist Catechism*, published in 1881, which became a basic text for the renewal of Buddhism in Sri Lanka. Recalling the effectiveness of the Christian catechism, he proposed a similar Buddhist volume prepared by one of the monks; the high priest Sumangala encouraged him to undertake the work himself. He boasted that he read nearly ten thousand pages of Buddhist translations in carrying out the labor, with most of the reading in English and French translations by such scholars as T. W. Rhys Davids, R. C. Childers, Samuel Beal, and Spence Hardy.[24] The following suggests the primitive level of the *Catechism*:

1. Q. *Of what religion are you?*
   A. The Buddhist.
2. Q. *What is a Buddhist?*
   A. One who professes to be a follower of our Lord Buddha, and accepts his doctrine.
3. Q. *Was Buddha a God?*
   A. No.
4. Q. *Was he a man?*
   A. In form a man, but internally not like other men; that is to say, in moral and mental qualities he excelled all other men of his own or subsequent times.[25]

Though committed to presenting the pure Buddhist doctrine, he was unable to eliminate Theosophical preconceptions as revealed by his portrayal of Buddhism as an activistic religion consistent with modern science and his assertion that Buddhists accepted the existence of "Devas" or higher beings.[26]

It was crucial that the *Catechism* be acceptable to the Buddhist hierarchy, so as soon as the text had been translated into Sinhalese, Olcott took the manuscript to the high priest Sumangala. Inevitably, conflict arose over the handling of nirvana; the high priest threatened to oppose the text publicly unless the formulation was redrafted. After the colonel complied, Sumangala endorsed the volume as "in agreement with the Canon of the Southern Buddhist Church" and recommended the work to teachers in Buddhist schools.[27] Over the next several decades the *Catechism* was widely used in Buddhist schools not only in Sri Lanka but in other Asian countries as well and went through more than forty editions. In retrospect, Olcott's role as Buddhist educator seems almost incredible.

The colonel also became a leader in world Buddhism. He was instrumental in persuading British authorities in Sri Lanka to declare the Buddhist festival Wesak a public holiday; and he led in the move to establish a Buddhist flag, which was subsequently adopted as the official flag of the

World Fellowship of Buddhists. He also became a leader in the drive to reunite the separate schools of Buddhism, compiling a common statement of principles, which Northern and Southern Buddhists were called upon to embrace. Though unsuccessful, he was able to get official endorsements from Buddhist leaders in several Asian countries. Traveling to Japan he urged that Buddhist tract societies be established and that Buddhist missionaries be dispatched to the United States and Europe, actions that were soon taken. In recognition of the colonel's many contributions, modern Buddhists in Sri Lanka and India observe "Olcott Day."[28]

Theosophy contributed to the Buddhist revival in other ways, a fact pointed up by the career of Anagarika Dharmapala (1864-1933), now recognized as a major prophet of resurgent Buddhism.[29] Born into a well-to-do Sinhalese family and educated in Christian schools, the boy was becoming rapidly Westernized when he discovered Theosophy.[30] He began to read *The Theosophist* regularly and eagerly attended Olcott's lectures; he was initiated as a member of the Theosophical Society in 1884. Over the next fifteen years he assisted Olcott as interpreter during a lecture tour in Sri Lanka, served as general secretary of the society's Buddhist Section, and accompanied the colonel on a lecture tour to Japan in 1889. When he launched the Maha-Bodhi Society in 1891, he asked Olcott to serve as its honorary director and chief adviser. At the colonel's suggestion he went to the 1893 Chicago World's Parliament of Religions, where he gained the wide acclaim and American financial backing required for his later work.[31] His lectures, *Maha-Bodhi* articles, and creation of a Maha-Bodhi Society were critical influences in stimulating Buddhist revival. Though he later broke with Theosophy, he never denied indebtedness to either of the society's founders. Blavatsky, he once declared, "gave me the key to open the door of my spiritual nature," while Olcott "taught me to work forgetting my self."[32]

The nineteenth-century revival of Hinduism also owed a good deal to Theosophy. Annie Besant, a dynamic Englishwoman who would become a venerated figure among Hindu militants, played the major role. Before her alignment with Theosophy, she had been well known in England as a freethinker and close collaborator of Charles Bradlaugh. (She was also well known in America; she wrote a well-received series on free thought for *The Index* in the 1870s.[33]) Converted to Theosophy after being asked to review one of Blavatsky's books, she went to India in 1893. Never one to do things halfway, she avowed herself a Hindu and adopted Hindu food and dress styles. Paralleling Olcott's work in Sri Lanka, she took up the defense of Hinduism and inaugurated Hindu schools based on the traditional religious ideals. In subsequent years she became increasingly active in the Indian nationalist movement: she founded the Indian Home Rule League, was instrumental in uniting Hindus and Muslims in the cause of independence, and in 1917 was elected president of the Indian National Congress—a unique honor for a Westerner. D. S. Sarma, who has written one of the most important accounts of the Hindu revival movement, devotes an entire chapter to Besant's large contribution.[34]

Besant's prominent identification with Hinduism placed new strains on Theosophy's platform of universalism, although—as Colonel Olcott recognized—it also alleviated some of the fears raised by his and Blavatsky's earlier support of Buddhism. He suggested that Besant's lectures proved that the society "is doing the very same thing for Hinduism that it is doing for Buddhism in Buddhist countries and Parsiism at Bombay, *viz.*, giving it renewed vitality."[35] Unfortunately, new complications arose. If Besant's advocacy of Hinduism promoted Theosophy's appeal in India, it did much to undermine the promising collaboration with Buddhists in Sri Lanka. By 1907 the *Maha-Bodhi* was denouncing Olcott's treachery, charging that thanks to Besant, Theosophy had become little more than a front for Hinduism.[36] For a few years Theosophists might claim to speak for Buddhism in one country, for Hinduism in another, and for universal religion in the West; however, the nationalistic fever that accompanied Asian religious revival made such a policy increasingly difficult. Seeking to attract converts throughout the world by its universalism, in the end Theosophy was rejected everywhere as a dangerous eclecticism.

An analysis of Blavatsky's *The Secret Doctrine*, seems a fitting close to the discussion of the Indian years. Published in 1888, it reflected much greater indebtedness to Oriental thought than *Isis Unveiled*. *Isis* had outlined Theosophy's major teachings; *Secret Doctrine* attempted to provide a systematic explanation. The subtitles suggest the difference in scale: where *Isis* promised a "Master-key" to the "Mysteries of Ancient and Modern Science and Theology," *Secret Doctrine* proposed a more ambitious "Synthesis" of "Science, Religion, and Philosophy." Henceforth, students of Theosophy were instructed that *Isis* offered the primer of Theosophical belief, *Secret Doctrine* the definitive statement.

The work's basic argument is the assertion of an ancient Wisdom Religion going back to earliest times that had survived as a "Secret Doctrine." No religion, including Hinduism and Buddhism, could claim to embody the Secret Doctrine; it was the "essence" of all religions. The Secret Doctrine in all ages had been based on the affirmation of three "fundamental propositions": first, the existence of an "Omnipresent, Eternal, Boundless, and Immutable PRINCIPLE," which no human mind could grasp, since it was the "absolute Reality" which preceded "manifested, conditioned, being"; second, the "Eternity of the Universe *in toto* as a boundless plane," which periodically became the "playground of numberless Universes incessantly manifesting and disappearing"; and finally, the "fundamental identity of all Souls with the Universal Over-Soul," which included an "obligatory pilgrimage for every Soul . . . through the Cycle of Incarnation (or 'Necessity') in accordance with Cyclic and Karmic law. . . ."[37] The language is Blavatsky's, but the doctrines come from traditional Hindu philosophy; *Brahman, maya, atman,* and karma have been reformulated in Theosophical terminology. The third proposition—the "identity of all Souls with the Universal Over-Soul"—of course restates the *Vedantic* conclusion, "*Tat tvam asi*": "That art thou." According to the *Vedantist,* the Self or *atman* is one with the Ultimate or *Brahman.*

For most modern readers the book is likely to remain a "secret" doctrine. Though packed with obscure information, the analysis is so convoluted and fantastic that it is often impossible to follow. Consider the following passage, where Blavatsky is clarifying(!) the third principle concerning the identity of individual souls with the Over-Soul:

> In other words, no purely spiritual Buddhi (divine Soul) can have an independent (conscious) existence before the spark which issued from the pure Essence of the Universal Sixth principle,—or the OVER-SOUL,—has (a) passed through every elemental form of the phenomenal world of that Manvantara, and (b) acquired individuality, first by natural impulse, and then by self-induced and self-devised efforts (checked by its Karma), thus ascending through all the degrees of intelligence, from the lowest to the highest Manas, from mineral and plant, up to the holiest archangel (Dhyani-Buddha).[38]

What, one wonders, did the average nineteenth-century reader make of this? Unfortunately, the passage is quite characteristic. Much of the obscurity may be traced to the occultism that pervades the two volumes. Human evolution, for example, is explained as the simultaneous evolution of seven different races in seven different parts of the globe, the "astral" body preceding the "physical." There are frequent references to the "Book of Dzyan," the "oldest book in the world"; however, Blavatsky explains that it was "not in the possession of European Libraries" and "utterly unknown" to Western philologists.[39] Thus, much of the *Secret Doctrine* was based on the exposition of an ancient text known only to Blavatsky.

The great successes of the early years were overshadowed in the mid-1880s by charges of fraud that almost destroyed the movement. The controversy revolved about claims concerning the Mahatmas whose secret powers became increasingly prominent. It was charged that Blavatsky had rigged her Indian quarters with sliding panels and false doors through which she passed the sacred communications that she claimed came from the Masters. The London Society for Psychical Research—which was eager to establish the scientific credibility of study of psychic phenomena—took the claims so seriously that it dispatched a young investigator to India to examine the charges. The resulting Hodgson Report was devastating, confirming that the mysterious "Mahatma Letters" had indeed come from Blavatsky's hand and that her quarters had been especially designed to conceal transmission of the letters. In an unusual testimony, the report concluded that Blavatsky should be viewed "neither as the mouthpiece of hidden seers, nor as a mere vulgar adventuress," but as "one of the most accomplished, ingenious, and interesting impostors in history."[40] Though bitterly denounced by Theosophists, the report was widely accepted as conclusive evidence of the bankruptcy of the movement. Under a cloud, Blavatsky retreated to London where she would spend her last years. Olcott was left behind to gather up the pieces.

While Theosophy was attracting wide notice in Asia, it nearly disappeared in the United States. The man Olcott left in charge as president *pro tempore* was General Abner Doubleday, better remembered as the father of baseball. An old friend of the colonel's—they had worked together in the War Department during the Civil War—Doubleday was one of Blavatsky's earliest American disciples and an active Theosophist throughout his life.[41] For a time the American society was known as the "Theosophical Society of the Arya Samaj or Arya Vart," a change necessitated by Blavatsky's and Olcott's brief alliance with Dayananda.[42] The society continued to meet sporadically, but the American movement simply was not prospering.

William Quan Judge's emergence in the 1880s marked a new era, and under his dynamic leadership American Theosophy rose rapidly to become the largest and most active wing of the international movement. Despite his prominence, he is the most obscure founder of Theosophy. Born in Ireland in 1851 and brought to New York as a child, he had attended the original organizational meeting of the society in 1875, but his legal practice and business interests had at first prevented full participation in the body's activities.[43] He began to take charge of the American movement in the 1880s, utilizing the Aryan Theosophical Society of New York as his base of operations. He quickly achieved a leadership position in the larger movement, traveling to Europe in 1884 to renew contact with Blavatsky and on to India to assist the society through the trials brought on by the Hodgson Report. By 1888, five years after he assumed command, the total number of American Theosophical branches was listed as twenty-five; at his death in 1896 the number had grown to more than one hundred.[44]

The Aryan Society served as the dynamo in revitalizing the American movement. Public meetings at which a paper was read were scheduled twice a month; private meetings were also regularly held with the notes printed for distribution to all American Theosophists.[45] A library of occult, Oriental, and Theosophical books was established for circulation among the society's members. (Abner Doubleday's gift of more than seventy volumes served as the nucleus of the library.) *The Path* began to appear in 1886, and soon after the Aryan Press was created to reprint cheap editions of Theosophical classics. And in 1888, following Blavatsky's lead, an Esoteric Section was announced for more advanced students of Theosophy.

Once the Aryan Society was operating smoothly, Judge moved to consolidate the scattered American branches into a more centralized operation. A "Board of Control" was established to have jurisdiction over the "general and routine work" of all American branches, with the right to certify official Theosophical publications. Upon word from India, however, the plan was soon abandoned for an "American Council" made up of branch presidents and other elected representatives who were to meet regularly to submit reports to the Indian headquarters. Looking back, it is apparent that tensions were already rising between Olcott and Judge that would eventually lead most of the American societies to secede.[46] However, for the moment, Judge acquiesced while continuing to tighten the organization. These measures were not well received in all quarters, some members openly questioning what such mundane considerations had to do with Theosophy. Judge responded, "While we are working in the world we must use the things of the world. . . ." and "Nothing encourages people so much as results of work. . . ."[47] Despite a preference for otherworldly Oriental philosophies, Theosophists did not abandon Western attitudes.

Spiritualism had captured greatest attention in the original American movement, but Orientalism was soon completely overshadowing it despite the fact that the society's official objectives include no reference to Hinduism, Buddhism, or any other Oriental religion. The Society was committed

1. To form a nucleus of the Universal Brotherhood of Humanity, without distinction of race, creed, sex, caste or colour.
2. To encourage the study of comparative religion, philosophy and science.
3. To investigate unexplained laws of Nature and the powers latent in man.[48]

Nevertheless, the promotion of Oriental ideas, particularly Hindu and Buddhist conceptions, had become the society's major concern by the 1880s. Indeed, no contemporary Western group spent more energy explaining and encouraging the adoption of Eastern conceptions.

The pages of *The Path*, Judge's mouthpiece and the leading American organ, provide an excellent gauge of the attitude toward Oriental religions in American Theosophy. The journal is literally filled with articles about the sacred writings and key doctrines of Hinduism and Buddhism. These include the high priest Sumangala's exposition of "The Nature and Office of Buddha's Religion," Isaac Meyer's "Hindu Symbolism," E. D. Walker's "Reincarnation," Charles Johnston's "The Lessons of Karma," J. H. Connelly's "Yoga and Common Sense," Kyo-Ryo-Ya-Sha's "Japanese Buddhist Sects," G. R. S. Mead's "Yoga," and K. P. Mukherji's "Hindu Deities and their Worship."[49] Judge justified the heavy emphasis on Asian thought on the ground that the Eastern masters had already arrived at the religious truths that were just being discovered in the West. Listing the *Vedas*, Patanjali's *Yoga Aphorisms*, the *Bhagavad-Gita*, and "hundreds of other works," he remarked, "What need, then, to bother with crude beginnings of the same things put forth in Europe . . .?"[50] Practically all the leading writers also produced book-length expositions, including Judge's *Bhagavad-Gita*, E. D. Walker's *Reincarnation*, Charles Johnston's *A Compendium of the Raja Yoga Philosophy*, and A. P. Sinnett's *Esoteric Buddhism*.

Theosophists also indicated interest in developing Oriental libraries and promoting Oriental scholarship. The Indian section had the best opportunities for such work because it had direct access to native scholars and ancient manuscript sources. Olcott initiated the most notable effort in 1886 with the founding of the Adyar Library, which included both Western and Oriental collections. By 1901 the colonel could boast that the Oriental collection included some four thousand volumes of palm-leaf manuscripts and an equal number of printed books in Sanskrit, Siamese, Burmese, Sinhalese, Persian, Arabic, Chinese, Japanese, and Pali. There were "more than 200 important Sanskrit works" in the holding "not to be found in any other library in the world. . . ."[51] The collection has come to be highly regarded by Western scholars: writing in 1965, Professor Daniel Ingalls, a distinguished Harvard Sanskritist, referred to the Adyar Library as "one of the chief repositories of Sanskrit manuscripts in the world."[52]

Judge launched several scholarly projects in America, though none were successful. In 1891 he proposed an "Oriental Department" to employ native scholars in India to translate and write articles concerning the religious, philosophical, and social life of the East, with the results to be published and regularly transmitted to American Theosophists.[53] An announcement appeared that Professor Manilal Dvivedi of India had agreed to supply articles; however, the scheme soon collapsed.[54] In 1893 Judge announced the formation of another society, the "Nigamagama Dharma Sabha." The society was to work for the revival of Hinduism in India through the translation of rare manuscripts and employment of a pandit to instruct Hindus in their ancestral religion. Several hundred dollars were spent, but apparently with little result.[55]

In 1894 Judge proposed a still grander body, the "American Asiatic and Sanskrit Revival Society," to conduct historical and scientific research, collect and translate palm-leaf manuscripts, establish an Oriental library, and employ Hindu scholars to lead the revival of Sanskrit learning in India.[56] Embroilment in Theosophical politics and premature death ended any possibility for Judge to implement the ambitious scheme. Judge emphasized that ". . . India is our great storehouse and as such ought to be used with all the means at our command. . . ."[57]

Not all Theosophists were defenders of Oriental thought. In a strange twist, Judge eventually became a leading critic. Politics undoubtedly had much to do with his reversal, which became obvious after the break with Olcott and the secession of the American movement. Once he broke with Indian control, Judge seemed driven to accentuate a Western orientation. There were hints of doubt before the break, however. In a typical piece, Judge explained "Why Yoga Practice Is Dangerous"; in another, a reviewer of a new book on raja yoga warned that "popularizing" any "foreign system of abstruse philosophy" was "difficult" since "language, ideas, and modes of thought . . . rarely transplanted" with success.[58] When a subscriber asked whether he should go to India to develop higher spiritual powers, Judge urged him to remain at home. Judge explained that he would "get no more there than here" and that the "Hindus of to-day" were "not those of the past. . . ." And in a series of "Theosophical Don'ts," the American leader admonished readers not to "think or say that the only true occultism is found in the East."[59]

Following the break with India, these occasional warnings hardened into a definite shift of policy. In a crucial article entitled "The Truth About East and West," Judge charged that modern Hinduism had become stagnant. The "great majority of Brahmans" were as "fixed and dogmatic as the Romish Church" and engaged in "idol-worship and a great number of degrading caste observances." He concluded that future leadership would have to come from the West: though the East would continue to provide "storehouses for the world," the West would "teach the East" to use these riches.[60] Occasionally, he sounded more like a Christian missionary than a Theosophist. Noting the American vogue of Buddhism and Hinduism, he blasted," . . . If the people knew fully the superstitions and absurdities of those two old religions they would never call themselves by either name."[61]

Theosophy's dream of establishing a universal religion was decisively shattered by a series of schisms in the 1890s. For a period, the movement precariously balanced between Olcott in India, Blavatsky in England, and Judge in the United States. Blavatsky's death in 1891 precipitated a drawn-out contest over succession, culminating in a permanent division between the Indian and American sections. Judge's early death in 1896 precipitated the new American schisms. Leadership passed to Katherine Tingley, who moved the American headquarters to California and radically recast the society's work. E. T. Hargrove then broke away and formed a new body committed to the revival of the "original" Theosophical Society.[62] Within a short time Theosophy in America fragmented into three groups: those who remained loyal to Olcott and Besant, the "Adyar" group; those who followed Tingley; and those, including the United Lodge of Theosophy, who emphasized a return to Theosophy's original teachings. In 1951, the authors of a new history of the movement would sadly conclude that the society had "largely degenerated into not one, but several sects." The authors argued that the "dogma of succession in spiritual authority" had been the chief cause of dissension: "No other claim ever rent the Society so much as this one; no other presemption has so betrayed the great impersonality of the Movement."[63] The dream of a universal religion that would unite East and West had produced merely another small and divided sect.

The Theosophical Society's large contribution to the nineteenth-century discovery of Oriental ideas should be obvious. What is not so obvious is the important but indirect role it played in leading other American movements toward the East. Indeed, it is probable that Theosophy's greatest influence came through outside groups. Certainly, that seems to be the conclusion of Charles Braden, who has made the most searching examination of modern religious cults. He cites Unity, New Thought, Rosicrucianism, Psychiana, and the I Am movement as the groups most clearly indebted to Theosophy for Oriental elements; all had drawn a "great deal from Theosophy," but achieved a "mass basis never achieved" by that body.[64]

Though not a religious body in a strict sense, one should add the Nationalist movement to the list; it arose in response to Edward Bellamy's *Looking Backward*. As Arthur Morgan points out, Theosophists played a leading role in the movement's early history.[65] Cyrus Field Willard and Sylvester Baxter, who led in the establishment of the first Nationalist Club, were both Theosophists; Theosophists also dominated *The Nationalist*, the magazine of the movement. Reviewing Bellamy's "wonderful little book," one Theosophical writer went so far as to declare that the Nationalist movement is "essentially theosophical. Many of our most active and ardent fellows have gone into it with enthusiasm. . . ."[66] Morgan concludes, "No description of Nationalism can be adequate which does not take into account its relation to the Theosophical society."[67] Though direct evidence of Oriental influence is meager, Morgan emphasizes that Bellamy was definitely influenced by Indian thought.

The New Thought movement, which rose to prominence in the 1890s and flourished under a variety of names (Mental Science, Divine Science, Unity School of Christianity, Mind Cure, and Practical Metaphysics), offers the best example of Theosophy's intermediary role in leading other movements to the East. An examination of leading New Thought journals—particularly *Mind*, *Metaphysical Magazine*, *Nautilus*, and *Advanced Thought*—reveals widespread evidence of interest in the *Vedanta* philosophy, yoga, reincarnation, and karma.[68] Theosophy was a major stimulus in this interest. The debt to Theosophy was freely acknowledged. Thomas Cuyler spoke of Theosophy as one of the "leading direct sources" of New Thought. The indebtedness included Oriental ideas: "The Theosophical doctrine of Reincarnation and Karma have found much favor among many of the followers of 'New Thought'," Cuyler wrote.[69] Leading New Thought writers who revealed a close acquaintance with Theosophy include Prentice Mulford, William J. Colville, Kate Boehme, Ursula Gestefeld, C. H. A. Bjerregaard, and Ella Wheeler Wilcox. Prominent Theosophists also wrote frequently in New Thought journals, including Charles Johnston, Franz Hartmann, Alexander Fullerton, and Elliott Coues. Members frequently crossed back and forth between the movements. One prominent New Thought leader, Ursula Gestefeld, believed the two were practically identical: she wrote that after "years of attention to both 'Theosophy' and 'Divine Science,'" she had concluded that the "essence of the two is one and the same. . . ."[70] Enjoying a mass appeal, New Thought broadcast the doctrines of the East to a much wider audience than Theosophy.

T. W. Rhys Davids, the great English scholar whose writings did much to remove Western misconceptions concerning Buddhism, may be given the last word. He reminded readers in 1896 that one must always remember that there were "Theosophists and Theosophists." While one could hardly ignore the unhappy aberrations associated with "esoteric Buddhism," one must not forget the Theosophists who were "doing good service" in breaking down Western parochialism; a good number had "really devoted themselves" to the study of Eastern religion. The other Theosophists—who dwelled on "obscure questions of psycho-physics" and "half-savage practices of magic"—had given the whole movement a bad name.[71] Rhys Davids is surely correct. If there have been few modern movements that deserve harsher condemnation, few deserve higher praise for promoting the modern Western awareness of Oriental thought.

Notes

1. *The Theosophical Movement, 1875-1950* (Los Angeles: Cunningham Press, 1951), pp. 39-40. Prepared by the editors of *Theosophy*, the volume offers one of the most dependable "inside" histories of the movement. The controlling viewpoint is that of the United Lodge of Theosophists: there is a pro-Blavatsky, anti-Olcott, pro-Judge bias throughout. See also Henry Steel Olcott, *Old Diary Leaves: The True Story of the Theosophical Society* (New York: G. P. Putnam's, 1895), pp. 113-25. In order to distinguish this work from a five-volume series by the same title, the 1895 publication will always be listed as *Old Diary Leaves: The True Story*.

2. No biographer has done justice to Blavatsky. A. P. Sinnett, ed., *Incidents*

in the Life of Madame Blavatsky Compiled from Information Supplied by her Relatives and Friends (London: George Redway, 1886), provides a sympathetic contemporary account; Vsevolod S. Solovyoff, *A Modern Priestess of Isis* (New York: Longmans, Green, 1895) offers a harshly critical view. Gertrude M. Williams, *Priestess of the Occult (Madame Blavatsky)* (New York: Alfred Knopf, 1946) remains the best modern biography. The accounts vary widely even on the basic details; caution is obviously in order.

3. Olcott, *Old Diary Leaves: The True Story*, p. vii and William Butler Yeats, *The Autobiography of William Butler Yeats* (New York: Macmillan, 1953), p. 107. William Y. Tindall argues that her influence on the poet was profound. Cf. his "Transcendentalism in Contemporary Literature," in Arthur Christy, ed., *The Asian Legacy and American Life* (New York: John Day, 1942), especially pp. 177-86. Yeats's distinguished compatriot, the poet AE (George Russell) was also deeply indebted to Blavatsky.

4. William T. Stead, "Two Views of Madame Blavatsky," *Review of Reviews* 3 (June 1891): 613.

5. The basic source is the multivolume *Old Diary Leaves, The Only Authentic History of the Theosophical Society*, 5 vols. 2nd ed. (Madras, India: Thesophical Publishing House, 1928-35). The five volumes were published as volumes 2-6, since the already published 1895 *Old Diary Leaves: The True Story* had covered the first period. Also see the obituary in *The Theosophist* 28 (March 1907): 433-38, and the recent "inside" biography by Howard Murphet, *Hammer on the Mountain: Life of Henry Steel Olcott (1832-1907)* (Wheaton, Ill.: Theosophical Publishing House, 1972). Olcott deserves a critical modern study.

6. Olcott, *Old Diary Leaves*, pp. 1, 4.

7. Ibid., p. 6.

8. Olcott, *Old Diary Leaves*, 4:23.

9. Cf. Williams, *Priestess of the Occult*, p. 52 and Olcott, *Old Diary Leaves: The True Story*, pp. 25, 132, 330.

10. Helena P. Blavatsky, *Isis Unveiled: A Master-Key to the Mysteries of Ancient and Modern Science and Theology*, 2 vols. (New York: J. W. Bouton, 1877), 1: v, vi.

11. Ibid., 1: vii and 2: 639.

12. Dale Riepe, *The Philosophy of India and Its Impact on American Thought* (Springfield, Ill.: Charles C. Thomas Publishers, 1970), p. 65.

13. Williams, *Priestess of the Occult*, p. 112. For Coleman's general critique, see "The Sources of Madame Blavatsky's Writings," published as Appendix C in Solovyoff, *Modern Priestess of Isis*, pp. 353-66.

14. Olcott, *Old Diary Leaves: The True Story*, pp. 7, 278.

15. I. Kislingbury, "Spiritualism in its Relation to Theosophy," *The Theosophist* 13 (June 1892): 571.

16. Henry Steel Olcott, "Inaugural Address of the President of the Theosophical Society," *The Theosophist* 28 (February 1907): 321-27, continued in 28 (March 1907): 401-7. See particularly pp. 402-5; the quote is from p. 405. For further evidence, see Eugene R. Corson, ed., *Some Unpublished Letters of Helena Petrovna Blavatsky* (London: Rider & Co., 1929), pp. 127-29 and 175, where Blavatsky comments: "My dear Mr. Corson, will you doubt me being a spiritualist?"

17. Henry Steel Olcott, "Theosophy and Theosophists," *Overland Monthly*, Second Series 37 (February 1901): 993.

18. Olcott, *Old Diary Leaves*, pp. 394-407 and *Theosophical Movement, 1875-1950*, pp. 56-59. See also Idem, *Theosophy, Religion and Occult Science* (London: George Redway, 1885), p. x.

19. Williams, *Priestess of the Occult*, p. 141 and Murphet, *Hammer on the Mountain*, pp. 109-10.

20. John N. Farquhar, *Modern Religious Movements in India* (New York: Macmillan, 1915), p. 233. The sketch of Theosophy on pp. 209-91 is one of the best early surveys.

21. Olcott, *Old Diary Leaves*, 2: 165-69.

22. Ibid., 2: 168-69.

23. "Colonel Olcott and the Buddhist Revival Movement," *Maha-Bodhi* 15 (January, February, March 1907): 26. It should be said that as the Buddhist revival spread, its leaders turned away from Theosophy.

24. Olcott, *Old Diary Leaves*, 2: 198-99.

25. Henry Steel Olcott, *A Buddhist Catechism, According to the Canon of the Southern Church* (Boston: Estes & Lauriat, 1885), pp. 11-13.

26. Ibid., pp. 34-35, 39, 77-78.

27. Olcott, *Old Diary Leaves*, 2: 301. The high priest's endorsement appears on p. iv. of the *Buddhist Catechism*. Sumangala later recalled his endorsement, citing major discrepancies between the *Catechism* and Theravada doctrine. Cf. "High Priest Sumangala and the Theosophical Society," *Maha-Bodhi* 14 (April 1906): 57-58.

28. Olcott, *Old Diary Leaves*, 3: 352-53; 4: 114-23, 432-37; "Olcott Day," *The Middleway* (London) 29 (August 1954): 85.

29. See Ernst Benz, *Buddhism or Communism: Which Holds the Future of Asia?* (New York: Doubleday, 1965), pp. 19-27, 61-65.

30. Anagarika Dharmapala, "Reminiscences of my Early Life," *Maha-Bodhi* 41 (May-June 1933): 151-62, and Sri Chandra Sen, "The Ven'ble Sri Devamitta Dhammapala," *Maha-Bodhi* 41 (July-September 1933): 326-56.

31. Anagarika Dharmapala, "Diary Leaves," *Maha-Bodhi* 2 (December 1893): 6-7. For Dharmapala's appearance at the Parliament of Religions, see chap. 13.

32. D. Valisenha, "Diary Leaves of the Late Ven. Anagarika Dharmapala," *Maha-Bodhi* 64 (March 1956): 99.

33. The first installment appeared in *The Index* 7 (March 16, 1876): 128-29, and continued over several issues. Unlike other Theosophical leaders, she has received serious scholarly treatment. See Arthur H. Nethercot's *The First Five Lives of Annie Besant* (London: Rupert Hart-Davis, 1961) and *The Last Four Lives of Annie Besant* (Chicago: University of Chicago Press, 1963). For a recent evaluation by an Oriental scholar, see Daniel H. H. Ingalls, "The Heritage of a Fallible Saint: Annie Besant's Gifts to India," *Proceedings of the American Philosophical Society* 109 (April 9, 1965): 85-88.

34. See his appreciative account, "Annie Besant and the Theosophic Society," pp. 193-227 in D. S. Sarma, *Studies in the Renaissance of Hinduism in the Nineteenth and Twentieth Centuries* (Benares, India: Benares Hindu University, 1944).

35. H. S. O. [Henry Steel Olcott], "The Hindu Revival," *The Theosophist* 15 (April 1894): 424.

36. *Maha-Bodhi* 15 (January, February, March 1907): 19-20, 26-28.

37. Helena P. Blavatsky, *The Secret Doctrine: The Synthesis of Science, Religion, and Philosophy*, 2 vols. (London, 1888; reprint ed., Pasadena, Calif.: Theosophical University Press, 1952), 1: 14, 16, 17.

38. Ibid., 1: 17.

39. Ibid., 1: xxii.

40. *Theosophical Movement, 1875-1950*, p. 96. See also Williams, *Priestess of the Occult*, pp. 237-57.

41. H. S. O. [Henry Steel Olcott], "Major-General Doubleday, F.T.S." *The Theosophist* 14 (May 1893): 499; see also *The Path* 7 (February 1893): 362.

42. *The Path* 10 (May 1894): 58.

43. See Jasper Niemand, "William Q. Judge," serialized in the *Irish Theosophist* (Dublin) 4 (1896): 90-92, 112-16, 141-45, 165-68. "Jasper Niemand" was the pen name used by Mrs. Archibald Keightley.

44. Figures cited in *The Path* 3 (December 1888). 394 and *North American Review* 162 (June 1896): 700.

45. *The Path* 1 (June 1886): 95-96. The society's activities may be followed in successive issues of the journal.

46. *The Path* 1 (May 1886): 63-64, and 1 (September 1886): 191-92.

47. *The Path* 3 (February 1889): 352.

48. "Rules of the Theosophical Society," *The Theosophist* 19 (January 1898): Supplement, 72. This is the standard codification; there are some significant differences from earlier formulations.

49. *The Path* 1 (April 1886): 24-26; 1 (October 1886): 220-22; 1 (March 1887): 370-72; 2 (May 1887): 33-44; 2 (February 1888): 335-39; 4 (January 1890): 297-301; 5 (November 1890): 240-41, continued; 7 (June 1892): 75-79, continued; and 7 (July 1892): 115-16.

50. [William Q. Judge], "Two Years on the Path," *The Path* 2 (March 1888): 358-59.

51. Olcott, *Overland Monthly*, Second Series 37 (February 1901): 997.

52. Daniel H. H. Ingalls, "The Heritage of a Fallible Saint: Annie Besant's Gifts to India," *Proceedings of the American Philosophical Society* 109 (April 9, 1965): 86.

53. "The Oriental Department," *The Path* 5 (February 1891): 359.

54. Cf. *The Path* 6 (June 1891): 91, and 8 (July 1893): 126.

55. William Q. Judge, "Nigamagama Dharma Sabha," *The Path* 9 (July 1894): 117-19.

56. "The American Asiatic and Sanskrit Revival Society," *The Path* 9 (December 1894): 296.

57. [William Q. Judge], "India a Storehouse for Us," *The Path* 5 (February 1891): 345.

58. *The Path* 5 (March 1891): 367-68 and 3 (January 1889): 330.

59. *The Path* 7 (July 1892): 124, and 9 (December 1894): 277.

60. William Q. Judge, "The Truth about East and West," *The Path* 10 (April 1895): 3, 5.

61. William Q. Judge, "Questions and Answers," *The Path* 10 (November 1895): 257.

62. *Theosophical Movement, 1875-1950,* pp. 190-289. Emmett A. Greenwalt, *The Point Loma Community in California, 1897-1942: A Theosophical Experiment* (Berkeley, Calif.: University of California Press, 1955) is a first-rate account of the Tingley wing of the movement.

63. *Theosophical Movement, 1875-1950,* pp. 284-85.

64. Charles S. Braden, *These Also Believe. A Study of Modern American Cults and Minority Religious Movements* (New York: Macmillan, 1949), p. 255.

65. Arthur E. Morgan, *Edward Bellamy* (New York: Columbia University Press, 1944), pp. 260-75.

66. J. Hudson Markam, "Who Invented Altruism?" *The Theosophist* 11 (April 1890): 397.

67. Morgan, *Bellamy*, p. 260.

68. See my article, "The New Thought Movement and the Nineteenth Century Discovery of Oriental Philosophy," *Journal of Popular Culture* 9 (Winter 1975): 523-48.

69. Thomas H. Cuyler, "The Crucible of Modern Thought," *Progress Magazine* 9 (February 1910): 41.

70. Ursula N. Gestefeld, "Another View of Metaphysical Healing," *The Path* 6 (February 1892): 342.

71. Thomas W. Rhys Davids, *Buddhism: Its History and Literature*, 3rd rev. ed. (New York: G. P. Putnam's, 1896), pp. 213-14.

10
The Emergence of the Oriental Scholar

Despite an intense interest in Oriental thought, Transcendental and Unitarian intellectuals were always handicapped by their inability to read Asian languages. They consulted translations by English and French scholars, but no translation could substitute for reading texts in the original. Theosophists enthusiastically supported the idea of Oriental scholarship, but few had the background to engage in such activity. Popular accounts of Oriental thought were useful, but something more was needed. Fortunately, by the end of the century the country could boast of a number of outstanding Oriental scholars.

One of the earliest men to demonstrate scholarly interest in Asian languages was the gifted Franco-American Peter Du Ponceau (1760-1844).[1] A passionate supporter of the American Revolution, he had come to America in 1777 as Baron von Steuben's personal secretary. After the war he settled in Pennsylvania where he entered upon a distinguished career as a lawyer and author. Drawn to the study of philology, he published several highly regarded treatises on the languages of North American Indians before turning to Oriental languages. His one attempt at Oriental scholarship, *A Dissertation on the Nature and Character of the Chinese System of Writing*, was published in 1838.

Du Ponceau set out in the *Dissertation* to provide an analysis of the grammatical structure and principles underlying Chinese. (The nature of the language has long preoccupied Westerners, with many novel theories advanced to explain its peculiarities.) He argued that the written language was "lexigraphic" rather than "ideographic," that is, the written characters did not represent ideas or representations of the objective world, as some European scholars had claimed, but simply sounds or syllables.[2] Did he read Chinese and did he know anything about Chinese thought? Apparently, the answer to both questions is "no," since he remarks that he did not intend to master Chinese literature or even to memorize the major characters of the language. Not that he was a complete novice; he notes that he had heard Chinese converse and he cites such European Orientalists as Rémusat, Morrison, Marshman, Klaproth. The *Dissertation* was largely ignored by contemporaries. Modern scholars have come to regard it as a pioneer work: Franklin Edgerton, a distinguished twentieth-century Orientalist, acclaims it as a "brilliant" work whose argument modern Sinologists have increasingly come to accept.[3] Du Ponceau was a gifted amateur; the country still awaited the emergence of the first professionals.

The true beginning of Oriental scholarship in America dates from 1842, the year of the formation of the American Oriental Society. Once again, New Englanders played the leading role. John Pickering of Salem served as the organization's first president; much of the membership came from the Boston area. The body's chief activities included calling meetings where scholarly papers could be read, acquiring an Oriental library, and sponsoring the *Journal of the American Oriental Society*.[4] Though a few years after its formation the society's corresponding secretary was lamenting that "our poor Oriental Society seems to languish," the organization grew from 65 members listed in 1846-47 to 288 members by 1900.[5] Over the next fifty years it would do more than any other organization to establish the scholarly study of Asian thought in America.

Leafing through the early proceedings of the society, one is immediately impressed by the prominence of missionaries in the first years. In the very first presidential address, John Pickering emphasized the key role that missionaries must play. American missionaries were "more active" and provided a "greater number of proficients in various languages of the East" than any other nation.[6] Indeed, with the exception of a few academicians like Professor Cornelius Felton of Harvard or Professor Edward Salisbury of Yale, the typical member seems to have been a minister, theologian, or missionary—the three professions providing most of the names listed on the society's early rolls. Following Pickering's death, Edward Robinson—of the Union Theological Seminary—filled the presidency for the next seventeen years (1846-1863). All three of the organization's first vice-presidents were men of the cloth: Robinson, who shortly succeeded to the presidency, the Reverend William Jenks, and Moses Stuart, who was professor of Hebrew at Andover Theological Seminary.[7] The society made strenuous efforts to contact missionaries in the field and to encourage communications to its journal. Excluding printed proceedings, membership lists, and miscellaneous notes, forty-five of the ninety-six major pieces published in the first ten volumes of the *Journal* (1843-1880)—almost half—were contributed by missionaries.[8] The church, not the university, was the dominant force in early American Oriental scholarship.

An examination of the *Journal* indicates that the society's original conception of the field of its inquiry was quite broad. Indeed, until 1900, the term "Orient" was applied to all areas of the Old World except Europe. (The society subsequently subdivided the work into three parts: a Section for Semitic Studies, a Section for Indic and Iranian Studies, and a Section for Far Eastern Studies.) Of the three centers of Asian civilization, India received most attention, China much less, and Japan almost none at all. A rough count for the period until 1900 reveals that while some sixty articles pertain to India, only ten were devoted to China and two to Japan. This disproportion, though less extreme in later years, has remained a problem throughout the society's history.[9]

Asian religion received much attention, but practically all the contributions focused on Hinduism. The emphasis varied widely: there were bibliographical essays such as Professor William Whitney's report on *Vedic* researches in Germany; translations of religious texts such as missionary Henry Hoisington's translation of a treatise from the Tamil; essays such as Professor Rudolph Roth's "On the Morality of the Veda"; and more philosophical pieces such as Professor Charles Everett's "The Psychology of the Vedanta and Sankhya Philosophies."[10] Buddhism was the only other Asian religion to receive attention, though much less than Hinduism. Examples include Edward Salisbury's scholarly "Memoir on the History of Buddhism"; the Reverend Francis Mason's "Hints on the Introduction of Buddhism into Burmah"; and diplomat William Rockhill's translation of Tibetan Buddhist Birth stories.[11] Several articles concerned China, but none were specifically devoted to Confucianism or Taoism. For the most part, the pieces were written for the scholar and advanced student, not the layman.

Perhaps half the contributions were philological in emphasis, the dominant note in early American Oriental scholarship. Random but representative pieces from the first four volumes reveal the emphasis: Samuel Wells Williams's "Note on Japanese Syllabaries," the Reverend Henry Ballantine on the relations between the Maratha and the Sanskrit, Professor John Avery's "Contributions to the History of Verb-Inflection in Sanskrit," and the Reverend Moses White's "Chinese Local Dialects Reduced to Writing."[12] Several reasons may undoubtedly be advanced for this heavy concentration on language, but the most important surely was the European example, especially the German influence. Inspired by Franz Bopp's studies in comparative philology, which emphasized the common Aryan roots of

Sanskrit and the major European languages, scholars had increasingly looked to language as the master key to knowledge. As a large proportion of America's first Oriental scholars received their training in Germany—the center of so much of the philological research—it was to be expected that they should manifest the same enthusiasm. Young scholars quickly learned that a meticulously annotated translation of a formerly untranslated manuscript was the best path to a scholarly reputation.

Despite some very impressive monographs, the heavy emphasis on language was unfortunate in a number of ways. For one thing it tended to divert attention from the larger pattern and significance of the texts. Looking back, one may criticize Samuel Johnson's lack of linguistic skills but wish that more of the new Orientalists had shared his desire to map the larger contours of Oriental thought. From a humanistic perspective, less attention to Sanskrit verb inflections and more to the explanation of Hindu doctrines would surely have been more fruitful. One might further question whether American scholars were wise to place such high priority on duplicating work already being done in Europe when there were other areas of inquiry open where they might have broken new ground. Such doubts seem especially appropriate in the case of the missionary scholars who contributed so much in the first period. Based in Asian countries, they were in positions to do what few European scholars could do: to observe and analyze the actual ethnographic, economic, social, and religious peculiarities of the Eastern societies in which they resided. Instead, most confined themselves to linguistic analysis.[13]

The narrow philological emphasis won out, but there were always advocates of a broader focus. The first volumes of the *Journal* offered a good deal to interest a general reader, including Edward Salisbury's "Memoir on the History of Buddhism," Klaproth's "The History of Paper Money in China," William Greenough's "China: Its Population—Trade—and the Prospect of a Treaty," and William Turner's "Account of a Japanese Romance."[14] On several occasions the society's officers expressed concern over the small number of Americans who showed interest in the Orient and indicated interest in broadening the organization's appeal. Though in part motivated by the small membership and shaky financial condition of the society, the concern also reflected a deeper commitment to awaken Americans to the significance of Oriental cultures. In 1849 the society actually amended its statement of objectives to emphasize a broader, more humanistic approach.[15] Unfortunately, there is little indication that the constitutional change widened the society's work.

Missionaries played a significant role in the American Oriental Society's first decades, but professional Orientalists soon emerged to dominate it.

The man who led the transition to professionalism, who deserves the title of father of American Oriental studies, was Edward Salisbury. Born in 1815 in Boston and educated at Yale, Salisbury had originally intended to enter the ministry.[16] However, Josiah Willard Gibbs, professor of biblical literature at Yale, diverted his interest to comparative philology, and, during a subsequent English visit, Horace Hayman Wilson, professor of Sanskrit at Oxford, diverted him toward Oriental studies.[17] Salisbury remained in Europe for several years, studying Arabic with Professors Garcin De Tassy and Sylvester De Sacy in Paris and Sanskrit with Franz Bopp in Berlin. When he returned home in 1841, Yale asked him to fill a new professorship in Arabic and Sanskrit, the first such position in an American university. After another year of European study with Sanskritist Christian Lassen of the University of Bonn, he took up his duties in 1843.

Salisbury took a leading role in the fledgling American Oriental Society. Made the society's corresponding secretary in 1846, he carried on most of its correspondence for decades, began the Oriental library, and even provided funds to underwrite the *Journal*'s repeated deficits. He served as president of the society from 1863 to 1866 and again from 1873 to 1881. He also became one of the *Journal*'s most dependable contributors, commencing with a "Memoir on the History of Buddhism" in the first volume. Altogether, he published eleven major contributions. The diversity is amazing: there are pieces on Buddhism, the Persian cuneiform alphabet, the genuineness of a Nestorian monument in China, the progress of Oriental studies, the Islamic doctrines of predestination and free will, as well as several translations of Arabic texts.[18] If most summarized new developments in European scholarship, several were works of original research.

Salisbury was the first American to demonstrate serious acquaintance with Buddhism—a major development considering the previous ignorance that had dominated discussions of Buddha. His fifty-five-page "Memoir on the History of Buddhism" appeared in 1844. He indicated indebtedness to the best European authorities, including Henry Thomas Colebrooke, Brian H. Hodgson, and Alexander Csoma de Körös. Generally synthetic and historical in emphasis, the article discussed the origins and key doctrines of Buddhism, the historical facts of Buddha's life, and the subsequent spread of Buddhism throughout Asia.[19] Salisbury stressed that Buddhism was not atheistic and that nirvana referred to a higher state of realization, not annihilation—questions that would be sharply debated later in the century. Another pioneering article, a review-essay of Burnouf's *Introduction a l'histoire du Buddhisme Indien*, was less ambitious, but provided an informative discussion of Indian Buddhism based on Nepalese sources—a form of Buddhism unknown in the United States. Salisbury summarized Burnouf's arguments and quoted extensively from the Buddhist texts.[20]

Despite his real accomplishments, Salisbury came to regard his career as a disappointment. In an astonishing confession near the end of his life, he expressed regret that he had given up plans for the ministry.[21] Apparently, much of his sense of failure stemmed from his inability to specialize as the new scholarship required. Referring to his articles in the Oriental Society *Journal*, he would declare that he had written more as an "amateur student" than as a "master with authority."[22] He seemed overwhelmed by his very title as professor of Arabic and Sanskrit, dismissing it as an "absurdly named professorship" which had "discouraged" him from the first. "I never advanced much beyond the position where I stood at the start," he sadly confessed.[23] One might be tempted to dismiss such assertions were it not that his actions reveal a tendency toward withdrawal. Within a decade of his acceptance of the Yale appointment, while still in his early forties, he began to phase out his position. He turned the Sanskrit half of the professorship over to a former student in 1854 and resigned the Arabic half as well in 1856. His publications in the *Journal* ceased in the 1860s—when he was still only in his mid-fifties, with more than thirty years of life remaining. He devoted his last years to genealogical studies.

Though Salisbury's professional training and European residence pointed the way of the future, his scholarly preferences pointed backward to the previous age of genteel scholarship. As Orientalist Edward Washburn Hopkins declared at his death in 1901, Salisbury had always worked in a surprisingly old-fashioned manner. There were "no technical studies, no statistics, almost no investigation in the confined sense we give to that word to-day"; Hopkins concluded that Salisbury's taste had been "literary and historical rather than philological. . . ."[24] The shift from a broad literary emphasis to philological specialization represented the basic difference between the old and new scholarship.

Salisbury need not have judged his life a failure if for no other reason than his role in launching the brilliant career of William Dwight Whitney. Tough-minded, self-confident, and a fantastic worker, with the scholar's passion for detail, Whitney had all the traits that his mentor seemed to lack. Succeeding Salisbury as corresponding secretary and eventually president of the American Oriental Society, the younger man oversaw the society's transformation from a loose association of missionaries, theologians, and amateurs into a disciplined organization of professionals dedicated to the most demanding standards of scholarship. Whitney was the greatest Oriental scholar produced by nineteenth-century America, perhaps ever. He was also the first American to make major scholarly contributions to the study of Hinduism.

Born and raised in Northampton, Massachusetts, Whitney's sturdy New England roots have appeared to most biographers as the source of much of his later success.[25] In fact, the secret seems to have been sturdy New England parents, for all the Whitney children were remarkable achievers. William's older brother Josiah became a distinguished professor of geology at Harvard; another brother, James Lyman, became head of the Boston Public Library; a third brother, Henry Mitchell, was professor of English literature at Beloit College; and sister Maria was professor of modern languages at Smith College. At first, William seemed predestined for a scientific career, revealing a youthful passion for natural history. His earliest writings were not devoted to Sanskrit, but to the pine grosbeak and snowy owl, published while he was still an undergraduate at Williams College.[26]

Whitney's first encounter with Sanskrit reveals the often obscure paths by which America's early Orientalists found their vocations. His brother Josiah had gone to Germany to pursue studies in geology; among the books he brought back was a Sanskrit grammar by Professor Bopp. Looking through the book, William was fascinated and commenced to teach himself Sanskrit.[27] Nothing might have come of this had not a local minister discovered the boy's strange enthusiasm and persuaded his businessman father to permit him to pursue Sanskrit studies. Thus, Whitney came to Yale in 1849 to study under Salisbury—the only man then in America equipped to offer the instruction he desired.[28] After a year, he proceeded to Germany where he studied for the next three years under Bopp, Albrecht Weber, Karl Lepsius, and Rudolph Roth.

One of the remarkable aspects of Whitney's subsequent career is the large role that Salisbury played. Few teachers have been more devoted to their students. Having taught the younger man what he knew and sent him off to Europe, he personally raised the funds necessary to establish the new Yale professorship in Sanskrit, which awaited Whitney on his return in 1853. On the one occasion Whitney was tempted to leave Yale as the result of an attractive offer from Harvard, Salisbury quickly intervened, advancing funds out of his own pocket to establish a full chair for him to occupy. Salisbury also promoted Whitney in the American Oriental Society: he read his papers in his absence, acclaimed his work in *Journal* reviews, and encouraged his leadership in the organization. Though enormous talent and hard work would undoubtedly have assured Whitney's success, Salibury's constant support made for a faster rise.

Whitney's phenomenal productiveness as a scholar fully justified Salisbury's confidence. The bibliography of his total writings stretches to 360 items, extending from his youthful ventures in natural history through the 2,459 page manuscript of the second volume of his magisterial translation of the *Atharva Veda.* His earliest publication as an aspiring Oriental scholar dates from 1849, an article "On the Grammatical Structure of the Sanskrit."[29] Most of his scholarly writing appeared in the *Journal of the American Oriental Society.* The first contribution, "On the Main Results of the Later Vedic Researches in Germany," offered a summary of the work of his German mentors, Roth and Weber. Over the next forty years hardly a year passed in which a major article or an abstract of a paper did not appear in the *Journal's* pages, including general essays on the *Vedas* as well as more specialized pieces on Sanskrit grammar.[30] Between 1857 and 1885, the period of his greatest productivity, more than half of the *Journal*'s contents came from his pen alone.[31]

Whitney's reputation as America's greatest Oriental scholar rests primarily on two accomplishments: his *Vedic* translations and his *Sanskrit Grammar*. As the oldest and most venerated scriptures of Hinduism, the *Vedas* are crucial. Despite an interest that went back at least to Colebrooke's famous 1805 "Essay on the Vedas," *Vedic* studies in the West were still in their infancy at midcentury. Roth, Weber, and Max Müller had just begun to open the field when Whitney appeared.[32] The first need was accurate translations of the four *Vedas*—which required a search for all available texts and a collation of their contents. Whitney was largely responsible for establishing the scholar's text of the fourth and least known of the ancient works, the *Atharva Veda*. He began to copy texts for the translation at Professor Roth's suggestion and published the first volume in 1855-1856. (Roth is listed as a full collaborator, although Whitney did most of the labor.) The second volume was completed and published posthumously in the 1890s. In addition, he completed a translation of the *Atharva Veda Pratisakhya*, a major commentary on the *Atharva Veda*, and a complete index, the *Index Verborum to the Atharva-Veda*.

For scholarly studies of Hinduism to advance very far, Sanskrit was essential. Here Whitney made his second major contribution, his *Sanskrit Grammar*, which revolutionized the teaching of Sanskrit in America. Traditionally, students had approached the study of Sanskrit through the grammar of Panini, a Hindu grammarian of the fourth century B.C., who had succeeded in codifying the four thousand rules of the language so brilliantly that his pronouncements had dominated study ever after. Unfortunately, Panini's rules were so complicated and his presentation so terse that Westerners had great difficulty following them.[33] In his *Grammar* Whitney recast the entire subject according to the principles of modern philology. Previously, following Panini, Sanskrit had been treated as a static language whose rules had remained constant; Whitney approached it historically with the assumption that the language had constantly changed. (It seems safe to say that no field in the late nineteenth century escaped the pervasive influence of evolution.) The *Grammar* quickly became the basic text for beginning students. Writing as late as the 1940s, the eminent Orientalist Franklin Edgerton still spoke of the *Grammar* as a "supreme triumph," which after sixty years remained "unequalled in its field as a descriptive account of the language. . . ."[34] Few nineteenth-century books have stood up so well.

Though uncompromising in his view of scholarship, Whitney recognized the need to bridge the gap between the specialist and the general public. The need grew as the new scholarship became more technical. Such pieces as "The British in India" and "China and the Chinese," published in the *New Englander*, and "The Translation of the Veda" and "Histories of India," published in the *North American Review*, indicate his ability to write for a lay audience. Hindu religion came under discussion in his "On the Vedic Doctrine of a Future Life."[35] Most of these popular essays were subsequently reissued in book form as *Oriental and Linguistic Essays*. Whitney also regularly reviewed books dealing with the East in the columns of the *Nation*.

William Hayes Ward, who subsequently became president of the American Oriental Society, declared in 1898 that "every one of the Sanskritists of this country" had in some sense been Whitney's pupil.[36] The estimate is not far off. By 1900 a new generation of young Oriental scholars had emerged, and few were not in some way indebted to Whitney. A brief resume of the careers of three—Charles Rockwell Lanman, Maurice Bloomfield, and Edward Washburn Hopkins—indicates the rising maturity of American Oriental scholarship by century's end. All three were born in the decade before the Civil War and entered careers in Oriental scholarship in the late 1870s or early 1880s.[37] All three made significant contributions to the study of Oriental religion.

Charles Rockwell Lanman (1850-1941), one of Whitney's first doctoral students at Yale, was one of the earliest Americans to complete a doctorate in Sanskrit studies in an American university.[38] He completed his training in Germany, studying under Weber, Roth, and Curtius. He began teaching at Johns Hopkins, which established the second Sanskrit professorship in the United States, but he soon moved to Harvard where he remained for the next forty-five years. His publications include several articles dealing with *Vedic* research in the Oriental Society *Journal*, several pieces on yoga including "Hindu Ascetics and their Powers" and "The Hindu Yoga System,"[39] a book *The Beginnings of Hindu Pantheism* (1890), and his *Sanskrit Reader* (1884), a companion volume to Whitney's *Grammar* which became a standard text for introductory students.

However, Lanman's greatest contribution was his editorship of the *Harvard Oriental Series*, which published scholarly translations of major Oriental works. Whitney's *Atharva Veda*, Henry Clarke Warren's *Buddhism in Translation*, Maurice Bloomfield's *Vedic Concordance*, and James Haughton Woods's *The Yoga-System of Patanjali* are only a few of the notable volumes published in the series. One of Lanman's students, Henry Clarke Warren, provided the funds necessary to underwrite the series. The statement of purpose appended to the 1920 publication list indicates that the series was conceived as a crucial link in East-West encounter. Lanman spoke glowingly of the great value Westerners would derive from better acquaintance with the Oriental religions, and he described the volumes in the series as making available the "incomparable lessons" which "Wise Men of the East" could "teach us."[40] Like Max Müller's famous *Sacred Books of the East*, the *Harvard Oriental Series* indicates the important role scholars could play in Western acquaintance with the Asian religions.

Maurice Bloomfield (1855-1928) is one of the few American Orientalists in the nineteenth century who did not come from New England. (Salisbury, Whitney, Hopkins, and Warren were all from Massachusetts, Lanman from Connecticut.) Born in Austria, Bloomfield immigrated to the United States at the age of four.[41] Graduating from Furman University in South Carolina, he spent a year with Whitney at Yale and then transferred to Johns Hopkins to complete his doctorate under Lanman. After further work at Berlin and Leipzig, in 1881 he succeeded Lanman at Johns Hopkins, a position he filled for the next forty-five years. In many ways he was Whitney's nearest successor, publishing a translation of the *Hymns of the Atharva Veda* in 1897 and a *Vedic Concordance* in 1906. His meticulous translation of the *Hymns* is apparent in the fact that in a work of nearly eight hundred pages, only two hundred pages actually provide the translations with the remaining pages devoted to explanation and scholarly analysis. Whitney himself would not have been more thorough! In later years he moved on to the *Rig-Veda*, publishing a work entitled *Rig-Veda Repetitions*.

If most of his writing was forbiddingly technical, Bloomfield could adapt to a more general audience, a fact pointed up by articles on "The Foundation of Buddhism" and "Brahmanical Riddles and the Origin of Theosophy,"[42] as well as his book, *Religion of the Vedas* (1908). Prepared as lectures for student audiences at Johns Hopkins, Union Theological Seminary, and Hartford Theological Seminary, the book offered a suitable introduction to Indian religion. In Bloomfield's interpretation Hinduism was rooted in paradox: "tolerant, liberal, latitudinarian" in abstract belief, it was at the same time "tyrannous, illiberal, [and] narrow-minded" in its social practices. The result was a curious combination of "fluidity" in doctrine and "rigidity" in practice.[43] Running to nearly two hundred items, Bloomfield's publication record is extremely impressive—though his total fell well below Whitney's prodigious output.

Since he was never actually Whitney's student, Edward Washburn Hopkins (1857-1932) cannot be considered a protégé in the same sense as Lanman and Bloomfield. However, there were important links: since Columbia University did not yet offer Sanskrit studies when he matriculated, Hopkins taught himself to read Sanskrit with the help of Whitney's *Grammar*; he also inherited Whitney's post as Salisbury professor of Sanskrit and comparative philology at Yale upon the great scholar's death. Finally, he spent several crucial years in Germany where he studied with one of Whitney's mentors, Albrecht Weber. Receiving his Ph.D. from the University of Leipzig in 1881, he served brief stints at Columbia and Bryn Mawr before assuming the position at Yale in 1895. He would remain for the next thirty years.[44] The most active publisher of the younger group, he authored *The Religion of India, The Great Epic of India, India Old and New, Epic Mythology, The History of Religions, Ethics of India, Legends of India,* and *The Origin and Evolution of Religion.* Hopkins pointed to important changes that were emerging in Oriental scholarship. One was the decline of fixation on philology and the emergence of a broader, more cross-disciplinary perspective; another was a much greater emphasis on historical and comparative perspectives. Both tendencies dominate Hopkins's books; he was much more concerned with Hindu ethics, sociology, and philosophy than language.

Hopkins's *Religions of India* indicates the growing sophistication of American writing on Oriental religion. Originally published in 1895 and reissued in 1902, it was apparently one of the period's most influential books on Indian religion.[45] The book is dedicated to Whitney. Embracing a perspective that was adopted increasingly, Hopkins set out to view Indian religion "from within," allowing Hindu spokesmen "to reveal themselves."[46] Although harsh judgments still occur, the general tone is much more objective than in earlier accounts. The book's most impressive feature is Hopkins's success in laying out the successive stages in the evolution of Hinduism—that is, in placing Indian religion in history. Following an analysis of the entry of Aryans into India and several chapters on the *Vedas,* subsequent chapters trace the crystallization of early Hinduism, the Jainist and Buddhist revolts, and the later emergence of sectarian movements such as Vaishnavism and Sivaism. The volume climaxes in two final chapters on "Modern Hindu Sects" and "India and the West," bringing the treatment to the 1890s. Another virtue of the work is Hopkins's insistence on including popular forms of Hinduism; he rightly complained that the philosophical view presented in the *Upanishads* and *Vedanta* always tended to be exaggerated. He recognized that many primitive elements in Hinduism had survived into the nineteenth century.

The last chapter, "India and the West," deserves special notice as one of the earliest American attempts to evaluate the contemporary impact of Oriental religions. Despite intense interest in Indian thought, Hopkins was clearly hostile to the idea of Eastern influence. He conceded that there was considerable Western interest in "Indic superstition and spiritualism," but credited this to the ignorance of "half-educated people." If Buddhism seemed to be having "some influence on popular thought," he explained the phenomenon as a "very unreal Buddhism. . . ."[47] What, then, was the value of studying the Oriental religions? His answer: "Not, we venture to think, in their face value for the religious or philosophical life of the Occident," but as a case study of the "origin and growth of theistic ideas" and of the "prodigious significance of the religious factor in the development of a race. . . ."[48] While minimizing the appeal of the Oriental religions, the very fact that Hopkins recognized the increasing attraction and felt the need to minimize it signals an important change. Fifty years earlier it is difficult to imagine an American scholar feeling the need to mention the matter.

While American scholars poured out new books on Hinduism almost annually, Buddhism seemed almost forgotten. It is true that Salisbury had helped launch American Oriental scholarship in the 1840s with several important articles on Buddhism, but he worked almost alone. The lack of scholarly attention became all the more obvious in the wake of the popular interest generated by Sir Edwin Arnold's *Light of Asia*. The probable explanations for this strange omission include a lack of background in Pali and other languages necessary for Buddhist studies and the already well-established concentration on Indic studies. However, the situation was to change dramatically in the 1890s.

Mention may be first made of Albert J. Edmunds (1857-1914), who though self-trained, deserves recognition as a pioneer of Buddhist studies in America. Already middle-aged when he took up Buddhist scholarship and never connected with a university, he was unquestionably an amateur. The details of his life are obscure. English and a Quaker in background, he immigrated to the United States in 1885, living most of his life in the vicinity of Philadelphia. A student of psychic phenomena and Swedenborgianism, he was apparently drawn to Buddhism as much out of religious as scholarly motivation.[49] Teaching himself to read Pali, the ancient language of Theravada Buddhism, in 1902 he published a translation of the *Dhammapada* entitled *Hymns of the Faith*, and two years later brought out his two-volume *Buddhist and Christian Gospels Now First Compared from the Originals*. In addition, he published several pieces in the *Buddhist Review*, organ of the Buddhist Society of Great Britain and Ireland, and was a regular contributor to the *Open Court*, the well-known journal edited by Paul Carus.[50] Through Carus he became acquainted with D. T. Suzuki, who was then assisting with the *Open Court*—to become an internationally famous authority on Mahayana and Zen Buddhism. As they became friends, Edmunds introduced Suzuki to Swedenborgianism, while Suzuki in turn encouraged Edmunds's Buddhist studies.[51]

Edmunds concentrated most of his scholarly energy on the comparative study of Buddhist and Christian sacred writings. Although European scholars had been debating parallels between the lives and legends of Buddha and Jesus since midcentury, unfortunately, much of the discussion was marred by sensationalism, including the claims that Christianity had borrowed heavily from Buddhism and that Jesus had studied in the Orient. Edmunds approached the matter much more cautiously. He explained that he neither sought to prove that Christianity was derived from Buddhism nor that Buddhism came from Christianity, but only to compare passages in the sacred literatures of the two traditions. Much of his analysis consists of parallel columns of extracts drawn from the two religions, grouped under such headings as "Healing the Sick," "Prayer," "Psychical Powers," and "The Second Coming." After a line-by-line analysis, he concluded that there was some evidence of Buddhist influence on the Christian scriptures, especially in the book of Saint Luke, but also evidence that Christianity had touched later Buddhism. Altogether, he identified 102 parallels of the Christian scriptures with the Buddhist canonical literature and 13 with the uncanonical literature.[52]

For some reason, Edmunds's effort was practically ignored. He experienced great difficulty getting a publisher for the *Buddhist and Christian Gospels,* finally preparing an abstract of the book out of his own meager funds for circulation among scholars. A Japanese scholar recommended by D. T. Suzuki, Masaharu Anesaki, finally came to his rescue, and the two volumes were published.[53] Several eminent European Orientalists praised his effort. T. W. Rhys Davids welcomed the *Buddhist and Christian Gospels,* remarking that the volumes would do much to settle the controversy over bothersome parallels. Many years later, Maurice Winternitz, a German Sanskritist, would emphasize that Edmunds had improved on previous scholars as the result of "far more accurate knowledge of the Pali and Sanskrit texts. . . ."[54] These were obviously minority voices: Edmunds later lamented that the book had been misunderstood by nearly all who reviewed it.[55] Despite limitations, Albert Edmunds was certainly no charlatan; he deserves a place as a transitional figure in the history of American Orientalism.

No one has seriously questioned the scholarship of Henry Clarke Warren (1854-1899), the man usually credited with launching systematic Buddhist studies in America. He began his study of Sanskrit as an undergraduate at Harvard and continued under Charles Lanman and Maurice Bloomfield at Johns Hopkins.[56] A trip to England and a visit with Rhys Davids led him to shift his major interest to Pali and Buddhism. Badly crippled throughout his life as the result of a childhood fall, Warren worked under the most difficult circumstances, which undoubtedly explains his small publication list. With the exception of several papers published in the American Oriental Society *Journal,* his scholarly reputation has had to stand on one work, *Buddhism in Translations*, published in 1896 in the *Harvard Oriental Series*. (Although it was hailed as the first Pali translation published in the United States, Levi H. Elwell, a classics professor at Amherst, had published a Pali translation entitled the *Nine Jatakas* ten years earlier.[57]) Happily, it is an outstanding work that has been reprinted frequently. President Eliot included nearly half of the volume in his *Harvard Classics*, which gave it a much wider readership.[58]

Buddhism in Translations offers more than one hundred extracts translated from Pali texts. Many of the translations were made from Burmese manuscripts originally placed in Brown University by J. N. Cushing, a Baptist missionary to Burma—one more testimony to the missionary contribution. The book is divided into five chapters: the first focuses on Buddha's life, the next three on key philosophical doctrines, and the last on the Buddhist monastic order. Warren agreed with Rhys Davids that the Pali texts provided the truest statement of Buddhism and expressed regret that so much reliance had been placed on non-Pali sources. (The assumption that the Pali texts were earlier and thus embodied a purer version of Buddha's teachings has been seriously questioned by later scholars.) An avid student of philosophy since his days at Harvard, Warren focused on Buddhism as a religio-philosophical system; the three inner chapters are entitled "Sentient Existence," "Karma and Rebirth," and "Meditation and Nirvana." He especially emphasized Buddhism's practicality, remarking that one could find little in Buddha's sayings that did not have a "direct and practical bearing." As a system, it offered "applied philosophy."[59]

The incredible career of William Woodville Rockhill (1853-1914) suggests that Oriental studies need not be dull. Warren had focused on the ascetic Theravada Buddhism of southeast Asia; Rockhill characteristically preferred the more flamboyant Tibetan Buddhism of central Asia. Though born in the United States, he was educated mostly in France where his widowed mother took him at the age of eleven. He graduated from St. Cyr, the French equivalent to West Point, and served several years in the French Foreign Legion. In 1876 he returned to the United States, married, and moved to frontier New Mexico to engage in ranching.[60]

Rockhill's special obsession, which began while he was still in France, was Tibet. He was particularly influenced by the Abbé Huc's *Souvenirs d'un voyage dans la Tartarie et le Thibet*, an account of a French priest's travels in central Asia in the 1840s. He had studied Tibetan under a French teacher and spent many hours in the Bibliothèque Nationale reading the few European books available on that country. Though ranching could have left little time for scholarship, he apparently made the best of the situation in New Mexico. His biographer Paul Varg explains that he resumed his Chinese and Sanskrit studies during the off-season. During these periods,

"It was well understood that he was not to be disturbed, and weeks would pass when he hardly spoke."[61]

Three years on the frontier convinced Rockhill that he had a more serious mission in life than herding cattle. Returning to France in 1881, he threw himself back into Oriental studies, publishing three works on Tibetan Buddhism in rapid succession. Two were translations: the *Udanavarga* (1883), a Tibetan version of the *Dhammapada*, and *Pratimoksha Sutra* (1884), a Tibetan Buddhist scripture. His most substantial work was *The Life of the Buddha and the Early History of his Order* (1884), which offered a connected life based on Tibetan sources. Rockhill emphasized that he had not attempted a critical evaluation of the texts, but sought to provide the "materials" that later scholars could use to compile a full life.[62] In view of the meager knowledge of Tibetan Buddhism at the time, few Americans were in a position to judge Rockhill's success in these pioneering works. William Dwight Whitney did express appreciation of his work.[63]

In 1884 Rockhill launched a new phase in his many-sided career when he entered the American diplomatic service as second secretary to the American legation in Peking. In subsequent years he served as secretary of the Peking legation, chargé d'affaires in Korea, assistant secretary of state in Washington, and, at varying times, minister to China, Russia, and Turkey. By the turn of the century he was recognized as America's most influential Far Eastern expert, capping his career in 1899 by drafting a joint memorandum with his English friend, Alfred Hippisley, which John Hay promulgated as the Open Door policy. Indeed, Paul Varg asserts that as late as World War II, the "Rockhill policy" served as the "basic plan for American diplomacy in the Far East."[64] He also served as the American commissioner in the negotiations following the Boxer Rebellion and was instrumental in the American decision to remit the Chinese indemnity for use in the education of Chinese youths. It is safe to say that no Oriental scholar has had greater influence upon American history.

Despite many years as a diplomat, Rockhill rarely allowed his duties to keep him from scholarship. Immediately after his first arrival in China in 1884, he sought out a lama under whom he studied Tibetan for the next four years. Indeed, his studiousness eventually led to a quarrel with his superior, and he was dismissed.[65] It is apparent that his eagerness to serve in China was connected with his dream of reaching Tibet. He was finally successful, undertaking long and arduous expeditions across northern China into Tibet in 1888-1889 and again in 1891-1892. He described his experiences in *The Land of the Lamas* and a *Diary of a Journey through Mongolia and Tibet in 1891 and 1892*.

The Land of the Lamas is the more readable report, providing a compelling account of the first expedition. "Tibet has been my life hobby," he explained on the first page.[66] The story the book unfolds is one of incredible difficulties surmounted. He had laboriously mastered spoken Tibetan and then carefully concealed his Western identity, since to be recognized would have led to immediate expulsion. By donning a "big Mongol gown and fur cap," shaving his head, and traveling in the traditional central Asian style, he succeeded in passing, facing the threat of discovery on only one occasion. The book provides a description of the historical, geographical, and ethnographical features of the areas through which he passed, including a sizable section on Tibetan religion. At one point he recounts a fascinating discussion with three Tibetan lamas which deserves repeating. Shown a copy of one of Rockhill's books and informed of his great interest in their land, the lamas had responded with awe. Rockhill writes:

> They took the book, raised it to their foreheads in sign of respect, and declared that I was a great *pundib*. Then they asked endless questions concerning the state of Buddhism in foreign lands. They were astonished that it no longer existed in India. . . . When told of our esoteric Buddhists, the Mahatmâs, and of the wonderful doctrines they claimed to have obtained from Tibet [a reference to the Theosophical Society and its claim that powerful religious sages or Mahatmas who resided in Tibet were directing their movement], they were immensely amused. They declared that though in ancient times there were, doubtless, saints and sages who could perform some of the miracles now claimed by the Esoterists, none were living at the present day. . . .[67]

The fact that an American scholar traveling in central Asia was instructing Tibetan lamas in the history of their Buddhist faith should leave little doubt that by the end of the century East and West were coming together as never before.

By the time of his second expedition, Rockhill felt completely at ease in central Asia. He confessed in *Diary of a Journey* that he was "so accustomed now to being all the time with Asiatics" that it was "more of a strain to converse with Europeans than with them"; he also found it "more irksome to comply with the foreign customs" of the few European missionaries he encountered than with "those of Chinese and Tibetans."[68] The *Diary* leaves little doubt concerning the real dangers of such travel. At one point Rockhill's horse fell through the ice and the horse was swept away and drowned while Rockhill clung precariously to the ice shelf. On another occasion the expedition ran out of food, and he and his guides were faced with eating their horses in order to stay alive. Rockhill reports these misadventures matter-of-factly, suggesting the coolness and self-possession that undoubtedly saved his life on a number of occasions.

Obviously, Rockhill is a unique figure. His cosmopolitan background, long years in diplomatic service, and intimate acquaintance with Asian life place him apart from all other American Orientalists. He succeeded in knowing Asian life more intimately than any contemporary American scholar. Alice Roosevelt Longworth, after meeting him in Peking, remarked that he had "grown to look curiously Chinese." She suggested that "China had gotten into his blood"; that had he "let his mustache grow and pulled it down at the corners in a long twist, and wore Chinese clothes," he would have passed as a "serene expounder" of Confucian philosophy.[69] Though hardly a familiar figure in the United States (he spent a total of only thirteen years here from the time he left home at the age of eleven), he maintained his American ties. He published a number of articles in the American Oriental Society *Journal* and serialized parts of the account of his first Tibetan journey in *Century Magazine*.[70] At his death his magnificent collection of more than six thousand volumes of rare Chinese and Tibetan works went to the Library of Congress.

From Edward Salisbury to Henry Clarke Warren certain commonalities stand out that define the strengths, limitations, and direction of nineteenth-century American Oriental scholarship. First, one can hardly escape the all-enveloping impact of German scholars. Practically all America's first-generation Orientalists trained with a few German mentors: Franz Bopp, Rudolph Roth, and Albrecht Weber. There were other eminent European Orientalists—Sylvain Lévi, Louis de las Vallée, and Thomas Rhys Davids, to name several—but few American students sought them out. In the late nineteenth century Germany was regarded as the fountainhead of scholarship, not only in Oriental studies but in many other fields as well. The heavy philological emphasis in American scholarship was one major consequence of the German training.

Second, one notes a heavy Indological emphasis. For all practical purposes Oriental scholarship in nineteenth-century America meant Indian scholarship carried on through the medium of Sanskrit. Looking through the pages of the *Journal of the American Oriental Society* as well as the publications of the leading American Orientalists, one rarely finds any attention to China, Japan, and Southeast Asia or to the Chinese, Japanese, and Pali languages. It is true that several Pali and Tibetan scholars appeared near the end of the century, but Sanskritists still dominated overwhelmingly. The only American Sinologist of note in the whole century was Samuel Wells Williams, a missionary scholar of great learning—but he stands alone.[71] Once institutionalized in the university, the tendency naturally persisted: Sanskrit scholars trained more Sanskrit scholars.

Third, and most relevant to this study, it is striking how much of the new research is focused on religions of India. If the dominant geographical area is the Indian subcontinent and the language Sanskrit, the dominant subject matter is Hinduism. The fact is that most of the early scholarship and most of the books produced by American Oriental scholars were devoted to Hindu religion. Interestingly enough, much of the scholarly writing on Buddhism also revealed the same focus, with a heavy concentration on ancient Indian Buddhism. Other varieties of Buddhism in China, Japan, and Southeast Asia as well as other major religions such as Confucianism, Taoism, and Shintoism were almost entirely ignored. In view of increasing contacts with Asia during the century, it seems surprising that scholars showed so little interest in the variety and modern forms of Asian religion.

Notes

1. Cf. John Pickering's obituary in the *Journal of the American Oriental Society* [hereafter cited as *JAOS*] 1 (1843-1849): 161-70, and Robley Dunglison, "Biographical Sketch of Peter S. Du Ponceau," *American Law Magazine*, no. 9 (April 1845): 1-33. Du Ponceau's autobiography was edited by James L. Whitehead and published in the April, July, and October 1939 and January and April 1940 issues of the *Pennsylvania Magazine of History*; unfortunately, it runs only through 1783.

2. Peter S. Du Ponceau, *A Dissertation on the Nature and Character of the Chinese System of Writing* . . . (Philadelphia: American Philosophical Society, 1838), pp. xxxi-xxxii.

3. Ibid., pp. 5-6, 63 and Franklin Edgerton, "Notes on Early American Work in Linguistics," *Proceedings of the American Philosophical Society* 87 (July 1943): 28-29.

4. See *JAOS* 1 (1843-1849): ii-viii and 16 (1892-1895): lix-lxiv. It seems astonishing that no book-length study has yet been devoted to this crucial chapter in America's cultural history. See Myrl Young's brief discussion in "The Impact of the Far East on the United States, 1840-1860," (Ph.D. diss., University of Chicago, 1951), pp. 99-127.

5. William H. Greenough to John Pickering, November 11, 1845, quoted in Mary Orne Pickering, *Life of John Pickering* (Boston: Privately Printed, 1887), p. 508. Membership figures in *JAOS* 1 (1843-1849): xi; 21 (1901): 218-26.

6. John Pickering, "Address at the First Annual Meeting," *JAOS* 1 (1843-1849): 47-48.

7. *JAOS* 32 (1912): vi; 10 (1871-1879): cix.

8. See *JAOS* 1 (1843-1849): xl-xlvii, xlviii-xlix; also 9 (1866-1870): xxxviii.

9. See *JAOS* 76 (October-December 1956): 251, where the editor calls for more Far Eastern contributions.

10. *JAOS* 3 (1852-1853): 289-328; 4 (1853-1854): 31-102; 3 (1852-1853): 329-49; and 20 (July-December 1899): 309-16.

11. *JAOS* 1 (1843-1849): 79-135; 2 (1851): 334-37; and 18 (January-June 1897): 1-14.

12. *JAOS* 2 (1851): 55-60; 3 (1852-1853): 367-85; 10 (1872-1880): 219-324; and 4 (1853-1854): 327-34.

13. Several later presidents complained of the narrowness and expressed the conviction that the society should broaden its approach. See particularly Cyrus Adler's remarks in "East and West," *JAOS* 44 (September 1924): 177-85.

14. *JAOS* 1 (1843-1849): 79-135; 1 (1843-1849): 136-42; 1 (1843-1849): 143-61; and 2 (1851): 27-54.

15. *JAOS* 2 (1849-1850): xxi.

16. [Edward W. Hopkins], "In Memoriam," *JAOS* 22 (January-July 1901): 1-6.

17. Franklin Edgerton, "A Salisbury Letter," *JAOS* 64 (April-June 1944): 60.

18. Among others, see *JAOS* 1 (1843-1849): 79-135, 275-98, 299-316, 317-36, 517-58; 2 (1851): 257-324; 3 (1852-1853): 399-419; 7 (1862): 60-142; 8 (1866): 105-82.

19. Edward Salisbury, "Memoir on the History of Buddhism," *JAOS* 1 (1843-1849): 79-135.

20. Edward Salisbury, "M. Burnouf on the History of Buddhism in India," *JAOS* 1 (1843-1849): 275-98.

21. Edgerton, "A Salisbury Letter," pp. 58-61.

22. Quoted in *JAOS* 22 (January-July 1901): 4.

23. Edgerton, "A Salisbury Letter," p. 60.

24. E. Washburn Hopkins, *India Old and New* (New York: Charles Scribners, 1901), pp. 4, 6.

25. See Thomas D. Seymour, "William Dwight Whitney," *American Journal of Philology* 15 (1894): 271-98, by far the best sketch of his life and work. But see also Charles R. Lanman, "William Dwight Whitney," *Atlantic Monthly* 75 (March 1895): 398-406; Thomas R. Lounsbury, "William Dwight Whitney," *Proceedings of the American Academy of Arts and Sciences* 30 (May 1894-May 1895): 579-89; O. W. Long, "William Dwight Whitney," *New England Quarterly* 2 (January 1929): 105-19; and H. H. B. [Harold H. Bender], "William Dwight Whitney," *Dictionary of American Biography (DAB)*, 20: 166-69. Whitney is still another overlooked nineteenth-century figure of major importance who awaits a modern biographer.

26. For a comprehensive list, see Charles R. Lanman, "Chronological Bibliography of the Writings of William Dwight Whitney," *JAOS [The Whitney Memorial Issue]* 19 (January-June 1898): 121-50.

27. Seymour, "William Dwight Whitney," p. 273.

28. Ibid.: 273-74.

29. Lanman, "Chronological Bibliography," pp. 121-50; William Dwight Whitney, "On the Grammatical Structure of the Sanskrit," *Bibliotheca Sacra* 6 (August 1849): 471-86.

30. William Dwight Whitney, "On the Main Results of the Later Vedic Researches in Germany," *JAOS* 3 (1852-1853): 289-328; Idem, "On the History of the Vedic Texts," 4 (1853-1854): 245-61; Idem, "Bopp's Comparative Accentuation of the Greek and Sanskrit Languages," 5 (1855-1856): 195-218; and Idem, "The Atharva-Veda-Praticakhya . . . Text, Translation, and Notes," 7 (1862): 333-615.

31. *JAOS* 15 (1890-1892): iii.

32. See Whitney's own evaluation, *JAOS* 3 (1851-1852): 289-93.

33. Cf. A. L. Basham, *The Wonder That Was India*, rev. ed. (New York: Hawthorn Books, 1963), pp. 390-91.

34. Franklin Edgerton, "Notes on Early American Work in Linguistics," *Proceedings of the American Philosophical Society* 87 (July 1943): 33.

35. *New Englander* 16 (1858): 100-141, and 17 (1859): 111-43; *North American*

Review 106 (April 1868): 515-42, and (January 1868): 340-45; *Bibliotheca Sacra* 16 (1859): 404-20.

36. *JAOS* 19 (January-June 1898): 55.

37. Cf. E. Washburn Hopkins, "Thirty Years of Indo-European Studies," in *Thirty Years of Oriental Studies . . .*, ed. Roland G. Kent (Philadelphia, 1918), pp. 73-84 and W. Norman Brown, "South Asian Studies in the United States," *Indian Studies Abroad*, ed. Indian Council for Cultural Relations (New York: Asia Publishing House, 1964), pp. 106-10.

38. Walter Eugene Clark, "Charles Rockwell Lanman, 1850-1941," *JAOS* 61 (September 1941): 191-92.

39. Charles R. Lanman, "Hindu Ascetics and their Powers," *American Philological Association Transactions and Proceedings* 48 (1917): 133-51, and Idem, "The Hindu Yoga System," *Harvard Theological Review* 11 (October 1918): 355-75.

40. Charles R. Lanman, *Harvard Oriental Series. Descriptive List Thereof, Revised to 1920 . . .* (Cambridge, Mass.: Harvard University Press, 1920), n.p.

41. Franklin Edgerton, "Maurice Bloomfield, 1855-1928," *JAOS* 48 (September 1928): 193-99, and A. V. W. J. [A. V. Williams Jackson], "Maurice Bloomfield," *DAB*, 2: 386-88.

42. Maurice Bloomfield, "The Foundation of Buddhism," *New World* 1 (June 1892): 246-63, and Idem, "Brahmanical Riddles and the Origin of Theosophy," in *International Congress of Arts and Science, St. Louis, 1904 Congress of Arts and Science*, ed. Howard J. Rogers, 8 vols. (Boston: Houghton Mifflin, 1905-1907), 2: 481-92.

43. Maurice Bloomfield, *The Religion of the Veda: The Ancient Religion of India* (New York: G. P. Putnam's, 1908), p. 8.

44. Franklin Edgerton, "Edward Washburn Hopkins, 1857-1932," *JAOS* 52 (December 1932): 311-15.

45. Cf. Franklin Edgerton's remark: "It remained for many years almost the only comprehensive and scholarly treatment of the subject." *DAB, Supplement One*, 21: 434.

46. E. Washburn Hopkins, *The Religions of India* (Boston: Ginn & Co., 1895), pp. xi, xii.

47. Ibid., chap. 19, "India and the West," pp. 543-71. Quote on p. 562.

48. Ibid., pp. 564-65.

49. See *Open Court* 23 (August 1909): 510-12, and Albert J. Edmunds, *Buddhist and Christian Gospels Now First Compared from the Originals . . .*, 4th ed., 2 vols. (Philadelphia: Innes & Sons, 1909), 2: 202-19.

50. *Buddhist Review* (London) 1 (July 1909): 191-97 and 5 (October, November, December 1913): 272-76. As examples see Albert J. Edmunds, "The Canonical Account of the Birth of Gotama the Buddha," *Open Court* 12 (August 1898): 485-90, Idem, "Buddhist Omissions in Hasting's Dictionary of Religion and Ethics," ibid. 29 (November 1915): 698-700. He also published a series of translations in vols. 14 and 15, which were later incorporated into the *Buddhist and Christian Gospels*.

51. See the comment in a notice of Edmunds's books, *Eastern Buddhist* (Kyoto) 2 (May-June, July-August 1922): 92.

52. Albert J. Edmunds, "Buddhist and Christian Gospels. Replies to Critics,"

Buddhist Review 1 (July 1909): 192, and Idem, *Buddhist and Christian Gospels,* 2: 71-72, 237.

53. [Albert J. Edmunds], "Professor Anesaki at Harvard," *Buddhist Review* 5 (October, November, December 1913): 272-76.

54. *International Quarterly* 7 (May-June 1903): Maurice Winternitz, *A History of Indian Literature,* 2 vols., rev. ed. (Calcutta: University of Calcutta Press, 1933), 2: 404. (Italics omitted)

55. *Buddhist Review* 1 (July 1909): 191-97.

56. Charles Lanman, "Henry Clarke Warren: An Obituary Notice," *JAOS* 20 (July-December 1899): 332-37, and W. E. C. [Walter E. Clark], "Henry Clarke Warren," *DAB,* 19: 474-75.

57. *JAOS* 37 (May 1917): 4-5.

58. William Peiris, *The Western Contribution to Buddhism* (Delhi, India: Motilal Banarsidass, 1973), pp. 244-45.

59. Henry C. Warren, *Buddhism in Translations* (Cambridge, Mass.: Harvard University Press, 1909), p. 112.

60. Paul Varg's excellent *Open Door Diplomat: The Life of W. W. Rockhill* (Urbana, Ill.: University of Illinois Press, 1952) has been relied on heavily throughout. Also see Alfred E. Hippisley, "William Woodville Rockhill," *Journal of the Royal Asiatic Society of Great Britain and Ireland* 47 (April 1915): 367-74.

61. Varg, *Open Door Diplomat,* p. 9.

62. William W. Rockhill, *The Life of the Buddha and the Early History of his Order . . .* (London: Kegan, Paul, Trench, Trübner, 1884), p. x.

63. Varg, *Open Door Diplomat,* p. 9.

64. Ibid., p. 36.

65. Ibid., p. 2.

66. William W. Rockhill, *The Land of the Lamas. Notes of a Journey through China, Mongolia, and Tibet* (London: Longmans, Green, 1891), p. 1.

67. Ibid., p. 102.

68. William W. Rockhill, *Diary of a Journey through Mongolia and Tibet in 1891 and 1892* (Washington, D.C.: Smithsonian Institution, 1894), p. 103.

69. Varg, *Open Door Diplomat,* p. 2.

70. William W. Rockhill, "Korea in its Relations with China," *JAOS* 13 (1889): 1-33, and Idem, "Tibetan Buddhist Birth Stories," ibid. 18 (January-June 1897): 1-14; Idem, "An American in Tibet," *Century Magazine* 41 (November 1890): 3-17. Other installments: *Century Magazine* 41 (December 1890, January 1891-March 1891): 250-63, 350-61, 599-606, 720-30.

71. See Frederick Williams, *Life and Letters of Samuel Wells Williams* (New York: G. P. Putnam's, 1889).

11
Spiritual Discoveries in Japan—Edward Morse to Ernest Fenollosa

As possibilities of travel improved, a handful of privileged Americans set out to investigate the East at first hand. Only recently opened to Westerners, Japan was to exercise a special attraction. For the first who came, it was an irresistible land of immense charm and mystery. A sizable number came away from several months in Japan convinced that the ancient, spiritual, and aesthetic civilizations of the East had much to teach Western man. Ernest Fenollosa, who had gone to teach Western philosophy and instead discovered the beauties of Eastern art, evokes the excited mood in the following letter written to his friend Edward Morse in 1884. Just returned from an extensive search for art treasures in out-of-the-way Japanese temples, he wrote:

> For myself, I must confess to you, who will hear me in private without thinking me conceited, that I cannot see why my work this summer was not just as important at bottom as much of that which the world's archaeologists are doing in Greece and Turkey. Of course people don't see the practical importance of Eastern Civilization for the world with the same vividness as they do that of Greek culture. . . . I expect the time will come when it will be considered as necessary for a liberally educated man to know the names and deeds of man's great benefactors in the East, and the steps of advance in their culture, as it is now to know Greek and Latin dates and the flavor of their production.[1]

Although appreciation of the immense achievements of Eastern civilization has still not become general in America, the idea would certainly no longer seem fanciful. Much credit for this increased appreciation is due to early explorers like Fenollosa.

Fenollosa stands out, but he was only one of a remarkable collection of young Americans who congregated in Japan in the 1870s and 1880s. The others include Edward Morse, William Sturgis Bigelow, Percival Lowell, Henry Adams, and John La Farge. (Lafcadio Hearn also belongs, but his case will be reserved for separate treatment.) Van Wyck Brooks was to memorialize the group as "Fenollosa and his Circle," but a case could be made for "Morse and his Circle," since Morse preceded Fenollosa to Japan. Morse's enthusiastic reports did much to stimulate the interest of the others. The high creativity of the men in the Morse Circle, their view of Japanese culture soon after the country's opening to Western visitors, and the pioneering books they wrote all emphasize the importance of their exploration of Japan.[2]

As we will see, Japan affected each of the men's lives in different ways. Bigelow and Fenollosa were most profoundly touched, going so far as to become Buddhists; Morse limited his enthusiasm to brachiopods and ceramics and remained a Christian. However, all appear to have discovered something mysteriously different in the Japanese way that altered their thinking and in most cases their careers. Fenollosa, who left the United States as a teacher of philosophy returned to become America's first great expert on Japanese and Chinese art; Morse, who set out as a scientist was soon spending much of his time searching out Japanese pottery and is mainly remembered today not for his work with brachiopods, but for his great ceramic collection; Bigelow and Lowell both gave up promising careers in medicine and business to explore Oriental thought and culture. The impact is less certain in the cases of Adams and La Farge: they spent the least time in Japan, and perhaps the country had not yet had time to work its spell. Aesthetic considerations were crucial in the positive reactions of all the men. Attracted by Japan's great art, they went on to explore the culture and religious conceptions that had made such works possible. The Japanese experience awakened their interest in Oriental religion, particularly Buddhism, but in many ways Japan itself was the revelation.

It should be said that Japan had already begun to exercise its special magic on Americans well before Morse's discovery in the 1870s. Nathan Hale was calling attention to the island kingdom in the pages of the *North American Review* as early as 1820. "There is probably no part of the world," Hale wrote, "which is so little known, and at the same time so worthy of exciting a rational curiosity, as the empire of Japan." He listed its "immense population," "great wealth and industry," "progress in the useful arts," and the "peculiarity of its civil and religious government" as the attractions that gave Japan a "hold on our curiosity over almost every other part of the East."[3] The Japanese government's policy of isolation from the outside world, adopted in the late sixteenth century, had minimized Western knowledge, but European writers had provided occasional glimpses of the Flowery Kingdom. Karl Thunberg, a Swedish scientist who had served as physician to the Dutch outpost on the island of Deshima, provided one of the earliest accounts, published in the *Massachusetts Magazine* in 1789. Isaac Titsingh, a Dutch trader, and Philipp von Siebold, a German natural scientist, also wrote early accounts, which were circulated in America.[4] The Perry expedition naturally quickened American interest. Edward Everett Hale reflected the possessive pride Americans felt in the commodore's historic voyage: "Under the auspices of an expedition sent out, as we are proud to remember, by our own government, the world's knowledge of Japan has just now been doubled. . . ." Reviewing several new books on Japan, Hale admonished: "Let the reader disabuse himself, as quickly as he can, of the notion that this is a nation of barbarians."[5]

Barbaric or not, Japan remained a mystery to most Americans until the century's later decades. Following the overthrow of the Tokugawas in 1868, however, American educators, scientists, and technical advisers were welcomed by the new Meiji government. Among the first to arrive was Edward Sylvester Morse, who came in 1877 to study Pacific Ocean brachiopods. Quickly recruited by the government to teach zoology at Tokyo Imperial University, he lived in Japan about five years (1877-1879 and 1882-1883).[6]

Morse arrived early and stimulated others to follow, but he made little effort to probe the Japanese soul. His biographer, Dorothy Wayman, laments, "Arriving on his fortieth birthday in Japan, the most picturesque country of his day, he wrote barely two paragraphs of description of its landscape in his thousand-page journal during the next two years. Privileged to visit a land only ten years removed from actual medieval feudalism, he overlooked the poetry and romance. . . . Anything beyond the evidence of Morse's senses was beyond his interest."[7] It was not that Morse lacked curiosity or talent as an observer, but rather that his interests were extremely selective. Passing up politics, religion, and philosophy, he concentrated his studies in three areas: the country's sea life, homes, and ceramics. The result of his Japanese sojourn was a magnificent pottery collection, which became the foundation of the celebrated collection at the Boston Museum of Fine Arts, a book *Japanese Homes and their Surroundings*, and a now-classic article on "Latrines of the East"—the latter leaving little doubt concerning his intimate acquaintance with Japanese life.

Fortunately, there was one other artifact, a book he never intended to publish, which reveals much about his personal feelings. This is his *Japan Day by Day*, a private journal he recorded in the 1870s and 1880s but did not publish until 1917. He was finally pushed into publishing the journal by his friend William Sturgis Bigelow, who complained that Morse had frittered away his time on the "lower forms of animal life" instead of devoting himself "to the highest," the "manners and customs" about which no one was so well qualified to speak. "Honestly, now," Bigelow had upbraided him, "Isn't a Japanese a higher organism than a worm?"[8]

The book reveals that Morse shared many of the stereotypes common in the period, but that he was also aware of the danger of stereotypes. Thus, he noted the Japanese tendency of doing things in reverse, their permissive child-raising practices, which made the country a paradise for children, and the unintelligibility and unpleasantness of their music—common and distorted conceptions held by many Westerners in the period—but he also dismissed the idea that the Japanese were given to mindless imitation or that Japanese civilization was inferior to that of the West.[9] He observed that "after remaining a few months in Japan," a foreigner "slowly begins to realize that, whereas he thought he would teach the Japanese everything, he finds, to his amazement and chagrin, that those virtues . . . [which] are the burden of our moral teachings at home, the Japanese seem to be born with." He went on to list such virtues as "simplicity of dress, neatness of home, cleanliness of surroundings, a love of nature and of all natural things, a simple and fascinating art, courtesy of manner, [and] considerations for the feelings of others" as characteristic of the low as well as the upper classes.[10] One might say that he had discovered the Oriental soul in the commonplace practices of Japanese life.

One searches in vain for Morse's views concerning Japanese religion. If philosophy and politics were generally excluded, religion was even more so. This may have stemmed from scars he carried from a narrow religious upbringing. At least, this is the suggestion of one biographer who has described Morse as an "intensely emotional" and "often prejudiced" man who omitted religion in his writings on Japan because of "antireligious bias."[11] At the outset of *Japan Day by Day*, Morse confessed that he had "made no effort to record or collect data" on subjects in "which I was not especially interested," and he specifically noted the omission of Japanese religion, mythology, and folklore. He visited the famous temples at Nikko, but characteristically moved on, lamely apologizing for his "utter inability of doing the slightest justice to the temples and tombs, so wonderful are they, so elaborate, so vast and magnificent."[12] At the same time he did not approve Christian missionary attacks on Japanese religion. He lashed out at the misrepresentations of missionary propagandists: "When I read in the papers from home letters by missionaries saying that the temples are being deserted and the faith dying out, and then see the actual facts of temples crowded every day . . . with every evidence of prosperity, I wonder at such false reports."[13]

Upon his return, Morse delivered a series of twelve lectures at Boston's

Lowell Institute in the winter of 1881-1882 distilling his several years of experience in Japan. The topics included (the summary is his): "1. Country; people, language. 2. Traits of the people. 3. Houses; food; toilet. 4. Homes and their surroundings. 5. Children; toys; games. 6. Temples; theatres; music. 7. City life and health matters. 8. Country life and natural scenery. 9. Educational matters and students. 10. Industrial occupations. 11. Ceramic and pictorial art. 12. Antiquities."[14] The talks were one of the hits of the lecture season. They served as turning points for both Sturgis Bigelow and Percival Lowell, who departed soon after to see Japan for themselves. Lydia Maria Child, who had been an enthusiastic student of Oriental ideas since the 1840s, was also present, applauding Morse's observation that Americans had much to learn from the Japanese.[15] And Isabella Gardner was so charmed that she prevailed on Morse to give another series of lectures in her home in Fenway Court, a celebrated salon for Boston's intelligentsia. These so fired her interest that she and her husband also set off for Japan. (She found the country's Buddhist temples irresistible. She confided, "When I get into one I never want to come away—I could lie on the mats and look forever through the dim light."[16]) Having cracked the door to the Flowery Kingdom, Morse stood aside, allowing others to explore its religious and philosophical offerings.

One of the first to step forward was Morse's friend, William Sturgis Bigelow. The scion of a notable New England medical family who graduated from the Harvard Medical School in 1874, Bigelow had studied with Pasteur in France before returning to the United States to set up a bacteriological laboratory.[17] He persuaded Morse to allow him to accompany him on his return to Japan in 1882; the trip proved the turning point in his life. Abandoning medicine, he remained in Japan until 1889, where he studied Buddhism, collected Oriental art, and conducted tours for friends he could persuade to join him. His impressive collection of 26,000 swords, together with Morse's pottery collection, later became the core of the Boston Museum of Fine Arts' magnificent Oriental holding.[18]

Bigelow's eccentric behavior and championship of Buddhism made him something of a legend among his contemporaries. Theodore Roosevelt, who met him through Henry Cabot Lodge, later wrote to Lodge that he had found Bigelow "most charming," but he wondered "*why*" he had not warned him that Bigelow was an "esoteric Buddhist." He complained that he might have "been spared some frantic floundering" when the subject of religion had come up.[19] Despite a great disparity in religious viewpoints, the two men became good friends. Bigelow stayed occasionally in the Roosevelt home, while Roosevelt recommended Bigelow's qualifications as an expert in Oriental art. Bigelow was also a friend of Phillips Brooks. When the famous

Boston divine visited Japan in 1889, Bigelow showed him the temples at Nikko. According to Brooks's biographer, the two men were "strangely drawn to each other. . . ." They "discussed the non-Christian religions which both had studied," and subsequently Brooks wrote Bigelow a "long letter continuing their discussion of the relation of these religions to Christianity. . . ."[20]

Bigelow was apparently very serious about Buddhism. He received personal instruction in its doctrines from a Japanese priest for several years and considered the priesthood for himself. One of his closest friends reported that he had actually gone through the "preliminary stages of induction"; received his "name in religion"; and would have been ordained a priest "had he thought his physical health good enough to enable him to lead the required life."[21] When he died, he was buried—at his request—in the cloak of a Buddhist priest, with part of his ashes deposited at a Japanese Buddhist temple.

Despite intense interest, Bigelow wrote little concerning Oriental thought. His one major publication is a seventy-six-page monograph, *Buddhism and Immortality*, delivered at Harvard University as the Ingersoll Lecture of 1908. A sober attempt to summarize Buddhist doctrine, the monograph indicates Bigelow's special attraction to the Tendai and Shingon schools. He warned of the added difficulty of understanding "such a vast and intricate system of thought" if the student began by classifying Buddhism as some form of "Pantheism, Polytheism, Monotheism, Materialism, Idealism, and the like."[22] At the same time, the doctor insisted on the compatibility of Buddhist doctrine with modern science, and in particular with the theories of Darwin and Mendel. Although it was regarded in the West as a very exotic philosophy, Buddhism, he insisted, was quite up-to-date. Another contribution was an introduction for Chi Ki's *On the Method of Practicing Concentration and Contemplation*, a work on Buddhist meditation. He emphasized the valuable psychological insights that Buddhism offered. "Broadly speaking," Bigelow explained, "in the East men have studied themselves; in the West, what is outside themselves. . . ."[23]

In 1883, Bigelow's friend Percival Lowell joined him in Japan. Also the descendant of a distinguished New England family, Lowell was the brother of Amy Lowell, the famous Imagist poet. Following graduation from Harvard, he had entered the family business, but within six years retired to pursue more intellectual interests.[24] He would divide the rest of his life between Oriental studies and astronomy. Despite striking similarities in background, Lowell approached Oriental thought much differently than Bigelow. Where Bigelow revealed a deep personal interest in Buddhism, Lowell was fascinated by the larger pattern of Far Eastern civilization. Where Bigelow looked to Japan as a spiritual seeker, Lowell approached it more as a philosophical anthropologist.

The Oriental phase of Lowell's career was actually fairly brief, extending over the decade between 1883 and 1893. However, in that short time, he published four sizable books on the Orient. Perhaps it is well to begin with the Eastern chronology. Inspired by Morse's lectures, he sailed for Japan in 1883 and immediately began studies of Japanese life. However, soon after his arrival, he was invited to accompany a special diplomatic mission from Korea to the United States—the first such mission to any Western nation. Following the trip, he received an invitation to come to Korea as a guest of the king, where he spent the winter months of 1883-1884. The result was his first book, *Chösön,* one of the earliest Western examinations of Korean society. (The book is an astonishing effort. Altogether, Lowell had spent only about two months in Korea, mostly in Seoul; he knew only a few words in Korean; yet he set out to reveal the inner spirit of the Korean people![25]) He returned to Japan for much of the remainder of 1884, then sailed back to the United States where he remained for the next four years. Returning to Japan in 1889, he visited one of the most inaccessible areas of western Japan. The result of these hurried visits was three more books: *The Soul of the Far East* (1888), *Notto* (1891), and *Occult Japan* (1894).

Where Morse had been content to collect pottery and describe the latrines of the East, Lowell's dream was the discovery of the Eastern soul. More precisely, he aspired to define the esssence of Oriental civilizations, which would allow a definition of the essence of Western civilization as well. In a key passage in *Chöson,* he confessed his deeper interest in Oriental societies: "It is because the far-East holds up the mirror to our own civilization,—a mirror that like all mirrors gives us back left for right . . . that she is so very interesting. It is in this that her great attraction lies. It is for this that men have gone to Japan intending to stay weeks, and have tarried years."[26] The concern pervades all his Eastern books, but it is most systematically stated in his *The Soul of the Far East,* a work that writer Lafcadio Hearn hailed as "incomparably the greatest of all books on Japan, and the deepest. . . ."[27] One of the most ambitious efforts ever made by an American to define the essence of Eastern civilization, *The Soul of the Far East* deserves close examination.

Several far-reaching assumptions dominate Lowell's treatment in the book (and, indeed, in his other three books as well). First, East and West define opposites in all areas of life. He had sensed this polarity from the first moment he set foot in Yokohama. If the Japanese people were not literally standing on their heads, as their geographic position seemed to demand, nevertheless they seemed to view everything from a topsy-turvy perspective. "What we regard intuitively in one way from our standpoint," Lowell observed, "they as intuitively observe in a diametrically opposite manner from theirs. To speak backwards, write backwards, read backwards, is but the *a b c* of their contrariety." This "inversion" extended beyond "mere modes of expression" right down to the "very matter of thought."[28]

Second, all Eastern societies share a uniform viewpoint. "Whatever portion of the Far East we examine," Lowell wrote, "we find its mental history to be the same story with variations. However unlike China, Korea, and Japan are in some respects, through the careers of all three we can trace the same life-spirit."[29] It is significant that he ignored India, which would have created tensions in his analysis. The assumption of uniformity was convenient since Japan (or Korea) could be treated as the microcosm of the Far Eastern mind. Apparently, there was no need to test the formulations by a visit to China.

Third, the key to the Far Eastern soul is its "Impersonality." Indeed, the theory of Impersonality ultimately defines the difference between East and West. Lowell explained that if one traced a line around the globe, it was clear that the sense of self steadily declined as one moved from West to East—from America to Europe to the Middle East to Japan. "If with us the *I* seems to be of the very essence of the soul," he claimed, "then the soul of the Far East may be said to be Impersonality."[30] He found evidence of impersonality in three major areas of Far Eastern life: language, everyday thought, and religion. Examples included the subordination of individual desires to family needs, the elimination of romantic love in marriage, the absence of personal nouns in the Japanese language, and the emphasis on self-denial in Far Eastern religion. If impersonality defined the Eastern view, "individuality" was central in the Western view.

The attraction of *The Soul of the Far East* is its sweep and certainty. Unlike most Western travelers who were content to report surface appearances, Lowell probed for the Far East's deepest roots. If his generalizations are too sweeping, he at least sought the larger pattern and offered an original and provocative thesis in his theory of Impersonality. He also reveals much ingenuity in discovering examples to support his interpretations.

But the work is also open to serious criticism. Lowell would have written a better book had he concentrated on the "Souls" rather than the "Soul" of the Far East. There are basic similarities between Japanese, Chinese, and Korean culture—reflecting the dispersion of Chinese influences throughout the Far East—but the differences are even more obvious and should have been emphasized. His Impersonality thesis is difficult to accept—or to rebut —because one is unsure what he meant by impersonality and individuality. He also manipulates his evidence. He cites numerous examples to support the Impersonality thesis; however, other examples would surely have contradicted it. A contemporary Japanese critic complained that Lowell's method was completely arbitrary: "When he cannot find what he wants among the Japanese, then, without saying anything, he goes directly to the Celestial Empire and gets his illustrations there!"[31] Lowell based his argument concerning the impersonality of Far Eastern languages on the lack of personal pronouns in Japanese; however, when he turned to the impersonality of family life, he shifted to family patterns in China.

Though not personally drawn to Oriental religion, Lowell acknowledged its importance. In *The Soul of the Far East* Buddhism is offered as a crucial instance of the pervasive impersonalism of the Far East. (He arbitrarily omits Shintoism, Confucianism, and Taoism on the strange ground that none of these emphasized the human soul.) He noted surprising similarities in Buddhism and Christianity, remarking that if Buddhism seemed "exceedingly foreign" when viewed as a "system of philosophy," it looked "unexpectedly familiar" as a "faith." "Indeed, the one religion might well pass for the counterfeit . . . of the other."[32] Both inculcated a sense of charity and emphasized similar moral injunctions. However, the resemblances were external as indicated by their radical divergence on the self. "Christianity," he wrote, "is a personal religion; Buddhism, an impersonal one. . . . Christianity tells us to purify ourselves that we may enjoy countless aeons of that bettered self hereafter; Buddhism would have us purify ourselves that we may lose all sense of self for evermore."[33] Christianity offered a "gospel of optimism"; Buddhism emphasized a pessimistic view.

As he became better acquainted with Japan, Lowell developed greater appreciation of the importance of Shintoism in the formation of Japanese character. This may be seen in his last book, *Occult Japan*. On a journey to Mount Ontaké, one of Japan's sacred peaks, he came upon several Japanese pilgrims undergoing trances. He quickly recognized that he had stumbled upon something very important, which might be termed "esoteric Shintoism," an "esoteric cult imbedded in the very heart and core of the Japanese character and instinct. . . ."[34] The more he considered the evidence, the more Lowell was convinced that, despite Westernization, Shintoism remained central to the Japanese experience. Fusing the worship of nature with ancestor worship, it was peculiarly Japanese.

Shintoism's strangeness greatly intrigued Lowell. Despite its primitive conceptions and lack of philosophy, he declared that he found "something fine" in its "sweet simplicity." "The very barrenness of the faith's buildings has a beauty of its own, touched as it is by Japanese taste," he wrote.[35] Much of *Occult Japan* is given over to a description of trances, possessions, and "miracles"; Lowell emphasized that he had personally witnessed a number of these in his own house. One is not quite sure what to make of this: did he approach the unusual experiences as a clinical observer or as spiritual seeker? He did insist on the reality of the experiences; however, he credited them more to the faith of the believer than to the operation of the divine. Of all Oriental religions, Shintoism was the most unapproachable; Lowell was one of the first Americans to explore its ancient practices.

If he maintained a critical distance, Lowell emphasized that the East had a good deal to offer Westerners. He suggested in *Chöson* that a study of Far Eastern societies would reveal much about the West's early development. Here the emphasis was on knowledge: from an evolutionary viewpoint, the arrested societies of the Far East might provide an "historical parallax" for the "determination of our common remote past" as well as of the "possibilities and adaptabilities of the human race."[36] In *The Soul of the Far East* he argued for mutual exchange, emphasizing that, neither being perfect, the Far Eastern and Western views might complement one another. He spoke of using the Far Eastern point of view "stereoptically." Merging the two viewpoints would "help us to realize humanity." Indeed, he suggested, it was only "by such a combination of two different aspects that we ever perceive substance and distinguish reality from illusion. What our two eyes make possible for material objects, the earth's two hemispheres may enable us to do for mental traits."[37] In 1893 Lowell left Japan and closed his account with the Orient; he seems to have never looked back. Enthusiastic about astronomy since childhood, he established an observatory at Flagstaff, Arizona; at his death he was a leading proponent of the theory that life had once flourished on the planet Mars.

Lowell had required a full decade and four books to explore Japan's mysteries; Henry Adams found that three months sufficed and he repeatedly announced that the Japanese journey had been something of a personal disappointment. Obviously, not everyone who followed Morse to Japan in the late nineteenth century found their lives altered by the event. However, Adams often confessed disappointment: the evidence suggests that he, too, was drawn to Oriental thought.

William Sturgis Bigelow had convinced Adams to take the Japanese journey. (Bigelow was his wife's cousin.) Adams was undoubtedly attracted by the prospect of escaping the constant reminders of his recent, painful bereavement, the suicide of his wife. There is also some suggestion that he hoped to find a larger consolation. Accompanied by John La Farge, an artist friend he persuaded to join him, Adams set off by rail in 1886 for San Francisco. While stopped in Omaha, they were appraoched by a young reporter who asked why they were going to Japan; La Farge had beamed and replied that they "were in search of Nirvana. . . ." Adams repeated the phrase in a subsequent letter, describing himself and La Farge as "two woe-begone Pagans, searching Nirvana. . . ."[38] Though he enjoyed misleading his readers, Adams was unquestionably drawn to something he vaguely referred to as the "Asian mystery."

In fact, as Ernest Samuels emphasizes, Adams had already indicated a rising interest in Asian culture well before he set out for Japan. His friends and associates, including La Farge who had written a pioneering sketch on

Japanese art; Raphael Pumpelly, the geologist-traveler who had written a book on his Asian travels; and, of course, Bigelow would have made ignoring the Orient difficult. Adams had certainly begun to look to the East by 1869; he spoke of Asian travel as early as 1871. "Early and late," Samuels writes, "Japanese and Chinese art and life had attracted the Adamses. . . . Adams's collector's judgment was already a byword among their friends."[39] Adams had also cultivated the Japanese and Chinese envoys in Washington; Baron Yoshida had introduced him to the game of Go-Bang and discussed the laws of archaic Japan with him. Adams's second novel, *Esther*, published in 1884, contains a number of references to Asia and Buddhism—as well as a very revealing allusion to Japan. One of the characters turns to Esther and remarks, "How pleasant it would be to go off to Japan together and fill our sketch-books with drawings."[40]

Altogether, Adams and La Farge spent about three months in Japan, constantly assisted by Bigelow, their "courier and master of ceremonies." Bigelow introduced them to Ernest Fenollosa and found them a neighboring house. Though he enjoyed certain moments of the stay, Adams did not adapt to his surroundings. (As the trip followed his wife's death so closely, perhaps he would not have enjoyed Chartres itself.) His letters are filled with complaints concerning the intense heat, unrivaled street smells, and cesspool conditions of Japanese homes. He was also irritated by Fenollosa, who attempted to improve his taste in Oriental art. "Fenollosa is a tyrant who says we shall not like any work done under the Tokugawa Shoguns," he erupted at one point.[41] When not complaining, he found himself amused and astonished by the dwarfish appearance of everything. Looking back on his first ten days in Yokohama and Tokyo, he confessed that he had "not often been more amused. . . . Everything was new, and opposite to all fundamental principles. . . ." In their daily sight-seeing expeditions with Bigelow, he and La Farge always ended with the feeling that "we were playing baby, and living in doll-land." He became convinced that the Japanese regarded nothing, except the tea ceremony, as worthy of seriousness. "I am still in search of something serious in this country," Adams wrote at one point; the people treated their religion as "a high old joke" while death was dismissed as a "pleasant conceit."[42]

Adams's spirits seemed to rise after the party moved on to Nikko, a beautiful and historic center of imperial tombs and temples, which became their home base. "In truth the place is worth coming to see," he wrote his friend John Hay. "Japan is not the last word of humanity, and Japanese art has a well-developed genius for annoying my prejudices; but Nikko is, after all, one of the sights of the world."[43] He spent a good deal of time purchasing art pieces or what he called his "curios." His new sense of contentment is visible in the following letter: "La Farge and I have found shelter in the mountains from the heat and hotels of Japan. We have a little box of a Japanese house, where we look out on a Japanese temple-garden, and on Japanese mountains, all like the pictures that one sees on plates." Describing their "princely" style of life, he continued, "The dealers in *curios* send us, from far and wide, whatever they can find that we like, and our rooms are full of such rubbish. La Farge sketches. I waste time as I can. . . ."[44] He was also charmed with Kyoto, which they visited on the way out of the country. The only real irritation that seemed to linger was Fenollosa, whom Adams continued to fulminate against. Worrying that he would dismiss his art purchases as "Tokugawa rot" and that he would "bully me into letting them go," Adams now attacked Fenollosa as "a kind of St. Dominic." "He is now trying to prevent my having a collection of Hokusai's books," he complained.[45]

Certainly, there is little indication in his letters that Adam's visit made much impression upon him. His observations concerning Japanese life are more graceful but no more perceptive than those of the usual tourist. It seemed that although he saw Japan, his mind was elsewhere. What then of his earlier references to seeking nirvana in Japan? And what of his admission to Hay that during the train ride to San Francisco he had "read Buddhism and slept," while La Farge sketched? There is also his remark with regard to Fenollosa—who seems to have alienated him in more ways than one—that "He has joined a Buddhist sect; I was myself a Buddhist when I left America, but he has converted me to Calvinism with leanings towards the Methodists."[46] Despite a playful spirit, it is clear that Adams was attracted to Oriental thought. He was sufficiently moved by the religious symbolism of the Japanese Buddhist goddess of mercy, Kwannon, that after returning to the United States he directed St. Gaudens to sculpt the famous hooded figure as a memorial to his wife.

Apparently nirvana continued to beckon, for in 1891 Adams set out once again with La Farge to seek the famous Sinhalese Buddhist temples in the ancient city of Anuradhpura. He declared they came not "for the historical or industrial part of the affair," but "to see the art," which was "older than anything in India" and belonged to the "earliest and probably purest Buddhist times." Mysterious as usual, he confessed, "I expected—never mind what—all sorts of things—which I have not found." He went on, "Of course we went at once to the sacred bo-tree, which is now only a sickly shoot or two from the original trunk, and under it I sat for half an hour, hoping to attain Nirvana. . . ." But instant nirvana had not come; he confessed that he "left the bo-tree without attaining Buddhaship." A month later he wrote that he now found Buddhism a "trifle flat and unsatisfactory," that he guessed he was "going on for a new avatar." At the same time, he remarked that, "Duty calls me back to Asia, and sooner or later that destiny will accomplish itself, for Brahma waits me. . . ."[47] One is not surprised that Adams failed to find salvation in the East. In the end France, not Japan, offered relief; characteristically, it was the France of Chartres and St. Michel, a France that had passed away centuries before.

Perhaps Adams would have found the answer he sought in China, which he often spoke of visiting, though this seems doubtful. He confided to his friend Hay that among the "chunks of wisdom" he had picked up during his travels was the "certainty that Japan and its art are only a sort of antechamber to China, and that China is the only mystery left to penetrate." He affirmed that as soon as possible he meant "to start for China, and stay there."[48] Meanwhile, he sought to increase his knowledge of the Middle Kingdom through William Woodville Rockhill, who had just returned from an expedition through China and Tibet. Rockhill had sent Adams a copy of his *Life of the Buddha*. Adams responded that the book had "interested me much" and that the "accidental presence" of a Japanese scholar had allowed him to "understand a little of it." He declared that he was "curious to understand more" and "to have your help"—ending with an invitation that Rockhill join him for dinner, to give him a "Chinese education."[49]

The attraction to the East seems to have faded in later years, or at least that is the suggestion of the *Education of Henry Adams*, which nowhere mentions the trip to Japan or the plan to travel to China. But of course the memoir also neglects to mention the suicide of his wife and other crucial details in his life. It is widely understood that the *Education* conceals as much as it reveals the secrets of Adams's life. Though he obviously failed to achieve nirvana, Adams published a final testimonial, "Buddha and Brahma," a blank-verse poem written twenty years earlier, which appeared in the *Yale Review* in 1915.[50] In the end Adams remains an enigma.

For John La Farge the summer in Japan was a much more positive experience. Like Adams, he was drawn to Eastern thought through Eastern art. His first interest traced back to his early years: he had joined his brothers in editing a small paper entitled *Le Chinois* while still a child. In college he became acquainted with a Jesuit missionary who had brought a number of Oriental art objects from Japan.[51] His friendship with Raphael Pumpelly, the globe-trotting American geologist, was especially important. Commissioned by the Japanese government to conduct mineral explorations, Pumpelly lived in Japan several years and traveled through China and central Asia. He came home in 1865 loaded down with hundreds of art pieces from Japan and China, which he allowed La Farge to see.[52]

The result was La Farge's "An Essay on Japanese Art," included in Pumpelly's account of his travels, *Across America and Asia*. One of the earliest American treatments of Japanese art, the sketch establishes La Farge as a pioneer of Oriental art. La Farge extolled the "inimitable" lacquers and celebrated the "novelty" of the design and the "grandeur" of the style revealed by Japanese art. "We feel," he wrote, "that we are looking at perfect work, that we are in [the] presence of a distinct civilization, where art is happily married to industry."[53] Earlier Americans had dismissed Oriental art almost contemptuously.

When La Farge sailed for Japan in 1886, the country was not entirely unknown to him. Unlike Adams, he decided to write a book about his experiences, which he entitled *An Artist's Letters from Japan*. (He originally published the letters in the *Century Magazine*.) Dedicating the work to Adams, La Farge declared, "If anything worth repeating has been said by me in these letters, it has probably come from you, or has been suggested by being with you—perhaps even in the way of contradiction."[54] If the book reveals Adams's influence, La Farge's description suggests a quite different perception of the Japanese world. Perhaps because he was an artist, he was immediately entranced by the beauties of the exotic environment and so found it possible to ignore the petty inconveniences of which Adams constantly complained. La Farge remarks that the two men had agreed from the outset "that we should bring no books, read no books, but come as innocently as we could. . . ."[55] Innocence was, of course, impossible, but La Farge seems to have been much more successful than Adams in opening himself to the strange country.

Although *Artist's Letters* indicates a more intimate grasp of Japanese art, the book echoes most of the views of his essay of a quarter of a century earlier. "The Japanese sensitiveness to the beauties of the outside world," he wrote in a characteristic passage, "is something much more delicate and complex and contemplative, and at the same time more natural, than ours has ever been." Where the block prints of Hokusai and the Ukioye school seem to have been the basis for his generalizations in the earlier essay, he now realized the significance of the more ancient religious art and the impact of Buddhism and Taoism. Of all the images he saw, he testified that the "one that touches me most—partly, perhaps, because of the Eternal Feminine"—was the "incarnation that is called Kuwannon [Kwannon], when shown absorbed in the meditations of Nirvana." Taken to see Fenollosa's collection of Oriental paintings, he confessed that the view of only a few of the masterpieces had "lifted me away from to-day into an indefinite great past."[56] He also expressed sympathy for the Taoist spirit, which enfused much of Japanese art.

Good Catholic that he was, La Farge was apparently never tempted to embrace the Oriental conceptions that had inspired much of the art he so admired; however, he retained a lifelong affection for Japanese culture. Resuming work on the "Ascension" mural, which he had abandoned to join Adams, he chose to draw in the serene landscape of Japan as a backdrop to one of the supreme episodes in the Christian drama. He became a close friend of Kakuzo Okakura, the Japanese are expert who came to Boston in 1904 to serve as a curator with the Boston Museum of Fine Arts. Reaching back for his earliest memories of his father, La Farge's son would later recall that his father had frequently prowled their home in a Japanese kimono; he also remembered the delight of Okakura's visits when the family would gather to drink tea from a special lacquer set his father always brought out on such occasions.[57]

It is fitting that this chapter end with Ernest Fenollosa, who in many ways derived the most from the Japanese years and who most clearly grasped the larger significance of the encounter with Eastern civilization. Edward Morse is once again a critical link. Asked by the president of Tokyo University to recommend a candidate to fill the university's new chair of philosophy, Morse had appealed to Charles Eliot Norton, who suggested young Fenollosa. The son of a Spanish musician who fled to America during the Carlist Wars, his mother a member of a prominent New England family, Fenollosa grew up in Salem and graduated from Harvard in 1874.[58] He had been drawn to philosophy as an undergraduate and took two years of advanced philosophical studies at Harvard; however, he finally turned to art. Arriving in Japan in 1878, he recapitulated his educational experience: he taught philosophy for several years, then took up the study and collection of Japanese art. In 1890 he came back to the United States as curator of Oriental art at the Boston Museum of Fine Arts, but returned to Japan in 1897 for three more years as professor of English literature at the Imperial Normal School at Tokyo.

Fenollosa has been remembered mainly as a seminal figure in inaugurating twentieth-century Western interest in Oriental art, and rightly so. Though increasing numbers of Westerners were turning to Oriental art, he was one of the first to study with Japanese teachers and to achieve mastery in the field. His most notable works were a study of *The Masters of Ukioye* (1896), the great Japanese school of wood-block artists culminating in Hokusai, and the more wide-ranging *Epochs of Chinese and Japanese Art* (1912), a path-breaking effort to classify the main schools of Far Eastern art. He also played a crucial role in the revival of traditional arts in Japan and the introduction of Western audiences to the classical Noh plays. His interest in Japanese classical drama led to two books: *Certain Noble Plays of Japan* and *"Noh"; or, Accomplishment, a Study in the Classical Stage of Japan,* both published in 1916 from notes by his admirer Ezra Pound. Certainly, few Westerners and no American has played a more significant role in stimulating modern interest in Oriental art.

However, our main concern is not with Fenollosa's career in Oriental art, but with his interest in Oriental thought—though his profound interest in the art had much to do with his attraction to the thought. In the West, he had wavered between naturalism and idealism. As an undergraduate at Harvard, he had organized a Spencer Club and avowed the cosmic philosopher's ideas; but he soon shifted allegiance to Hegel. He also admired Emerson and delivered a "Transcendental" address at his Harvard commencement in 1874.[59] (It is intriguing that Samuel Johnson, the aging Transcendentalist and author of *Oriental Religions,* was present. Johnson cheered young Fenollosa's "charming disquisition" for its "unqualified advocacy of Pantheism in its highest and purest form. . . ."[60]) In the end, however, Buddha became his spiritual hero.

Apparently, Fenollosa originally investigated Buddhism as the result of his art work; he soon recognized that medieval art in Japan and China was "as much involved with Buddhism" as the art of medieval Europe had been with Christianity.[61] At some point professional investigation gave way to personal interest: he sought instruction from a Buddhist abbot and, in 1885, was confirmed in the doctrines of the Tendai sect. He rarely spoke of his conversion, but he seems to have remained a Buddhist for the remainder of his life. Several years after returning to America, he remarked that he "still" looked upon his Japanese mentor as "my most inspired and devoutly liberal teacher in matters religious"; he also confessed that the "days and nights I had the privilege of spending with him in the vicinities of Kioto, Nara, and Nikko" would always remain "precious."[62] Upon his death Fenollosa's ashes were deposited at a Buddhist temple in Japan.

Returning to America after more than a decade in Japan, Fenollosa was almost inevitably drawn to a comparison of the two civilizations he had come to know—as well as the probable consequences of their increasing encounter. The result is one of the most profound efforts to explore the meeting of East and West in the century. Fenollosa offered his views in two important articles and a lengthy poem, all published in the 1890s.

In "Chinese and Japanese Traits," published in the *Atlantic Monthly* in 1892, he confronted the West's misunderstanding of the Orient, emphasizing that Eastern societies had been much more dynamic than most Westerners realized. The conventional conceptions of the Chinese as a stolid, unchanging people and the Japanese as an imitative, fickle one are both dismissed; throughout their histories both peoples had, in fact, exhibited a powerful mixture of both "individuality and formalism," change and stability, the new and the old—just as in the West. Though he does not name names, Fenollosa's insistence that individuality had played large roles in both Chinese and Japanese history represented a frontal assault on Percival Lowell's Impersonality thesis. He suggested that misunderstanding had arisen because of confusion concerning the meaning of "individuality." The term should be understood not as that "sickly cast of thought" and "morbid self-consciousness" so often associated with individuality, but rather as the "power to produce freshly from within" and to "react and adapt under rapid change of environment."[63] Obviously, Eastern and Western societies had both demonstrated such individuality.

In addition to correcting Western misconceptions, the article includes a startling prediction concerning the future world role of the Japanese. Fenollosa prophesied that as East and West fused, a new "civilized man" would appear who would "prevail throughout the world for the next thousand years"; he went on to proclaim that the new man would first appear on Japanese shores.[64] He explained that, of all the countries in the world, Japan had most successfully preserved the traditional elements of her heritage while embracing the dynamic changes forced by modernization —the essence of the future fusion of East and West. There is no better example of the radical reversal in perspective that residence in a country like Japan could cause: Americans had always been taught that the future rested with the United States.

Fenollosa spelled out his dream of a new world civilization in "East and West," a poem he read before the Phi Beta Kappa Society at Harvard in 1892. Forty-five pages in length, the poem is divided into five parts. Part 1, "The First Meeting of East and West," celebrates the original encounter of civilizations, when Alexander the Great "brought the arts of Greece face to face with the mystical thought of India." Parts 2 and 3 trace the subsequent separation of East and West following the breakup of the Roman Empire, while Parts 4 and 5 focus on "The Present Meeting of East and West" and "The Future Union of East and West." In brief, Fenollosa affirmed three propositions: that East and West needed one another, that they had come together once before, and that they were coming together once again —marking the end of the century as a "unique dramatic epoch in human affairs" and the "end of a great cycle." The merging of the "two halves of the world" would result in the creation of a new civilization and a more cosmic man.[65]

In the poem Fenollosa portrayed the East as a feminine society, the West as a masculine one—a popular formulation. However, he added a subtle modification, suggesting that religion had softened the dominant tendency in both centers of civilization. The result was not the usual antithesis, but what Fenollosa called "This stupendous double antithesis." Christianity had exercised a softening, feminine influence on the West, just as the Samurai tradition and elements in Buddhism had exercised a hardening, masculine influence on the East. Thus, the West's proclivity for violence had been moderated by a "feminine faith" in love, renunciation, and obedience; while the "peaceful impotence of the East" had been modified by a "martial faith" in "spiritual knighthood" and self-reliance.[66] There was, then, a basic distinction between the feminine East and the masculine West, but each contained elements of the opposite civilization. His "double antithesis" represents a much more sophisticated view than the usual contrast.

Fenollosa had seen too much of the corrosive effects of Westernization in Japan to overlook the fact that in the early phases of East-West synthesis, the infusion of alien elements would be harmful to both. Western industrialism and materialism would nearly destroy the traditional East. He wrote: "O you West in the East like the slime of a beast,/ Why must you devour that exquisite flower?/ Why poison the peace of the far Japanese?" In turn, the West would become choked with a pseudo-Oriental spirituality: "O this spirituality of pure externality!/ Which can patch up disasters with arnica plasters." However, in the end a true synthesis would occur: "Scientific Analysis" would merge with "Spiritual Wisdom" and "Aesthetic Synthesis" with "Spiritual Love."[67] Though the poetry may not be distinguished, "East and West" presents one of the most significant visions of the meeting of East and West proposed by an American.

Fenollosa returned to the theme in 1898 in an article entitled "The Coming Fusion of East and West." Despite the confidence of his title, the article suggests new doubts about the results of East-West encounter. He now warned that if Western nations persisted in disparaging Oriental civilization and in minimizing the world-shaking developments in the East, the very survival of the West could be in doubt. The closure process seemed to be accelerating, marked by widening power struggles in the Far East, China's movement toward modernization, and, for America, the Spanish-American War and new commitments in the Philippines. More aware of international politics and the dangers of war than before, he now urged that the Western appropriation of the East must be "no conquest, but a fusion." The Western benefits of fusion remained very large. "We shall," he predicted, "regain in this East magnificent enthusiasm long grown cold, living ideals that shall lend wings to our own. There is hardly a mooted topic—art, literature, philosophy, morals, manners, family organization—that shall not find its parallax of computation wonderfully enlarged."[68]

Hailing Fenollosa's cosmic vision, his recent biographer Lawrence Chisolm has claimed that he was "the first philosopher, perhaps the first modern writer in any field, to think in a genuinely historical world perspective. . . ."[69] Fenollosa deserves the highest praise, but he was hardly the first to adopt a world perspective. As the earlier pages of this study demonstrate, a more universal outlook based on a growing respect for the achievement of Eastern societies was in the air. Fenollosa merely put into words what increasing numbers were recognizing by the last decade of the century.

Notes

1. Lawrence Chisolm, *Fenollosa: The Far East and American Culture* (New Haven, Conn.: Yale University Press, 1963), pp. 58-59.

2. See Earl Miner, *The Japanese Tradition in British and American Literature* (Princeton, N.J.: Princeton University Press, 1958) and the long opening essay in Van Wyck Brooks, *Fenollosa and his Circle, with Other Essays in Biography* (New York: E. P. Dutton, 1962), pp. 1-68.

3. [Nathan Hale], "Adventures of Golownin in Japan," *North American Review* 10 (January 1820): 33.

4. For the pre-1853 period, see Henry F. Graff, "Introduction," *Bluejackets with Perry in Japan: A Day-by-Day Account Kept by Master's Mate John R. C. Lewis and Cabin Boy William B. Allen* (New York: New York Public Library, 1952), pp. 11-70. For earlier European contacts, see Donald Lach, *Asia in the Making of Europe*. Vol. 1, Bk. 2: *The Century of Discovery* (Chicago: University of Chicago Press, 1965), 651-729.

5. [Edward Everett Hale], "The American Expedition to Japan," *North American Review* 83 (July 1856): 235-36, 240.

6. See Dorothy Wayman, *Edward Sylvester Morse: A Biography* (Cambridge, Mass.: Harvard University Press, 1942). Much of the following biographical detail has been culled from Wayman's useful study.

7. Ibid., p. 234.

8. Edward S. Morse, *Japan Day by Day. 1877, 1878-79, 1882-83* (1917; reprint ed., Tokyo: Kobunsha Publishing Co., 1936), pp. ix-x.

9. Ibid., Part 1, pp. 25, 41, 115; Part 2, p. 198. (The pagination starts over in Part 2.)

10. Ibid., Part 1, p. 44.

11. F. W. C. [Frederick W. Coburn], "Edward Sylvester Morse," *Dictionary of American Biography (DAB)*, 13: 242.

12. Morse, *Japan*, Part 1, pp. vii, 72.

13. Ibid., Part 2, p. 89.

14. Ibid., Part 1, p. x.

15. Cf. *The Index* 15 (April 3, 1884): 473, and Lydia M. Child, *Letters of Lydia Maria Child*, (1883; reprint ed., New York: Negro Universities Press, 1969), p. 246.

16. Morris Carter, *Isabella Stewart Gardner and Fenway Court* (Boston: Houghton Mifflin, 1925), pp. 59-62. Quote on p. 62.

17. See Frederick C. Shattuck, "William Sturgis Bigelow," *Proceedings of the Massachusetts Historical Society* 60 (October 1926-June 1927): 15-19.

18. W. T. Councilman, "William Sturgis Bigelow, 1850-1926," in M. A. De Wolfe Howe, *Later Years of the Saturday Club, 1870-1920* (Boston: Houghton Mifflin, 1927), p. 267.

19. Theodore Roosevelt, *The Letters of Theodore Roosevelt*, ed. Elting E. Morison, 8 vols. (Cambridge, Mass.: Harvard University Press, 1951-1954), 1: 125. Also see the letters in 5: 117; 5: 296; and 7: 541.

20. Raymond W. Albright, *Focus on Infinity: A Life of Phillips Brooks* (New York: Macmillan, 1961), p. 332.

21. George C. Shattuck, "Personal Letter About Dr. William Sturgis Bigelow (1850-1926) from John E. Lodge to Frederick Cheever Shattuck," *Proceedings of the Massachusetts Historical Society* 75 (January-December 1963): 109.

22. William S. Bigelow, *Buddhism and Immortality* (Boston: Houghton Mifflin, 1908), pp. 5-6.

23. William S. Bigelow, "Prefatory Note," in Chi Ki, *On the Method of Practicing Concentration and Contemplation*, p. 111. A pamphlet in Harvard University Library, reprinted from the *Harvard Theological Review* 16 (April 1923): 109-41.

24. Cf. A. Lawrence Lowell, *Biography of Percival Lowell* (New York: Macmillian, 1935), pp. 1-7.

25. Cf. Percival Lowell, *Chöson: The Land of the Morning Calm. A Sketch of Korea* (Boston: Ticknor, 1886); Lowell, *Percival Lowell*, pp. 13-19.

26. Lowell, *Chöson*, p. 107.

27. Elizabeth Bisland, *Life and Letters of Lafcadio Hearn*, 2 vols. (Boston: Houghton Mifflin, 1906), 2: 487.

28. Percival Lowell, *The Soul of the Far East* (Boston: Houghton Mifflin, 1888), pp. 1-3. Quotes on pp. 2-3.

29. Ibid., p. 9.

30. Ibid., p. 15.

31. Rikizo Nakashima, "Mr. Percival Lowell's Misconception of the Character of the Japanese," *New Englander and Yale Review* 50 (February 1899): 100.

32. Lowell, *Soul of Far East*, p. 173.

33. Ibid., pp. 184-85.

34. Percival Lowell, *Occult Japan or The Way of the Gods. An Esoteric Study of Japanese Personality and Possession* (Boston: Houghton Mifflin, 1894), p. 13.

35. Ibid., p. 25.

36. Lowell, *Chöson*, pp. 107, 108-9. Quote on p. 109.

37. Lowell, *Soul of the Far East*, pp. 4-5.

38. Worthington C. Ford, ed., *Letters of Henry Adams (1858-1891)* (Boston: Houghton Mifflin, 1930), p. 366, and Harold D. Cater, ed., *Henry Adams and his Friends: A Collection of his Unpublished Letters* (Boston: Houghton Mifflin, 1947), p. 163.

39. Ernest Samuels, *Henry Adams: The Middle Years* (Cambridge, Mass.: Belknap Press of Harvard University Press, 1965), p. 293, the second of a magnificent three-volume work.

40. *Letters of Adams*, p. 309, and Samuels, *Adams: Middle Years*, pp. 245-46, 290. Quote on p. 290.

41. *Letters of Adams*, pp. 366, 367.

42. Cater, *Adams and Friends*, p. 165.

43. *Letters of Adams*, pp. 371-72.

44. Ibid., pp. 372-73.

45. Ibid., p. 372.

46. Ibid., pp. 365, 372.

47. Ibid., pp. 525, 526, 532. Also see, Ernest Samuels, *Henry Adams: The Major*

Phase (Cambridge, Mass.: Belknap Press of Harvard University Press, 1964), pp. 53-58.

48. Cater, *Adams and Friends*, p. 174. Also see *Letters of Adams*, p. 309.

49. Cater, *Adams and Friends*, pp. 189, 178.

50. Samuels, *Adams: Major Phase*, p. 58.

51. John La Farge, S.J., *The Manner Is Ordinary* (New York: Harcourt, Brace, 1954), pp. 17-18.

52. Raphael Pumpelly, *My Reminiscences*, 2 vols. (New York: Henry Holt, 1918), 2: 582.

53. John La Farge, "An Essay on Japanese Art," in Raphael Pumpelly, *Across America and Asia*, 2nd rev. ed. (New York: Leypoldt & Holt, 1870), p. 196.

54. John La Farge, *An Artist's Letters from Japan* (New York: Century Co., 1897), p. vii.

55. Ibid., p. 17.

56. Ibid., pp. 30, 175, 14.

57. La Farge, *Manner Is Ordinary*, pp. 4, 11, 12-14.

58. See Lawrence Chisolm, *Fenollosa: The Far East and American Culture*, a brilliant, far-ranging study. But also refer to the sketch by his widow, Mary Fenollosa, in Ernest F. Fenollosa, *Epochs of Chinese and Japanese Art. An Outline History of East Asiatic Design*, 2 vols. (London: William Heinemann, 1912), 1: vii-xxii.

59. Chisolm, *Fenollosa*, pp. 23-26.

60. Samuel Longfellow, "Memoir," in Samuel Johnson, *Lectures, Essays, and Sermons* (Boston: Houghton Mifflin, 1883), p. 112.

61. Mary Fenollosa in Fenollosa, *Epochs of Chinese and Japanese Art*, 1: xv.

62. Ernest Fenollosa, *East and West. The Discovery of America and Other Poems* (New York: Thomas Y. Crowell, 1893), p. 211.

63. Ernest Fenollosa, "Chinese and Japanese Traits," *Atlantic Monthly* 69 (June 1892): 770.

64. Ibid.: 774.

65. See the "Preface" in Fenollosa, *East and West*, pp. v-vii. Quotes on p. v.

66. Ibid., pp. v-vi.

67. Ibid., pp. 39, 42, vi.

68. Ernest Fenollosa, "The Coming Fusion of East and West," *Harper's New Monthly* 98 (December 1898): 116, 121.

69. Chisolm, *Fenollosa*, p. 6.

12
Lafcadio Hearn and the Higher Buddhism

Lafcadio Hearn shared his friend Fenollosa's fascination with Japan. Though he ultimately arrived at many of the same perceptions and conclusions as Morse, Bigelow, Lowell, Adams, La Farge, and Fenollosa, his path was radically different. The Morse-Fenollosa group nearly all had strong roots in the Boston area, Harvard educations, and New England identities; Hearn was an immigrant, a self-taught writer who missed a college education, and a wanderer in search of an identity. Despite overlapping years and a mutual fascination with Japan, Hearn would have little contact with the group. While they congregated and trooped about the streets together, he preferred his solitude. The exception was his warm friendship with Fenollosa, but he finally broke that off, too, explaining that though he greatly enjoyed his visits, he must avoid the Fenollosa home in order to concentrate on his writing. "Enjoyment is not for me,—excepting in the completion of work," he apologized.[1] Deeply influenced by Lowell's *The Soul of the Far East*, he barely knew the author and made little effort to cultivate his acquaintance. To a considerable extent he was always an outsider—in the West as well as the East. Unique in so many ways, Lafcadio Hearn is nevertheless a crucial figure in the study of the impact of Oriental ideas in nineteenth-century America. Of the sizable number who visited the East in the period, none explored Asian thought more deeply or went further toward embracing the Oriental viewpoint, including adoption of Japanese ways, marriage to an Asian woman, and immersion in Oriental religion. In many ways he represents the outer limit in the nineteenth-century American exploration of Oriental thought.

Hearn's early life began in romance but quickly gave way to tragedy. Born in 1850 on one of the islands in the Ionian Sea, he was the son of an Anglo-Irish soldier and a beautiful Greek woman whom his father met while in service with the British army.[2] He was taken to Dublin at the age of two, and then everything seemed to turn sour: his parents' marriage fell apart, his mother fled back to Greece, and he was handed over to a stern aunt to be raised. He would never see either parent again. Although there must have been good moments, new setbacks followed. At sixteen he lost an eye, a condition that repeatedly threatened his writing career and left a permanent trauma. At nineteen he sought to begin life anew by moving to the United States. Certain of his later idiosyncracies—a morbid self-consciousness, a tendency to retreat into himself, and difficult interpersonal relations—undoubtedly stemmed from these repeated shocks.

Though he never became an American citizen, Hearn lived the next twenty-odd years in the United States. In a sense he was never a citizen of any country, though he held on to his British citizenship until external pressures forced him to take out Japanese citizenship. He would spend much of his adult life in the United States and publish practically all his books with American publishers. He drifted into the newspaper business, working first as a reporter in Cincinnati and then in New Orleans. When he sailed away to Japan in 1890, never to return, he was forty years old.

Hearn once declared that everyone had to specialize in order to succeed and that, accordingly, he had chosen "the worship of the Odd, the Queer, the Strange, the Exotic, the Monstrous."[3] The statement offers a good characterization of the romantic cast of his thought as well as the appeal of the Orient. He had an itch to travel to exotic places, confessing in 1880 to a "spirit of restlessness" whenever he observed ships arriving in New Orleans. And he remarked, ". . . I would give anything to be a literary Columbus,—to discover a Romantic America in some West Indian or North African or Oriental region,—to describe the life that is only fully treated of in universal geographies or ethnological researches."[4] Meanwhile, he sought out the "Orient at home" as he sometimes said, living for extended periods in the French Quarter in New Orleans and on Martinique in the West Indies.

The first references to Oriental thought appear in Hearn's letters in the 1870s and became more frequent and more extended in the 1880s. It is difficult to say what first drew his attention to the East. The fact that he was reading Free Religious materials in 1869 soon after reaching Cincinnati would certainly have exposed him to references to Oriental thought. He penned an unfriendly piece on caste as early as 1873, apparently the first of his writings to concern India.[5]

Hearn's sustained interest in Eastern thought may be traced from the late 1870s and his acquaintance with H. E. Krehbiel, a fellow newspaperman, music critic, and, most crucially, an early student of Oriental music. Hearn revealed in 1877 that Krehbiel had "for several years devoted himself to the study of Oriental music and the chants of the ancient peoples of the East," and that he was then preparing a series of essays on the subject.[6] Whether Krehbiel stimulated Hearn's interest or whether the two arrived at a common interest independently, they were soon trading information on Asian matters generally. In 1879, for example, Hearn wrote Krehbiel to correct a reference concerning the Hindu god Siva, using the occasion to pontificate about the Hindu trinity. In a succeeding letter the subject was mythology. "Your Hindoo legends charmed me," Hearn wrote—although his characterization of the legends as "superhumanly vast, wild, and terrible" and as "typhoons of the tropical imagination" hardly suggest charm. He remarked that the Greek mind seemed "infantile" when compared to the Indian; the Greek had been a "pure naturalist," while the Hindu had "fathomed the deepest deeps of human thought. . . ."[7]

Hearn's interest in the Orient was clearly rising, but it by no means monopolized his attention. Elizabeth Stevenson claims that throughout the 1880s Hearn lacked any special "sense of a destiny" that beckoned him toward the East and that he "was at least as interested in Arabic and Jewish folklore, and in Finnish mythology." The decision to go to Japan was largely "an accident."[8] A key letter in 1882 leaves no doubt of his quickening interest: he notes that he has been using his leisure hours "studying the theories of the East, the poetry of antique India, the teachings of the wise concerning absorption and emanation, the illusions of existence, and happiness as the equivalent of annihilation." As a result he now thought that the Eastern teachers "were wiser than the wisest of the Occidental ecclesiastics."[9]

Edwin Arnold's *Light of Asia,* which Hearn reviewed for a New Orleans paper in 1879, seems to have played a special role in increasing his enthusiasm. Hearn returned to it again and again in the 1880s. "Have you seen the exquisite new edition of Arnold's 'Light of Asia'?" he wrote a friend in 1883. "It has enchanted me,—perfumed my mind as with the incense of a strangely new and beautiful worship."[10] Arnold greatly increased his special interest in Buddhism and, indeed, seemed to hint an imminent conversion. "After all," Hearn now declared, "Buddhism in some esoteric form may prove the religion of the future. . . . Is not the tendency of all modern philosophy toward the acceptance of the ancient Indian teaching that the visible is but an emanation of the Invisible. . .?" He speculated that the "Right Man" might very well "revolutionize the whole Occidental religious world by preaching the Oriental faith."[11] And in an adulatory article published in the

New Orleans *Times-Democrat* in 1883, Hearn claimed that the English poet had accomplished what no Oriental scholar had ever done—he had conveyed the true spirit of Buddhism, the inner side that scholars always seemed to miss. The trouble with the day's leading Buddhist scholars was their compulsion to prove that Buddhism was inferior to Christianity. "Edwin Arnold," Hearn proclaimed, "first taught the vast reading public of Great Britain and of this country . . . what Buddha's life was, and what his doctrines were."[12] Though disappointed by Arnold's later writings, he never wavered in his praise of *Light of Asia*.

In addition to wide reading, Hearn was making other intriguing Oriental contacts in the 1880s. In 1886 he exuberantly informed Krehbiel that "I think I shall soon be able to send you a Hindoo. Yes, a Hindoo,—with Orientally white teeth, the result of vegetal diet and Brahmanic abstemiousness. . . ." A worker at a local factory in New Orleans, the Hindu actually sought Hearn out to protest his editorials concerning India. Delighted to discover that he spoke English and had been in the Indian civil service, Hearn quizzed him concerning Hindu literature, reporting that the Hindu was "somewhat familiar" with the great Hindu religious classics and that he had even consented to sing temple chants for him.[13] Hearn records a subsequent acquaintance with a Chinese doctor who "tried to teach me Chinese. . . ."[14] He was never very successful with any of his Oriental language studies.

By 1885 Hearn was devoting so much attention to Oriental thought in his New Orleans newspaper column that, as he confided to a friend, the paper was being condemned from some pulpits as "A Buddhist Newspaper" and "Infidel sheet." He wrote on Theosophy, Buddhism, the *Mahabharata*, Oriental scholarship, Indian and Japanese poetry, transmigration, and Chinese religion: he contemplated bringing the pieces together as a book, but decided that he did not know enough to execute the project.[15] (Albert Mordell, the pioneer Hearn scholar, later published a selection of the pieces in the *American Miscellany*, *Occidental Gleanings*, and *Essays in European and Oriental Literature*.)

Hearn did publish two volumes, *Stray Leaves from Strange Literature* (1884) and *Some Chinese Ghosts* (1887), which incorporated some of his Oriental reading. *Stray Leaves* consisted of ancient tales and parables from Egyptian, Eskimo, Indian, Scandinavian, Islamic, and Hebrew sources, which Hearn reworked from translations. He freely added to, cut from, fused, and rephrased the selections so that the result was more a reflection of Hearn than an accurate reproduction of his sources. It is significant that much the largest section consisted of the Hindu and Buddhist tales. *Some Chinese Ghosts* presented a retelling of six Chinese tales marked by the same editorial liberties taken in *Stray Leaves*. The criterion for selection, Hearn explained, was "*weird* beauty."[16] Neither work demonstrated much acquaintance with Asian civilization; Hearn later apologized for their jejune quality.

Surveying the early articles and letters, the most significant generalization that emerges is that Hearn had already reached the conclusions concerning Oriental thought that would dominate his books after he sailed to Japan in 1890. The point needs emphasis, since most students of Hearn's thought have tended to pass over his early interest in Oriental ideas. His preoccupation with Buddhism, for example, was already emerging in the early 1880s—years before his departure for Japan. Indeed, he had even begun to speak of a "higher Buddhism," which he subsequently featured in *Japan: An Attempt at Interpretation*, his summing up of the Japanese experience. The tendency of his thought may be seen in a letter penned in 1883 in which he argued, "Buddhism only needs to be known to make its influence felt in America." Dismissing Olcott's and other Theosophical writings for being "too metaphysical" and smacking too much of "Spiritualistic humbug," he prophesied that "the higher Buddhism,— that suggested by men like Emerson, John Weiss, etc.,—will yet have an apostle."[17] He penned a series of articles on Buddhist doctrines and literature in the New Orleans *Times-Democrat* between 1883 and 1886, including one called "What Buddhism Is."[18]

Despite a profound personal attraction to Buddhism, Hearn always held back from full commitment to it or any other sectarian religious viewpoint. The desired goal, he repeatedly emphasized, was universality, not dogma, Oriental or Occidental. Like the Buddhism, this universalist motif is evident in his thought well before Japan. Writing in 1879, he admonished, "You know that I have no faith in any 'faiths' or dogmas; I regard thought as a mechanical process, and individual life as a particle of that eternal force of which we know so little. . . ." And a few years later he remarked to a friend, "What matter creeds, myths, traditions, to you or me, who perceive in all faiths one vast truth,—one phase of the Universal Life?"[19] He attacked James Freeman Clarke's writings on comparative religion for failure to recognize this religious universality. Clarke, he charged, had "sat down to study with the preconceived purpose of belittling other beliefs by comparison with Christianity. . . ." His own "humble studies in comparative mythology" had led him to a "totally different conclusion," namely, a recognition of a "universal aspiration of mankind toward the Infinite and Supreme." Indeed, he now found himself unable "to perceive the least absurdity in any general idea of worship," whatever the form.[20]

Finally, one should mention Hearn's devotion to Herbert Spencer. No intellectual influence more profoundly conditioned his view of Japanese life—or more clearly testifies to the importance of the preconceptions he brought from America. Although recent scholars have cast doubts about Spencer's impact, especially with regard to businessmen,[21] in Hearn's case there can be no doubt: Spencer was unquestionably the major intellectual and religious event in his life. He had been converted into a Spencerian in 1885 or 1886 after reading the cosmic philosopher. Describing the experience as a "very positive change," he declared that the Englishman "completely converted me away from all 'isms, or sympathies with 'isms. . . ."[22] At first, he was so bowled over that he seemed willing to repudiate Oriental philosophy. "Talking of change in opinions, I am really astonished at myself," he informed his friend Krehbiel. "You know what my fantastic metaphysics were. A friend disciplined me to read Herbert Spencer. I suddenly discovered what a waste of time all my Oriental metaphysics had been." He now spoke of spending several years devouring Spencer's "oceanic philosophy," and, beginning with the *First Principles,* could soon report that he had worked his way through two volumes of the "Biology" and one volume of the "Sociology," with the "Psychology" to come next.[23]

Hearn's decision to travel to Japan seems inevitable in retrospect; yet, he had shown little prior interest in the land. He did publish an article on Japanese poetry in 1883 in which he pondered the differences between European and Oriental peoples, but the piece would not be worth mentioning were it not for later developments.[24] The event that finally riveted his attention on Japan was the New Orleans World Industrial Exposition held in 1884-1885. He was greatly taken by the Japanese exhibits which he referred to repeatedly in a series of articles in *Harper's Weekly* and *Harper's Bazaar*. Contemplating the strange hodge-podge of religious artifacts displayed at the exposition, he was led to wonder whether it was "utterly unreasonable" to believe that the "dream of a universal religion" would be achieved by such industrial gatherings.[25] Hearn went to New York in 1889 and, at the casual suggestion of a Harper editor, agreed to do a book on Japan.[26] It was the most fateful decision in his life.

Hearn's sojourn in Japan began in euphoria and, predictably, ended a few years later in considerable disillusionment—although not with traditional Japan or with Oriental ideals. "I feel indescribably towards Japan," he wrote to Elizabeth Bisland shortly after his arrival in 1890. In the first flush of arrival, everything seemed to win his approval: "What I love in Japan is the Japanese,—the poor simple humanity of the country. . . .There is nothing in this world approaching the naive natural charm of them. . . . And I love their gods, their customs, their dress, their bird-like quavering songs, their houses, their superstitions, their faults. And I believe that their art is as far in advance of our art as old Greek art was superior to that of the earliest European art-gropings. . . . *We* are the barbarians! I do not merely *think* these things: I am as sure of them as of death."[27]

Almost immediately he broke with Harper's and set out on his own, seeking to immerse himself in the life of the people. He took a job as an English teacher in Matsue, a nearly feudal city in western Japan where few Europeans had ever penetrated. As the Japanese eagerly adopted Western styles, Hearn characteristically chose to move in the opposite direction. He moved into a typical Japanese dwelling, learned to squat in the absence of Western furniture, cast off his Western clothing (after work) for kimono and sandals, and gave up European food for a Japanese diet. And, in the most radical step of all, he allowed his friends to arrange marriage to a young Japanese woman, daughter of an impoverished samurai. However, he quickly learned that lifelong habits were not so easily cast aside: within a year, declining health forced him to resume his old beef diet and not long after to hire carpenters to install a Western-style stove in place of the traditional hibachi. As he sadly confessed, he was forced to return "to the flesh-pots of Egypt."[28]

Hearn's shifting attitude toward Japan can be best followed through his correspondence with Basil Hall Chamberlain, a crucial new friend. An Englishman who had arrived in Japan in 1873, Chamberlain had become one of the West's foremost authorities: a master of both written and spoken Japanese, translator of the *Kojiki* ("Record of Ancient Things"), the oldest Japanese record, and editor of a book on Japanese customs, *Things Japanese*.[29] Knowledgeable and compassionate, Chamberlain was an ideal friend; Hearn was soon confiding his innermost thoughts. Writing to introduce himself, Hearn wasted no time in confessing that he was "more anxious than I could tell you to make a good book upon Japan. . . ." He spoke of quickly mastering the Japanese language and penetrating the emotional nature of the people.[30] As with American correspondents, Hearn was unable to restrain his original enthusiasm. "The little I have already seen of this marvellous country," he wrote Chamberlain in 1890, "so far surpasses anticipation that I am almost afraid to see more for the moment: impressions so multitudinous and so sharply novel come to me every day that the mind refuses to digest them. Everything seems enchanted. . . ."[31]

The euphoric mood dominated Hearn's first Japanese book, *Glimpses of Unfamiliar Japan*, published in 1894. By the time the book appeared, however, Hearn had already begun to reveal a more critical attitude; the surprising thing is how early this happened. Indeed, the letters to Chamberlain suggest the beginnings of a shift as early as 1891, only a year after his arrival. The conventional view that Hearn was an uncritical and incurable admirer of all things Japanese obviously will not do. He wrote in May 1891, "I am constantly more and more impressed with the unspeculative character of the Japanese. . . . They do not seem to find pleasure in the suggestions of philosophy:—they read Herbert Spencer without a suspicion of the tremendous ghostly fact behind his whole system. . . ." Considering

Hearn's respect for Spencer, this was a serious criticism. Several months later he went even further. "What you say about your experience with Japanese poetry," he wrote Chamberlain, "is indeed very telling and very painful to one who loves Japan. Depth, I have long suspected, does not exist in the Japanese soul-stream."[32] And in the most revealing admission of all, in August 1891, he observed, "The oscillation of one's thoughts concerning the Japanese—the swaying you describe—is and has for some time been mine also. There are times when they seem so small!"[33] It is true that such doubts are mainly confined to private letters and that Hearn nearly always finds reasons to minimize the limitations. In the very letter complaining of the smallness of the people, for example, Hearn quickly adds that "whatever doubts or vexations one has in Japan," it is only necessary to ask oneself, "Well, who are the best people to live with?"[34]

Events in 1893 and 1894 deepened Hearn's doubts as he found himself caught up in a rising antiforeign movement. As a foreigner married to a Japanese woman, he was confronted by the Japanese government with a hard decision: in order to have his marriage and new child legally recognized, he must become a Japanese citizen, but in doing so he would automatically lose his former privileged status as a foreigner and his salary would be sharply cut. If he refused Japanese citizenship, it seemed probable that his teaching contract would not be renewed. Dazed by these successive blows, at one point he abruptly dismissed his class and went home to write out his resignation. He now described himself to Chamberlain as a "disillusioned enthusiast."[35]

By 1895 Hearn had concluded "that the charm of Japanese life is largely the charm of childhood, and that the most beautiful of all race childhoods is passing into an adolescence which threatens to prove repulsive." And he now admitted that recent events had forced him to change a "good many" of his prior conclusions concerning the Japanese. The "tone" of *Glimpses* had been "true in being the feeling of a place and time," he wrote, but since then he had seen "how thoroughly detestable" the Japanese could be.[36] Though he talked of returning to the West, inquiring about employment possibilities in the United States, he remained. Years before, when he still resided in New Orleans, Hearn had made the observation, "There is such a delightful pleasantness about the *first* relations with people in strange places. . . . Stay long enough in any one place and the illusion is over. . . ."[37] The statement was prophetic.

Hearn had originally come to Japan to make a "good book"; before he was through, he had written twelve. It took several years to complete the first, but after that there was rarely a year without a new volume. *Glimpses of Unfamiliar Japan* records Hearn's preliminary opinion of the Japanese, while the next three volumes represent deeper probes: *Out of the East*

(1895), *Kokoro* (1896), and *Gleanings in Buddha-Fields* (1897). The three works offer a rich and impressionistic record of Japanese life—including vivid descriptions of street scenes, temples, festivals, children at play, and Japanese faces—and also several of Hearn's most sustained essays on the philosophical and religious tendencies of Japanese thought. *Exotics and Retrospectives*, published in 1898, represents a kind of climax—the "theoretical zenith of all his Japanese books" as one recent student has called it —a work that displays his dual commitments to Buddhism and evolutionism.[38] The later books are less theoretical: *In Ghostly Japan* (1899), *Shadowings* (1900), *A Japanese Miscellany* (1901), and *Kotto* (1902). He returned to the large view in a final retrospective survey, *Japan: An Attempt at Interpretation*, published in 1904, the year of his death.

Despite talk of rejecting "Oriental metaphysics" following his conversion to Spencerianism, Hearn clearly did nothing of the kind. He remained captivated by the Asian religious experience, a fascination evident in his twelve Japanese books, which are filled with accounts of temples and shrines he faithfully sought out, talks he held with monks, and essays he continued to write. "The Stone Buddha" essay in *Out of the East*, "The Idea of Pre-existence" essay in *Kokoro*, "Nirvana" in *Gleanings in Buddha-Fields*, and, most revealing of all, "The Higher Buddhism" in *Japan* are the mature reflections of his continuing interest. Moreover, the religious preoccupation is present almost from the moment of his arrival in Japan. He exulted, "Here I am in the land of dreams,—surrounded by strange Gods. I seem to have known and loved them before somewhere: I burn incense before them. I pass much of my time in the temples, trying to see into the heart of this mysterious people." Again, "I have been living in temples and old Buddhist cemeteries, making pilgrimages and sounding enormous bells and worshipping astounding Buddhas."[39] The most extended statement is to be found in his final book, *Japan: An Attempt at Interpretation*, which is almost entirely focused on the Japanese religious experience. He observed that as long as Japanese religion was ignored and misrepresented, "no real knowledge of Japan" was possible.[40]

Hearn's interest in Oriental religion was intellectual, but also deeply personal. A religious seeker during much of his life, he recalled on one occasion that he had already given up Christianity for pantheism at fifteen;[41] subsequently he went through a free thought, then a Buddhist, and finally a Spencerian phase. Like many of his contemporaries, he was a fall-away Christian in search of a substitute religion. Even Spencer failed to fill the void, for however satisfying intellectually, the Spencerian system offered little to satisfy emotional needs. Hearn may have been a committed evolutionist and agnostic in mind, but in his heart he was a pantheist and gnostic. He lamented the passing of the older religious viewpoint and hailed any sign of revival. He observed that at one time, men had endowed all forms and substances with spirit, but "becoming wiser in their own conceit," began to talk "about 'the Inanimate' and 'the Inert,'" replacing spirit by force, matter, and mind. "Yet," he concluded, "we now discover that the primitive fancies were, after all, closer to probable truth."[42] He was a harsh critic of materialism.

A major attraction of the Oriental religions was the survival of the "primitive fancies," of the inner, emotional side of religion that had been almost entirely eliminated in modern Western thought. He describes the wonder of discovering the survival of this inner religion in *Glimpses of Unfamiliar Japan*. Following a visit to a temple at Kōshin, he could only contrast the dryness of his former book study of Buddhism with the revelation of finding its force still "*alive* all around you. . . ." He had discovered that "these quaint Gods of Roads and Gods of Earth are really living still. . . ."[43] Hearn's predicament was that he no longer believed in these gods; he merely wished that he did. This perhaps explains why he so often referred to "ghosts." He could believe that the gods had once been alive to their worshipers and that the ancient faiths had served a profoundly constructive role, but he recognized the sad fact that such belief was largely a matter of the past. Still the original religious impulse—the "ghost"—lingered on in out-of-the-way places. He wrote to Chamberlain, "Now I believe in ghosts. Because I saw them? Not at all. I believe in ghosts, though I disbelieve in souls. I believe in ghosts because there are no ghosts now in the modern world."[44] Dead in the West, the ghosts were still alive in the Orient.

His previous reading naturally inclined him to Buddhism, and he reported in one of his first letters from Japan that ". . . Of course, I am studying Buddhism with heart and soul."[45] He engaged a young Buddhist to take him around to the temples and to interpret for him. But then he discovered Shintoism, still a living force in the backward province where he first took up teaching duties. Soon after, he was communicating his surprised discovery to Chamberlain: "The importance of Shinto here as compared with Buddhism impresses me more and more every day." And some time later, he confessed that of course he was still very fond of Buddhism, but "Shinto seems to me like an occult force,—vast, extraordinary,—which has not been seriously taken into account as a force."[46] He now devoted himself to Japan's native religion; the result was *Glimpses of Unfamiliar Japan*.

One of Shintoism's major fascinations was its primordial quality. Primitive, amorphous, yet powerful, to Hearn it embodied the mysterious force at the root of all religions—that, astonishingly, still survived in the modern world. Shinto disclosed the primal source of religious experience. "In certain of its primitive rites," he wrote, "in its archaic prayers and texts and symbols

. . . it is plainly revealed as the most ancient of all forms of worship, —that which Herbert Spencer terms 'the root of all religions'. . . ." Raw and unmediated, it represented a "religion of the heart"; Buddhism, by contrast, was a "religion of the head," as indicated by a "voluminous theology, a profound philosophy, a literature vast as the sea." Shinto had "no philosophy, no code of ethics, no metaphysics. . . ." Despite its simple forms, *because* of the simplicity, Hearn came to feel that Shintoism possessed a "far more profound vitality" than Buddhism, which "although omnipotent as an art-influence, had never found deep root in the intellectual soul of Japan."[47] It was, as he said on several occasions, the "Soul of the Race."

Another attraction in Shintoism was its emphasis upon ancestor-worship, which Hearn hailed as a primitive form of evolution and a confirmation of what he called the "Idea of Pre-existence." He wrote to Chamberlain,

> . . . I think we Occidentals have yet to learn the worship of ancestors; and evolution is going to teach it to us. When we become conscious that we owe whatever is wise or good or strong or beautiful in each one of us, not to one particular inner individuality, but to the struggles and sufferings and experiences of the whole unknown chain of human lives behind us, reaching back into mystery unthinkable, —the worship of ancestors seems an extremely righteous thing.[48]

Of all Oriental religions, none has seemed less attractive or more alien to Westerners than Shintoism; Hearn is one of the few Westerners to appreciate its mysterious observances. Although he was drawn back to Buddhism, his studies of Shinto show up in all his Japanese books; he devoted several chapters to it in *Japan*.

On his first day in Japan Hearn recalled that he had immediately entered a temple to make an offering to Buddha. Discovering that the attendant spoke English, they had conversed.

> "Are you a Christian?"
>
> And I answer truthfully:—
>
> "No."
>
> "Are you a Buddhist?"
>
> "Not exactly."
>
> "Why do you make offerings if you do not believe in Buddha?"
>
> "I revere the beauty of his teaching, and the faith of those who follow it."[49]

The phraseology is precise, providing a compressed statement of Hearn's mature attitude toward Buddhism. "Not exactly" a Buddhist, he yet revered its doctrines. He confessed on another occasion that, "If it were possible for me to adopt a faith, I should adopt it."[50] In the end he was more a Spencerian than a Buddhist; nevertheless, he continued to be deeply drawn to Buddhism, a fact documented by his continuous references to it. In 1892 he lamented that his "project to study Buddhism" had been delayed; a year later he wrote Chamberlain, "If ever I get into a good place for it, I must begin Buddhist studies. I have a splendid idea for a popular book on the subject."[51]

Buddhism was pushed aside briefly by his discovery of Shintoism, but his old enthusiasm quickly reasserted itself. His learned friend Chamberlain seems to have affected his thinking, for Hearn wrote, "I am now all at one with you on the subject of Buddhism; and my first enthusiasm for Shinto, I fear, was wrong. I thought I saw in Shinto, the soul of the Japanese Loyalty. . . ."[52] He even spoke of modifying certain statements concerning the two religions in the proofs of *Glimpses*. *Out of the East, Kokoro, Gleanings in Buddha-Fields*, and *Exotics and Retrospectives*, his next four books, all point to a deepening immersion in Buddhism. By late 1894 he was writing to an American friend, "When one has lived alone five years in a Buddhist atmosphere, one naturally becomes penetrated by the thoughts that hover in it; my whole thinking, I must acknowledge, has been changed, in spite of my long studies of Spencer and of Schopenhauer. I do not mean that I am a Buddhist, but I mean that the inherited ancestral feelings about the universe—the Occidental ideas every Englishman has—have been totally transformed."[53]

Though extremely sympathetic with the popular forms he found Buddhism taking in Japan, Hearn's personal preference was for a philosophical Buddhism—what he called the "Higher Buddhism" in an essay by that title.[54] Nonsectarian in form, the Higher Buddhism represented what was best in Buddhism; it included the following:

> That there is but one Reality;—
>
> That the consciousness is not the real Self;—
>
> That Matter is an aggregate of phenomena created by the force of acts and thoughts;—
>
> That all objective and subjective existence is made by Karma,—the present being the creation of the past, and the actions of the present and the past, in combination, determining the conditions of the future. . . .[55]

Hearn was at pains to emphasize that the Higher Buddhism was completely compatible with a Western scientific viewpoint. (Much of the essay is devoted to the parallel conceptions in Buddhist and Western thought.) A "kind of Monism," its doctrines accorded "in the most surprising manner" with the scientific theories of German and English monists. It was monistic because it held that the only Reality was the Absolute and because it insisted that the distinctions between mind and matter and the "I" and "Not-I" were ultimately unreal. Spencer had said much the same thing in the *First Principles,* but he had spoken of the "Unknown Reality." The Higher Buddhism was "also a theory of evolution," with karma the key to Buddhist evolution. The universe as well as consciousness were "aggregates of Karma" that had evolved over an enormous past. The difference between Western and Buddhist conceptions was that the Western view emphasized a mechanical and materialistic evolution, while Buddhism stressed a moral and spiritual evolution. Again, Hearn pointed to a special closeness with Spencer's ideas.[56]

One suprising omission in the "Higher Buddhism" essay is any discussion of nirvana. The reason is that Hearn had already dealt with it elsewhere in "Nirvana: A Study in Synthetic Buddhism," included in *Gleanings in Buddha-Fields.*[57] Like the "Higher Buddhism" essay, it is a crucial statement. Hearn complained that although nirvana was fundamental to Buddhism, few Westerners had understood it. Most seemed to believe that it entailed a belief in "complete annihilation," a half-truth at best. The outer "Self" or "Ego" was annihilated, but not the "Real Self." Like most American students of Buddhism, Hearn preferred to view nirvana as a positive doctrine: "Nirvana is no cessation, but an emancipation," he declared. "It means only the passing of conditioned being into unconditioned being. . . ."[58]

The belief that all Buddhists accepted nirvana was another common Western misconception. In fact, Hearn insisted, most Buddhists did *not* accept nirvana, preferring belief in a heaven that one immediately entered after death. Nirvana might appeal to the philosophically minded, but it would never attain a wide hold among the population at large. And what was true of nirvana was true of philosophical Buddhism generally. Hearn concluded that the "few glimpses" he had provided into the "fantastic world of Buddhist metaphysics" would surely "convince any intelligent reader that the higher Buddhism," including the "little-comprehended doctrine of Nirvana," could never become a popular faith. "It is," he declared, "a religion of metaphysicians. . . ."[59] Despite a nonsectarian, universalistic message, the Higher Buddhism was to be reserved for the intellectual elite.

If Hearn often wrote as a Buddhist, he continued to insist that he was a Spencerian. He constantly quoted the English philosopher in the Japanese books and referred to him matter-of-factly as the "world's greatest thinker." And in an 1898 letter he asserted unequivocally, ". . . I am not a Buddhist, but still a follower of Herbert Spencer."[60] How much clearer could he be? But writing in 1904, he also declared: "I venture to call myself a student of Herbert Spencer; and it was because of my acquaintance with the Synthetic Philosophy that I came to find in Buddhist philosophy a more than romantic interest."[61] The phrasing is somewhat different, more accurate, and his final word. Ultimately, Hearn was a Spencerian and a Buddhist. By seeking out the similarities and downplaying the differences, he suggested that the viewpoints were very close; both were monistic, evolutionary systems. What Buddhism had been able to do, Hearn wrote, was "to give us the revelation of larger religious possibilities,—the suggestions of a universal scientific creed nobler than any which has ever existed."[62] Spencer had offered the world a "Synthetic Philosophy"; Hearn proposed a "Synthetic Buddhism."

Hearn's attempt to penetrate the mystery of the Oriental soul recalls the effort that Percival Lowell had made some years before, and, in fact, Lowell was a crucial influence and the standard by which Hearn measured his own efforts. "If I had Lowell's genius and Lowell's independence, how happy I should be," Hearn confessed to Chamberlain.[63] Hearn had come upon the *Soul of the Far East* in 1889 just before he decided to go to Japan. "Gooley!" he wrote his new friend George Gould, "—I have found a marvellous book,—a book of books!—a colossal, splendid, godlike book. You must read every line of it. . . . The book is called 'The Soul of the Far East'. . . ."[64] Lowell's daring generalizations, intimate personal acquaintance with Asia, and theoretical orientation all appealed to Hearn. He would come back to the volume again and again, and as late as 1902, urge a Japanese friend to read Lowell's "charming book" as the "very best book in the English language on the old Japanese life and character. . . ." On another occasion he acclaimed it as "incomparably the greatest of all books on Japan, and the deepest. . . ."[65]

Residence in Japan made him more critical. He wrote Chamberlain that he had discovered it was "one thing" to read *The Soul of the Far East* in Philadelphia, and "quite another" to take it up again after "a year and a half in Japan." Though still impressed by the book's power and charm, he now confessed that he was "horrified" by some of the book's conclusions —including the antithesis between Eastern Impersonality and Western Individuality.[66] Had Lowell merely emphasized East-West differences, there would have been no difficulty, but he had posited that the higher the development of Individuality, the higher the place in intellectual evolution. Refusing to accept the conclusion of the inferiority of the East, Hearn questioned Lowell's claims. "In brief," he explained to Chamberlain, "I doubt, or rather I wish to doubt, that the development of individuality is a lofty or desirable tendency. Much of what is called personality and individuality is intensely repellent, and makes the principal misery of Occidental life."[67]

In time, he found other reasons to object to Lowell's contentions, among them his own increasing difficulties with Japanese officialdom. Exasperated by the frustrations of teaching, he burst out at one point, "Yet Lowell says the Japanese have no individuality! I wish he had to teach here for a year, and he would discover some of the most extraordinary individuality he ever saw."[68] The longer he remained in the Orient, the more he realized that all generalizations were misleading. Thus, he wrote: "All my Japanese experiences convinces me of this fact: '*There is nothing absent from Japanese life which we imagine to be absent; all we have is there,—only the colour is different!*' "He now recognized that there were "millions of individualities," but one had "to live close to them to discover them."[69] The tone of Lowell's subsequent books increased Hearn's disquiet. Though still impressed by Lowell's brilliant insights in *Occult Japan*, for example, he complained, "It is painfully unsympathetic—Mephistophelian in a way that chills me." In a subsequent letter he expressed an even more critical judgment, observing that the book's tone struck him as an "ugly, supercilious one, verging on the wickedness of a wish to hurt."[70]

Lowell not only influenced the way Hearn perceived Japan, but also the themes emphasized in his writings. There was simply no point, Hearn seems to have concluded, in duplicating what Lowell had done. "I am not vain enough to think I can ever write anything so beautiful as his 'Choson' or 'Soul of the Far East,' " Hearn remarked. "But I am not going to try to do anything in his line. My work will deal wholly with exceptional things (chiefly popular). . . ."[71] As his work appeared, it became apparent that there were, indeed, basic differences between the two men's writings. Hearn was more concerned with ordinary people, with emphasis on their emotional and religious life; his writings also reveal an attention to detail, a sensitivity, and a compassion that was largely missing in Lowell's writings. "I have tried to study from the bottom what he has observed from the top," Hearn remarked.[72]

Even after his books were published and he had won acclaim as an observer of Japanese folkways, Hearn continued to measure his achievement by Lowell's standard—although with increasing confidence. "I don't wish to say that my work is as good as Lowell's 'Soul of the Far East,' " he wrote in 1895, "but it is a curious fact that in at least a majority of the favourable criticisms I have been spoken of as far more successful than Lowell." Pondering the question "Why?" he concluded that it "certainly" was not because he was Lowell's intellectual equal. "The reason is simply that the world considers the sympathetic mood more just than the analytical or critical."[73] Lowell was still the model as late as 1902: contemplating a possible visit to the United States, Hearn suggested that he might offer a series of lectures that would evoke an "idea of Japan different from that which is given in books. Something, perhaps, in the manner of Mr. Lowell's 'Soul of the Far East' . . . but from a different point of view."[74] Indeed, he never really overcame a sense of inferiority where Lowell was concerned. The two offer a case study in contrast: Lowell excelled in generalization, Hearn in evoking specific situations; Lowell's strength was a powerful analytical mind, Hearn's a capacity for close emotional identification; Lowell was the cold, dispassionate "outsider" looking in, Hearn the warm, sympathetic "insider" looking out.

A bare fifty years separate Emerson's and Thoreau's excited discovery of Oriental thought from Hearn's end-of-the-century exploration. In certain respects Hearn viewed the East much as the Transcendentalists had: he tended to idealize Oriental civilization, which he contrasted to a more grasping Western culture; he often wrote as a romantic. But much had changed over the half-century: where Emerson and Thoreau might still approach Asian civilization in 1850 as a unified, unchanging society, by 1900 Hearn could hardly ignore the degree to which Western modernization was transforming everything.

Hearn viewed the changes as inevitable but deplorable, undermining the Old Japan he loved for a New Japan he disliked. He had sensed the change soon after his arrival when he had visited the temple of Kōshin, where he lovingly examined the statuary remains of the ancient gods ("these kind, queer, artless, mouldering gods, who have given ease to so many troubled minds, who have gladdened so many simple hearts," etc.). As he stepped out of the temple, the whistle of a locomotive had shattered the silence, forcing him to recognize that, after all, Western civilization was not to be avoided. He realized that "the old gods are dying. . . ."[75] He repeatedly lamented the change in subsequent years: "I cannot like the new Japan," he wrote to a Japanese acquaintance in 1893. "I dislike the officials, the imitation of foreign ways, the airs, the conceits. . . . Now to my poor mind, all that was good and noble and true was Old Japan: I wish I could fly out of Meiji forever. . . ."[76] In many ways this homeless man finally found a home in traditional Japan.

Notes

1. Elizabeth Bisland, *Life and Letters of Lafcadio Hearn*, 2 vols. (Boston: Houghton Mifflin, 1906), 2: 414.

2. The indispensable reference is still Bisland's two-volume *Life and Letters of Lafcadio Hearn*, but see also Elizabeth Stevenson's *Lafcadio Hearn* (New York: Macmillan, 1961), good on biographical detail, and Beongcheon Yu's *An Ape of Gods: The Art and Thought of Lafcadio Hearn* (Detroit, Mich.: Wayne State University Press, 1964), which focuses on Hearn's intellectual views. Earl Miner offers a perceptive sketch in *The Japanese Tradition in British and American Literature* (Princeton, N.J.: Princeton University Press, 1958), pp. 61-65, 87-96.

3. Bisland, *Life & Letters*, 1:328.

4. Ibid., 1: 215, 294-95.

5. Lafcadio Hearn, *Oriental Articles*, ed. Ichiro Nishizaki (Tokyo: Hokuseido Press, 1939), pp. 90-94.

6. Lafcadio Hearn, *An American Miscellany*, 2 vols., ed. Albert Mordell (New York: Dodd, Mead, 1924), 1: 206.

7. Bisland, *Life & Letters*, 1: 211, 227, 228. Quotes on pp. 227, 228.

8. Stevenson, *Lafcadio Hearn*, pp. 117, 196.

9. Milton Bronner, ed., *Letters from the Raven; Being the Correspondence of Lafcadio Hearn with Henry Watkin* (New York: Brentano's, 1907), p. 77.

10. Hearn, *Oriental Articles*, p. 77; Bisland, *Life & Letters*, 1: 291-92. Quote on p. 291.

11. Bisland, *Life & Letters*, 1: 291, 292.

12. Lafcadio Hearn, "The Two Arnolds," *Essays in European and Oriental Literature*, ed. Albert Mordell (1923; reprint ed., Freeport, N.Y.: Books for Libraries Press, 1968), p. 202.

13. Bisland, *Life & Letters*, 1: 367-68.

14. Ibid., 1: 404.

15. Ibid., 1: 345, 346, 349-50.

16. Lafcadio Hearn, *Stray Leaves from Strange Literature*, in *The Writings of Lafcadio Hearn* [*Koizumi Edition*], 16 vols. (Boston: Houghton Mifflin, 1923), 2: 1-194, Idem, *Some Chinese Ghosts* (1887; reprint ed., New York: Modern Library, 1927), quoted reference on p. 7.

17. Bisland, *Life & Letters*, 1: 265.

18. Lafcadio Hearn, "What Buddhism Is," *Essays European and Oriental*, p. 280. See also ibid., pp. 79-82, 101-3, and "The Shadow of the *Light of Asia*," in Lafcadio Hearn, *Occidental Gleanings*, 2 vols., ed. Albert Mordell (New York: Dodd, Mead, 1925), 2: 107-8.

19. Bisland, *Life & Letters*, 1: 208-9, 347.

20. Ibid., 1: 345.

21. Cf. Richard Hofstadter, *Social Darwinism in American Thought* (1955; paperback reprint, rev. ed., Boston: Beacon Press, 1944), pp. 31-50, and Irvin Wylie, *The Self-Made Man in America* (1954; paperback reprint ed., New York: Free Press, 1966), pp. 83-87.

22. Bisland, *Life & Letters*, 1: 364-65.

23. Ibid., 1: 374-75, 392.

24. Lafcadio Hearn, "A Peep at Japanese Poetry," *Essays European and Oriental*, pp. 330-39.

25. Lafcadio Hearn, "The New Orleans Exposition: The Japanese Exhibit," originally published in *Harper's Weekly*, January 31, 1885, and reprinted in *Occidental Gleanings*, 2: 209-14, and Idem, "Notes of a Curiosity-Hunter," *Harper's Bazaar*, April 4, 1885, reprinted in *Occidental Gleanings*, 2: 230-35. Quote on p. 230.

26. Stevenson, *Lafcadio Hearn*, p. 196.

27. Bisland, *Life & Letters*, 2: 3-4.

28. Ibid., 2: 93 and Elizabeth Bisland, ed., *The Japanese Letters of Lafcadio Hearn* (Boston: Houghton Mifflin, 1910), p. 26.

29. Stevenson, *Lafcadio Hearn*, p. 208.

30. Bisland, *Japanese Letters*, pp. 3, 4.

31. Ibid., p. 5.

32. Ibid., p. 10 and Bisland, *Life & Letters*, 2: 40.

33. Bisland, *Life & Letters*, 2: 56.
34. Ibid., 2: 57.
35. Bisland, *Japanese Letters*, p. 323.
36. Bisland, *Life & Letters*, 2: 207, 209.
37. Ibid., 1: 398.
38. Yu, *Ape of Gods*, p. 95.
39. Bronner, *Letters from the Raven*, p. 94; Bisland, *Life & Letters*, 2: 5.
40. Lafcadio Hearn, *Japan: An Attempt at Interpretation* (1904; reprint ed., New York: Macmillan, 1924), p. 4.
41. Lafcadio Hearn, *Exotics and Retrospectives* (1898; reprint ed., Boston: Little, Brown, 1905), p. 176.
42. Ibid., p. 179.
43. Lafcadio Hearn, *Glimpses of Unfamiliar Japan*, 2 vols. (Boston: Houghton Mifflin, 1894), 1: 102.
44. Bisland, *Japanese Letters*, p. 214.
45. Bisland, *Life & Letters*, 2: 4.
46. Ibid., 2: 15, 26-27.
47. Hearn, *Glimpses of Unfamiliar Japan*, 1: 209; 2: 387, 392.
48. Bisland, *Life & Letters*, 2: 27-28.
49. Hearn, *Glimpses of Unfamiliar Japan*, 1: 15.
50. Bisland, *Life & Letters*, 2: 26.
51. Ibid., 2: 82; Bisland, *Japanese Letters*, p. 111.
52. Bisland, *Japanese Letters*, p. 128.
53. Bronner, *Letters from the Raven*, p. 99.
54. Lafcadio Hearn, "The Higher Buddhism," *Japan*, pp. 229-50.
55. Ibid., p. 233. Italicized in the original.
56. Ibid., pp. 232ff.
57. Lafcadio Hearn, *Gleanings in Buddha-Fields: Studies of Hand and Soul in the Far East* (Boston: Houghton Mifflin, 1897), pp. 211-66.
58. Ibid., pp. 211-12, 255.
59. Hearn, *Japan*, p. 249.
60. Lafcadio Hearn, *"Out of the East." Reveries and Studies in New Japan* (Boston: Houghton Mifflin, 1895), p. 75; Bisland, *Life & Letters*, 2: 409.
61. Hearn, *Japan*, p. 232.
62. Hearn, *Gleanings in Buddha-Fields*, p. 265.
63. Bisland, *Japanese Letters*, p. 33. See Allen E. Tuttle, "Lafcadio Hearn and the Soul of the Far East," *Contemporary Japan* (Tokyo) 23 (1955): 529-52, for a more detailed analysis.
64. George M. Gould, *Concerning Lafcadio Hearn* (London: T. Fisher Unwin, 1908), p. 82.
65. Bisland, *Life & Letters*, 2: 479, 487.
66. Ibid., 2: 39. See chap. 11 for a fuller treatment of Lowell's views.
67. Bisland, *Life & Letters*, 2: 40.
68. Bisland, *Japanese Letters*, p. 322.
69. Ibid., p. 163. See also his reservations in *Glimpses of Unfamiliar Japan*, 2: 682n.
70. Bisland, *Life & Letters*, 2: 200, 208.

71. Ibid., 2: 30.
72. Bisland, *Japanese Letters*, p. 31.
73. Bisland, *Life & Letters*, 2: 208.
74. Ibid., 2: 487.
75. Hearn, *Glimpses of Unfamiliar Japan*, 1: 103, 104.
76. Bisland, *Life & Letters*, 2: 154.

13
The Parliament of Religions: The Closing of One Era and The Opening of Another

To sympathetic observers the World's Parliament of Religions, held in conjunction with the Chicago World's Fair in 1893, was one of the triumphs, some believed *the* climactic event, of the nineteenth century. Even its critics were forced to admit that the parliament offered one of the century's rare and splendid spectacles. Certainly, this was true of the opening ceremonies on September 11, witnessed by four thousand people who jammed the newly constructed Hall of Columbus.[1] After a brief delay the first of the delegates stepped out to march two by two up the center aisle. As the procession passed, all eyes turned toward the thronelike chair in the stage's center, where His Eminence James Cardinal Gibbons, highest prelate of the Roman Catholic Church in America, soon sat in his scarlet robes. It was to be his privilege to deliver the parliament's opening prayer. Among the delegates who soon overflowed the stage, the Asian representatives were the most exotic: garbed in their distinctive dress, enveloped in brilliant color, they must have appeared more like strange birds than the spokesmen for far-reaching religious establishments. The Confucian delegate was outfitted in the picturesque clothing of a Chinese mandarin, the tall Buddhist representative, Dharmapala, in a robe of purest white, and the Indian monk Vivekananda in the simple ochre cloth of the Hindu *sannyasin*.[2] Numerous dark-suited Protestant representatives completed the unusual tableau.

After the commotion had subsided somewhat, the meeting was called to order by the president of the World's Congress Auxiliary, Charles C. Bonney; a hymn was sung; and Cardinal Gibbons led majestically in the

Lord's Prayer. At last the speeches of welcome began, to stretch on throughout the morning and long afternoon sessions, broken again and again by staccato outbursts of applause. Cardinal Gibbons, introduced amid loud cheers, explained that he had come in spite of a recent illness, feeling that nothing must prevent him from appearing at such a convocation. Remarks by the Reverend Dionysios Latas, the archibishop of Zante, who had traveled from far-away Athens to appear on behalf of the Greek Orthodox Church, led Bonney to exclaim, "This indeed is glorious." The loudest clappings, however, were reserved for the Honorable Pung Kwang Yu, delegated by the Chinese emperor to present Confucianism to the Parliament. When President Bonney in introducing Yu, apologized, "We have not treated China very well in this country," the auditorium rafters vibrated with the greatest outburst of the day. An admiring observer noted that "men and women rose to their feet in the audience, and there was wild waving of hats and handkerchiefs."[3] During the course of the Parliament such outbursts were almost daily occurences.

Underlying the sheer spectacle, filled with scenes that might easily have been taken from Gilbert and Sullivan, the 1893 World's Parliament of Religions was a serious undertaking; with respect to the history of the Oriental religions in America it is not too much to claim that it was a decisive event. The original proposal for the parliament came from Charles Carroll Bonney, a Chicago lawyer, who had long had an interest in comparative religions. In 1889 soon after the World's Fair had been announced, Bonney suggested that a series of congresses, including one devoted to religion, should be held concurrently with the fair.[4] In 1890 a World's Congress Auxiliary was established to plan the congresses with Bonney as chairman; John Henry Barrows, pastor of the First Presbyterian Church in Chicago, was appointed head of the committee to organize the religious congress. Eventually twenty separate congresses, including women's progress, the press, temperance, commerce and finance, literature, engineering, music, labor, Sunday rest, agriculture—and religion, were scheduled, and more than two hundred smaller congresses were also planned. The undertaking was massive: the programs of the proceedings of all the congresses alone made up a book of 160 pages.[5]

The response of American Christianity to the Parliament was generally favorable, a significant fact considering the prominence given the Oriental religions.[6] Perhaps the most stunning surprise was the decision of the Roman Catholic Church to participate. Traditionally insistent upon its claim as the transmitter of Christian truth, the church might have been expected to oppose such an enterprise. Indeed, several European Catholic theologians expressed the strongest misgivings concerning participation in the parliament. However, the parliament's backers had prevailed, and eventually the Catholic archbishops of America gave their approval for participation. One enthusiastic supporter, William Onahan, subsequently went so far as to argue that the Roman church might actually lay prior claim to originating the idea of the parliament, since a Catholic gathering in 1889 had voted to assemble a future "international congress" in Baltimore.[7]

The ground rules for the parliament were astutely designed to attract the widest possible support. As Chairman Barrows emphasized, the "parliament" was not to be a mere platform for debate, the "counting of votes," or the "passing of resolutions." The speakers would be encouraged to "state their own beliefs, and the reasons for them, with the greatest frankness," though Barrows hoped, without "employing unfriendly criticism of other faiths."[8] This arrangement allowed the Catholic church—and every other religious body—to participate without conceding any claim to supremacy among the world's religions. There was further inducement in the option of scheduling separate denominational congresses, where each body could more thoroughly present its distinctive doctrines.

Despite such assurances, several prominent bodies refused to give the parliament official sanction. Embarrassingly enough, the General Assembly of Barrows's own Presbyterian church was one of these. Worldwide, the two most notable holdouts were the sultan of Turkey, who refused to send a representative of the Islamic religion, and the archbishop of Canterbury.[9] The archbishop voiced the doubts of many orthodox believers when he wrote that, believing Christianity to be the one true religion, he did "not understand" how Christians could participate "without assuming the equality" of the other members as well as the "parity of their position and claims."[10] The archbishop's sentiment was widely echoed in the more conservative religious press. Professor Herrick Johnson of the McCormick Theological Seminary fumed that inviting "all the false faiths of the world" to "exhibit their religious goods" and to scatter their "detestable and pestiferous doctrines" before Christian audiences was a "monstrous absurdity."[11] In spite of an intention not to notice adverse criticism, Chairman Barrows was finally goaded into undertaking a strenuous speaking campaign to demonstrate that there were Christian and scriptural foundations for the undertaking. Controversy continued during the summer and right up to the parliament's opening day.

The parliament lasted from September 11 through 27, a total of seventeen days. From the moment the doors were thrown open, the sessions at the Hall of Columbus were thronged, and by the fourth day the adjoining Hall of Washington was also opened to handle the overflow. A clumsy arrangement was worked out that permitted speakers to shuttle between the two halls, with each delivering his address first at the Hall of Columbus and then at the Hall of Washington. The addresses ranged widely over the whole spectrum of religion.[12] There were defenses of the older faiths (Cardinal Gibbons's "The Needs of Humanity Supplied by the Catholic Religion"), abstract philosophic discourses (William T. Harris's "Proofs of the Existence of God") as well as personal testimonies (Serge Wolkonsky's "Men Are Already Brothers"). And, most significantly for this study, unprecedented attention was given the Oriental religions—with the novel opportunity of hearing the beliefs expounded directly by their Asian believers.

The attendance of so many Asian delegates was a major tribute to the indefatigable labors of Barrows's committee. Distances were very great, and expenses of travel almost prohibitive. Appeals to missionaries in the field, a steady barrage of bulletins, the staging of contests for the best essays on the Oriental religions, and an endless correspondence were successful in overcoming the obstacles. By August 1893 Barrows could happily report that the Asians were on their way—including the Chinese representative who would be accompanied by his official interpreter, body servant, and cook.[13] Few foreign delegates traveled so luxuriously. Swami Vivekananda, who came from Calcutta to speak for Hinduism, was surely more typical. The swami had landed in the United States in July 1893 after a difficult passage due to the inadequacy of his clothing and the cold Pacific winds. Unfortunately, he had arrived more than a month before the parliament's opening, with no immediate means of surviving; even more dismaying, he discovered that the official list of delegates had already been drawn up and that his name was not on the list. In the end all difficulties were surmounted, though the swami spent the final anxious night before the parliament's opening in a wooden box he found abandoned by the railroad tracks.[14]

Though there were some obvious omissions, the Oriental religions were impressively represented at the parliament: Hinduism by the long-suffering Vivekananda and by a young man from Madras, identified as Nara Sima Charyar or sometimes Narasima Chari; Confucianism by Pung Kwang Yu, secretary of the Chinese legation in Washinton, D.C.; Jainism by Virchand R. Gandhi, who was sent by the Jain Association of India; Shintoism by Reuchi Shibata, president of the Jikko sect in Japan; the Brahmo Samaj by Protap Chunder Mozoomdar and B. B. Nagarkar. Buddhism had by far the largest Asian contingent: it included Anagarika Dharmapala of Sri Lanka, general secretary of the Maha-Bodhi Society, who came as the delegate of Theravada Buddhism, and Kinza Hirai, Soyen Shaku, Zitsuzen Ashitsu, Horin Toki, Banriu Yatsubuchi, Zenshiro Noguchi, and Yoshigiro Kawai, all representing various schools of Japanese Buddhism. Several other Asians who took active parts in the Parliament elude simple classification: these include Jeanne Sorabji, a Christian convert from Bombay, who read a paper on Parseeism; Professor G. N. Chakravarti, an Indian convert to Theosophy, who joined Vivekananda in the defense of Hinduism; and Horiuchi Kozaki, president of Doshisha University, who spoke on the future of Christianity in Japan.[15]

The ideal was a personal spokesman for every religion; in practice, this proved impossible. Thus, Confucianism had an official spokesman, Taoism did not; the Singalese school of Buddhism was represented, but the Buddhism of Burma, Thailand, and Vietnam was not. If Japanese Buddhists were present in force, no delegate came forward to speak for Chinese Buddhism or for Tibetan Lamaism.[16] The more popular expressions of the Asian religious experience were also notable by their absence. Audiences were treated to expositions of the philosophical doctrines of Hinduism, interpreted from the perspective of the *Vedanta*, but learned little about popular forms of Hinduism as embodied in the Sivaite or Vaishnavite movements. One critic objected that the presentations revealed as "little of the actual and popular religious thought and feeling of Asia" as "Thomas Aquinas or Meister Eckhart" revealed of the "actual religious life of mediaeval Europe."[17] Sensitive to the problem, Barrows's committee sought written statements where no delegate was available: thus, an essay on Taoism was received from China; Prince Chandradat Chudhadharn, brother of the king of Siam, sent a presentation of "The Buddhism of Siam"; and Miss Sorabji read Jinanji Jamshedji Modi's statement on "The Religious System of the Parsees".

The number and wide diversity of the addresses by the Oriental delegates make generalization about their contents difficult. The only sure observation is that Americans were offered an unprecedented feast. Most of the addresses presented highly condensed and necessarily simplified statements of the Oriental faiths. In his original instructions Barrows had warned against a technical exposition, emphasizing the need to adapt the remarks for an unfamiliar American audience.[18] Most of the Asian delegates complied with his request, although several made difficult, scholarly presentations. As befitted such a gathering, the papers were ecumenical in spirit with an emphasis on areas of agreement between Western and Eastern religions. Again, however, there were exceptions: several Asian delegates bitterly denounced the misrepresentations of Oriental religions common in the West; practically all complained of the misguided zeal and arrogance of Christian missionaries in the East. Surveying the papers today, one cannot resist the feeling that much of the enthusiasm they generated stemmed from the unique atmosphere and pageantry of the parliament as much as from what was said. Though extremely impressionistic, several examples, chosen more or less at random, will suggest the range and spirit of the Oriental contributions.

One impressive contribution was a paper on Hinduism by Manilal Dvivedi.[19] Identified as a member of the Philosophical Society of Bombay, Dvivedi was unable to attend the parliament; however, his countryman Virchand Gandhi read the address in his place. In a few highly compressed pages he traced the development of Hinduism from the *Vedas* to the contemporary period. Given the huge time span covered, the sketch is surprisingly complete; he not only managed to outline major stages in the history of Hinduism, but also found space, even if only a few lines, to comment upon the origins of the caste system, differences between the six major philosophical schools, and the intellectual impact of English rule on modern India, culminating in the rise of such reform societies as the Arya Samaj and Brahmo Samaj. Dvivedi's frequent references to Western philosophic conceptions indicate familiarity with Western as well as Eastern philosophy.[20] Though one may wonder whether the average listener at the parliament understood very much of the pandit's analysis, subsequent readers of the address in Barrows's two-volume work would have found it a useful survey.

Anagarika Dharmapala's address on "The World's Debt to Buddha," to cite a second example, was less informative and more popular in style, yet his moving testimonial to India's great sage was persuasive.[21] Everyone at the parliament was much taken with the youthful visitor from Sri Lanka, whose gentle manner and amiable disposition seemed to personify the best in Buddhism. Where Dvivedi had emphasized the philosophical profundities of Hinduism, Dharmapala accentuated the modern relevance and universality of Buddhism. The teachings of Buddha, he suggested, provided a "Synthetic Religion" which might answer to modern man's quest for meaning. Buddha had studied all the religions known in his day and recognized their underlying essentials. Despite its great antiquity, Buddhism was a "scientific religion": nothing was to be accepted on faith; Buddha had in fact taught evolution. If the message is Oriental, the emphasis reveals much indebtedness to Western conceptions as well as to Western scholarship. Among others, Max Müller, Thomas Huxley, and Sir Edwin Arnold are quoted approvingly; the list of works treating Buddhism at the end of the address includes most of the famous nineteenth-century European Buddhist scholars. Interestingly, Samuel Johnson's *Oriental Religions*, Rockhill's *Life of Buddha*, and Olcott's *Golden Rules of Buddhism* also appear on the list. The parliament revealed a meeting of East and West in more ways than one.

Thanks to a longtime interest in the Brahmo Samaj and the fact that he had made an earlier lecture visit to the United States in 1884, Protap Chunder Mozoomdar's several appearances before the parliament were regarded with special interest. A reformer who condemned the social abuses of India as sharply as the most ferocious missionary, Mozoomdar at the same time proclaimed "The World's Religious Debt to Asia"—to cite the title of his most memorable address.[22] Asia had made a series of great religious discoveries, which all men needed. These included a higher view of nature, recognition of the crucial importance of introspection, realization of the centrality of the spiritual realm, and an understanding of the crucial role of devotional activity and self-discipline in developing a full religious life. Mozoomdar both acclaimed the unique achievements of the West and urged the need for the counterbalancing spirituality of the Orient. "In the West you work incessantly, and your work is your worship. In the East we meditate and worship for long hours, and worship is our work," he noted. He prophesied that "perhaps one day," after the parliament had "achieved its success," Western and Eastern man would combine "to support each other's strength and supply each other's deficiencies."[23]

Language was unquestionably a problem for most Asian delegates, handicapping their effectiveness at the parliament. In the sizable Japanese delegation, apparently only Kinza Hirai and Zenshiro Noguchi had full command of English. On the other hand, Swami Vivekananda revealed unusual talents. Demonstrating a fluent command of English, impressive stage manner, and gift for the memorable phrase, the Hindu spokesman was a sensation from his first address. Together with Dharmapala and Mozoomdar, he became one of the parliament's celebrities.[24] His blunt rejection of the stereotypical view of Hinduism raised the hackles of missionary-minded Christians but attracted wide public attention. Throwing out one of the most familiar charges, he stated flatly, "On the very outset, I may tell you that there is no polytheism in India." He was equally curt in dismissing the indictment of Hinduism for idolatry: "One thing I must tell you. Idolatry in India does not mean a horror." He went on to explain that the use of images in India was an "attempt of undeveloped minds to grasp high spiritual truths." He conceded, "The Hindus have their own faults . . . but mark this, it is always towards punishing their own bodies, and never to cut the throats of their neighbors. If the Hindu fanatic burns himself on the pyre, he never lights the fire of inquisition. . . ." His pointed anecdotes demonstrate his gifts as a polemicist:

> I remember, when a boy, A Christian man was preaching to a crowd in India. Among other sweet things he was telling the people that if he gave a blow to their idol with his stick, what could it do? One of his hearers sharply answered, "If I abuse your God what can he do?" "You would be punished," said the preacher, "when you die." "So my idol will punish you when you die," said the villager.[25]

At the same time that the swami attacked Western distortions of Indian religion, he extolled tolerance toward other faiths as the essence of Hinduism.

Other representative papers read at the parliament include Mozoomdar's "The Brahmo-Somaj," Reuchi Shibata's "Shintoism," Kung Hsien Ho's "Confucianism," Horin Toki's "The History of Buddhism and its Sects in Japan," B. B. Nagarkar's "The Work of Social Reform in India," Soyen Shaku's "The Law of Cause and Effect as Taught by Buddha," H. Sumangala's "Orthodox Southern Buddhism," Virchand Gandhi's "The History and Tenets of the Jains of India," and S. Parthacarathy Arjangar's "The Visishtadvaita School of Hinduism." The wide range is impressive and unprecedented. On several occasions an entire program was devoted to one of the religions: there was, for example, a "Conference on the Modern Religions of India," with papers by Vivekananda and other Hindus; a conference on Shintoism, including papers on "The Origin of Shintoism" and "Shintoism in the Past and the Present"; and "A Presentation of Buddhism," with papers by Dharmapala and others. The Japanese delegates also handed out several thousand copies of "Outlines of the Mahayana, as Taught by Buddha," "A Brief Account of Shinshu," and "A Shin shu Catechism."[26]

Observers at the sessions repeatedly noted the positive impression that the Asian lecturers made. Affirming that the parliament had become a "fact" whose "principles and lessons" could "never again be eliminated" from the American Christian consciousness, Florence Winslow ascribed much of the impact to the "strong personalities" of the men who had represented Hinduism, Buddhism, Confucianism, and Shintoism at the congress. Their "seriousness, earnestness, devoutness and spirituality" precluded any thought that the Oriental religions would "fall or melt into mist" before a triumphant Christianity. She lauded Dharmapala as the "gentlest of men, almost Christian in his reverence for Christ" and eulogized Vivekananda as "one of the most thoroughly and broadly educated men" of the day as well as a "magnificent orator."[27] Lucy Monroe, who provided a running coverage of the sessions in *The Critic*, was also deeply struck by Dharmapala and Vivekananda, whom she proclaimed the "most impressive figures of the Parliament." She suggested that perhaps the "most tangible result" of the parliament had been the "feeling it aroused in regard to foreign missions." "The impertinence of sending half-educated theological students to instruct these wise and erudite Orientals was never brought home to an English-speaking audience more forcibly."[28]

Following the close of the parliament some question arose concerning the qualifications of the Asian delegates to speak for their respective religious traditions. The remark of the Indian *Christian Patriot* that there was "something amusing" in the "celebrity suddenly acquired at Chicago by men wholly obscure in their own lands" was publicized in the American religious press.[29] Though the criticisms seem to have originated with Christian missionaries—hardly a disinterested source—a brief examination of the backgrounds of the Asians at the parliament suggests some basis for question. Despite strenuous efforts to obtain the best spokesmen, Barrows's committee often had to make do with whoever happened to be available. The official representative of Confucianism, Pung Kwang Yu, is a case in point. As China's minister to the United States Yu was on hand, and so the emperor deputed him to represent Chinese religion at the parliament. Yu took his duties seriously, boning up on his ancestral religion to the extent of compiling a pamphlet-length summary of Confucianism, which Barrows inserted in his two-volume history.[30] However, the Chinese diplomat was the first to admit that he was no scholar. He apologized that during long service with the Chinese government his knowledge of Confucianism had grown "somewhat rusty." He also confessed that finding it "inconvenient" to carry "many books" when he came to America, he had "trusted" to his memory in the preparation of his remarks.[31]

It should also be noted that a number of the Asian representatives had been Theosophists, including Kinza Hirai and Dharmapala, the chief exponents of Buddhism at the congress. Though devoted to the renewal of Hinduism and Buddhism, Theosophists could hardly be viewed as orthodox representatives of those traditions. Five years before the parliament opened, a leading organ of the Theosophical Society in America recorded that a charter had just been granted to a "Mr. Kinzo Hirai and associates" for a branch society in Kyoto.[32] Hirai was something of a religious seeker: a Theosophist, then a Buddhist, he subsequently turns up as a spokesman for Japanese Unitarianism. His parliament address on "Synthetic Religion," in which he envisioned the merging of all religions, definitely suggests the influence of Theosophy.[33] Dharmapala, as already noted, had even closer Theosophical ties: he had served as Olcott's loyal assistant and personal secretary in the Sri Lanka work.[34]

The most controversial delegate at the parliament, Alexander Russell Webb—or "Mohammed" Webb as he now preferred—had also been a Theosophist. Converted to Islam after six years of investigation of Oriental religions, he had opened an Islamic center in New York City shortly before the convoking of the parliament and launched a journal known as *The Moslem World*.[35] Olcott, who had interviewed Webb in 1892 shortly after his resignation as American consul in Manilla, declares that Webb had been a "strenuous advocate of Buddhism" up to a "few months of his acceptance of Islam." Asked about his change of allegiance, Webb had informed Olcott that "although he had become a Muslim he had not ceased to be an ardent Theosophist," that "Islam, as he understood it," was "distinctly in accord" with Theosophy.[36] Webb's unflinching defense of Islam at the parliament created a sensation. Finally, there is Professor G. N. Chakravarti who joined Vivekananda in presenting Hinduism at the Parliament—and had been an active member of the Allahabad branch of the Indian Theosophical Society since 1883.[37] Understandably, Theosophists rejoiced in the parliament as "distinctly a Theosophical step."[38]

While emphasis has been focused upon the Asian presentations at the parliament, one must not overlook the active participation of Western delegates in the discussion of Asian religions. Much of this discussion was dominated by a comparative religions viewpoint, which had been growing in the United States since the 1870s. Comparative religionists were almost unfailingly sympathetic toward the Oriental faiths, even when their personal commitments favored Christianity. Professor J. Estlin Carpenter, the Oxford scholar, spoke for many when he declared that the older classification of non-Christian faiths as "false religions" would no longer do, since all religions revealed a common core of spiritual truth. "They may be more or less clearly articulate," he wrote, "less or more crude and confused or pure and elevated, but they are in substance the same."[39] In addition to greater sympathy, the papers reveal a more acute consciousness of the importance of seeing the Oriental religions from the inside. Charles D'Harlez, professor of Oriental languages at the University of Louvain, emphasized the "necessity of penetrating oneself with the spirit of the people who form the object of particular research. It is necessary," he declared, ". . . to think with their mind and to see with their eyes. . . ."[40] The parliament offered a unique opportunity to view the Oriental religions from the new perspective.

Many of the papers on the Oriental religions were authored by Christian missionaries, who, like the Asian delegates, could speak from direct acquaintance. These included presentations by the Reverend Maurice Phillips on "The Ancient Religion of India and Primitive Revelation," Robert Hume's "The Contact of Christian and Hindu Thought: Points of Likeness and of Contrast," and the Reverend M. L. Gordon's "Some Characteristics of Buddhism as It Exists in Japan which Indicate that It Is not a Final Religion"—all the results of many years in the field.[41] Though apologetic, the missionary papers were often generous in their evaluations of the Asian faiths. Drawing upon many year's residence in India, the Reverend Thomas Slater of the London Missionary Society warned that it was "hard for foreigners to understand the habits of thought and life that prevail in a strange country," and he expressed regret for the West's quick denunciation of religious traditions that had a "deep and sacred root." He observed, "The Hindus, by instinct and tradition, are the most religious people in the world."[42] It was not that missionary contributors failed to criticize the Oriental religions, but that they sought to balance the criticisms with positive aspects. The fiercely antagonistic view of the older Christian dogmatist was out of place at the parliament (but not entirely absent, as indicated by William Wilkinson's characterization of the proper Christian attitude toward other religions as "absolute, eternal, unappeasable hostility. . . ."[43])

The Parliament of Religions closed on September 27 amidst scenes that elicited comparisons with the greatest moments of the past. As in the opening session, the sheer spectacle was overwhelming, with the exhausted but elated delegates gathering one more time for an emotional leave-taking. Seeking words to characterize the feeling at the final meeting, Chairman Barrows confessed that he found it almost "impossible to describe" for "those who were not there"; however, he finally suggested that it was "quite within bounds" to speak of the spirit as "Pentecostal." "Seldom, if ever," wrote another participant, had the world "witnessed a more impressive religious scene than the closing session of the great Religious Parliament in Chicago."[44] The addresses were nearly unanimous concerning the significance of the parliament. "It is the greatest event so far in the history of the world," Alfred Momerie declared, a sentiment repeated again and again during the evening. Writing soon after the close of the congress, Paul Carus hailed the parliament as "undoubtedly the most noteworthy event of this decade," marking a "new era in the evolution of man's religious life."[45] For some the enthusiasm raised by the parliament did not dim with passing years. Writing more than a decade after the close of the congress, Washington Gladden, a leader in the Social Gospel movement, wrote, "We have had, once, upon this planet, a great Parliament of Religions, in which the representatives of all the great faiths . . . were gathered together for comparison of beliefs and experiences. It was, perhaps, the most important religious gathering which has ever assembled."[46]

Such reactions must not be allowed to obscure the fact that most Americans —and most of the people in the world—were quite unaware of the parliament. Indeed, some Americans who were in Chicago in September 1893 and who attended the Columbian Expostion did not even notice the event. Henry Adams tells us in his *Education* that he found the exposition so fascinating that he decided to spend an entire fortnight in Chicago, having discovered "matter of study to fill a hundred years. . . . Education," he observed, "ran riot at Chicago, at least for retarded minds which had never faced in concrete form so many matters of which they were ignorant."[47] Curiously, he does not even mention the Parliament of Religions. Adams believed that what was happening in Chicago in 1893 was important, indeed crucial, but he was thinking of dynamos rather than doctrines, of the dynamic tendency of history rather than the meeting of East and West. Much the same may be said of Hamlin Garland, who had just moved back to Chicago. "Like everyone else who saw it at this time," Garland declares,

"I was amazed at the grandeur of 'The White City'. . . ." Eager to share the wonders of the exposition with relatives and friends, he advised his father on the farm in Dakota to "Sell the cook stove if necessary and come. You *must* see this fair."[48] Again, nothing is said of the parliament.

On the other hand, the Parliament of Religions did make a profound impression on many, as we have seen; some viewed it as one of the critical events of the century. They saw a number of far-reaching consequences stemming from the congress. One of the results most frequently cited was a new sense of religious unity. In some cases the reference was to a unity between denomination and denomination, more often to a larger unity between Christians everywhere, but in many instances to an even wider unity between the separate world religions. As Crawford Toy, professor of religion at Harvard, pointed out, it had been "no small thing" for the parliament to meet at all. A "great point" had been gained "when men of different faiths" indicated willingness "to stand on the same platform and give expression, together, each to his own convictions." The implication was that "these other persons" were "human beings" who had ideas to which "it could not be wrong, and might not be unprofitable, to listen."[49]

Jabez Sunderland, a prominent Unitarian leader, agreed, although he warned enthusiasts against the impression that the parliament meant that the "religious millennium has come" or that "all forms of religion are equally true or equally good." Sunderland's warning was timely for such views were, indeed, being expressed in the period following the congress. The parliament did mean that, despite "many and important differences," the world's religions did have "much in common." It did mean a "growing conviction" that the things which believers held in common were "more important than those about which they disagree," and it indicated a "deepening and widening consciousness that tolerance and charity" were essential attributes of all the higher religions.[50] The growth of ecumenicism among and within the world's religions was one obvious result of the parliament.

Another valuable result frequently cited was that the parliament had created a new appreciation of Oriental religions. This was especially marked in the reactions of several well-known Christian participants who testified to radical shifts in perspective. The parliament "has become an epoch in my own intellectual life, as doubtless it has in that of many others," the Reverend George Candlin, a missionary to the Chinese, declared. The "central fact" established by the congress was the "good which lies at the heart of every religion, however erroneous" its "intellectual propositions" and "however superstitious" its practices.[51] Lyman Abbott, Henry Ward Beecher's successor at Plymouth Congregational Church and editor of *The Outlook*, echoed Candlin's view. "The first effect of this Parliament of Religions," he wrote, "must be to correct the opinion too often entertained" that "all forms of religion but our own are a mixture of ignorance and superstition." He concluded, "The Shinto priest, the Buddhist philosopher, and the Roman Catholic Archbishop were not one whit less serious in their quest for truth and righteousness than the Protestant theologian."[52] Although, according to biographer Ira Brown, Abbott "never developed a very keen appreciation of other religions." He always maintained the superiority of Christianity, but he nevertheless gave more attention to Oriental religions after the parliament than before. Thus, in 1897 *The Outlook* introduced a new series on "The Message of the World's Religions," including sketches of Buddhism, Brahmanism, and Confucianism.[53] Abbott was convinced that Christians must know more about Oriental religions. Another Christian spokesman, the Reverend D. S. Schaff, confessed that he had originally opposed the parliament, but now found himself an advocate; he predicted that the congress would "be looked back to as an epoch in religious thought" as well as a crucial event in the "onward and conquering progress of the Christian faith." A stout defender of the superiority of Christianity, Schaff insisted that the parliament made a closer acquaintance with the Oriental religions necessary. "The reports from the ethnic religions cannot be suppressed," he wrote. "Oriental theosophy is in the air. The great religious movements in India, China, and of Islam appeal to the serious examination of increasingly large Christian constituencies."[54]

There was another opinion, of course. Admitting that the "cultivated representatives from the far remote East" had added a certain "picturesque element" to the parliament, the Reverend F. A. Noble questioned whether they had contributed anything more. "Not an atom was added by what these men said to the stock of the common knowledge concerning the Oriental religions," he insisted. "That people in India and China and Japan" had "some right ideas of God" was "no surprise." The "only surprising thing" about the Brahmin, Buddhist, and Confucian statements at the parliament was that "anybody should be surprised by them."[55] Professor Crawford Toy took perhaps the most intelligent position, stationing himself somewhere between those who hailed the parliament as a milliennial event and those who dismissed it as an affair of no consequence. He did feel that it had opened new avenues toward better knowledge of the Asian religions. He noted that the "actual appearance" of spokesmen for the non-Christian faiths at the congress would give greater "reality to people's conceptions of these faiths"; moreover, those who had witnessed or read the parliament's proceedings would "probably feel more or less concerned to know something of the history of the systems of belief" represented there. On the other hand, he discounted the likelihood of any fundamental alteration in view: "The general public will no doubt go on as before," he predicted, "content to know that such things exist, incurious as to their nature."[56]

Finally, there is the parliament's impact upon the missionary movement. Almost inevitably as the estimation of the Oriental religions rose, the foreign work of the missionary was called into question. Missionaries were placed under attack by the Asian delegates from the first, compelled to respond to the claim that, possessing their own religions, the non-Christian world did not need a foreign faith. On September 22 an entire session was devoted to a "Criticism and Discussion of Missionary Methods," with Dharmapala, Narasima Charya, and Swami Vivekananda making the criticisms, pitted against Robert Hume and George Candlin, who spoke for the missionary. Dharmapala warned that the "platform" established "must be entirely reconstructed" if Christianity was "to make progress in the East"; a different, more tolerant missionary, who knew more about the indigenous religions would have to be trained. Narasima Charya flatly declared that if success was the criterion of measurement and if "missionary success" meant the "conversion of the Hindu," then it was obvious that "missionary work in India" had been "a failure."[57] On the defensive, the missionaries were conciliatory. In a mild rebuttal, Hume questioned that the Christian effort in India had, indeed, failed, but conceded, "we do make our mistakes." He agreed that missionaries needed better training: "We ought to study their books more deeply, more intelligently, more constantly."[58] The issue was debated throughout the parliament.

The reverberations were to continue for years. Interestingly enough, missionary leaders seemed prone to agree with the more extreme claims concerning the parliament's deep influence; unfortunately, that influence had been almost entirely harmful. In 1895 Arthur Pierson, editor of the influential *Missionary Review of the World,* formulated one of the most comprehensive statements. In a long and detailed indictment, Pierson explained why the parliament had been an unmitigated disaster. In essence, he argued that the congress had been stacked in favor of the non-Christian religions. Leaders of evangelical Christianity had refused to participate in the parliament, leaving control in the hands of the enemy. Pierson complained that the "advocates of these foreign faiths," had enjoyed the advantage of addressing audiences in which there were "few who were competent to answer them," and in which "no reply or rejoinder was allowable."[59] In addition to giving a false view of the non-Christian religions, the parliament had set a bad precedent by encouraging talk of still other congresses; it had given undeserved prominence to propagandists for alien faiths; and it had substituted a policy of laxity for liberality. Most of all, the parliament had done a great disservice by its implication that salvation could be found outside Christianity. Confessing that he badly feared that the parliament's effect would be to "raise new walls" between Christian missionaries and those they sought to convert, Pierson closed dramatically: " 'With charity toward all and malice toward none,' we now dismiss the Parliament of Religions from these pages, praying God that such a gathering may never again give occasion to the enemies of the Lord to blaspheme!"[60]

Pierson's anguished reaction was fairly characteristic of the missionary view. However, a small number of missionaries and laymen looked upon the parliament as initiating a new era in missionary activity. It had, one such writer declared, removed mutual misunderstandings, emphasized the importance of more knowledge of the non-Christian faiths, and underlined the need for a more positive approach to the people they wished to convert.[61] But this was definitely a minority view. Negative or positive, missionary writers revealed a new awareness of the appeals of Oriental religion as well as the need for changes in missionary methods.

Asian writers continued their attacks on missions for several years, stimulating a series of exchanges with Western defenders. Virchand Gandhi, the Jain delegate, opened the exchange with a sharply critical article on "Why Christian Missions Have Failed in India"; Fred Powers answered with a piece on "The Success of Christian Missions in India." Purushotam R. Telang came back with an article on "Christian Missions as Seen by a Brahmin," answered by Bishop J. M. Thoburn's "Christian Missions as Seen by a Missionary." Gandhi offered a final rejoinder and J. H. Mueller a final reply.[62] To be sure, mounting criticism in the 1880s and 1890s indicates that the missionary movement was already under attack and that some reevaluation was taking place before 1893.[63] However, it is clear that the successes scored by the Oriental religions at the parliament increased doubts and deepened the missionary debate. By 1914 many missionaries were taking a more favorable attitude toward Hinduism, Buddhism, and other non-Christian faiths.

The 1893 Parliament of Religions provides a good point at which to close our study of the nineteenth-century American discovery of Asian religion. In the years since Emerson had hailed the East, a series of events and movements had pushed the Asian religions into growing prominence. The parliament was in many respects the culmination. Several writers would argue that such a congress, in which representatives of all religious viewpoints met on a common platform to present their distinctive doctrines, could not have taken place in any other country at any other time. An exaggeration perhaps, yet it does seem that the United States offered a peculiarly hospitable site for the parliament. If the Parliament of Religions marked a culmination of preceding developments, it also pointed to the future. The appearance of Asians at the parliament heralded the twentieth-century situation in which Asian spokesmen and Asian movements have increasingly taken the lead in bringing Oriental religion to Americans. In this sense, the Parliament of Religions marked the closing of one era but also the opening of another.

Notes

1. The intense interest generated by the parliament resulted in the publication of a number of contemporary histories of varying usefulness. By far the most valuable is John Henry Barrows, ed., *The World's Parliament of Religions*, 2 vols. (Chicago: The Parliament Publishing Co., 1893). Including all major papers delivered, Barrows's work has been the basic reference throughout. The addresses in the first volume were published almost verbatim; unfortunately, many in the second volume have been condensed. Also see: Walter R. Houghton, ed., *Neely's History of the Parliament of Religions and Religious Congresses of the World's Congress Auxiliary of the World's Columbian Exposition. Chicago, 1893,* 2 vols. (Chicago: Rand McNally, 1893), and Egal Feldman's "American Ecumenicism: Chicago's World's Parliament of Religions of 1893," *A Journal of Church and State* 9 (Spring 1967): 180-99. Barrows, *World's Parliament*, 1: 62-109 and Houghton, *Neely's History*, 1: 33-71 provide vivid descriptions of the spectacle of the first day.

2. "The World's Parliament of Religions. The First Week," *The Independent* 45 (September 21, 1893): 1278. Also see Jabez T. Sunderland, "The World's Parliament of Religions," *The Unitarian* 8 (October 1893): 442.

3. Barrows, *World's Parliament*, 1: 86, 88.

4. Charles C. Bonney, "The Genesis of the World's Religious Congresses of 1893," *New Church Review* 1 (January 1894): 73-100 and [Paul Carus], "The Hon. C. C. Bonney, the Inaugurator of the Parliament of Religions," *Open Court* 14 (January 1900): 4-8. Such an idea had, of course, occurred to others, including the Free Religious Association, which had sponsored a miniature congress as early as 1870.

5. Houghton, *Neely's History*, 1: 19.

6. Barrows, *World's Parliament*, 1: 11.

7. William J. Onahan, "Columbian Catholic Congress at Chicago," *Catholic World* 57 (August 1893): 606-7. See also "An Epoch in Catholicism," ibid. 58 (October 1893): 126-32 and Thomas T. McAvoy, *The Americanist Heresy in Roman Catholicism, 1895-1900* (South Bend, Ind.: Notre Dame University Press, 1963), pp. 71-72, 78-79, 83-85 (paperback edition).

8. John H. Barrows, "A Parliament of Religions," *The Independent* 44 (February 4, 1892): 152.

9. Barrows, *World's Parliament*, 1: 18-20.

10. The archbishop's letter is reprinted in William Pipe, "The Parliament of Religions," *The Outlook* 48 (August 26, 1893): 385.

11. Herrick Johnson, "The Proposed Parliament of Religions at the World's Fair," *The Independent* 44 (March 24, 1892): 401.

12. See the summaries listed in the table of contents of Barrows, *World's Parliament*, 1: xvii-xxiv; 2: 810-15.

13. John H. Barrows, "The Approaching Parliament of Religions," *The Independent* 45 (August 17, 1893): 1106.

14. Cf. *The Complete Works of the Swami Vivekananda. . . .*, 7 vols. (Mayavati, India: Advaita Ashrama, 1924-1932), 5: 1-10 and Eastern and Western Disciples, *Life of Swami Vivekananda* (Calcutta, India: Advaita Ashrama, 1955), pp. 286ff.

15. See Barrows, *World's Parliament*, 2: 1584-90, for brief profiles of the Asian delegates.

16. A Special Correspondent, "Final Impressions of the World's Parliament of Religions," *The Independent* 45 (October 5, 1893): 1341-42.

17. Charles J. Little, "The Chicago Parliament of Religions," *Methodist Review* 76 (March-April 1894): 213.

18. Barrows, *World's Parliament*, 1: 375.

19. Manilal N. Dvivedi, "Hinduism," reprinted in ibid., 1: 316-32; see also his "Answers of the Mimansa Vedanta or Advaita Philosophy—(Orthodox Hinduism) —to Religious Problems," ibid., 1: 333-39, appended to the address.

20. Dvivedi, *Monism or Advaitism? An Introduction to the Advaita Philosophy* (Bombay: Subodha-Praka's Press, 1889) and *The Imitation of S'ankara* (London: G. Redway, 1895) were known in America and commended as useful expositions of Hindu thought. See *Open Court* 4 (July 10, 1890): 2388 and 6 (April 1896): 471-72.

21. Reprinted in Barrows, *World's Parliament*, 2: 862-80.

22. Reprinted in ibid., 2: 1083-92. The address has been condensed for Barrows's work, but the spirit and line of argument are clear.

23. Ibid., 2: 1092.

24. See Harriet Monroe's testimony, *A Poet's Life: Seventy Years in a Changing World* (New York: Macmillan, 1938), p. 137.

25. Vivekananda, "Hinduism," in Barrows, *World's Parliament*, 2: 975, 976.

26. Culled from Barrows, *World's Parliament*. The Buddhist tracts are mentioned in ibid., 1: 441-42.

27. Florence E. Winslow, "A Pen Picture of the Parliament," *Christian Thought* 11 (1893-1894): 223, 224, 227-28, 229, originally published in *Outlook*.

28. Lucy Monroe, "Chicago Letter," *The Critic* 23 (October 7, 1893): 232, 233.

29. "The Parliament of Religions as Seen on Foreign Mission Fields," *Methodist Review* 78 (July-August 1896): 649.

30. Pung Kwang Yu, "Confucianism," reprinted in Barrows, *World's Parliament*, 1: 374-439.

31. Ibid., 1: 387.

32. *The Path* 2 (January 1888): 319. Despite the slight discrepancy in first names, there is little doubt that the same Hirai was present at the parliament.

33. Barrows, *World's Parliament*, 2: 1286-88.

34. See chap. 9.

35. See *The Theosophist* 14 (August 1893): 691; also *The Path* 8 (April 1893): 27-28.

36. Henry S. Olcott, "Old Diary Leaves," *The Theosophist* 23 (April 1902): 387. Webb explains his views in *Islam in America; A Brief Statement of Mohammedanism*

and an Outline of the American Islamic Propaganda (New York: The Oriental Publishing Co., 1893).

37. "Faces of Friends," *The Path* 8 (October 1893): 204-6.

38. "The Theosophical Congress and the Parliament of Religions," ibid. 8 (November 1893): 248.

39. J. Estlin Carpenter, "The Need of a Wider Conception of Revelation, or Lessons from the Sacred Books of the World," in Barrows, *World's Parliament*, 2: 848.

40. Charles D'Harlez, "The Comparative Study of the World's Religions," ibid., 1: 620.

41. Phillips, ibid., 1: 296-305; Hume, ibid., 2: 1269-76; and Gordon, ibid., 2: 1293-96.

42. Thomas Slater, "Concession to Native Ideas, Having Special Reference to Hinduism," ibid., 1: 456-57.

43. William Wilkinson, "The Attitude of Christianity toward Other Religions," ibid., 2: 1249.

44. Barrows, ibid., 1: 157, 158; Jabez T. Sunderland, "The Close of the Great Parliament of Religions," *The Unitarian* 8 (November 1893): 497.

45. Barrows, *World's Parliament*, 1: 160; Paul Carus, "The Dawn of a New Religious Era," *The Monist* 4 (April 1894): Appendix, 16, originally published in the *Forum*, November 1893.

46. Washington Gladden, *The Church and Modern Life* (Boston: Houghton Mifflin, 1908), pp. 37-38. Also see his remark in *Recollections* (Boston: Houghton Mifflin, 1909), p. 359. He had delivered a paper on "Religion and Wealth" at the parliament.

47. Henry Adams, *The Education of Henry Adams. An Autobiography*, 1918; Sentry paperback edition, (Boston: Houghton Mifflin, 1961), pp. 339, 342.

48. Hamlin Garland, *A Son of the Middle Border* (New York: Grosset & Dunlap, 1917), p. 458.

49. Crawford Toy, "The Parliament of Religions," *New World* 2 (December 1893): 728, 734.

50. Jabez Sunderland, "The World's Parliament of Religions," *The Unitarian* 8 (October 1893): 447, 448. The italics have been omitted.

51. George T. Candlin, "Results and Mission of the Parliament of Religions," *Biblical World* 5 (May 1895): 371.

52. Lyman Abbott, "The Parliament of Religions," *The Outlook* 48 (September 30, 1893): 583.

53. Ira V. Brown, *Lyman Abbott: Christian Evolutionist. A Study in Religious Liberalism* (Cambridge, Mass.: Harvard University Press, 1953), p. 136.

54. D. S. Schaff, "The Parliament of Religions and the Christian Faith," *Homiletic Review* 26 (December 1893): 553.

55. F. A. Noble, "The Parliament of Religions," *Our Day* 12 (1893): 419, 420.

56. Crawford Toy, "The Parliament of Religions," *New World* 2 (December 1893): 739-40.

57. Barrows, *World's Parliament*, 2: 1093, 1094.

58. Ibid., 2: 1095.

59. Arthur T. Pierson, "The Parliament of Religions: A Review," *Chinese*

Recorder 26 (April 1895): 162. Pierson's article originally appeared in *Missionary Review of the World* 7 (December 1894): 881-94.

60. Pierson, "The Parliament of Religions," pp. 171, 175. See also the blistering attack by Herrick Johnson, "The World's Parliament of Religions," *The Independent* 47 (February 28, 1895): 266-67.

61. H. R. Bender, "Missions as Seen at the Parliament of Religions," *Methodist Review* 77 (November-December 1895): 907-12. See also George T. Candlin, "Results and Mission of the Parliament of Religions," *Biblical World* 5 (May 1895): 371-73.

62. Virchand Gandhi, "Why Christian Missions Have Failed in India," *Forum* 17 (April 1894): 160-66; Fred Powers, "The Success of Christian Missions in India," ibid. 17 (June 1894): 475-83; Purushotam Telang, "Christian Missions as Seen by a Brahmin," ibid. 18 (December 1894): 481-89; J. M. Thoburn, "Christian Missions as Seen by a Missionary," ibid. 18 (December 1894): 490-501; Virchand Gandhi, "Christian Missions in India," *The Arena* 11 (January 1895): 157-66; J. H. Mueller, "Are Our Christian Missionaries in India Frauds?" ibid. 16 (October 1896): 806-12.

63. See J. M. Thoburn, "Recent Missionary Discussions," *Methodist Review* 73 (November-December 1891): 867-81. The rising Asian disaffection is clear in Nobuta Kishimoto, "The Present Religious Crisis in Japan," *Andover Review* 15 (June 1891): 598-613. Robert Hume, "Missions in India Not a Failure," *Missionary Herald* 82 (February 1886): 53-57, indicates that the debate was not a new phenomenon.

Conclusion

The significance of the growing American awareness of Oriental religion is still unclear, despite a rising curve of interest. Obviously, much will hinge upon whether the Asian influence continues to spread. The dilemma, of course, is a familiar one that all historians who deal with contemporary movements have to confront. Living close to events that are still unfolding, it is difficult to ascertain the direction in which history is moving. This disturbing fact explains why historians have been cautious about undertaking contemporary history. "Stick to the past, leave the present to the journalists," historians admonish one another. But the mere passage of time does not guarantee perspective, and sooner or later all historians are forced to posit some pattern within which the events are to be fitted. Until the pattern is formulated, there is no sense in the events.[1]

To this historian it seems likely that the contemporary American interest in Asian thought will one day be viewed as an important phase in an unprecedented encounter of Eastern and Western societies, crucial to understanding American, and, indeed, world history. Several twentieth-century prophets have already hailed this meeting of East and West as the turning event of the modern era. Arnold Toynbee seems to have adopted such a view in the later volumes of his famous *A Study of History*. After tracing the cyclical rise and fall of civilizations over the first six volumes of the study, Toynbee shifted to the view that events were forcing a recognition of the similar teachings of the world's "higher religions"—Christianity, Islam, Mahayana Buddhism, and Hindusim—which would lay the foundations of a new world civilization.[2] In *The Meeting of East and West*, F. S. C. Northrop, the Yale philosopher, envisioned an ideological rather than a religious transformation based on the interaction of the dominantly "aesthetic" viewpoint of Oriental cultures with the "theoretic" viewpoint of the West. Northrop believed the blending of the two viewpoints would provide the philosophical framework for world unity.[3] Both thinkers may be criticized for simplifying the complexities of history and forcing events to conform to personal philosophies.

University of Chicago historian William McNeill has recently offered a less sweeping analysis that seems to avoid Toynbee's and Northrop's simplifications. I refer to his impressive *The Rise of the West*, which spends a good deal of time tracing historical contacts between East and West in the course of analyzing the modern ascendancy of Europe. McNeill reminds us that contacts between West and East are hardly a recent phenomenon: one can trace the first encounter back at least 30,000 years, when *Homo sapiens* crossed from western Asia into Europe, displacing Neanderthal man. He demonstrates that contacts across the Eurasian steppe have been frequent from earliest times, with peoples, tools, and ideas constantly flowing in both directions.[4]

Sensitive to the chronology of interaction, McNeill goes on to suggest that in the long process of encounter between Asian and Western societies, two periods of "closure" have been most important. The first, the "Closure of the Eurasian Ecumene," reached a peak between 200 B.C. and A.D. 200 with Hellenic, Middle Eastern, Indian, and Chinese civilizations drawn into more intimate contact than in any previous period. Since the four civilizations were roughly equal in technological and cultural development, McNeill suggests that borrowing between the civilizations was "selective" and of relatively minor significance. Nevertheless, blending did occur as pointed up by Gandharan art, which featured sculptures of Buddha done in the Hellenistic style. In some areas the meeting of East and West was well under way thousands of years ago.

Contact between Europe and Asia greatly diminished between A.D. 500 and 1500, except for a brief interlude during the thirteenth and early fourteenth centuries, when Genghiz and Kublai Khan opened China to European monks and traders. Vasco da Gama's historic voyage to India in 1497-1498 inaugurated the second period of intensive contact, the "Closure of the Global Ecumene." In McNeill's view the contemporary world is still caught in the throes of the revolutionary changes introduced by this second East-West confrontation. The West has been dominant during the second closure, unlike the first, thanks to military and technological superiority.[5]

My brief summary does not do justice to McNeill's provocative analysis, which is notable for its balanced judgments and rich supporting evidence. The book and the concept of a "Closure of the World Ecumene" provide an excellent framework within which to fit the rising American interest in Asian religion. Surprisingly for one so attuned to East-West interaction, McNeill underestimates the significance of recent Asian influence in the West. If the West has clearly dominated over the past two or three centuries, Eastern influences have also been at work. The obvious changes in Asian life caused by Western technology are impossible to miss; the more intangible effects of Asian religious influence in the West must be searched out.

Whatever happens in the future, it is already clear that American influence has not only impinged upon the lives of countless Asian peoples from Iran to Japan, but that Asian conceptions have also begun to impinge upon Americans. The outcome may remain a riddle, but a close observer of the contemporary scene can already see that Oriental religious and philosophical ideas constitute a significant intellectual force in twentieth-century American culture. The role of the Oriental religions in the United States has just begun to be widely noted, but, as this study has sought to show, the perception and rising appreciation of the Oriental religions must be traced back to the eighteenth and nineteenth centuries. Indeed, I have sought to show that the American encounter with Asian religion was already well advanced by the end of the nineteenth century.

What conclusions may be drawn? One fundamental point is that the American discovery of Oriental religion was largely a literary enterprise based on indirect encounter through the printed page. For nineteenth-century Americans the meeting of East and West was primarily an intellectual experience. It is true that a handful of New England shippers engaged in the China and India trade had some opportunity to investigate the Oriental religions directly and that Protestant missionaries had more extended contact with Asian peoples, but most early students of Oriental conceptions were forced to rely on the written word. Few Americans traveled to the East, and even fewer Asians traveled to the United States. A major difference in the contemporary scene has been the large numbers of Americans—soldiers, technicians, businessmen, and students—who have traveled and lived in Asia for extended periods, as well as the steady arrival of Asian students and teachers in the United States. The modern student has much more opportunity to investigate the Oriental religions at first hand.

European writers and scholars played a tremendous role in the American reaction to Asian thought. Indeed, much of the history of the American discovery of the Oriental religions may be explained as an integral part of European discovery. European misconceptions of Asia and Asian religion were at the root of early American misconceptions, just as more accurate representations followed improvements in European knowledge. It is difficult to imagine the American discovery without the impetus of Sir William Jones's writings in the first half of the nineteenth century or Max Müller's in the second half. Charles Wilkins's translation of the *Bhagavad-Gita* played a crucial role in awakening interest in Hindu thought, while Sir Edwin Arnold's *Light of Asia* ignited popular interest in Buddhism. The Transcendentalists deserve major credit for recognizing the importance of the Oriental religions, but in many ways they merely echo European Romantic writers who had acclaimed Oriental spirituality earlier. Characteristically, America's first Oriental scholars learned their craft, not by going to India or China, but by going to Germany.

If it is hard to imagine the growth of interest in Oriental religion without European stimulus, it is impossible to understand the reaction to Asian thought without knowledge of the peculiar religious climate in nineteenth-century America. On the surface more vital than ever, American Christianity was undergoing a deepening crisis as the century advanced. Doubts about Christianity among intellectuals was again and again crucial in promoting a favorable response to Asian conceptions. Indeed, an affirmative reaction to Oriental religion was often a vote against doctrinaire Christianity, not a vote for an alternative religious system. The more critical American thinkers became of the tribalism of traditional Christianity, the more sympathetic many became to the Oriental religions. One senses another key difference between the nineteenth- and twentieth-century responses. In a post-Christian era, twentieth-century Americans have felt free to investigate Oriental conceptions because they are intrigued by them, not because they are rebelling against the mother church. The nineteenth-century response was much more rooted in a negative reaction to Christianity.

Our investigation has sought to trace the American discovery of Oriental religions, but in fact, most of the treatment has been focused on Hinduism and Buddhism. Hinduism attracted the greater interest in the first half of the nineteenth century, Buddhism in the second half. Since both religions arose in India, one should perhaps speak of the discovery of Indian thought. Chinese and Japanese religion tended to be passed over. Confucianism was frequently noticed, but never exerted the fascination that Hinduism and Buddhism did. This seems surprising: the humanism and practical emphasis of Confucius' teachings seem better suited to pragmatic American taste than Hindu or Buddhist mysticism. The other major Asian religions—Taoism, Shintoism, Zen Buddhism, and Tibetan Buddism—were practically unknown in nineteenth-century America. In many ways, preferences seem to have reversed in the twentieth century, with greater fascination now shown in Zen Buddhism, Taoism, and Tibetan religions.

None of the men or women surveyed were able to treat Oriental conceptions without altering them in important ways. The problem was partly fragmentary sources and faulty knowledge, but the root cause was more fundamental. Even the most sympathetic American investigator could not escape deeply held Western preconceptions. Emerson approached Hinduism as an Eastern Platonism; Free Religionists viewed Confucius as a rationalist and reformer; and Lafcadio Hearn confused Higher Buddhism with Spencerianism. Critics have repeatedly charged that Western sympathizers misunderstand and distort the Oriental religions, superimposing more familiar Western conceptions over the Asian ones. And so they have. Much of the fascination of the study of the West's reception of Oriental religion concerns the strange transformations that Asian conceptions undergo when introduced into a new environment. But that, after all, is one inevitable consequence of the meeting of East and West.

Notes

1. Edward H. Carr gracefully analyzes the importance of the larger pattern in *What Is History?* (1961; paperback reprint ed., New York: Vintage, 1967). See particularly chaps. 1 and 4.

2. Arnold Toynbee, *A Study of History* (New York: Oxford University Press, 1947-1957), the authorized two-volume Somervell abridgment. See particularly 2: 87-93. See also his *Christianity Among the Religions of the World* (New York: Charles Scribners, 1957).

3. F. S. C. Northrop, *The Meeting of East and West: An Inquiry Concerning World Understanding* (New York: Macmillan, 1946).

4. William McNeill, *The Rise of the West: A History of the Human Community* (Chicago: University of Chicago Press, 1963).

5. McNeill discusses the two periods of closure in ibid., pp. 295-360 and 565-793. For other surveys of European and Asian contacts, see H. G. Rawlinson, "India in European Literature and Thought" in *The Legacy of India*, ed. G. T. Garratt (Oxford: Clarendon Press, 1937), pp. 1-21; Geoffrey F. Hudson, *Europe and China: A Survey of their Relations from the Earliest Times to 1800* (Boston: Beacon Press, 1931), and Wolfgang Francke, *China and the West: The Cultural Encounter, 13th to 20th Centuries* (New York: Harper & Row, 1967), a paperback reprint.

Bibliography

This bibliography includes a number of recent works that came to my attention too late to incorporate, as well as articles and general surveys useful to any student of East-West cultural contacts.

Periodicals

Andover Review, vols. 1-19 (1884-1893).
The Arena, vols. 1-41 (1889-1909).
Atlantic Monthly, vols. 1-86 (1857-1900).
Biblical World, vols. 1-16 (1893-1900).
Catholic World, vols. 57-60 (1893-1895).
Chinese Recorder and Missionary Journal, vols. 1-31 (1868-1900).
Chinese Repository, vols. 1-20 (1832-1851).
Christian Examiner, vols. 1-87 (1824-1869).
The Dial (Boston), vols. 1-4 (1840-1844).
The Dial (Cincinnati), vol. 1 (1860).
Edinburgh Review, vols. 1-52 (1802-1830).
The Harbinger, vols. 1-8 (1845-1849)
Homiletic Review, vols. 23-40 (1892-1900).
The Index, vols. 1-18 (1870-1886).
International Review, vols. 1-14 (1874-1883).
Journal of the American Oriental Society, vols. 1-21 (1843-1900).
Maha-Bodhi, vols. 1-83 (1892-1975).
Massachusetts Quarterly Review, vols. 1-3 (1847-1850).
Methodist Review, vols. 72-82 (1890-1900).

Missionary Herald, vols. 17-96 (1821-1900).
Missionary Review of the World, vols. 16-20 (1893-1897).
The Monist, vols. 1-46 (1890-1936).
New World, vols. 1-9 (1892-1900).
North American Review, vols. 1-171 (1815-1900).
Open Court, vols. 1-50 (1887-1936).
The Panoplist, vols. 1-16 (1805-1820). [Became *Missionary Herald* in 1821.]
The Path, vols. 1-15 (1886-1901).
The Present, vol. 1 (1843-1844).
Princeton Review, vols. 1-16 (1878-1885).
The Radical, vols. 1-10 (1865-1872).
Spirit of the Age, vols. 1-2 (1849-1850).
The Theosophist, vols. 11-30 (1889-1909).
The Unitarian, vols. 1-12 (1886-1897).
The Western, vols. 1-6 (1875-1880).
Western Messenger, vols. 1-8 (1835-1841).

Books and Articles

Abeel, David. *Journal of a Residence in China, and the Neighboring Countries, from 1829 to 1833*. New York: Leavitt, Lord, 1834.

Adams, Hannah. *A Memoir of Miss Hannah Adams, Written by Herself*. Boston: Gray & Bowen, 1832.

———. *A View of Religions in Two Parts, . . .* 3rd rev. ed. Boston: Manning & Loring, 1801.

Ahlstrom, Sydney E. *The American Protestant Encounter with World Religions*. Beloit, Wis.: Beloit College, 1962.

Alcott, A. Bronson. *Concord Days*. Boston: Roberts Bros., 1872.

———. *Tablets*. Boston: Roberts Brothers, 1868.

Aldridge, Alfred O. *Benjamin Franklin and Nature's God*. Durham, N.C.: Duke University Press, 1967.

[Alger, William R.] "The Brahmanic and Buddhist Doctrine of a Future Life." *North American Review* 86 (April 1858): 435-63.

Allen, Alexander V. G. *Life and Letters of Phillips Brooks*. 2 vols. New York: E. P. Dutton, 1900.

Allen, Joseph H. *Sequel to "Our Liberal Movement."* Boston: Roberts Brothers, 1897.

Anderson, Rufus. *History of the Missions of the American Board of Commissioners for Foreign Missions in India*. Boston: Congregational Publishing Society, 1884.

Appleton, William W. *A Cycle of Cathay: The Chinese Vogue in England during the Seventeenth and Eighteenth Centuries*. New York: Columbia University Press, 1951.

Arnold, Sir Edwin. "A Book from the Iliad of India." *International Review* 10 (January, April 1881): 36-51, 297-306.

A Special Correspondent. "Final Impressions of the World's Parliament of Religions." *The Independent* 45 (October 5, 1893): 1341-42.

Baer, Helene G. *The Heart Is Like Heaven: The Life of Lydia Maria Child*. Philadelphia: University of Pennsylvania Press, 1964.

Barrows, John H. "A Parliament of Religions." *The Independent* 44 (February 4, 1892): 152-53.

———. "The Approaching Parliament of Religions." *The Independent* 45 (August 17, 1893): 1105-06.

———, ed. *The World's Parliament of Religions*. . . . 2 vols. Chicago: The Parliament Publishing Co., 1893.

Barrows, Mary E. *John Henry Barrows. A Memoir*. New York: Fleming H. Revell, 1904.

Bender, H. R. "Missions as Seen at the Parliament of Religions." *Methodist Review* 77 (November-December 1895): 907-12.

Bentley, William. *The Diary of William Bentley. D.D. Pastor of the East Church, Salem, Massachusetts*. 4 vols. 1905; reprint, Gloucester, Mass.: Peter Smith, 1962.

Benz, Ernst. *Buddhism or Communism: Which Holds the Future of Asia?* New York: Doubleday, 1965.

———. "The Pietist and Puritan Sources of Early Protestant World Missions (Cotton Mather and A. H. Francke)." *Church History* 20 (June 1951): 28-55.

Bhagat, Goberdhan. *Americans in India, 1784-1860*. New York: New York University Press, 1970.

Bigelow, William S. *Buddhism and Immortality*. Boston: Houghton Mifflin, 1908.

Bingham, Hiram. *Elihu Yale: The American Nabob of Queen Square*. New York: Dodd, Mead, 1939.

Bishop, Donald H. "Religious Confrontation, A Case Study: The 1893 Parliament of Religions." *Numen* (Leiden) 16 (April 1969): 63-76.

Bisland, Elizabeth, ed. *The Japanese Letters of Lafcadio Hearn*. Boston: Houghton Mifflin, 1910.

———. *The Life and Letters of Lafcadio Hearn*. 2 vols. Boston: Houghton Mifflin, 1906.

Bixby, James T. "The Buddha's Path of Salvation." *Biblical World* 12 (November 1898): 307-17.

Blavatsky, Helena P. *Isis Unveiled: A Master-Key to the Mysteries of Ancient and Modern Science and Theology*. 2 vols. New York: J. W. Bouton, 1877.

———. "Recent Progress in Theosophy." *North American Review* 151 (August 1890): 173-86.

———. *The Secret Doctrine: The Synthesis of Science, Religion, and Philosophy*. 2 vols. 1888; reprint, Pasadena, Calif.: Theosophical University Press, 1952.

Bloomfield, Maurice. "The Foundation of Buddhism." *New World* 1 (June 1892): 246-63.

———. *The Religion of the Veda: The Ancient Religion of India*. New York: G. P. Putnam's, 1908.

Bolster, Arthur S., Jr. *James Freeman Clarke: Disciple to Advancing Truth*. Boston: Beacon Press, 1954.

Bonney, Charles C. "The Genesis of the World's Religious Congresses of 1893." *New Church Review* 1 (January 1894): 73-100.

———. "The World's Parliament of Religions." *The Monist* 5 (April 1895): 321-44.

Braden, Charles S. *These Also Believe: A Study of Modern American Cults and Minority Religious Movements*. New York: Macmillan, 1949.

[Bridgman, E. C.] "Intellectual Character of the Chinese." *Chinese Repository* 7 (May 1838): 1-8.

———. "Remarks on the Philosophy of the Chinese. . . ." *Chinese Repository* 18 (January 1849): 43-48.

Bridgman, Eliza J. G. *The Life and Labors of Elijah Coleman Bridgman*. New York: Anson D. F. Randolph, 1864.

Bronner, Milton, ed. *Letters from the Raven; Being the Correspondence of Lafcadio Hearn with Henry Watkin*. New York: Brentano's, 1907.

Brooks, Van Wyck. *Fenollosa and his Circle, with Other Essays in Biography*. New York: E. P. Dutton, 1962.

———. *The Flowering of New England, 1815-1865*. Rev. ed. New York: E. P. Dutton, 1937.

Bryant, William M. "Buddhism and Christianity." *Andover Review* 2 (September and October 1884): 255-68, 365-81.

Burger, G. H. "Religious Worship of the Japanese." *Chinese Repository* 2 (November 1833): 318-24.

Burtis, Mary E. *Moncure Conway. 1832-1907*. New Brunswick, N.J.: Rutgers University Press, 1952.

Cabot, James E. *A Memoir of Ralph Waldo Emerson*. 2 vols. Boston: Houghton Mifflin, 1899.

Cady, Lyman V. "Thoreau's Quotations from the Confucian Books in Walden." *American Literature* 33 (March 1961): 20-32.

Cameron, Kenneth W. " 'Indian Superstition' and Orientalism in Emerson's Harvard." *Emerson Society Quarterly*, no. 33 (4th Quarter 1963): 7-16.

———. "More Notes on Orientalism in Emerson's Harvard." *Emerson Society Quarterly, no. 22 (1st Quarter 1961): 81-90.*

———. *The Transcendentalists and Minerva. Cultural Backgrounds of the American Renaissance with Fresh Discoveries in the Intellectual Climate of Emerson, Alcott and Thoreau*. 3 vols. Hartford, Conn.: Transcendental Books, 1958.

Candlin, George T. "Results and Mission of the Parliament of Religions." *Biblical World* 5 (May 1895): 371-73.

Cannon, Garland H. *Oriental Jones. A Biography of Sir William Jones (1746-1794)*. New York: Asia Publishing House, 1964.

Cappon, Lester J., ed., *The Adams-Jefferson Letters: The Complete Correspondence between Thomas Jefferson and Abigail and John Adams*. 2 vols. Chapel Hill, N.C.: University of North Carolina Press for The Institute of Early American History and Culture, 1959.

Carpenter, Frederic I. *Emerson and Asia*. Cambridge, Mass.: Harvard University Press, 1930.

———. *Emerson Handbook*. New York: Hendricks House, 1953.

Carpenter, J. Estlin. "The Theistic Evolution of Buddhism." *New World* 1 (March 1892): 89-106.

Carter, Paul A. *The Spiritual Crisis of the Gilded Age*. DeKalb, Ill.: Northern Illinois University Press, 1971.

Carus, Paul. "The Dawn of a New Religious Era." *The Monist* 4 (April 1894): Appendix, 1-20.

[Carus, Paul.] "The Hon. C. C. Bonney, the Inaugurator of the Parliament of Religions." *Open Court* 14 (January 1900): 4-8.

Caruthers, J. Wade. *Octavius Brooks Frothingham, Gentle Radical*. University, Ala.: University of Alabama Press, 1977.

Cater, Harold D., ed. *Henry Adams and his Friends: A Collection of his Unpublished Letters*. Boston: Houghton Mifflin, 1947.

Chadwick, John W. *Theodore Parker: Preacher and Reformer*. Boston: Houghton Mifflin, 1900.

Chandrasekharan, K. R. "Emerson's Brahma: An Indian Interpretation." *New England Quarterly* 33 (December 1960): 506-12.

[Channing, E. T.] "Lalla Rookh, an Oriental Romance." *North American Review* 6 (November 1817): 1-25.

Channing, William E. *Thoreau the Poet-Naturalist*. Ed. F. B. Sanborn. Rev. ed.; Boston: Charles E. Goodspeed, 1902.

Channing, William H. *Religions of China. Address before the Free Religious Association. Boston, May 27, 1870*. Boston: John Wilson, 1870.

Chapman, John J. "Emerson, Sixty Years After." *Atlantic Monthly* 79 (January 1897): 27-41.

Chari, V. K. *Whitman in the Light of Vedantic Mysticism. An Interpretation*. Lincoln, Neb.: University of Nebraska Press, 1964.

Chaudhuri, Nirad C. *Scholar Extraordinary. The Life of Professor the Rt. Hon. Friedrich Max Müller, P.C.* London: Chatto & Windus, 1974.

Child, Lydia M., ed. *Aspirations of the World. A Chain of Opals*. Boston: Roberts Brothers, 1878.

———. "The Intermingling of Religions." *Atlantic Monthly* 28 (October 1871): 385-95.

———. *Letters of Lydia Maria Child*. 1883; reprint, New York: Negro Universities Press, 1969.

———. "Resemblances Between the Buddhist and the Roman Catholic Religions." *Atlantic Monthly* 26 (December 1870): 660-65.

———. *The Progress of Religious Ideas through Successive Ages*. 3 vols. New York: C. S. Francis, 1855.

Chisolm, Lawrence W. *Fenollosa: The Far East and American Culture*. New Haven, Conn.: Yale University Press, 1963.

Christy, Arthur E., ed., *The Asian Legacy and American Life*. New York: John Day, 1942.

———. "Orientalism in New England: Whittier." *American Literature* 1 (January 1930): 372-92.

———. "The Orientalism of Whittier." *American Literature* 5 (November 1933): 247-57.

———. *The Orient in American Transcendentalism: A Study of Emerson, Thoreau, and Alcott*. 1932; reprint, New York: Octagon Books, 1963.

Clark, Walter E. "Charles Rockwell Lanman, 1850-1941." *Journal of the American Oriental Society* 61 (September 1941): 191-92.

[Clarke, James F.] J. F. C. "Comparative Theology of Heathen Religions." *Christian Examiner* 62 (March 1857): 183-99.

Clarke, James F. "Affinities of Buddhism and Christianity." *North American Review* 136 (May 1883): 467-77.

———. "Brahmanism: According to the Latest Researches." *Atlantic Monthly* 23 (May 1869): 548-62.

———. "Buddhism; or, the Protestantism of the East." *Atlantic Monthly* 23 (June 1869): 713-28.

———. *Ten Great Religions: An Essay in Comparative Theology*. Boston: James R. Osgood, 1871.

———. "Why I Am Not a Free-Religionist." *North American Review* 145 (October 1887): 378-83.

Collet, Sophia D. *The Life and Letters of Raja Rammohun Roy*. 3rd ed. Calcutta, India: Sadharan Brahmo Samaj, 1962.

"Colonel Olcott and the Buddhist Revival Movement." *Maha-Bodhi* 15 (January, February, March 1907): 26-28.

Commager, Henry Steele. *Theodore Parker. Yankee Crusader*. 2nd ed. Boston: Beacon Press, 1960.

Conant, Martha P. *The Oriental Tale in England in the Eighteenth Century*. New York: Columbia University Press, 1908.

Conger, Arthur L., ed. *Practical Occultism: From the Private Letters of William Q. Judge*. Pasadena, Calif: Theosophical University Press, 1951.

Conway, Moncure D. *Autobiography. Memories and Experiences of Moncure Daniel Conway*. 2 vols. Boston: Houghton Mifflin, 1904.

———. *Emerson at Home and Abroad*. London: Trübner, 1883.

———. "Madame Blavatsky at Adyar." *The Arena* 4 (October 1891): 579-90.

———. "Memories of Max Müller." *North American Review* 171 (December 1900): 884-93.

———. *My Pilgrimage to the Wise Men of the East*. Boston: Houghton Mifflin, 1906.

———, ed. *The Sacred Anthology. A Book of Ethnical Scriptures*. 5th ed. London: Trübner, 1876.

Cooke, George W. *An Historical and Biographical Introduction to Accompany "The Dial."* 2 vols. 1902; reprint, New York: Russell & Russell, 1961.

———. *Unitarianism in America. A History of its Origin and Development*. Boston: American Unitarian Association, 1902.

Corner, George W., ed. *The Autobiography of Benjamin Rush: His "Travels Through Life" together with his Commonplace Book for 1789-1813*. Princeton, N.J.: Princeton University Press for the American Philosophical Society, 1948.

Corson, Eugene R., ed. *Some Unpublished Letters of Helena Petrovna Blavatsky*. London: Rider & Co., 1929.

Courtney, W. L. "Socrates, Buddha, and Christ." *North American Review* 140 (January 1885): 63-77.

Dall, Caroline H. "Kami No Michi, or 'The Way of the Gods.'" *The Index* 13 (November 24, 1881): 247-48.

Dall, Charles H. A. "The Buddha and the Christ." *Unitarian Review* 18 (September 1882): 230-41.

Danton, George H. *The Culture Contacts of the United States and China: The Earliest Sino-American Culture Contacts, 1784-1844*. New York: Columbia University Press, 1931.

——— and Carl Bode, eds. *The Correspondence of Henry David Thoreau*. New York: New York University Press, 1958.

Harris, William T. "Emerson's 'Brahma' and the 'Bhagavad Gita.'" *Poet-Lore* 1 (June 1889): 253-59.

Hearn, Lafcadio. *An American Miscellany*. Ed. Albert Mordell. 2 vols. New York: Dodd, Mead, 1924.

———. *Essays in European and Oriental Literature*. Ed. Albert Mordell. 1923; reprint, Freeport, N.Y.: Books for Libraries Press, 1968.

———. *Exotics and Retrospectives*. 1898; reprint, Boston: Little, Brown, 1905.

———. *Gleanings in Buddha-Fields: Studies of Hand and Soul in the Far East*. Boston: Houghton Mifflin, 1897.

———. *Glimpses of Unfamiliar Japan*. 2 vols. Boston: Houghton Mifflin, 1894.

———. *Japan. An Attempt at Interpretation*. 1904; reprint, New York: Macmillan, 1924.

———. *Kokoro. Hints and Echoes of Japanese Inner Life*. Boston: Houghton Mifflin, 1896.

———. *Occidental Gleanings*. Ed. Albert Mordell. 2 vols. New York: Dodd, Mead, 1925.

———. *Oriental Articles*. Ed. Ichiro Nishizaki. Tokyo, Japan: Hokuseido Press, 1939.

———. *Out of the East. Reveries and Studies in New Japan*. Boston: Houghton Mifflin, 1895.

———. *Some Chinese Ghosts*. 1887; reprint, New York: Modern Library, 1927.

———. *The Writings of Lafcadio Hearn [Koizumi Edition]*. 16 vols. Boston: Houghton Mifflin, 1923.

Herrnstadt, Richard L., ed. *The Letters of A. Bronson Alcott*. Ames, Iowa: Iowa State University Press, 1969.

Higginson, Thomas W. *Cheerful Yesterdays*. Boston: Houghton Mifflin, 1898.

———. "The Character of Buddha." *The Index* 3 (March 16, 1872): 81-83.

———. "The Sympathy of Religions." *The Radical* 8 (February 1871): 1-23.

Hippisley, Alfred E. "William Woodville Rockhill." *Journal of the Royal Asiatic Society of Great Britain and Ireland* 47 (April 1915): 367-74.

Holmes, Oliver Wendell. "The Light of Asia." *International Review* 7 (October 1879): 345-72.

Hopkins, E. Washburn. *India Old and New with a Memorial*. New York: Charles Scribners, 1901.

———. "In Memoriam." [Edward Salisbury] *Journal of the American Oriental Society* 22 (January-July 1901): 1-6.

———. *The Religions of India*. Boston: Ginn & Co., 1895.

Houghton, Walter R., ed. *Neely's History of the Parliament of Religions and Religious Congresses of the World's Congress Auxiliary of the World's Columbian Exposition. Chicago, 1893*. 2 vols. Chicago: Rand McNally, 1893.

Hudson, Geoffrey F. *Europe and China: A Survey of their Relations from the Earliest Times to 1800*. Boston: Beacon Press, 1931.

Hume, Robert A. "Missions in India Not a Failure." *Missionary Herald* 82 (February 1886): 53-57.

Hummel, Arthur W. "Some American Pioneers in Chinese Studies." *Notes on Far Eastern Studies in America*, no. 9 (1941): 1-6.

Davies, William. "The Religion of Gotama Buddha." *Atlantic Monthly* 74 (September 1894): 334-40.

Dawson, Raymond. *The Chinese Chameleon: An Analysis of European Conceptions of Chinese Civilization*. London: Oxford University Press, 1967.

———, ed. *The Legacy of China*. London: Oxford University Press, 1964.

De Bary, William T., ed. *Sources of Indian Tradition*. New York: Columbia University Press, 1958.

Delano, Amasa. *Narrative of Voyages and Travels in the Northern and Southern Hemispheres: Comprising Three Voyages Round the World; Together with A Voyage of Survey and Discovery, in the Pacific Ocean and Oriental Islands*. Boston: E. G. House, 1817.

DeWolfe Howe, M. A., ed. *Later Years of the Saturday Club, 1870-1920*. Boston: Houghton Mifflin, 1927.

Dharmapala, Anagarika. "Reminiscences of my Early Life." *Maha-Bodhi* 41 (May-June 1933): 151-62.

[Dickinson, James T.] "Asiatic Civilization." *Christian Examiner* 67 (July 1859): 1-31.

———. "The Chinese." *Christian Examiner* 65 (September 1858): 177-205.

———. "The Hindoos." *Christian Examiner* 64 (March 1858): 173-209.

Dictionary of American Biography. 20 vols. New York: Charles Scribners, 1928-1936.

Dictionary of National Biography. 21 vols. London: Oxford University Press, 1921-1922.

Dulles, Foster R. *China and America: The Story of their Relations since 1784*. Princeton, N.J.: Princeton University Press, 1946.

Dunglison, Robley. "Biographical Sketch of Peter S. Du Ponceau." *American Law Magazine*, no. 9 (April 1845): 1-33.

Du Ponceau, Peter S. *A Dissertation on the Nature and Character of the Chinese System of Writing. . . .* Philadelphia: American Philosophical Society, 1838.

Eastern and Western Disciples. *The Life of Swami Vivekananda*. Calcutta, India: Advaita Ashrama, 1955.

Edgerton, Franklin. "A Salisbury Letter." *Journal of the American Oriental Society* 64 (April-June 1944): 58-61.

———. "Edward Washburn Hopkins, 1857-1932." *Journal of the American Oriental Society* 52 (December 1932): 311-15.

———. "Maurice Bloomfield, 1855-1928." *Journal of the American Oriental Society* 48 (September 1928): 193-99.

———. "Notes on Early American Work in Linguistics." *Proceedings of the American Philosophical Society* 87 (July 1943): 25-34.

Edmunds, Albert J. *Buddhist and Christian Gospels Now First Compared from the Originals. . . .* 2 vols. 4th ed. Philadelphia: Innes & Sons, 1909.

———. "Buddhist and Christian Gospels. Replies to Critics." *Buddhist Review* 1 (July 1909): 191-97.

———. "The Canonical Account of the Birth of Gotama the Buddha." *Open Court* 12 (August 1898): 485-90.

Eliot, Samuel A., ed. *Heralds of a Liberal Faith*. 3 vols. Boston: American Unitarian Association, 1910.

Ellinwood, F. F. "A Hindu Missionary in America." *Homiletic Review* 28 (November, December 1894): 400-06, 494-99.

Ellsbree, Oliver W. "The Rise of the Missionary Spirit in New England, 1790-1815." *New England Quarterly* 1 (July 1928): 295-322.
Ellwood, Robert S. "Percival Lowell's Journey to the East." *Sewanee Review* 78 (Spring 1970): 285-309.
———. *Alternative Altars: Unconventional and Eastern Spirituality in America.* Chicago: University of Chicago Press, 1979.
Emerson, Edward W., ed. *The Complete Works of Ralph Waldo Emerson [Centenary Edition]* 12 vols. Boston: Houghton Mifflin, 1903-1904.
Emerson, Edward W. and Waldo E. Forbes, eds. *Journals of Ralph Waldo Emerson.* 10 vols. Boston: Houghton Mifflin, 1909-14.
Emerson, Ralph Waldo. *Indian Superstition. Edited with a Dissertation on Emerson's Orientalism at Harvard.* Ed. Kenneth W. Cameron. Hanover, N.H.: The Friends of the Dartmouth Library, 1954.
[Everett, Alexander H.] "Chinese Manners." *North American Review* 27 (October 1828): 524-62.
———. "Remusat's Chinese Grammar." *North American Review* 17 (July 1823): 1-13.
Fairbank, John K. *China Perceived. Images and Policies in Chinese-American Relations.* New York: Alfred Knopf, 1974.
———, ed. *The Missionary Enterprise in China and America.* Cambridge, Mass.: Harvard University Press, 1974.
———. *The United States and China.* Rev. ed. New York: Viking Press, 1962.
Farquhar, John N. *Modern Religious Movements in India.* New York: Macmillan, 1915.
Feldman, Egal. "American Ecumenicism: Chicago's World's Parliament of Religions of 1893." *A Journal of Church and State* 9 (Spring 1967): 180-99.
Fenollosa, Ernest F. "Chinese and Japanese Traits." *Atlantic Monthly* 69 (June 1892): 769-74.
———. *East and West. The Discovery of America and Other Poems.* New York: Thomas Y. Crowell, 1893.
———. *Epochs of Chinese and Japanese Art. An Outline History of East Asiatic Design.* 2 vols. London: William Heinemann, 1912.
———. "The Coming Fusion of East and West." *Harper's New Monthly* 98 (December 1898): 115-22.
Flower, Benjamin O. "Sir Edwin Arnold and Nineteenth-Century Religious Concepts and Ideals." *The Arena* 32 (July 1904): 80-82.
Ford, Worthington C., ed. *Letters of Henry Adams (1858-1891).* Boston: Houghton Mifflin, 1930.
Forsythe, Sidney A. *An American Missionary Community in China, 1895-1905.* Cambridge, Mass.: East Asian Research Center, Harvard University, 1971.
Francke, Kuno. "Cotton Mather and August Hermann Francke." *Harvard Studies in Philology and Literature* 10 (1896): 56-67.
———. "Further Documents Concerning Cotton Mather and August Hermann Francke." *Americana Germanica* 1 (1897): 31-66.
Francke, Wolfgang. *China and the West: The Cultural Encounter, 13th to 20th Centuries.* New York: Harper & Row, 1967.
Franklin, Benjamin. *The Works of Benjamin Franklin.* Ed. John Bigelow. 12 vols. New York: G. P. Putnam's, 1904.

Frothingham, Octavius B. *Memoir of William Henry Channing.* Boston: Hou Mifflin, 1886.
———. *Recollections and Impressions, 1822-1890.* New York: G. P. Putn 1891.
———. *Theodore Parker: A Biography.* Boston: James R. Osgood, 1874.
———. *Transcendentalism in New England. A History.* New York: G. P. Putn 1876.
———. "Why Am I a Free Religionist?" *North American Review* 145 (July 1 8-16.
Furber, Holden. "The Beginnings of American Trade with India, 1784-1812." *England Quarterly* 11 (June 1938): 235-65.
Gandhi, Virchand R. "Why Christian Missions Have Failed in India." *Foru* (April 1894): 160-66.
Garratt, G. T., ed. *The Legacy of India.* Oxford: Clarendon Press, 1937.
Gilman, William, et al., eds. *The Journals and Miscellaneous Notebook Ralph Waldo Emerson.* Vols. 1- . Cambridge, Mass.: Belknap Pres Harvard University Press, 1960-.
Gohdes, Clarence L. F. *The Periodicals of American Transcendentalism.* Durh N.C.: Duke University Press, 1931.
Goodspeed, Edgar J. *Strange New Gospels.* Chicago: University of Chicago P 1931.
Gordon, M. L. "The Buddhisms of Japan." *Andover Review* 5 (March 1886): 301-
Gould, George M. *Concerning Lafcadio Hearn.* London: T. Fisher Unwin, 1908.
Graff, Henry F., ed. *Bluejackets with Perry in Japan: A Day-by-Day Acc Kept by Master's Mate John R. C. Lewis and Cabin Boy William B. Al* New York: New York Public Library, 1952.
Greenwalt, Emmett A. *The Point Loma Community in California, 1897-1942 Theosophical Experiment.* Berkeley, Calif.: University of California Press, 1955.
[Gutzlaff, Charles.] "Remarks on Buddhism." *Chinese Repository* 2 (Septem 1833): 214-19.
———, ed. *James Freeman Clarke. Autobiography, Diary and Corresponder* Boston: Houghton Mifflin, 1891.
———. "The American Expedition to Japan." *North American Review* 83 (J 1856): 233-60.
Hale, Edward E. "The Unknown Life of Christ." *North American Review* 158 (M 1894): 594-601.
[Hale, Nathan.] "Adventures of Golownin in Japan." *North American Review* (January 1820): 33-62.
[Hamilton, Alexander.] Reviews of successive volumes of *Asiatic Researches. Ed burgh Review* 1 (October 1802): 26-43; 9 (October 1806): 92-101; 9 (Janua 1807): 278-304; 12 (April 1808): 36-50; (October 1809): 175-89; 16 (Aug 1810): 384-98.
———. Review of Edward Moor, *The Hindu Pantheon. Edinburgh Review* 17 (Fe ruary 1811): 311-30.
Harding, Walter R. *A Thoreau Handbook.* New York: New York Universi Press, 1959.
———. *The Days of Henry Thoreau.* New York: Alfred Knopf, 1966.

Indian Council for Cultural Relations, ed. *Indian Studies Abroad*. New York: Asia Publishing House, 1964.

Ingalls, Daniel H. H. "The Heritage of a Fallible Saint: Annie Besant's Gifts to India." *Proceedings of the American Philosophical Society* 109 (April 9, 1965): 85-88.

Isaacs, Harold R. *Images of Asia: American Views of China and India*. New York: Capricorn Books, 1962.

Isani, Mukhtar A. "Cotton Mather and the Orient." *New England Quarterly* 43 (March 1970): 46-58.

Iyer, Raghavan, ed. *The Glass Curtain Between Asia and Europe. A Symposium on the Historical Encounters and the Changing Attitudes of the Peoples of the East and the West*. London: Oxford University Press, 1965.

Jackson, Carl T. "Oriental Ideas in American Thought." *Dictionary of the History of Ideas*. Ed. Phillip P. Wiener. 4 vols. New York: Charles Scribners, 1973. 3: 427-39.

———. "The Meeting of East and West: The Case of Paul Carus." *Journal of the History of Ideas* 29 (January-March 1968): 73-92.

———. "The New Thought Movement and the Nineteenth-Century Discovery of Oriental Philosophy." *Journal of Popular Culture* 9 (Winter 1975): 523-48.

———. "The Orient in Post-Bellum American Thought: Three Pioneer Popularizers." *American Quarterly* 22 (Spring 1970): 67-81.

Jinarajadasa, C. *The Golden Book of the Theosophical Society: A Brief History of the Society's Growth from 1875-1925*. Adyar, India: Theosophical Publishing House, 1925.

Johnson, Herrick. "The World's Parliament of Religions." *The Independent* 47 (February 28, 1895): 266-77.

Johnson, Samuel. *Lectures, Essays, and Sermons*. Boston: Houghton Mifflin, 1883.

———. *Oriental Religions and their Relation to Universal Religion. China*. Boston: James R. Osgood, 1877.

———. *Oriental Religions and their Relation to Universal Religion. India*. Boston: James R. Osgood, 1872.

———. *Oriental Religions and their Relation to Universal Religion. Persia*. Boston: Houghton Mifflin, 1885.

———. "The Piety of Pantheism. As Illustrated in Hindu Philosophy and Faith." *The Radical* 5 (June 1869): 487-98.

[Jones, Samuel A.], ed. *Pertaining to Thoreau*. Detroit: Edwin B. Hill, 1901.

Jordan, Lewis H. *Comparative Religion. Its Genesis and Growth*. Edinburgh: T. & T. Clark, 1905.

J. T. S. [Jabez T. Sunderland]. "The Close of the Great Parliament of Religions." *The Unitarian* 8 (November 1893): 497-502.

[Judge, William Q.] "India a Storehouse for Us." *The Path* 5 (February 1891): 343-46.

———. "The Truth about East and West." *The Path* 10 (April 1895): 1-5.

———. "Two Years on the Path." *The Path* 2 (March 1888): 357-60.

Kellogg, Samuel H. *The Light of Asia and The Light of the World. A Comparison of the Legend, the Doctrine, and the Ethics of the Buddha with the Story, the Doctrine, and the Ethics of Christ*. London: Macmillan, 1885.

Kent, Roland G., ed. *Thirty Years of Oriental Studies. . . .* Philadelphia, 1918.

Kern, Alexander. "The Rise of Transcendentalism, 1815-1860," in *Transitions in American Literary History*. Ed. Harry H. Clark. Durham, N.C.: Duke University Press, 1953. Pp. 247-314.

Kuo, Ping C. "Canton and Salem: The Impact of Chinese Culture upon New England Life during the Post-Revolutionary Era." *New England Quarterly* 3 (July 1930): 420-42.

Lach, Donald F. *Asia in the Making of Europe*. Vol. 1, Book 2: *The Century of Discovery*. Chicago: University of Chicago Press, 1965.

La Farge, John. *An Artist's Letters from Japan*. New York: Century Co., 1897.

La Farge, John, S.J. *The Manner Is Ordinary*. New York: Harcourt, Brace, 1954.

Lanman, Charles R. "Chronological Bibliography of the Writings of William Dwight Whitney." *Journal of the American Oriental Society* [*The Whitney Memorial Issue*] 19 (January-June 1898): 121-50.

———. "Henry Clarke Warren: An Obituary Notice." *Journal of the American Oriental Society* 20 (July-December 1899): 332-37.

———. "Hindu Ascetics and their Powers." *American Philological Association Transactions and Proceedings*. 48 (1917): 133-51.

———. "The Hindu Yoga System." *Harvard Theological Review* 11 (October 1918): 355-75.

———, ed. "The Whitney Memorial Meeting." *Journal of the American Oriental Society* 19 (January-June 1898): entire issue.

———. "William Dwight Whitney." *Atlantic Monthly* 75 (March 1895): 398-406.

Latourette, Kenneth S. *A History of Christian Missions in China*. 1929; reprint, New York: Russell & Russell, 1967.

———. *The History of Early Relations between the United States and China, 1784-1844*. New Haven, Conn.: Yale University Press, 1917.

Leidecker, Kurt F. "Emerson and East-West Synthesis." *Philosophy East and West* 1 (July 1951): 40-50.

———. "Harris and Indian Philosophy." *The Monist* 46 (January 1936): 112-53.

———. "Oriental Philosophy in America," in *American Philosophy*. Ed. Ralph B. Winn. New York: Philosophical Library, 1955. Pp. 211-20.

Little, Charles J. "The Chicago Parliament of Religions." *Methodist Review* 76 (March-April 1894): 208-20.

Lockwood, William W. "Adam Smith and Asia." *Journal of Asian Studies* 23 (May 1964): 345-55.

Loines, Elma. "Houqua, Sometime Chief of the Co-Hong at Canton (1769-1843)." *Essex Institute Historical Collections* 89 (April 1953): 99-108.

Long, O. W. "William Dwight Whitney." *New England Quarterly* 2 (January 1929): 105-19.

Longfellow, Samuel. "The Unity and Universality of the Religious Ideas." *The Radical* 3 (March 1868): 433-57.

Lounsbury, Thomas R. "William Dwight Whitney." *Proceedings of the American Academy of Arts and Sciences* 30 (May 1894-May 1895): 579-89.

Lowell, A. Lawrence. *Biography of Percival Lowell*. New York: Macmillan, 1935.

Lowell, Percival. *Chöson: The Land of the Morning Calm. A Sketch of Korea*. Boston: Ticknor, 1886.

———. *Noto: An Unexplored Corner of Japan*. Boston: Houghton Mifflin, 1891.

———. *Occult Japan or The Way of the Gods. An Esoteric Study of Japanese Personality and Possession*. Boston: Houghton Mifflin, 1894.

———. *The Soul of the Far East*. Boston: Houghton Mifflin, 1888.

Lum, Dyer D. "Buddhism Notwithstanding: An Attempt to Interpret Buddha from a Buddhist Standpoint." *The Index* 6 (April 29, 1875): 194-96.

Macshane, Frank. "Walden and Yoga." *New England Quarterly* 37 (September 1964): 322-42.

Marshall, P. J., ed. *The British Discovery of Hinduism in the Eighteenth Century*. Cambridge: Cambridge University Press, 1970.

Mason, Mary G. *Western Concepts of China and the Chinese, 1840-1876*. New York: The Seeman Printery, 1939.

Mather, Cotton. *Diary of Cotton Mather*. 2 vols. New York: Frederick Ungar, 1957.

McKey, Richard H., Jr. "Elias Haskett Derby and the Founding of the Eastern Trade." *Essex Institute Historical Collections* 98 (January, April 1962): 1-25, 65-83.

McNeill, William H. *The Rise of the West: A History of the Human Community*. Chicago: University of Chicago Press, 1963.

Meltzer, Milton. *Tongue of Flame: The Life of Lydia Maria Child*. New York: Thomas Y. Crowell, 1965.

Miller, Stuart C. "The American Trader's Image of China, 1785-1840." *Pacific Historical Review* 36 (November 1967): 375-95.

———. *The Unwelcome Immigrant: The American Image of the Chinese, 1785-1882*. Berkeley, Calif.: University of California Press, 1969.

Mills, Charles D. B., ed. *Pebbles, Pearls and Gems of the Orient*. Boston: George H. Ellis, 1882.

———. *The Indian Saint; or, Buddha and Buddhism: A Sketch, Historical and Critical*. Northampton, Mass.: Journal and Free Press, 1876.

Miner, Earl. *The Japanese Tradition in British and American Literature*. Princeton, N.J.: Princeton University Press, 1958.

Moore, Adrienne. *Rammohun Roy and America*. Calcutta, India: Sadharan Brahmo Samaj, 1942.

Morais, Herbert M. *Deism in Eighteeth Century America*. 1934; reprint, New York: Russell & Russell, 1960.

Morgan, Arthur E. *Edward Bellamy*. New York: Columbia University Press, 1944.

Morison, Elting E., ed. *The Letters of Theodore Roosevelt*. 8 vols. Cambridge, Mass.: Harvard University Press, 1951-1954.

Morse, Edward S. *Japan Day by Day. 1877, 1878-79, 1882-83*. 1917; reprint, Tokyo, Japan: Kobunsha Publishing Co., 1936.

Mueller, J. H. "Are Our Christian Missionaries in India Frauds?" *The Arena* 16 (October 1896): 806-12.

Mueller, Roger C. "Samuel Johnson, American Transcendentalist: A Short Biography." *Essex Institute Historical Collections* 115 (January 1979): 9-60.

Mukherjee, S. N. *Sir William Jones: A Study in Eighteenth-Century British Attitudes to India*. London: Camridge University Press, 1968.

Müller, F. Max. "Buddhist Charity." *North American Review* 140 (March 1885): 221-36.

———. "The Alleged Sojourn of Christ in India." *Nineteenth Century* 39 (October 1894): 515-22.

———. "The Real Significance of the Parliament of Religions." *The Arena* 11 (December 1894): 1-14.

Müller, Georgina M. *The Life and Letters of the Right Honourable Friedrich Max Müller.* 2 vols. New York: Longmans, Green, 1902.

Murphet, Howard. *Hammer on the Mountain: Life of Henry Steel Olcott (1832-1907).* Wheaton, Ill.: Theosophical Publishing House, 1972.

Nagley, Winfield E. "Thoreau on Attachment, Detachment, and Non-Attachment." *Philosophy East and West* 3 (January 1954): 307-20.

Nakashima, Rikizo. "Mr. Percival Lowell's Misconception of the Character of the Japanese." *New Englander and Yale Review* 50 (February 1899): 97-102.

Nash, J. V. "India at the World's Parliament of Religions." *Open Court* 47 (June 1933): 217-30.

Nethercot, Arthur H. *The First Five Lives of Annie Besant.* London: Rupert Hart-Davis, 1961.

———. *The Last Four Lives of Annie Besant.* Chicago: University of Chicago Press, 1963.

Niemand, Jasper. [Mrs. Archibald Keightley] "William Q. Judge." *Irish Theosophist* (Dublin) 4 (1896): 90-92, 112-16, 141-45, 165-68.

Noble, F. A. "The Parliament of Religions." *Our Day* 12 (1893): 418-22.

Northrop, F. S. C. *The Meeting of East and West: An Inquiry Concerning World Understanding.* 1946; reprint, New York: Macmillan, 1960.

Norton, Charles E., ed. *Letters from Ralph Waldo Emerson to a Friend, 1838-1853.* 1899; reprint, Port Washington, N.Y.: Kennikat Press, 1971.

Notovitch, Nicholas [Notovich, Nicolai.] *The Unknown Life of Jesus Christ; from an Ancient Ms., Recently Discovered in a Buddhist Monastery in Thibet.* Chicago: Indo-American Book Co., 1907.

Olcott, Henry S. *A Buddhist Catechism, According to the Canon of the Southern Church.* Boston: Estes & Lauriat, 1885.

———. "Inaugural Address of the President of the Theosophical Society." *The Theosophist* 28 (February, March 1907): 321-27, 401-07.

———. *Old Diary Leaves, the Only Authentic History of the Theosophical Society.* 2nd ed. 5 vols. Madras: Theosophical Publishing House, 1928-1935.

———. *Old Diary Leaves: The True Story of the Theosophical Society.* New York: G. P. Putnam's, 1895.

———. *Theosophy, Religion and Occult Science.* London: George Redway, 1885.

Onahan, William J. "Columbian Catholic Congress at Chicago." *Catholic World* 57 (August 1893): 604-8.

Oswald, Felix. "The Secret of the East." *The Index* 14 (March 1, 1883): 410-11.

———. "Was Christ a Buddhist?" *The Arena* 3 (January 1891): 193-201.

Parker, Theodore. *The Works of Theodore Parker* [*Centenary Edition.*] 14 vols. Boston: American Unitarian Association, 1907-1911.

———. "The Writings of Ralph Waldo Emerson." *Massachusetts Quarterly Review* 3 (March 1850): 200-55.

[Parsons, Theophilus.] "Manners and Customs of India." *North American Review* 9 (June 1819): 36-58.

Pathak, Sushil M. *American Missionaries and Hinduism (A Study of Their Contacts from 1813 to 1910)*. Delhi, India: Munshiram, Manoharlal, 1967.

Paul, Sherman. *The Shores of America: Thoreau's Inward Exploration*. Urbana, Ill.: University of Illinois Press, 1958.

Peabody, Andrew P. "Memoir of James Freeman Clarke, D.D." *Proceedings of the Massachusetts Historical Society*, Second Series 4 (March 1889): 320-35.

Peiris, William. *The Western Contribution to Buddhism*. Delhi, India: Motilal Banarsidass, 1973.

Persons, Stow. *Free Religion. An American Faith*. 1947; reprint, Boston: Beacon Press, 1963.

[Perry, Thomas Sergeant.] "Clarke's Ten Great Religions." *North American Review* 113 (October 1871): 427-29.

Phillips, Clifton J. *Protestant America and the Pagan World: The First Half Century of the American Board of Commissioners for Foreign Missions, 1810-1860*. Cambridge, Mass.: Harvard East Asian Monographs #32, 1969.

Philosinensis [Charles Gutzlaff.] "Remarks on the History and Chronology of China from the Earliest Ages Down to the Present Time." *Chinese Repository* 2 (June, July 1833): 74-85, 111-28.

———. "Remarks on the Religion of the Chinese." *Chinese Repository* 4 (October 1835): 271-76.

Pickering, John. "Address at the First Annual Meeting." *Journal of the American Oriental Society* 1 (1843-1849): 1-60.

———. "Du Ponceau on the Chinese System of Writing." *North American Review* 48 (January 1839): 271-310.

Pickering, Mary O. *Life of John Pickering*. Boston: Privately Printed, 1887.

Pierson, Arthur T. "The Parliament of Religions." *The Chinese Recorder* 26 (April 1895): 161-75.

Powers, Fred P. "The Success of Christian Missions in India." *Forum* 17 (June 1894): 475-83.

Prescott, William H. "Memoir of Hon. John Pickering, LL.D." *Massachusetts Historical Society Collections*, Third Series 10 (1846): 204-24.

Priestley, Joseph. *The Doctrines of Heathen Philosophy, Compared with Those of Revelation*. Northumberland, Penn.: John Binns, 1804.

Pumpelly, Raphael. *Across America and Asia. Notes of a Five Years' Journey Around the World and of a Residence in Arizona, Japan and China*. 2nd rev. ed. New York: Leypoldt & Holt, 1870.

———. *My Reminiscences*. 2 vols. New York: Henry Holt, 1918.

Quincy, Josiah, ed. *The Journals of Major Samuel Shaw, The First American Consul at Canton*. Boston: William Crosby & H. P. Nichols, 1847.

Quincy, J. P. "Memoir of Octavius Brooks Frothingham." *Proceedings of the Massachusetts Historical Society*, Second Series 10 (March 1896): 507-39.

Rayapati, J. P. Rao. *Early American Interest in Vedanta: Pre-Emersonian Interest in Vedic Literature and Vedantic Philosophy*. New York: Asia Publishing House, 1973.

Reichwein, Adolf. *China and Europe: Intellectual and Artistic Contacts in the Eighteenth Century*. New York: Alfred Knopf, 1925.

Reischauer, Edwin O. *The United States and Japan*. 3rd ed. New York: Viking Press, 1967.

Review of John Barrow, *Travels in China. Edinburgh Review* 5 (January 1805): 259-88.

Review of Sir George Staunton, *Ta Tsing Leu Lee. Edinburgh Review* 16 (August 1810): 476-99.

Review of Thomas Moore, *Lalla Rookh. Edinburgh Review* 29 (November 1817): 1-35.

Review of William Ward, *Account of the Writings, Religion, and Manners of the Hindoos. . . . Edinburgh Review* 29 (February 1818): 377-403.

Rhys Davids, Thomas W. "Buddhism and Christianity." *International Quarterly* 7 (March-June 1903): 1-13.

———. *Buddhism. Its History and Literature*. 3rd rev. ed. New York: G. P. Putnam's, 1896.

Richardson, Lyon N. *A History of Early American Magazines, 1741-1789*. 1931; reprint, New York: Octagon Books, 1966.

Riepe, Dale. "Contributions of American Sanskritists in the Spread of Indian Philosophy in the United States." *Buffalo Studies* 3 (1967): 35-72.

———. "Emerson and Indian Philosophy." *Journal of the History of Ideas* 28 (January-March 1967): 115-22.

———. *The Philosophy of India and its Impact on American Thought*. Springfield, Ill.: Charles C. Thomas Publishers, 1970.

Rocher, Rosane. *Alexander Hamilton (1762-1824). A Chapter in the Early History of Sanskrit Philology*. New Haven, Conn.: American Oriental Society, 1968.

Rockhill, William W. "An American in Tibet." *Century Magazine* 41 (November, December, 1890, January, February, March 1891): 3-17, 250-63, 350-61, 599-606, 720-30.

———. *Diary of a Journey through Mongolia and Tibet in 1891 and 1892* Washington, D.C.: Smithsonian Institution, 1894.

———. *The Land of the Lamas. Notes of a Journey through China, Mongolia, and Tibet*. London: Longmans, Green, 1891.

———. *The Life of the Buddha and the Early History of his Order, Derived from the Tibetan Works in the Bkah-Hgyur and Bstan-Hgyur*. London: Kegan, Paul, Trench, Trübner, 1884.

Rusk, Ralph L., ed. *The Letters of Ralph Waldo Emerson*. 6 vols. New York: Columbia University Press, 1939.

———. *The Life of Ralph Waldo Emerson*. New York: Charles Scribners, 1949.

Rutt, John. T., ed. *The Theological and Miscellaneous Works of Joseph Priestley*. 25 vols. Hackney, England: George Smallfield, 1817.

Sakamaki, Shunzo. "Western Concepts of Japan and the Japanese, 1800-1854." *Pacific Historical Review* 6 (1937): 1-14.

Salisbury, Edward E. "M. Burnouf on the History of Buddhism in India." *Journal of the American Oriental Society* 1 (1843-1849): 275-98.

———. "Memoir on the History of Buddhism." *Journal of the American Oriental Society* 1 (1843-1849): 79-135.

Samuels, Ernest. *Henry Adams: The Major Phase*. Cambridge, Mass.: Belknap Press of Harvard University Press, 1964.

———. *Henry Adams: The Middle Years*. Cambridge, Mass.: Belknap Press of Harvard University Press, 1965.

Sanborn, Franklin B., *Henry D. Thoreau*. Rev. ed. Boston: Houghton Mifflin, 1910.

———, ed. *The Genius and Character of Emerson. Lectures at the Concord School of Philosophy*. Boston: James R. Osgood, 1885.

———. "Thoreau and his English Friend Thomas Cholmondeley." *Atlantic Monthly* 72 (December 1893): 741-56.

——— and William T. Harris. *A. Bronson Alcott. His Life and Philosophy*. 2 vols. Boston: Roberts Bros., 1893.

Sarma, D. S. *Studies in the Renaissance of Hinduism in the Nineteenth and Twentieth Centuries*. Benares, India: Benares Hindu University, 1944.

Sarma, Sreekrishna. "A Short Study of the Oriental Influence upon Henry David Thoreau with Special Reference to his *Walden*." *Jahrbuch für Amerikastudien* (Heidelberg) 1 (1956): 76-92.

Schaff, D. S. "The Parliament of Religions and the Christian Faith." *Homiletic Review* 26 (December 1893): 552-61.

Schlesinger, Arthur M., Sr. "A Critical Period in American Religion, 1875-1900." *Proceedings of the Massachusetts Historical Society* 64 (June 1932): 523-47.

Schwantes, Robert S. *Japanese and Americans: A Century of Cultural Relations*. New York: Harpers, 1955.

Sen, Sri Chandra. "The Ven'ble Sri Devamitta Dhammapala." *Maha-Bodhi* 41 (July-September 1933): 326-56.

Seymour, Thomas D. "William Dwight Whitney." *American Journal of Philology* 15 (1894): 271-98.

Sharpe, Eric L. *Comparative Religion. A History*. London: Gerald Duckworth, 1975.

Shattuck, Frederick C. "William Sturgis Bigelow." *Proceedings of the Massachusetts Historical Society* 60 (October 1926-June 1927): 15-19.

Shattuck, George C. "Personal Letter about Dr. William Sturgis Bigelow (1850-1926) from John E. Lodge to Frederick Cheever Shattuck." *Proceedings of the Massachusetts Historical Society* 75 (January-December 1963): 108-9.

Shepard, Odell. *Pedlar's Progress. The Life of Bronson Alcott*. Boston: Little, Brown, 1937.

———, ed. *The Journals of Bronson Alcott*. Boston: Little, Brown, 1938.

Silverman, Kenneth, ed. *Selected Letters of Cotton Mather*. Baton Rouge, La.: Louisiana State University Press, 1971.

Sinnett, A. P., ed. *Incidents in the Life of Madame Blavatsky Compiled from Information Supplied by her Relatives and Friends*. London: George Redway, 1886.

Solovyoff, Vsevolod S. *A Modern Priestess of Isis*. New York: Longmans, Green, 1895.

Stanley, Peter W. "The Making of an American Sinologist: William W. Rockhill and the Open Door." *Perspectives in American History* 11 (1977-1978): 419-60.

Stedman, Edmund C. *Octavius Brooks Frothingham and the New Faith*. New York: G. P. Putnam's, 1876.

Stein, William B. "Thoreau's First Book: A Spoor of Yoga." *Emerson Society Quarterly*, no. 41 (4th Quarter 1965): 4-25.

———, ed. *Two Brahman Sources of Emerson and Thoreau*. Gainesville, Fla.: Scholar's Facsimiles & Reprints, 1967.

Stevens, Abram W. "Confucius and his Religion." *The Index* 6 (September 2, 1875): 410-12.

Stevens, George B. *The Life, Letters, and Journals of the Rev. and Hon. Peter Parker, M.D.* Boston: Congregational Sunday-School & Publishing Society, 1896.

Stevenson, Elizabeth. *Lafcadio Hearn*. New York: Macmillan, 1961.

Stifler, Susan R. "Elijah Coleman Bridgman: The First American Sinologist." *Notes on Far Eastern Studies in America*, no. 10 (1942): 1-11.

Telang, Purushotam R. "Christian Missions as Seen by a Brahmin." *Forum* 18 (December 1894): 481-89.

Vivekananda, Swami. *The Complete Works of the Swami Vivekananda. . . .* 7 vols. Mayavati, India: Advaita Ashrama, 1924-32.

"The Parliament of Religions as Seen on Foreign Mission Fields." *Methodist Review* 78 (July-August 1896): 648-50.

"The Theosophical Congress and the Parliament of Religions." *The Path* 8 (November 1893): 247-49.

The Theosophical Movement, 1875-1950. Los Angeles: Cunningham Press, 1951.

Thoburn, J. M. "Christian Missions as Seen by a Missionary" *Forum* 18 (December 1894): 490-501.

———. "Recent Missionary Discussions." *Methodist Review* 73 (November-December 1891): 867-81.

Thomas, John W. *James Freeman Clarke. Apostle of German Culture to America.* Boston: John W. Luce, 1949.

Torrey, Bradford and Francis H. Allen, eds., *The Writings of Henry David Thoreau* [*Walden Edition.*] 20 vols. 1906; reprint, New York: AMS Press, 1968.

Toy, Crawford H. "The Parliament of Religions." *New World* 2 (December 1893): 728-41.

Toynbee, Arnold J. *A Study of History. Abridgment of Volumes I-X by D. C. Somervell.* 2 vols. New York: Oxford University Press, 1947-1957.

[Tudor, William.] "Theology of the Hindoos, as Taught by Ram Mohun Roy." *North American Review* 6 (March 1818): 386-93.

Tuttle, Allen E. "Lafcadio Hearn and the Soul of the Far East." *Contemporary Japan* (Tokyo) 23 (1955): 529-52.

Varg, Paul A. *Open Door Diplomat: The Life of W. W. Rockhill*. Urbana, Ill.: University of Illinois Press, 1952.

[Warner, Herman J.] "The Last Phase of Atheism." *Christian Examiner* 78 (January 1865): 78-88.

Warren, Henry C. *Buddhism in Translations*. Cambridge, Mass.: Harvard University Press, 1909.

Warren, Sidney. *American Freethought, 1860-1914*. New York: Columbia University Press, 1943

Washburn, Wilcomb E. "The Oriental 'Roots' of American Transcendentalism." *Southwestern Journal* 4 (Fall 1949): 141-55.

———. "The Orient in Mid-Nineteenth Century American Literature." *Southwestern Journal* 5 (Winter-Spring 1949-1950): 73-82.

Wayland, Francis. *A Memoir of the Life and Labors of the Rev. Adoniram Judson.* 2 vols. Boston: Phillips, Sampson, 1853.

Wayman, Dorothy G. *Edward Sylvester Morse: A Biography*. Cambridge, Mass.: Harvard University Press, 1942.

Weiss, John. *Life and Correspondence of Theodore Parker*. 2 vols. 1864; reprint, New York: Bergman Publishers, 1969.

Welbon, Guy R. *The Buddhist Nirvana and its Western Interpreters*. Chicago: University of Chicago Press, 1968.

Wells, Anna M. *Dear Preceptor: The Life and Times of Thomas Wentworth Higginson*. Boston: Houghton Mifflin, 1963.

Whitney, William D. "On the Main Results of the Later Vedic Researches in Germany." *Journal of the American Oriental Society* 3 (1852-1853): 289-328.

———. "On the Vedic Doctrine of a Future Life." *Bibliotheca Sacra* 16 (1859): 404-20.

———. *Oriental and Linguistic Studies. First Series*. New York: Charles Scribners, 1872.

———. *Oriental and Linguistic Studies. Second Series*. New York: Charles Scribner's, 1874.

———. "The Translation of the Veda." *North American Review* 106 (April 1868): 515-42.

Wilbur, Earl M. *A History of Unitarianism in Transylvania, England, and America*. 2 vols. Cambridge, Mass.: Harvard University Press, 1952.

Wilkinson, William C. "The Attitude of Christianity toward Other Religions." *Homiletic Review* 27 (January 1894): 3-15.

———. "The Sympathy of Religions." *Homiletic Review* 31 (February 1896): 109-14.

Williams, Frederick W. *The Life and Letters of Samuel Wells Williams, LL.D.: Missionary, Diplomatist, Sinologue*. New York: G. P. Putnam's, 1889.

Williams, Gertrude M. *Priestess of the Occult (Madame Blavatsky)*. New York: Alfred Knopf, 1946.

Williams, Leighton and Mornay, eds. *Serampore Letters Being the Unpublished Correspondence of William Carey and Others with John Williams, 1800-1816*. New York: G. P. Putnam's, 1892.

Williams, Stanley T., ed. "Unpublished Letters of Emerson." *Journal of English and Germanic Philology* 26 (October 1927): 475-84.

[Williams, S. Wells.] "Life and Times of Confucius." *Chinese Repository* 18 (July 1849): 337-42.

——— *The Middle Kingdom; A Survey of the Geography, Government, Education, Social Life, Arts, Religion, etc., of The Chinese Empire and its Inhabitants*. 2 vols. New York: Wiley & Putnam, 1848.

Willson, A. Leslie. *A Mythical Image: The Ideal of India in German Romanticism*. Durham, N.C.: Duke University Press, 1964.

Winternitz, Maurice. *A History of Indian Literature*. Rev. ed. 2 vols. Calcutta, India: University of Calcutta Press, 1927-1933.

Wright, Brooks. *Interpreter of Buddhism to the West: Sir Edwin Arnold*. New York: Bookman Associates, 1957.

Wright, Conrad. *The Beginnings of Unitarianism in America*. Boston: Beacon Press, 1955.

"Writings of Rammohum Roy." *Christian Disciple and Theological Review*, New Series 5 (September-October 1823): 363-92.

Yeats, William Butler. *The Autobiography of William Butler Yeats*. New York: Macmillan, 1953.

Yohannan, J. D. "Emerson's Translations of Persian Poetry from German Sources." *American Literature* 14 (January 1943): 407-20.

———. "The Influence of Persian Poetry upon Emerson's Work." *American Literature* 15 (March 1943): 25-41.

Yu, Beongcheon. *An Ape of Gods. The Art and Thought of Lafcadio Hearn.* Detroit, Mich.: Wayne State University Press, 1964.

Dissertations

Ashmead, John. "The Idea of Japan, 1853-1895: Japan as Described by American and Other Travellers from the West." Harvard University, 1951.

Bowditch, James R. "The Impact of Japanese Culture on the United States, 1853-1904." Harvard University, 1963.

Druyvesteyn, Kenten. "The World's Parliament of Religions." University of Chicago, 1976.

Foster, John B. "China and the Chinese in American Literature." University of Illinois, 1952.

Isani, Mukhtar A. "The Oriental Tale in America through 1865: A Study in American Fiction." Princeton University, 1962.

McCutcheon, James M. "The American and British Missionary Concept of Chinese Civilization in the Nineteenth Century." University of Wisconsin, 1959.

Mueller, Roger C. "The Orient in American Transcendental Periodicals (1835-1886)." University of Minnesota, 1968.

Schramm, Richard H. "The Image of India in Selected American Literary Periodicals, 1870-1900." Duke University, 1964.

Singh, Man M. "Emerson and India." University of Pennsylvania, 1946.

Stern, Bernard S. "American Views of India and Indians, 1857-1900." University of Pennsylvania, 1956.

Udy, James S. "Attitudes Within the Protestant Churches of the Occident Towards the Propagation of Christianity in the Orient: An Historical Survey to 1914." Boston University, 1952.

Young, Myrl M. "The Impact of the Far East on the United States, 1840-1860." University of Chicago, 1951.

Index

About the Author

Carl T. Jackson is Professor of History at the University of Texas at El Paso. His articles on Asian Religion and thought have appeared in the *Journal of the History of Ideas, American Quarterly,* and the *Journal of Popular Culture,* among other publications. *The Oriental Religions and American Thought: Nineteenth-Century Explorations* was chosen the winner of the Ralph Henry Gabriel Prize Competition in American Studies, 1979.